Language Diversity and Academic Writing

A BEDFORD SPOTLIGHT READER

Language Diversity and Academic Writing

A BEDFORD SPOTLIGHT READER

Samantha Looker-Koenigs
University of Wisconsin Oshkosh

bedford/st.martin's
Macmillan Learning

Boston | New York

For Bedford/St. Martin's

Vice President, Editorial, Macmillan Learning Humanities: Edwin Hill
Senior Program Director for English: Leasa Burton
Program Manager: John E. Sullivan III
Executive Marketing Manager: Joy Fisher Williams
Director of Content Development: Jane Knetzger
Development Editor: Kathy Retan
Associate Editors: Jennifer Prince, Lexi DeConti
Content Project Manager: Louis C. Bruno Jr.
Senior Workflow Supervisor: Joe Ford
Production Supervisor: Robin Besofsky
Media Project Manager: Rand Thomas
Manager of Publishing Services: Andrea Cava
Project Management: Lumina Datamatics, Inc.
Composition: Lumina Datamatics, Inc.
Director of Rights and Permissions: Hilary Newman
Photo Researcher: Candice Cheesman, Lumina Datamatics, Inc.
Photo Editor: Angela Boehler
Permissions Editor: Kalina Ingham
Permissions Researcher: Tom Wilcox, Lumina Datamatics, Inc.
Senior Art Director: Anna Palchik
Text Design: Castle Design; Janis Owens, Books By Design, Inc.; Claire
    Seng-Niemoeller
Cover Design: William Boardman
Cover Photo: Ganchev Anatolii/Shutterstock
Printing and Binding: LSC Communications, Harrisonburg

Copyright © 2018 by Bedford/St. Martin's.

Manufactured in the United States of America.

For information, write: Bedford/St. Martin's, 75 Arlington Street, Boston,
    MA 02116

ISBN 978-1-319-05509-7

Acknowledgments

Text acknowledgments and copyrights appear at the back of the book on pages 362–63, which constitute an extension of the copyright page. Art acknowledgments and copyrights appear on the same page as the art selections they cover.

About The Bedford Spotlight Reader Series

The Bedford Spotlight Reader Series is a growing line of single-theme readers, each featuring Bedford's trademark care and quality. The readers in the series collect thoughtfully chosen readings sufficient for an entire writing course—about thirty-five selections—to allow instructors to provide carefully developed, high-quality instruction at an affordable price. Bedford Spotlight Readers are designed to help students make inquiries from multiple perspectives, opening up topics such as borders, food, gender, happiness, humor, money, monsters, music, subcultures, and sustainability to critical analysis. An editorial board of a dozen compositionists whose programs focus on specific themes have assisted in the development of the series.

Bedford Spotlight Readers offer plenty of material for a composition course while keeping the price low. Each volume in the series offers multiple perspectives on the topic and its effects on individuals and society. Chapters are built around central questions such as, "How Does Language Reflect Who We Are?" and "What Do We Do When We Write?" and so offer numerous entry points for inquiry and discussion. High-interest readings, chosen for their suitability in the classroom, represent a mix of genres and disciplines as well as a choice of accessible and challenging selections to allow instructors to tailor their approach. Each chapter thus brings to light related—even surprising—questions and ideas.

A rich editorial apparatus provides a sound pedagogical foundation. A general introduction, chapter introductions, and headnotes provide context. Following each selection, writing prompts provide avenues of inquiry tuned to different levels of engagement, from reading comprehension ("Understanding the Text") to critical analysis ("Reflection and Response"), to the kind of integrative analysis appropriate to the research paper ("Making Connections"). An appendix, "Sentence Guides for Academic Writers," helps students with the most basic academic scenario: having to understand and respond to the ideas of others. This is a practical module that helps students develop an academic writing voice by giving them sentence guides, or templates, to follow in a variety of rhetorical situations and types of research conversations. A website for the series offers support for teaching, with a sample syllabus, additional readings, video links, and more; visit **macmillanlearning.com /spotlight**.

Language *Diversity and Academic Writing* presents a collection of readings that encourage students to understand the diversity within their own and others' language and apply that knowledge to their academic writing. I have created this collection because I believe firmly, based on both research and classroom experience, that language diversity is a necessary topic for first-year writing students.

For some students, academic discussion of language diversity presents an opportunity to apply academic terminology to everyday experiences. These students may be multilingual code-switchers, they may have experienced firsthand the effects of standard language ideologies, or they may be fluent speakers of an undervalued dialect that linguists have studied for decades. Few things scholarship could tell these students about the everyday workings of language diversity and ideology will be entirely new to them, but the fact that these issues inform entire academic careers is often a revelation. Finding one's own experience represented in scholarly venues is a richly rewarding and validating experience for college students (for all of us, really), and I for one find it exciting to watch students find new ways to think critically about their life experience.

For other students, "diversity" has nearly always read to them as code for "stuff involving other people." If they have encountered the phrase "language diversity," they have immediately thought of speakers of Spanish or African American English. If asked about the diversity present in their own language, they would likely say, as several of my students have said to me early on in the semester, "I just talk normal." For these students, discussion of language diversity presents opportunities for enormous growth. They can understand the complexity of their own language by understanding how their speech and writing are influenced by issues of social class, regional location, age, technology, education, gender, and race. They can also develop knowledge of unfamiliar linguistic varieties and experiences that will help them build the skills and empathy necessary to communicate as global citizens.

So language diversity is important for college students, yes. But why do this work in first-year writing? Simply put, because the conventions we teach student writers and the ways they learn and understand those conventions are inextricably intertwined with language and our ideologies around it. From a student perspective, understanding language diversity means understanding one's own array of linguistic resources and recognizing the skill that all people have in selecting from among those resources to suit a range of situations. In other words, discussing language diversity alongside academic writing can help students feel more capable as academic writers; it enables them to see academic writing as one among many codes that they command, and one to which they can apply many of their existing skills as communicators.[1]

On a pedagogical and theoretical level, discussing language diversity, and the assumptions and judgments that often accompany it, enables both students and teachers to develop a critical, complex understanding of academic writing expectations. Far from being the mythical monolith it often seems, the category of "academic" or "college-level" in writing and language is complex and difficult to pin down. Usages that qualify as "academic" in one discipline or to one professor may not be acceptable to another. Ideas about academic discourse have been constructed historically based on a collection of often-hidden assumptions and ideologies about language. Discussing ideas about academic writing alongside ideas about language diversity and standards, then, allows both students and instructors to ask questions and clarify unstated assumptions, leading to a deeper and more productive understanding of what it means to write academically.

This book is structured to lead students from their personal connections with language to its broader and subtler ideologies and standards; at the same time, it leads them from everyday experience to formal academic writing. In Chapters 1 and 2 especially, I had in mind the different ways our students may identify (or not) with the idea of diversity. The readings in these chapters have been selected to connect with a range of student experiences; students can receive validation and academic vocabulary for their experiences and build empathy and curiosity toward the experiences of others. They should finish Chapter 1 with an understanding of language's role in lives and cultures, and Chapter 2 with an understanding of its role in perceptions and judgments. Students are then ready to think in Chapter 3 about the processes of language change, which is driven by language's connection to culture, and language standardization, which relates closely to language-based judgments.

While many of the principles discussed in the first three chapters can apply to both spoken and written language, Chapters 4 and 5 are meant to turn students' attention specifically to writing. Chapter 4 serves two purposes: In the first half, it transitions into the focus on writing with readings that show how general principles of language apply to writing specifically; in the second half, it encourages attention to issues of process and cognition that are somewhat unique to written language. In addition to a transition

---

[1] I discuss my pedagogical rationale for a language-focused first-year writing class in the article "Writing about Language: Studying Language Diversity with First-Year Writers" (*Teaching English in the Two-Year College*, vol. 44, no. 2, December 2016). A version of this paragraph appears in that article.

in focus, Chapter 4 represents a shift in discipline from linguistics to writing studies, which sets up Chapter 5. Chapter 5 is intended as something of a culmination to the book, helping students see the connections between language diversity and academic writing that hold the book together. In it, students are invited to consider the range of genres and languages that can be present in academic writing. They can explore, in dialogue with writing studies scholars, how common criteria for "academic writing" can miss the full complexity of what academic writers do and expect. As Chris Thaiss and Terry Myers Zawacki note in their Chapter 5 selection, academic writing standards are never truly "as straightforward as 'avoid the first person' or 'use correct English' or 'have a clear thesis'" (p. 288).

By explaining the rationale behind my chapter sequence, I do not intend to say that these readings can be taught only, or even best, in the order I've placed them. (In fact, I decided to start my own class this semester with the Thaiss and Zawacki reading, since I felt it made an excellent catalyst for discussion of our purposes and goals for the class.) The chapters and individual pieces in this text talk back and forth well, so I encourage you to find the connections and sequences that you feel will make sense to your students; the alternative tables of contents will aid you. I have worked in my introductions to the chapters and individual readings to provide students with the necessary foundation for approaching each piece, wherever it falls in the trajectory of your course. I encourage you also to visit the accompanying website for additional resources, including supplementary online links and sample syllabi.

By the time students have finished working with *Language Diversity and Academic Writing*, I hope that they will have a solid foundation of knowledge that they can apply to their lives in academic contexts and beyond. I hope that they will become savvier communicators and more critical academic thinkers as we work together to lead them through thinking and writing about the situations, identities, and ideologies that shape their languages and their lives.

Acknowledgments

A great many people have made this book possible. For the ideas behind the book, I am most indebted to my many first-year writing students, whose inquisitiveness and engagement both inspired me to put this book together and helped me refine my approach to its theme. I extend particular thanks to my Fall 2016 Writing-Based Inquiry Seminar class, which was the best group of students a teacher could ask for during textbook crunch time; their kindness toward my scattered self and their excitement about the book sustained me through the semester.

For making the book happen, I have many folks at Macmillan to thank. Brook Hanson, Senior Sales Representative, and Laura Davidson,

Humanities Specialist, who brought me into the Bedford fold with their genuine interest in my program and courses. Through them, I met Program Manager for Readers and Literature John Sullivan and Senior Program Director for English Leasa Burton, who invited me to join the Bedford Spotlight Reader Series Editorial Board. As John got to know more about my first-year writing course, he encouraged me to make my theme the basis for my own Spotlight Reader Series book. John was my primary collaborator in developing the organization for the book and selecting appropriate readings; calling him essential to this project still feels like an understatement. One of my favorite of John's many contributions was his selection of Kathy Retan as Developmental Editor. It is truly amazing how a good editor can get into your brain and figure out exactly what you're trying to do before you've managed to enact it. Kathy did this over and over, not only helping me to articulate my ideas in words but also, when some of my original readings started to feel less than ideal and images needed to be selected, helping me decide on readings and images that would best achieve the learning goals I had in mind. Kathy is, in sum, a miracle. Throughout my work with Kathy and John, the contributions of Jennifer Prince, Associate Editor, were vital. Thank you, Jen, for keeping us organized and on track on so many fronts. I would also like to thank Edwin Hill, Vice President of Editorial Humanities, and Lexi DeConti, Associate Editor, at Macmillan Learning. Finally, I am grateful for the refinement and logistical help provided toward the end of the process by Andrea Cava, Publishing Services Manager; Lou Bruno, Content Project Manager; Tom Wilcox, permissions researcher; and Angela Boehler, photo researcher.

This book benefited enormously from the sharp insights and critiques of the faculty colleagues who reviewed an early version. My sincere thanks to Elizabeth Baldridge, Illinois Central College; Christopher Basgier, Auburn University; Anne Boyle, Wake Forest University; Marcia Buell, Northeastern Illinois University; Deborah Cole, University of Texas-Rio Grande Valley; Sheila Dooley, University of Texas-Rio Grande Valley; Errin Jordan, University of North Dakota; Jonathon Keller, Kent State University; Cat Mahaffey, University of North Carolina at Charlotte; Andrea Olinger, University of Louisville; Christa Olson, University of Wisconsin–Madison; and Martha Webber, California State University, Fullerton.

Finally, on a personal level, I am grateful to those who have supported me and believed in me throughout this process. There are too many to name here, but a few deserve special mention: my department chair, Roberta Maguire; my parents, George and Liane Waselus; my closest confidants, Brian Looker and Alexandra Cavallaro; and my husband and partner in all of life's most important endeavors, Trevor Koenigs. Thank you all.

Samantha Looker-Koenigs

Bedford/St. Martin's is as passionately committed to the discipline of English as ever, working hard to provide support and services that make it easier for you to teach your course your way.

Find **community support** at the Bedford/St. Martin's English Community (**community.macmillan.com**), where you can follow our *Bits* blog for new teaching ideas, download titles from our professional resource series, and review projects in the pipeline.

Choose **curriculum solutions** that offer flexible custom options, combining our carefully developed print and digital resources, acclaimed works from Macmillan's trade imprints, and your own course or program materials to provide the exact resources your students need.

Rely on **outstanding service** from your Bedford/St. Martin's sales representative and editorial team. Contact us or visit **macmillanlearning .com** to learn more about any of the options below.

Choose from Alternative Formats of *Language Diversity and Academic Writing*

Bedford/St. Martin's offers a range of formats. Choose what works best for you and your students.

- *Popular e-Book formats*: For details of our e-book partners, visit **macmillanlearning.com/ebooks**.

Select Value Packages

Add value to your text by packaging one of the following resources with *Language Diversity and Academic Writing*.

LaunchPad Solo for Readers and Writers allows students to work on what they need help with the most. At home or in class, students learn at their own pace, with instruction tailored to each student's unique needs. *LaunchPad Solo for Readers and Writers* features:

- **Pre-built units that support a learning arc.** Each easy-to-assign unit is comprised of a pretest check, multimedia instruction and assessment, and a post-test that assesses what students have learned about critical reading, writing process, using sources, grammar, style, and mechanics. Dedicated units also offer help for multilingual writers.

- **Diagnostics that help establish a baseline for instruction.** Assign diagnostics to identify areas of strength and for improvement and to help students plan a course of study. Use visual reports to track performance by topic, class, and student as well as improvement over time.

- **A video introduction to many topics.** Introductions offer an overview of the unit's topic, and many include a brief, accessible video to illustrate the concepts at hand.

- **Twenty-five reading selections with comprehension quizzes.** Assign a range of classic and contemporary essays each of which includes a label indicating Lexile level to help you scaffold instruction in critical reading.

- **Adaptive quizzing for targeted learning.** Most units include LearningCurve, gamelike adaptive quizzing that focuses on the areas in which each student needs the most help.

Order ISBN 978-1-319-05509-7 to package *LaunchPad Solo for Readers and Writers* with *Language Diversity and Academic Writing* at a significant discount. Students who rent or buy a used book can purchase access and instructors may request free access at **macmillanlearning.com /readwrite.**

Instructor Resources

You have a lot to do in your course. We want to make it easy for you to find the support you need — and to get it quickly. Instructor resources can be downloaded from **macmillanlearning.com**. Visit the instructor resources tab for *Language Diversity and Academic Writing* for additional resources, including supplementary online links and sample syllabi.

Contents

Introduction for Students   1

Chapter 1   How Does Language Reflect and Create Who We Are?   9

Lee Romney, *Revival of Nearly Extinct Yurok Language Is a Success Story*   **12**
In this *Los Angeles Times* article, journalist Romney follows the efforts of tribal elders and local schools to bring a Native American language in California back from "half a century of virtual silence."

Louise Erdrich, *Two Languages in Mind, but Just One in the Heart*   **18**
"To Ojibwe speakers the language is a deeply loved entity," says Erdrich, a novelist and poet who offers her thoughts on learning the language of her Ojibwe heritage as an adult.

Amy Tan, *Mother Tongue*   **24**
Bestselling writer Amy Tan describes her relationship with her Chinese mother's English. While others may view it as "broken," Tan says that her mother's English "helped shape the way I saw things, expressed things, made sense of the world."

Gloria Anzaldúa, *How to Tame a Wild Tongue*   **31**
Anzaldúa, a writer and cultural theorist, proclaims her connection to her Chicano Spanish language and defends the rights of herself and others to speak it: "Ethnic identity is twin skin to linguistic identity— I am my language."

Susan Tamasi and Lamont Antieau, *Social Variables*   **43**
Linguists Tamasi and Antieau explain some of the social factors that affect language, including gender, age, and sexual orientation, while

Chapter 3   How Does Language Change (Whether We Like It or Not)?   159

Chapter 5 What Does It Mean to Write "Academically"? 281

Writing researchers Sommers and Saltz observe that struggling students often see writing as "a game, where someone else makes up the rules and doles out the grades." Success as a college writer, they claim, requires seeing a "greater purpose in writing than completing an assignment."

Whitney, an education professor, describes how one student's experience inspired her to understand voice and source use in student writing: Students need to feel "entitled to speak alongside or even over the voices of more authoritative, published, and expert speakers."

Contents by Discipline

Media Studies

Psychology

Social Justice

Writing Studies

Contents by Theme

Age and Youth

American English Dialects

Bilingualism and Multilingualism

Gender and Sexuality

Identity and Self-Perception

Language Change and Evolution

Race and Ethnicity

Standards and Correctness

Teaching and Learning

Tools and Technologies

Writing Processes

Contents by Rhetorical Purpose

Analysis and Exemplification

Argument

Comparison and Contrast

Critique

Explanation

Narration and Reflection

Introduction for Students

Why Study Language Diversity?

One of the most exciting things about college-level learning, I often tell my students, is the opportunity to examine aspects of our everyday lives that we previously took for granted. Through academic investigation, we can deepen our understandings and find answers to questions we had not previously even thought to ask. This book will teach you many new concepts, most from the scholarly field of sociolinguistics (the study of how language and society interact). At the same time, it will encourage you to consider your experiences with and knowledge of language, raising your awareness of what you as a language user already know and do. By putting your own and others' experiences in dialogue with scholarly perspectives, you will gain a richer understanding of how language functions in your life and in society.

Few of us are consciously aware of everything we know about language. As we go through our lives as language users, we are constantly acquiring information, ideas, and abilities that influence how we use language and how we respond to others' language use. For one thing, each of us has acquired a set of unique language characteristics—our *idiolect*, in linguistic terms—which is based on who we are and what we have experienced. Our pronunciation, for instance, often reflects our upbringing. If you grew up in Wisconsin, you likely pronounce some of your vowels differently from someone who grew up in Alabama. If you grew up speaking Korean in Korea and then learned English in your early teens when you came to the United States, some of your English consonants likely sound different from those of someone whose first language is English. We could make a near-infinite number of similar statements relating to every aspect of your language and your background. Everything in your language—your pronunciation, vocabulary, grammar, spelling, intonation, and more—shows the influence of factors like your geographical location, age, ethnicity, and education.

Within our idiolects, then, all of us have a diverse store of language available to us. Another thing we acquire as we go through our lives as language users is the ability to pull selectively from that store of language as we move among different situations. We adjust our speech and writing to our situations naturally, often with very little conscious thought. If you are Spanish-English bilingual, you will automatically choose English, Spanish, or both depending on your conversation partner. If you are a biology major and a member of the tennis team, you will save your biology vocabulary for your classmates and your tennis vocabulary for your teammates. A text message about your week's schedule will have a different level of formality, including more or less use of features like slang and emoji, depending on whether it is intended for your best friend, your mom, or your boss.

The associations we make between situations and languages are based on our understandings of not only the situations but also language itself. And here is a third thing we acquire as we go through our lives as language users: We develop a set of attitudes toward language, which linguists sometimes call *language ideologies*. Language ideologies tell us that certain ways of speaking and writing are better (more correct, proper, educated, or appropriate) than others. These attitudes can be so deeply ingrained in our educational and cultural surroundings that we may not even recognize them as attitudes; they look, instead, like fact. Many of us grow up with parents telling us that profanities are "bad words." Many teachers in the United States tell young children that *ain't* is not "proper English." Yet, as language scholars argue, there can be nothing automatically good or bad about a particular collection of sounds, markings, or words. Language does nothing by itself, even at the simplest level; the letters *c-a-t* only combine to describe the four-legged animal that says "meow" because English speakers have agreed that they do. Similarly, you are told not to use *ain't* in an academic essay not because that word has something inherently wrong with it but because people in academic settings have agreed that they don't consider it appropriately formal. All parts of language rely on social agreement, and language ideology is no exception.

The attitudes and knowledge I've discussed so far are part of your everyday life, but they may or may not be within your conscious awareness.

Studying them from an academic perspective can, therefore, give you valuable new insight. By reading the texts in this book, you will come to see your language's unique characteristics as part of known linguistic patterns and phenomena, allowing you to understand yourself better through scholarly research that relates directly to aspects of your experience. You will come to see others' unique language features similarly, making you more effective at communicating with and understanding a broader range of people. Also, as you increase your awareness of both your language and your ideas about it, you will prepare yourself to investigate how you and others perceive and judge language according to complex standards.

Why engage in this study of language diversity in a writing class? Because, at its core, academic writing is just another one of our many ways of using language. To many undergraduate students, teachers' standards for and reactions to their academic writing feel completely mysterious. (Chris Thaiss and Terry Myers Zawacki make this point in their piece in Chapter 5, but I suspect that it also feels quite familiar from personal experience.) One of my goals in this book is to strip away some of that mystery. By understanding how we manage our language varieties and acquire our ideas about appropriate language, we can also see where academic writing standards come from. By understanding how we adjust our language to situations, we can also realize that there is no such thing as universally good writing or one "correct" way of writing in college. Like the choice to use more or less slang in a text message, your choices of particular vocabulary words, sentence structures, and tones in your academic writing are indeed *choices*, based on what you know, what you are doing, and what you want to achieve. As you raise your awareness of the contexts in which you write and the ideologies that influence others' expectations for your writing, you will become more comfortable making decisions about how to present yourself and your knowledge.

The Structure of This Book

This book is organized into five chapters, each focused on a central question related to language or writing. You will likely find, as I did, that these five questions are related in many interesting ways, and that often a reading in one chapter will help you answer questions posed by other chapters, too. Before you dive into this complex interrelatedness of ideas, though, I want to take a moment to give you an overview of the book's structure so that you can understand the key issue each chapter explores and why the chapters are sequenced in this particular order.

Chapter 1, "How Does Language Reflect and Create Who We Are?," anchors itself in the question of what language means to us personally. The writers in this chapter discuss the connection of language—whether that be an entire language, such as Yurok, or a variety such as youth slang or Chicano Spanish—to culture, community, and identity. As the scholarly and personal perspectives represented here illuminate, our dialects and languages continually work to shape and maintain our senses of identity and community membership.

Building on Chapter 1's exploration of our personal connections to language, Chapter 2, "How Does Language Affect How Others Perceive Us?," explores some of the judgments and stereotypes people tend to have about others' language. The identity topics introduced in Chapter 1 remain relevant here, for as the readings in Chapter 2 show, judgments about a particular language variety are often entangled with judgments about the people who speak that variety.

Chapter 3, "How Does Language Change (Whether We Like It or Not)?," builds on two themes from the previous chapters: variation within language and judgments about language. To supplement previous discussions of language variation between people and places, many of this chapter's authors consider some aspect of how language changes over time, including topics like how new words are added to the dictionary and how technological change influences language. Also, building on previous discussions about judgments toward language, this chapter considers common standards for language, how those standards develop, and how they affect attitudes toward language change.

Many of the language concepts discussed throughout this book apply to both written and spoken language, but Chapters 4 and 5 work toward applying these concepts specifically to academic writing. Chapter 4, "What Do We Do When We Write?," starts out by considering writing generally, including the similarities and differences between writing and speech. The writers, all scholars from the field of writing studies, show how writing involves many of the themes of identity and community that occur in all language use. Other articles in this chapter consider attitudes toward and processes for writing, so that you can consider mind-sets and circumstances that may be helping or hindering your writing.

This book's discussion of language diversity and academic writing culminates with Chapter 5, "What Does It Mean to Write 'Academically'?" Chapter 5 illuminates how issues of language variation and language ideology affect our understandings of academic writing. The writers here encourage careful consideration of how we define "academic" writing and draw attention to factors that can make that definition slippery. Ultimately, this chapter brings us to an important question: If there are few set standards for mechanical features of academic language and writing, what *does* matter in the teaching and learning of writing in academic settings? This is a question posed by many writing studies scholars, but student writers are not often brought into the conversation. I hope that you will benefit from this behind-the-scenes examination of the "mysterious" standards for academic writing.

Why a Single-Theme Reader?

Sometimes, my students will ask me, "Why are we focusing our entire class on a single topic?" In addition to what I have already said about why *this* particular topic is useful for a writing class, let me add a note about why focusing on a single theme is helpful for your learning and writing. Essentially, writing around a theme is designed to give you a more authentic academic writing experience, one that is closer to the experience of professional academics.

When professional academics write, they do so based on expertise and in the context of scholarly conversations and communities. They almost never start writing essays and articles about something right when they start learning about it. They do a great deal of reading to familiarize themselves with a topic — initially in their years of graduate school as they build their specialization, and then continually throughout their careers as new research is released or they shift to new interests. By doing this reading, they develop a strong sense of the scholarly conversation around their subject. You see, academic writers are, when they publish their books and articles, participating in a conversation. They are listening to what others have "said" (written) about a topic and then adding their own contribution to the conversation—offering some further information or ideas that future participants in the conversation can build on. As they read one another's writing and do their own writing in response, they are developing a shared understanding and shared vocabulary, much as you do when you cultivate a friendship with others who share your love of football, or form a study group with other students in your chemistry class.

By doing extensive reading on language diversity, you are making yourself part of a scholarly community that thinks about the topic of language and writing. You will come to the task of writing about this topic with a strong sense of what is already happening in that community's conversation, and you will be prepared with the background knowledge and vocabulary that will enable you to make an effective contribution to that conversation.

Tips for Active Reading

Many of us, when we start college, have had ample practice with reading two types of texts: novels, which we have read for plots, characters, and symbolism; and textbooks, which have helpfully announced necessary information to us with their bullet points, review sections, and bolded vocabulary words. We are much less likely to have substantial practice with the sorts of informative and opinion articles, both popular and academic, that are represented in this reader. Here, then, are some strategies that will help you to approach such articles:

- **Annotate the articles.** Highlighting or underlining is smart, but don't stop there. Write a label next to each significant point a writer makes; this practice will ensure that you don't have to reread an entire article to find a point you wanted to discuss in class or include in your essay. Make a note of any questions that come to mind as you read, or any points an author makes that surprise you. Use the margins of the text to "talk back" to an author when you disagree. By taking good notes, you are entering into the conversation around a topic, which will make you a stronger participant in class discussions and a more efficient essay writer.

- **Identify a "thesis," or organizing idea, for each piece you read.** Not all writers will state a thesis outright, but you should make it a priority to try to summarize their argument or main idea in a sentence or two. Having a sense of a writer's overall purpose will help you to understand all of the points made within an article and will guard you against misinterpreting or misusing any of them in your own writing.

- **Pay attention to how writers use their sources.** Coming out of high school, we often feel that the main reason for using a source is to say, "See, here is an expert who supports me." This is certainly one reason why writers use sources, but it is far from the only one. Some of the writers in this collection use sources for a very different purpose: to represent a provocative idea that they do *not* agree with. Keeping an author's overall purpose in mind becomes especially important when you need to understand how a writer is using the words or ideas of another. Consider Edwin Battistella's use of Jacques Barzun's ideas in the following passage from "Slang as Bad Language": "The argument is sometimes also made that slang is harmful to the language. For example, Jacques Barzun portrays slang as encroaching on the existing meanings of words" (p. 186). If I wrote in an essay that, according to Battistella, "slang is harmful to the language," my teacher would rightfully critique me for not noticing how Barzun's perspective functions in Battistella's essay. Barzun provides a point for Battistella to argue *against* rather than a point that he agrees with, and Battistella's overall argument in this selection is in fact that most criticisms of slang lack logical and factual support.

- **Look up unfamiliar words.** I have footnoted definitions of some words that have specific meanings in linguistics or writing studies, to ensure that you have a definition similar to the one the writer is using. But there are still plenty of other words in these readings that you may not have encountered. Sometimes you can skim past an unfamiliar word if it doesn't seem important—you may struggle to keep track of a writer's points if you pause to look up every other word—but if you don't stop to look up anything, you may quickly find that you are missing some of an article's meaning. As you read, keep a dictionary handy, or keep a tab open to a reliable dictionary website such as **merriam-webster.com**. Write those definitions down on the articles, so that you remember the meaning when you return to a selection in discussion and essay writing.

In addition to these general strategies, you have in this book some questions after each reading that are designed to deepen your understanding of the text. You will encounter three types of questions. "Understanding the Text" questions focus on summarizing the ideas and arguments presented in a reading, so that you can check that you understood some of the important points. "Reflection and Response" questions encourage you to think more deeply about the text, usually by either connecting it to your own experience or analyzing the writer's strategies and argument. "Making Connections" questions ask you to think about the current reading in dialogue with other texts, often ones elsewhere in this book. Your instructor may assign you to answer some of these questions in an essay or in preparation for discussion. If not, I encourage you to think about them on your own.

Overall, I encourage you to be aware of what works for you when reading, how you best prepare yourself to respond to and use what you read. Beyond that, I encourage you to approach your readings and the subject matter of this class with curiosity. I hope that this book will supplement your existing knowledge of language and writing in ways that will be both enjoyable and useful.

Ganchev Anatolii / Shutterstock

1 | How Does Language Reflect and Create Who We Are?

"Who are you?" That is a big question, but you likely have a lot of answers at the ready. We habitually label ourselves with words describing attributes like gender, race, sexuality, religion, or profession. It is interesting to note what we are doing when we say things like "I'm a woman," "I'm Mexican American," or "I'm a future nurse": We are asserting not only our understandings of ourselves but our status as part of a group, our identification with a community of people who share some aspect of our identity.

We're doing a similar thing when we use our languages, dialects, and registers. Speaking the Native American language Yurok, as the speakers in Lee Romney's article do, says not just "I speak Yurok" but "I am part of the Yurok tribe" or "I am part of the community that cares about saving the Yurok language." Likewise, when Louise Erdrich speaks Ojibwe, she asserts herself as one of the Ojibwe people, and she builds in herself the ability to think and communicate like other Ojibwe. Both Yurok and Ojibwe, like most Native American languages, were driven to extinction or near-extinction by the U.S. and Canadian governmental practices of educating Native children in English-only schools. Therefore, to assert oneself as a member of a tribe who speaks that tribe's language is a powerful act. "I am here," it says. "My tribe remains, and our language remains."

The languages we speak reflect our identity and membership in a community, and in turn serve to shape and maintain both our sense of ourselves and the identities of the communities we belong to. Each of us inhabits many identities and belongs to many communities of varying sizes and types. Amy Tan's family community is strengthened by her mother's Chinese-influenced English, which has become a family language that binds her to her loved ones and feels like home. Gloria Anzaldúa, meanwhile, is bound to her community of Chicanos by a list of languages reflecting their various backgrounds and locations; while her community is not as intimately connected as a family, a similar homelike familiarity is achieved through shared language. When Anzaldúa says, "I am my language" (p. 36), she makes a statement about the connection between language and identity that works well beyond the specific context of ethnic identity to which she applies it. As Susan Tamasi and Lamont Antieau explain, our language also connects us to group identities based on age, gender, and sexuality. Our use of vocabulary, intonation, or grammar that is associated with a particular group — such as the slang associated with young people or the rising ("questioning") intonation associated with women — ensures that we continue to be perceived as part of that group.

Part of our group identification, a part that is clearly reflected in language, is a group's values and priorities. When Connie Eble explores the slang of college students, she finds something that you likely know from your own experience: College slang illustrates how our language tends to reflect the things that are most important to us as individuals and communities. H. Samy Alim gives us a similar glimpse into the connection between language and group values for the Hip Hop Nation: a community tied together by hip hop culture, often connected to the everyday concerns of African Americans and/or residents of urban areas.

The communities and identities represented in this chapter — hip hop and Hispanic, youth and Yurok — are only a small sampling of the many communities and identities that we inhabit and that our language reflects. How does your language speak your identity?

Revival of Nearly Extinct Yurok Language Is a Success Story

Lee Romney

This article by journalist Lee Romney, which first appeared in the *Los Angeles Times* on February 6, 2013, focuses on the language of the Yurok Tribe, the largest group of American Indians in California. Today, the Yurok Tribe has a national membership of just under 6,000, over 4,000 of which is in California. These numbers represent enormous gains since the early 1900s, when white settlers' diseases and massacres had reduced the Yurok population to well under 1,000. While the population is strong today, the Yurok language is much less so. Yurok children, like those in most Native American tribes, were sent to government boarding schools in the 1800s and 1900s where they were severely punished for speaking languages other than English. As a result, Yurok is one of many indigenous languages that now have very few speakers. Efforts like those described in this article aim to save endangered languages from extinction. As you will see, saving a language from extinction also strengthens and preserves the corresponding culture's identity.

Carole Lewis throws herself into her work as if something big is at stake.

"*Pa'-ah,*" she tells her Eureka High School class, gesturing at a bottle of water. She whips around and doodles a crooked little fish on the blackboard, hinting at the dip she's prepared with "*ney-puy*" — salmon, key to the diet of California's largest Native American tribe.

For thousands of years before Western settlers arrived, the Yurok thrived in dozens of villages along the Klamath River. By the 1990s, however, academics had predicted their language soon would be extinct. As elders passed away, the number of native speakers dropped to six.

But tribal leaders would not let the language die.

Last fall, Eureka High became the fifth and largest school in Northern 5 California to launch a Yurok-language program, marking the latest victory in a Native American language revitalization program widely lauded as the most successful in the state.

At last count, there were more than 300 basic Yurok speakers, 60 with intermediate skills, 37 who are advanced and 17 who are considered conversationally fluent.

If all goes as planned, Lewis' 20 students will move on to a second year of study, satisfying the world language requirement for admission to University of California and Cal State schools.

But the teacher and tribe have some longer-term goals: boosting Native American high school graduation rates and college admissions numbers; deepening the Yurok youths' bonds to their culture; and ensuring that their language will regain prominence after half a century of virtual silence.

The decimation of the language dates to the first half of the 20th century, when tens of thousands of Native American youngsters across the country, Lewis' mom among them, were sent to government-run boarding schools. The effort to assimilate the youth into Euro-American culture pressed them to abandon their own. Often they were beaten for speaking in their native tongues.

"The schools had a big negative impact on us. It's how we lost our lan- 10
guage," said James Gensaw, 31, among the small staff of the tribal language program led by Lewis, 62. "Now the schools are helping us to keep it alive."

★ ★ ★ ★ ★

Jim McQuillen edged his SUV down Highway 101 from Crescent City and into the heart of Yurok ancestral territory. From Requa Hill—dotted with burial grounds—the tribe's education director pointed out 'O Re-gos, a rock shaped like a woman carrying a burden basket that is considered the spirit keeper of the mouth of the Klamath River.

A long sandbar blocks the river's exit, fostering a rich ecosystem. When the current breaks through into the ocean on the south side of the sandbar, one legend goes, the legs of 'O Re-gos are outstretched. When the mouth moves south, they are curled to her chest. Tribal members netted 80,000 salmon here last year. Canoes hand-built from fallen redwood ply the waters.

The ancient ways have seen a revival over the last 25 years or so, as have once-banned cultural traditions such as the White Deerskin Dance, part of a 30-day renewal ceremony meant to balance the physical and spiritual worlds.

For youth, the knowledge matters, said McQuillen, 50. "If they come from a family that was very bonded with the dances, they tend to do very well in higher ed. We call it success in both worlds."

But language revitalization proved complex. 15

Decades of dissuasion had silenced the tribal elders. As a 5-year-old, Archie Thompson attended boarding school in Hoopa Valley. "They didn't want Indian language spoken," recalled Thompson, now 93 with a rich head of gray hair and a luminous smile, "You couldn't do your own culture."

Thompson made his way back to his grandmother's ranch on the banks of the Klamath and was steeped in the language throughout his high school years. He hooked eels in the river and netted so many candlefish — *kwo'ror'* — that the bottom of his boat turned white. He is among the few remaining original speakers. But he raised his own eight kids in English, the language of accomplishment.

It's a familiar story.

Like others of their generation, McQuillen and his seven siblings didn't hear their fluent mother speak much Yurok. They knew the names for animals and birds, and couldn't help but soak up the scoldings: *"to'-woh"* (That's enough!) or *"Nee mokw we chpey-geyr'"* (don't you have ears?).

Some revival efforts began in the 1970s, but they did not take off until 20 after the nearly 6,000-member tribe received federal recognition and formed a government in 1992.

Soon Lewis was recruited, securing a grant from the federal Administration for Native Americans. She launched a master/apprentice program to pair elders with new learners and hired Barbara McQuillen, Jim's sister and now the language program's assistant coordinator.

Over the years, Lewis and McQuillen have worked with kids in elementary school, high school, after-school programs, preschoolers at the tribal-run Head Start program and adults in community classes.

Both had learned Yurok from elders, who soaked it up as babies with no knowledge of the rules of grammar. "The elders would say things one way one time and another way another time," McQuillen said. When asked why, they often could not answer.

Then in 2001, UC Berkeley linguists launched the Yurok Language Project.

Professor Andrew Garrett and a colleague reworked an early grammar 25 guide and collaborated with elders on a dictionary. The online written and audio version of the dictionary has been hailed as a national model.

There are sounds not found in English — "hi," for instance, made by putting the tongue against the back of the front teeth and blowing air out on both sides of the mouth, and "ew," which Lewis jokes is used in English only by Elmer Fudd when he says "I will."

The language also shines light on the Yurok worldview. The counting system depends on whether what's counted is round or flat, human or animal. There are no general terms for squirrel, owl or hawk — only names for specific types.

And certain terms have no true English counterpart: *Mue-neech*, for example, translates as "a foolish action," which misses the nuance. "When Coyote tries to do something to make himself look really good, and winds up looking really bad," Lewis said, "that's *mue-neech*."

*"*Ideally we'll be able to look back and say, 'Hey, we helped save a language. . . . How great is that?'"*

* * * * *

California is home to more than 80 Native American languages, making it the most diverse linguistic region in the Western hemisphere. And among revitalization efforts, Garrett said, the Yurok program has been "astonishingly successful."

Key to that was the push into the public schools. But making it happen wasn't easy: Yurok-language instructors in most instances lacked California teaching credentials. 30

The elders who first offered high school instruction—one as far back as the 1970s—were granted eminence credentials, or special waivers.

When McKinleyville High School relaunched its program in 2005 after a long lull, there were four students. There are now 23, said instructor Kathleen Vigil, who co-taught with her mother until the elder woman died four years ago at 95. To accommodate Vigil, the school has assigned a credentialed teacher to sit in class with her.

But it became clear a few years ago that such arrangements would not fly in larger districts. Lewis and the director of Indian education at Hoopa Valley High raised the issue at a statewide conference—and the Santa Ynez Band of Chumash Indians, a tribe with gaming resources, stepped up to press for legislation.

The Assembly bill signed into law in late 2009 requires the California Commission on Teacher Credentialing to issue an "American Indian languages credential" to teachers recommended by federally recognized tribes that are authorized to establish their own fluency tests.

The "squirming class of Klamath preschoolers" Romney describes, with Mike Carlson leading students in reviewing Yurok words for birds.
Robert Gauthier/Getty Images

By 2010, Barbara McQuillen was teaching Yurok at Crescent City's Del 35
Norte High School. Mike Carlson, 19, who graduated last year, is now an
apprentice instructor.

On a recent day, he reviewed the words for birds with a squirming
class of Klamath preschoolers.

"*Terkerkue,*" they squealed when shown an image of a quail.

The tribe has pushed for high school classes to be scheduled in the
early morning—to get students there and keep them there. It seems to
be working.

Alex Gensaw lives next door to tribal elder Archie Thompson and
craved a deeper connection to his culture. He came into McQuillen's
class three years ago knowing only 10 words of Yurok: It wasn't spoken
in his home. But the 16-year-old (a second cousin to Yurok teacher James
Gensaw) now is teaching his mom. And his feelings about the high
school have shifted. "It's like they care more," he said.

A number of non-native students have enrolled in Lewis' Eureka 40
High class, approved by the school board last summer as a pilot program. Principal Rick Jordan said he hopes the program will become
permanent.

"Ideally we'll be able to look back and say, 'Hey, we helped save a language,'" Jordan said. "How great is that?"

Understanding the Text

1. Summarize the history of the Yurok language: When was it thriving? What
   caused it to decline? What has helped to bring it back?

2. What have been some of the benefits for young people that have resulted
   from incorporating the Yurok revival effort into public schools?

Reflection and Response

3. Consider this chapter's title — "How Does Language Reflect and Create Who
   We Are?" — in reference to Romney's article. How does the Yurok language
   reflect who the Yurok people are? How has its revival helped to "create" or
   solidify their identity?

4. Romney's piece is an example of the sort of news article typically called a
   feature article. Unlike a hard news article, which tends to give all the basic
   facts up front, a feature article works its way toward the key information at a
   more leisurely pace, often first telling a story or describing a scene. Consider
   the beginnings of the first two sections of this article (pars. 1–2
   and 11–13). How do Romney's anecdotes about Carole Lewis and Jim

McQuillen prepare you for the information about the Yurok revival that
will follow? In what ways are these introductions similar to or different from
those you might find in an academic essay?

Making Connections

5. Louise Erdrich, in "Two Languages in Mind, but Just One in the Heart"
   (p. 18), and Gloria Anzaldúa, in "How to Tame a Wild Tongue" (p. 31), did
   not have the experience that the children in this article do of being free and
   encouraged to speak their culture's non-English language in school. How
   do you think Erdrich and Anzaldúa's stories would be different if Ojibwe or
   Chicano Spanish had been taught in their schools?

6. Citing Carole Lewis's example of *mue-neech*, Romney notes that "certain
   [Yurok] terms have no true English counterpart" (par. 28). Use Romney's
   article alongside Louise Erdrich's "Two Languages in Mind, but Just One in
   the Heart" (p. 18), Amy Tan's "Mother Tongue" (p. 24), and/or Gloria
   Anzaldúa's "How to Tame a Wild Tongue" (p. 31) to consider the idea of
   translation within this chapter's question of "How Does Language Reflect
   and Create Who We Are?" Why might it be difficult to translate concepts
   directly from one language to another, and how does this difficulty connect
   to cultural identity?

Two Languages in Mind, but Just One in the Heart

Louise Erdrich

Louise Erdrich is a novelist and a writer of poems, short stories, children's books, and memoirs. Her award-winning novels include *Love Medicine* (Holt, Rinehart and Winston, 1984) and *The Round House* (Harper, 2012). Her novels are set in the upper Midwest and tell the stories of Native American characters within the tribe known as the Ojibwe or Chippewa. Erdrich is herself a member of the Turtle Mountain Chippewa Nation of North Dakota, though she did not grow up on the reservation, nor did she learn the Ojibwe language (also called Ojibwemowin) as a child. In the article below, published in the *New York Times* in 2000, Erdrich describes her experience of learning to speak Ojibwe as an adult, an experience that has allowed her to connect more deeply with her culture and family history and has encouraged her to see the world in new ways.

For years now I have been in love with a language other than the English in which I write, and it is a rough affair. Every day I try to learn a little more Ojibwe. I have taken to carrying verb conjugation charts in my purse, along with the tiny notebook I've always kept for jotting down book ideas, overheard conversations, language detritus, phrases that pop into my head. Now that little notebook includes an increasing volume of Ojibwe words. My English is jealous, my Ojibwe elusive. Like a besieged unfaithful lover, I'm trying to appease them both.

Ojibwemowin, or Anishinabemowin, the Chippewa language, was last spoken in our family by Patrick Gourneau, my maternal grandfather, a Turtle Mountain Ojibwe who used it mainly in his prayers. Growing up off reservation, I thought Ojibwemowin mainly was a language for prayers, like Latin in the Catholic liturgy. I was unaware for many years that Ojibwemowin was spoken in Canada, Minnesota and Wisconsin, though by a dwindling number of people. By the time I began to study the language, I was living in New Hampshire, so for the first few years I used language tapes.

I never learned more than a few polite phrases that way, but the sound of the language in the author Basil Johnson's calm and dignified Anishinabe voice sustained me through bouts of homesickness. I spoke basic Ojibwe in the isolation of my car traveling here and there on twisting New England roads. Back then, as now, I carried my tapes everywhere.

The language bit deep into my heart, but it was an unfulfilled longing. I had nobody to speak it with, nobody who remembered my grandfather's standing with his sacred pipe in the woods next to a box elder tree, talking to the spirits. Not until I moved back to the Midwest and settled in Minneapolis did I find a fellow Ojibwe to learn with, and a teacher.

Mille Lac's Ojibwe elder Jim Clark—Naawi-giizis, or Center of the 5 Day—is a magnetically pleasant, sunny, crew-cut World War II veteran with a mysterious kindliness that shows in his slightest gesture. When he laughs, everything about him laughs; and when he is serious, his eyes round like a boy's.

Naawi-giizis introduced me to the deep intelligence of the language and forever set me on a quest to speak it for one reason: I want to get the jokes. I also want to understand the prayers and the *adisookaanug*, the sacred stories, but the irresistible part of language for me is the explosion of hilarity that attends every other minute of an Ojibwe visit. As most speakers are now bilingual, the language is spiked with puns on both English and Ojibwe, most playing on the oddness of *gichi-mookomaan*, that is, big knife or American, habits and behavior.

This desire to deepen my alternate language puts me in an odd relationship to my first love, English. It is, after all, the language stuffed into my mother's ancestors' mouths. English is the reason she didn't speak her native language and the reason I can barely limp along in mine. English is an all-devouring language that has moved across North America like the fabulous plagues of locusts that darkened the sky and devoured even the handles of rakes and hoes. Yet the omnivorous nature of a colonial language is a writer's gift. Raised in the English language, I partake of a mongrel feast.

A hundred years ago most Ojibwe people spoke Ojibwemowin, but the Bureau of Indian Affairs and religious boarding schools punished and humiliated children who spoke native languages. The program worked, and there are now almost no fluent speakers of Ojibwe in the United States under the age of 30. Speakers like Naawi-giizis value the language partly because it has been physically beaten out of so many people. Fluent speakers have had to fight for the language with their own flesh, have endured ridicule, have resisted shame and stubbornly pledged themselves to keep on talking the talk.

My relationship is of course very different. How do you go back to a language you never had? Why should a writer who loves her first language find it necessary and essential to complicate her life with another? Simple reasons, personal and impersonal. In the past few years I've found that I can talk to God only in this language, that somehow my grandfather's use of the language penetrated. The sound comforts me.

A group of girls from the Omaha tribe attending the Carlisle Indian School in Pennsylvania, ca. 1880. Most children attending government boarding schools in the 1800s and early 1900s, like the Ojibwe Erdrich discusses and the Omaha pictured here, were strictly forbidden from speaking their tribe's language or wearing any tribal clothing or hairstyle. Pictures of boarding school children in European-style dress were intended to display how "civilized" the children had become.
CORBIS/Corbis via Getty Images

What the Ojibwe call the Gizhe Manidoo, the great and kind spirit 10 residing in all that lives, what the Lakota call the Great Mystery, is associated for me with the flow of Ojibwemowin. My Catholic training touched me intellectually and symbolically but apparently never engaged my heart.

· There is also this: Ojibwemowin is one of the few surviving languages that evolved to the present here in North America. The intelligence of this language is adapted as no other to the philosophy bound up in northern land, lakes, rivers, forests arid plains; to the animals and their particular habits; to the shades of meaning in the very placement of stones. As a North American writer it is essential to me that I try to understand our human relationship to place in the deepest way possible, using my favorite tool, language.

There are place names in Ojibwe and Dakota for every physical feature of Minnesota, including recent additions like city parks and dredged lakes. Ojibwemowin is not static, not confined to describing the world of some out-of-reach and sacred past. There are words for e-mail, computers, internet, fax. For exotic animals in zoos. *Anaamibiig gookoosh*, the underwater pig, is a hippopotamus. *Nandookomeshiinh*, the lice hunter, is the monkey.

There are words for the serenity prayer used in 12-step programs and translations of nursery rhymes. The varieties of people other than Ojibwe or Anishinabe are also named: Aiibiishaabookewininiwag, the tea people, are Asians. Agongosininiwag, the chipmunk people, are Scandinavians. I'm still trying to find out why.

For years I saw only the surface of Ojibwemowin. With any study at all one looks deep into a stunning complex of verbs. Ojibwemowin is a language of verbs. All action. Two-thirds of the words are verbs, and for each verb there are as many as 6,000 forms. The storm of verb forms makes it a wildly adaptive and powerfully precise language. *Changite-ige* describes the way a duck tips itself up in the water butt first. There is a word for what would happen if a man fell off a motorcycle with a pipe in his mouth and the stem of it went through the back of his head. There can be a verb for anything.

When it comes to nouns, there is some relief. There aren't many 15 objects. With a modest if inadvertent political correctness, there are no designations of gender in Ojibwemowin. There are no feminine or masculine possessives or articles.

Nouns are mainly designated as alive or dead, animate or inanimate. The word for stone, *asin*, is animate. Stones are called grandfathers and grandmothers and are extremely important in Ojibwe philosophy. Once I began to think of stones as animate, I started to wonder whether I was picking up a stone or it was putting itself into my hand. Stones are not the same as they were to me in English. I can't write about a stone without considering it in Ojibwe and acknowledging that the Anishinabe universe began with a conversation between stones.

Ojibwemowin is also a language of emotions; shades of feeling can be mixed like paints. There is a word for what occurs when your heart is silently shedding tears. Ojibwe is especially good at describing intellectual states and the fine points of moral responsibility.

Ozozamenimaa pertains to a misuse of one's talents getting out of control. *Ozozamichige* implies you can still set things right. There are many more kinds of love than there are in English. There are myriad shades of emotional meaning to designate various family and clan members. It is a language that also recognizes the humanity of a creaturely God, and the absurd and wondrous sexuality of even the most deeply religious beings.

Slowly the language has crept into my writing, replacing a word here, a concept there, beginning to carry weight. I've thought of course of writing stories in

"However awkward my nouns, unstable my verbs, however stumbling my delivery, to engage in the language is to engage the spirit."

Ojibwe, like a reverse Nabokov. With my Ojibwe at the level of a dreamy 4-year-old child's, I probably won't.

Though it was not originally a written language, people simply 20 adapted the English alphabet and wrote phonetically. During the Second World War, Naawi-giizis wrote Ojibwe letters to his uncle from Europe. He spoke freely about his movements, as no censor could understand his writing. Ojibwe orthography has recently been standardized. Even so, it is an all-day task for me to write even one paragraph using verbs in their correct arcane forms. And even then, there are so many dialects of Ojibwe that, for many speakers, I'll still have gotten it wrong.

As awful as my own Ojibwe must sound to a fluent speaker, I have never, ever, been greeted with a moment of impatience or laughter. Perhaps people wait until I've left the room. But more likely, I think, there is an urgency about attempting to speak the language. To Ojibwe speakers the language is a deeply loved entity. There is a spirit or an originating genius belonging to each word.

Before attempting to speak this language, a learner must acknowledge these spirits with gifts of tobacco and food. Anyone who attempts Ojibwemowin is engaged in something more than learning tongue twisters. However awkward my nouns, unstable my verbs, however stumbling my delivery, to engage in the language is to engage the spirit. Perhaps that is what my teachers know, and what my English will forgive.

Understanding the Text

1. What reasons does Erdrich give for wanting to learn the Ojibwe language?
2. According to Erdrich's descriptions, in what ways are Ojibwe grammar and vocabulary different from those of English?

Reflection and Response

3. In an interview for *First Speakers*, a documentary that originally aired on Twin Cities Public Radio in 2010, Erdrich said, "You are entering another world when you begin to understand even bits and pieces of an indigenous language." In what ways does this article illustrate and support her statement? How has Ojibwe encouraged Erdrich to enter another world, or at least to see and think about her world differently?
4. Language and thought are often said to go hand in hand because languages reflect the experiences and values of their speakers. Can you identify any characteristics of the language(s) you speak that encourage you to think about your world in a certain way?

Making Connections

5. Erdrich spent much of her life believing that "Ojibwemowin mainly was a language for prayers" (par. 2); it wasn't until more recently that she realized the language is "not confined to describing the world of some out-of-reach and sacred past" (par. 12). Based on what you have read in this article and the previous one, supplemented by any relevant personal experience or research, why might people assume that American Indian languages belong only with religion and history? What problems come from such an assumption?

6. Erdrich's article is similar to Lee Romney's in subject matter, but they take rather different forms. Romney's is written in the third person by a reporter describing her observations and quoting from interviews with teachers and learners of Yurok; Erdrich's is written in the first person from the perspective of an Ojibwe learner. Compare the effects of these two different styles of writing: What types of information do you get from each article that you don't get from the other? Do you have a stronger emotional response to one article or the other? Why?

Mother Tongue

Amy Tan

Amy Tan is an award-winning fiction writer. Her best-known novels, including *The Joy Luck Club* (1989) and *The Kitchen God's Wife* (1991), focus on Chinese women — particularly mothers and daughters — with good reason: Her own mother has been a strong influence on Tan's life and writing. Tan's parents immigrated to the United States from China shortly before she was born, and her mother's English, like that of many immigrants who learn the language as adults, always retained traces of her native language's pronunciation and grammar. In this essay, which originally appeared in the Fall 1990 issue of *Threepenny Review*, Tan describes her mother's unique version of English and her own process of coming to understand and appreciate that language. The phrase "mother tongue" has a double meaning here: The language Tan is talking about is literally her mother's language, but it is also Tan's "mother tongue" — the first language she learned to speak growing up. As a result, Tan's understanding of her mother's language also deepens her understanding of herself.

I am not a scholar of English or literature. I cannot give you much more than personal opinions on the English language and its variations in this country or others.

I am a writer. And by that definition, I am someone who has always loved language. I am fascinated by language in daily life. I spend a great deal of my time thinking about the power of language — the way it can evoke an emotion, a visual image, a complex idea, or a simple truth. Language is the tool of my trade. And I use them all — all the Englishes I grew up with.

Recently, I was made keenly aware of the different Englishes I do use. I was giving a talk to a large group of people, the same talk I had already given to half a dozen other groups. The nature of the talk was about my writing, my life, and my book, *The Joy Luck Club*. The talk was going along well enough, until I remembered one major difference that made the whole talk sound wrong. My mother was in the room. And it was perhaps the first time she had heard me give a lengthy speech, using the kind of English I have never used with her. I was saying things like, "The intersection of memory upon imagination" and "There is an aspect of my fiction that relates to thus-and-thus" — a speech filled with carefully wrought grammatical phrases, burdened, it suddenly seemed to me, with nominalized forms, past perfect tenses, conditional phrases, all the forms of standard English that I had learned in school and through books, the forms of English I did not use at home with my mother.

Just last week, I was walking down the street with my mother, and I again found myself conscious of the English I was using, the English I do use with her. We were talking about the price of new and used furniture and I heard myself saying this: "Not waste money that way." My husband was with us as well, and he didn't notice any switch in my English. And then I realized why. It's because over the twenty years we've been together I've often used that same kind of English with him, and sometimes he even uses it with me. It has become our language of intimacy, a different sort of English that relates to family talk, the language I grew up with.

So you'll have some idea of what this family talk I heard sounds like, 5 I'll quote what my mother said during a recent conversation which I videotaped and then transcribed. During this conversation, my mother was talking about a political gangster in Shanghai who had the same last name as her family's, Du, and how the gangster in his early years wanted to be adopted by her family, which was rich by comparison. Later, the gangster became more powerful, far richer than my mother's family, and one day showed up at my mother's wedding to pay his respects. Here's what she said in part: "Du Yusong having business like fruit stand. Like off the street kind. He is Du like Du Zong—but not Tsung-ming Island people. The local people call putong, the river east side, he belong to that side local people. That man want to ask Du Zong father take him in like become own family. Du Zong father wasn't look down on him, but didn't take seriously, until that man big like become a mafia. Now important person, very hard to inviting him. Chinese way, came only to show respect, don't stay for dinner. Respect for making big celebration, he shows up. Mean gives lots of respect. Chinese custom. Chinese social life that way. If too important won't have to stay too long. He come to my wedding. I didn't see, I heard it. I gone to boy's side, they have YMCA dinner. Chinese age I was nineteen."

You should know that my mother's expressive command of English belies how much she actually understands. She reads the *Forbes* report, listens to *Wall Street Week*, converses daily with her stockbroker, reads all of Shirley MacLaine's books with ease—all kinds of things I can't begin to understand. Yet some of my friends tell me they understand 50 percent of what my mother says. Some say they understand 80 to 90 percent. Some say they understand none of it, as if she were speaking pure Chinese. But to me, my mother's English is perfectly clear, perfectly natural. It's my mother tongue.

> "Her language, as I hear it, is vivid, direct, full of observation and imagery. That was the language that helped shape the way I saw things, expressed things, made sense of the world."

Her language, as I hear it, is vivid, direct, full of observation and imagery. That was the language that helped shape the way I saw things, expressed things, made sense of the world.

Lately, I've been giving more thought to the kind of English my mother speaks. Like others, I have described it to people as "broken" or "fractured" English. But I wince when I say that. It has always bothered me that I can think of no way to describe it other than "broken," as if it were damaged and needed to be fixed, as if it lacked a certain wholeness and soundness. I've heard other terms used, "limited English," for example. But they seem just as bad, as if everything is limited, including people's perceptions of the limited English speaker.

I know this for a fact, because when I was growing up, my mother's "limited" English limited my perception of her. I was ashamed of her English. I believed that her English reflected the quality of what she had to say. That is, because she expressed them imperfectly her thoughts were imperfect. And I had plenty of empirical evidence to support me: the fact that people in department stores, at banks, and at restaurants did not take her seriously, did not give her good service, pretended not to understand her, or even acted as if they did not hear her.

My mother has long realized the limitations of her English as well. When I was fifteen, she used to have me call people on the phone to pretend I was she. In this guise, I was forced to ask for information or even to complain and yell at people who had been rude to her. One time it was a call to her stockbroker in New York. She had cashed out her small portfolio, and it just so happened we were going to go to New York the next week, our very first trip outside California. I had to get on the phone and say in an adolescent voice that was not very convincing, "This is Mrs. Tan."

And my mother was standing in the back whispering loudly, "Why he don't send me check, already two weeks late. So mad he lie to me, losing me money." 10

And then I said in perfect English, "Yes, I'm getting rather concerned. You had agreed to send the check two weeks ago, but it hasn't arrived."

Then she began to talk more loudly. "What he want, I come to New York tell him front of his boss, you cheating me?" And I was trying to calm her down, make her be quiet, while telling the stockbroker, "I can't tolerate any more excuses. If I don't receive the check immediately, I am going to have to speak to your manager when I'm in New York next week." And sure enough, the following week there we were in front of this astonished stockbroker, and I was sitting there red-faced and quiet, and my mother, the real Mrs. Tan, was shouting at his boss in her impeccable broken English.

We used a similar routine just five days ago, for a situation that was far less humorous. My mother had gone to the hospital for an appointment, to find out about a benign brain tumor a CAT scan had revealed a month ago. She said she had spoken very good English, her best English, no mistakes. Still, she said, the hospital did not apologize when they said they had lost the CAT scan and she had come for nothing. She said they did not seem to have any sympathy when she told them she was anxious to know the exact diagnosis, since her husband and son had both died of brain tumors. She said they would not give her any more information until the next time and she would have to make another appointment for that. So she said she would not leave until the doctor called her daughter. She wouldn't budge. And when the doctor finally called her daughter, me, who spoke in perfect English—lo and behold—we had assurances the CAT scan would be found, promises that a conference call on Monday would be held, and apologies for any suffering my mother had gone through for a most regrettable mistake.

I think my mother's English almost had an effect on limiting my possibilities in life as well. Sociologists and linguists probably will tell you that a person's developing language skills are more influenced by peers. But I do think that the language spoken in the family, especially in immigrant families which are more insular, plays a large role in shaping the language of the child. And I believe that it affected my results on achievement tests, I.Q. tests, and the SAT. While my English skills were never judged as poor, compared to math, English could not be considered my strong suit. In grade school I did moderately well, getting perhaps B's, sometimes B-pluses, in English and scoring perhaps in the sixtieth or seventieth percentile on achievement tests. But those scores were not good enough to override the opinion that my true abilities lay in math and science, because in those areas I achieved A's and scored in the ninetieth percentile or higher.

This was understandable. Math is precise; there is only one correct 15 answer. Whereas, for me at least, the answers on English tests were always a judgment call, a matter of opinion and personal experience. Those tests were constructed around items like fill-in-the-blank sentence completion, such as, "Even though Tom was ___, Mary thought he was ___." And the correct answer always seemed to be the most bland combinations of thoughts, for example, "Even though Tom was shy, Mary thought he was charming," with the grammatical structure "even though" limiting the correct answer to some sort of semantic opposites, so you wouldn't get answers like, "Even though Tom was foolish, Mary thought he was ridiculous." Well, according to my mother, there were very few limitations as to what Tom could have been and what Mary might have thought of him. So I never did well on tests like that.

The same was true with word analogies, pairs of words in which you were supposed to find some sort of logical, semantic relationship—for example, "*Sunset* is to *nightfall* as ___ is to ___." And here you would be presented with a list of four possible pairs, one of which showed the same kind of relationship: *red* is to *stoplight*, *bus* is to *arrival*, *chills* is to *fever*, *yawn* is to *boring*. Well, I could never think that way. I knew what the tests were asking, but I could not block out of my mind the images already created by the first pair, "*sunset* is to *nightfall*"—and I would see a burst of colors against a darkening sky, the moon rising, the lowering of a curtain of stars. And all the other pairs of words—*red, bus, stoplight, boring*—just threw up a mass of confusing images, making it impossible for me to sort out something as logical as saying: "A sunset precedes nightfall" is the same as "a chill precedes a fever." The only way I would have gotten that answer right would have been to imagine an associative situation, for example, my being disobedient and staying out past sunset, catching a chill at night, which turns into feverish pneumonia as punishment, which indeed did happen to me.

I have been thinking about all this lately, about my mother's English, about achievement tests. Because lately I've been asked, as a writer, why there are not more Asian Americans represented in American literature. Why are there few Asian Americans enrolled in creative writing programs? Why do so many Chinese students go into engineering? Well, these are broad sociological questions I can't begin to answer. But I have noticed in surveys—in fact, just last week—that Asian students, as a whole, always do significantly better on math achievement tests than in English. And this makes me think that there are other Asian American students whose English spoken in the home might also be described as "broken" or "limited." And perhaps they also have teachers who are steering them away from writing and into math and science, which is what happened to me.

Fortunately, I happen to be rebellious in nature and enjoy the challenge of disproving assumptions made about me. I became an English major my first year in college, after being enrolled as pre-med. I started writing nonfiction as a freelancer the week after I was told by my former boss that writing was my worst skill and I should hone my talents toward account management.

But it wasn't until 1985 that I finally began to write fiction. And at first I wrote using what I thought to be wittily crafted sentences, sentences that would finally prove I had mastery over the English language. Here's an example from the first draft of a story that later made its way into *The Joy Luck Club*, but without this line: "That was my mental quandary in its nascent state." A terrible line, which I can barely pronounce.

Fortunately, for reasons I won't get into today, I later decided I should 20 envision a reader for the stories I would write. And the reader I decided upon was my mother, because these were stories about mothers. So with this reader in mind—and in fact she did read my early drafts—I began to write stories using all the Englishes I grew up with: the English I spoke to my mother, which for lack of a better term might be described as "simple"; the English she used with me, which for lack of a better term might be described as "broken"; my translation of her Chinese, which could certainly be described as "watered down"; and what I imagined to be her translation of her Chinese if she could speak in perfect English, her internal language, and for that I sought to preserve the essence, but neither an English nor a Chinese structure. I wanted to capture what language ability tests can never reveal: her intent, her passion, her imagery, the rhythms of her speech and the nature of her thoughts.

Apart from what any critic had to say about my writing, I knew I had succeeded where it counted when my mother finished reading my book and gave me her verdict: "So easy to read."

Understanding the Text

1. Why does Tan dislike using phrases like "broken English" to describe her mother's speech?

2. What does Tan mean when she says that her mother's language "helped shape the way I saw things, expressed things, made sense of the world" (par. 6)?

Reflection and Response

3. How would you describe your own "mother tongue"? What is unique about the language you speak with family or others you grew up with?

4. Tan tells us that she decided to envision her mother as the reader for her stories, which helped her make choices about what language to use when writing. Whom do you imagine as your reader when you're writing, for school or in another context? How does that affect your choice of language?

5. Tan notes a contrast between her own perception of her mother's English, which to her is "perfectly clear, perfectly natural" (par. 6), and the perceptions of others, who claim to understand only some or even none of what her mother says. Why do you think there is this difference?

Making Connections

6. Tan explains that many people, herself included, "believed that her [mother's] English reflected the quality of what she had to say" (par. 8). Where do you see evidence of the belief that people have less valid ideas because of their speech in the readings by Marybeth Seitz-Brown ("Young Women Shouldn't Have to Talk Like Men to Be Taken Seriously," p. 92), Cheryl Boucher et al. ("Perceptions of Competency as a Function of Accent," p. 102), and/or John McWhorter ("Straight Talk: What Harry Reid Gets about Black English," p. 125)? What about in your own life experience?

7. Use Tan's discussion of SATs and other standardized tests (pars. 14–17) along with Rusty Barrett's "Rewarding Language" (p. 130) and/or Vershawn Ashanti Young's "The Problem of Linguistic Double Consciousness" (p. 325), supplemented by any applicable personal experience, to discuss the struggles that students from minority language backgrounds face in educational settings.

How to Tame a Wild Tongue

Gloria Anzaldúa

Gloria Anzaldúa (1942–2004) was a prolific writer who produced several award-winning book collections about feminism and Chicano/a culture, including *This Bridge Called My Back: Writings by Radical Women of Color* (1981), coedited with Cherríe Moraga. She also published several children's books and wrote many other unpublished essays, stories, and poems. In all of her work, she strove to encourage pride in one's heritage, language, and self. Though Anzaldúa lived in a number of places throughout her life, she identified perhaps most strongly as a Chicana *tejana*, or a Mexican-American Texan woman. Anzaldúa's book *Borderlands/ La Frontera* (1987), from which this essay is taken, was named one of the one hundred best books of the twentieth century by the magazines *Utne Reader* and *Hungry Mind Review*. As is the case in this essay, she often wrote in a mixture of dialects of English and Spanish. As you read, note the importance of language as both a topic of discussion and as Anzaldúa's method of communicating her ideas.

"We're going to have to control your tongue," the dentist says, pulling out all the metal from my mouth. Silver bits plop and tinkle into the basin. My mouth is a motherlode.

The dentist is cleaning out my roots. I get a whiff of the stench when I gasp. "I can't cap that tooth yet, you're still draining," he says.

"We're going to have to do something about your tongue," I hear the anger rising in his voice. My tongue keeps pushing out the wads of cotton, pushing back the drills, the long thin needles. "I've never seen anything as strong or as stubborn," he says. And I think, how do you tame a wild tongue, train it to be quiet, how do you bridle and saddle it? How do you make it lie down?

"Who is to say that robbing a people of its language is less violent than war?"

—RAY GWYN SMITH[1]

I remember being caught speaking Spanish at recess—that was good for three licks on the knuckles with a sharp ruler. I remember being sent to the corner of the classroom for "talking back" to the Anglo teacher when all I was trying to do was tell her how to pronounce my name. "If you want to be American, speak 'American.' If you don't like it, go back to Mexico where you belong."

"I want you to speak English, *Pa' hallar buen trabajo tienes que saber hablar* 5
el inglés bien. Qué vale toda tu educación si todavía hablas inglés con un 'accent,'"
my mother would say, mortified that I spoke English like a Mexican. At Pan
American University, I, and all Chicano students were required to take two
speech classes. Their purpose: to get rid of our accents.

Attacks on one's form of expression with the intent to censor are a
violation of the First Amendment. *El Anglo con cara de inocente nos arrancó
la lengua.* Wild tongues can't be tamed, they can only be cut out.

Overcoming the Tradition of Silence

Ahogadas, escupimos el oscuro.
Peleando con nuestra propia sombra
el silencio nos sepulta.

En boca cerrada no entran moscas. "Flies don't enter a closed mouth" is a
saying I kept hearing when I was a child. *Ser habladora* was to be a gossip and
a liar, to talk too much. *Muchachitas bien criadas*, well-bred girls don't answer
back. *Es una falta de respeto* to talk back to one's mother or father. I remember
one of the sins I'd recite to the priest in the confession box the few times I
went to confession: talking back to my mother, *hablar pa' 'trás, repelar. Hoci-
cona, repelona, chismosa*, having a big mouth, questioning, carrying tales are
all signs of being *mal criada*. In my culture they are all words that are derogatory if applied to women—I've never heard them applied to men.

The first time I heard two women, a Puerto Rican and a Cuban, say
the word *"nosotras,"*° I was shocked. I had not known the word existed.
Chicanas use *nosotros* whether we're male or female. We are robbed of
our female being by the masculine plural. Language is a male discourse.

And our tongues have become
dry   the wilderness has
dried out our tongues   and
we have forgotten speech.

—IRENA KLEPFISZ[2]

Even our own people, other Spanish speakers *nos quieren poner candados
en la boca.* They would hold us back with their bag of *reglas de academia.*

Oyé como ladra: el lenguaje de la frontera

Quien tiene boca se equivoca.

—MEXICAN SAYING

nosotros/nosotras: we; –os is a masculine ending, –as a feminine ending.

"Pocho, cultural traitor, you're speaking the oppressor's language by 10 speaking English, you're ruining the Spanish language," I have been accused by various Latinos and Latinas. Chicano Spanish is considered by the purist and by most Latinos deficient, a mutilation of Spanish.

But Chicano Spanish is a border tongue which developed naturally. Change, *evolución, enriquecimiento de palabras nuevas por invención o adopción* have created variants of Chicano Spanish, *un nuevo lenguaje. Un lenguaje que corresponde a un modo de vivir.* Chicano Spanish is not incorrect, it is a living language.

For a people who are neither Spanish nor live in a country in which Spanish is the first language; for a people who live in a country in which English is the reigning tongue but who are not Anglo; for a people who cannot entirely identify with either standard (formal, Castillian) Spanish nor standard English, what recourse is left to them but to cre-

> "Chicano Spanish sprang out of the Chicanos' need to identify ourselves as a distinct people. We needed a language with which we could communicate with ourselves, a secret language."

ate their own language? A language which they can connect their identity to, one capable of communicating the realities and values true to themselves—a language with terms that are neither *español ni inglés,* but both. We speak a patois, a forked tongue, a variation of two languages.

Chicano Spanish sprang out of the Chicanos' need to identify ourselves as a distinct people. We needed a language with which we could communicate with ourselves, a secret language. For some of us, language is a homeland closer than the Southwest—for many Chicanos today live in the Midwest and the East. And because we are a complex, heterogeneous people, we speak many languages. Some of the languages we speak are:

1. Standard English
2. Working class and slang English
3. Standard Spanish
4. Standard Mexican Spanish
5. North Mexican Spanish dialect
6. Chicano Spanish (Texas, New Mexico, Arizona and California have regional variations)
7. Tex-Mex
8. *Pachuco* (called *caló*)

My "home" tongues are the languages I speak with my sister and brothers, with my friends. They are the last five listed, with 6 and 7 being closest to my heart. From school, the media and job situations,

I've picked up standard and working class English. From Mamagrande Locha and from reading Spanish and Mexican literature, I've picked up Standard Spanish and Standard Mexican Spanish. From *los recién llegados*, Mexican immigrants, and *braceros*, I learned the North Mexican dialect. With Mexicans I'll try to speak either Standard Mexican Spanish or the North Mexican dialect. From my parents and Chicanos living in the Valley, I picked up Chicano Texas Spanish, and I speak it with my mom, younger brother (who married a Mexican and who rarely mixes Spanish with English), aunts and older relatives.

With Chicanas from *Nuevo México* or *Arizona* I will speak Chicano   15 Spanish a little, but often they don't understand what I'm saying. With most California Chicanas I speak entirely in English (unless I forget). When I first moved to San Francisco, I'd rattle off something in Spanish, unintentionally embarrassing them. Often it is only with another Chicana *tejana* that I can talk freely.

Words distorted by English are known as anglicisms or *pochismos*. The *pocho* is an anglicized Mexican or American of Mexican origin who speaks Spanish with an accent characteristic of North Americans and who distorts and reconstructs the language according to the influence of English.[3] Tex-Mex, or Spanglish, comes most naturally to me. I may switch back and forth from English to Spanish in the same sentence or in the same word. With my sister and my brother Nune and with Chicano *tejano* contemporaries I speak in Tex-Mex.

From kids and people my own age I picked up *Pachuco*. Pachuco (the language of the zoot suiters) is a language of rebellion, both against Standard Spanish and Standard English. It is a secret language. Adults of the culture and outsiders cannot understand it. It is made up of slang words from both English and Spanish. *Ruca* means girl or woman, *vato* means guy or dude, *chale* means no, *simón* means yes, *churo* is sure, talk is *periquiar, pigionear* means petting, *que gacho* means how nerdy, *ponte águila* means watch out, death is called *la pelona*. Through lack of practice and not having others who can speak it, I've lost most of the *Pachuco* tongue.

Chicano Spanish

Chicanos, after 250 years of Spanish/Anglo colonization have developed significant differences in the Spanish we speak. We collapse two adjacent vowels into a single syllable and sometimes shift the stress in certain words such as *maíz/maiz, cohete/cuete*. We leave out certain consonants when they appear between vowels: *lado/lao, mojado/mojao*. Chicanos from South Texas pronounced *f* as *j* as in *jue (fue)*. Chicanos use "archaisms," words that are no longer in the Spanish language, words that have been evolved out. We say *semos, truje, haiga, ansina,* and *naiden.* We retain the "archaic" *j,* as in *jalar,* that derives from an earlier *h* (the French *halar* or the Germanic *halon* which was lost to standard Spanish in the 16th century), but which is still found in several regional dialects such as the one spoken in South Texas. (Due to geography, Chicanos from the Valley of South Texas were cut off linguistically from other Spanish speakers. We tend to use words that the Spaniards brought over from Medieval Spain. The majority of the Spanish colonizers in Mexico and the Southwest came from Extremadura—Hernán Cortés was one of them—and Andalucía. Andalucians pronounce *ll* like a *y,* and their *d*'s tend to be absorbed by adjacent vowels: *tirado* becomes *tirao.* They brought *el lenguaje popular, dialectos y regionalismos.*[4])

Chicanos and other Spanish speakers also shift *ll* to *y* and *z* to *s.*[5] We leave out initial syllables, saying *tar* for *estar, toy* for *estoy, hora* for *ahora* (*cubanos* and *puertorriqueños* also leave out initial letters of some words). We also leave out the final syllable such as *pa* for *para.* The intervocalic *y,* the *ll* as in *tortilla, ella, botella,* gets replaced by *tortia* or *tortiya, ea, bota.* We add an additional syllable at the beginning of certain words: *atocar* for *tocar, agastar* for *gastar.* Sometimes we'll say *lavaste las vacijas,* other times *lavates* (substituting the *ates* verb endings for the *aste*).

We use anglicisms, words borrowed from English: *bola* from ball, 20 *carpeta* from carpet, *máchina de lavar* (instead of *lavadora*) from washing machine. Tex-Mex argot, created by adding a Spanish sound at the beginning or end of an English word such as *cookiar* for cook, *watchar* for watch, *parkiar* for park, and *rapiar* for rape, is the result of the pressures on Spanish speakers to adapt to English.

We don't use the word *vosotros/as* or its accompanying verb form. We don't say *claro* (to mean yes), *imagínate,* or *me emociona,* unless we picked up Spanish from Latinas, out of a book, or in a classroom. Other Spanish-speaking groups are going through the same, or similar, development in their Spanish.

Linguistic Terrorism

Deslenguadas. Somos los del español deficiente. We are your linguistic nightmare, your linguistic aberration, your linguistic *mestizaje,* the subject of your *burla.* Because we speak with tongues of fire we are culturally crucified. Racially, culturally and linguistically *somos huérfanos*—we speak an orphan tongue.

Chicanas who grew up speaking Chicano Spanish have internalized the belief that we speak poor Spanish. It is illegitimate, a bastard language. And because we internalize how our language has been used against us by the dominant culture, we use our language differences against each other.

Chicana feminists often skirt around each other with suspicion and hesitation. For the longest time I couldn't figure it out. Then it dawned on me. To be close to another Chicana is like looking into the mirror. We are afraid of what we'll see there. *Pena.* Shame. Low estimation of self. In childhood we are told that our language is wrong. Repeated attacks on our native tongue diminish our sense of self. The attacks continue throughout our lives.

Chicanas feel uncomfortable talking in Spanish to Latinas, afraid of 25 their censure. Their language was not outlawed in their countries. They had a whole lifetime of being immersed in their native tongue; generations, centuries in which Spanish was a first language, taught in school, heard on radio and TV, and read in the newspaper.

If a person, Chicana or Latina, has a low estimation of my native tongue, she also has a low estimation of me. Often with *mexicanas y latinas* we'll speak English as a neutral language. Even among Chicanas we tend to speak English at parties or conferences. Yet, at the same time, we're afraid the other will think we're *agringadas* because we don't speak Chicano Spanish. We oppress each other trying to out-Chicano each other, vying to be the "real" Chicanas, to speak like Chicanos. There is no one Chicano language just as there is no one Chicano experience. A monolingual Chicana whose first language is English or Spanish is just as much a Chicana as one who speaks several variants of Spanish. A Chicana from Michigan or Chicago or Detroit is just as much a Chicana as one from the Southwest. Chicano Spanish is as diverse linguistically as it is regionally.

By the end of this century, Spanish speakers will comprise the biggest minority group in the U.S., a country where students in high schools and colleges are encouraged to take French classes because French is considered more "cultured." But for a language to remain alive it must be used.[6] By the end of this century English, and not Spanish, will be the mother tongue of most Chicanos and Latinos.

So, if you want to really hurt me, talk badly about my language. Ethnic identity is twin skin to linguistic identity—I am my language. Until I can take pride in my language, I cannot take pride in myself. Until I can accept as legitimate Chicano Texas Spanish, Tex-Mex and all the other languages I speak, I cannot accept the legitimacy of myself. Until I am free to write bilingually and to switch codes without having always to translate, while I still have to speak English or Spanish when I would rather speak Spanglish, and as long as I have to accommodate the English speakers rather than having them accommodate me, my tongue will be illegitimate.

I will no longer be made to feel ashamed of existing. I will have my voice: Indian, Spanish, white. I will have my serpent's tongue—my woman's voice, my sexual voice, my poet's voice. I will overcome the tradition of silence.

> My fingers
> move sly against your palm
> Like women everywhere, we speak in code. . . .
>
> —MELANIE KAYE/KANTROWITZ[7]

"Vistas," corridos, y comida: My Native Tongue

In the 1960s, I read my first Chicano novel. It was *City of Night* by John Rechy, a gay Texan, son of a Scottish father and a Mexican mother. For days I walked around in stunned amazement that a Chicano could write and could get published. When I read *I Am Joaquín*[8] I was surprised to see a bilingual book by a Chicano in print. When I saw poetry written in Tex-Mex for the first time, a feeling of pure joy flashed through me. I felt like we really existed as a people. In 1971, when I started teaching High School English to Chicano students, I tried to supplement the required texts with works by Chicanos, only to be reprimanded and forbidden to do so by the principal. He claimed that I was supposed to teach "American" and English literature. At the risk of being fired, I swore my students to secrecy and slipped in Chicano short stories, poems, a play. In graduate school, while working toward a Ph.D., I had to "argue" with one advisor after the other, semester after semester, before I was allowed to make Chicano literature an area of focus.

Even before I read books by Chicanos or Mexicans, it was the Mexican movies I saw at the drive-in—the Thursday night special of $1.00 a carload—that gave me a sense of belonging. *"Vámonos a las vistas,"* my mother would call out and we'd all—grandmother, brothers, sister and cousins—squeeze into the car. We'd wolf down cheese and bologna white bread sandwiches while watching Pedro Infante in melodramatic tear-jerkers like *Nosotros los pobres,* the first "real" Mexican movie (that was not an imitation of European movies). I remember seeing *Cuando los hijos se van* and surmising that all Mexican movies played up the love a mother has for her children and what ungrateful sons and daughters suffer when they are not devoted to their mothers. I remember the singing-type "westerns" of Jorge Negrete and Miguel Aceves Mejía. When watching Mexican movies, I felt a sense of homecoming as well as alienation. People who were to amount to something didn't go to Mexican movies, or *bailes* or tune their radios to *bolero, rancherita,* and *corrido* music.

The whole time I was growing up, there was *norteño* music some-times called North Mexican border music, or Tex-Mex music, or Chicano music, or *cantina* (bar) music. I grew up listening to *conjuntos*, three- or four-piece bands made up of folk musicians playing guitar, *bajo sexto,* drums and button accordion, which Chicanos had borrowed from the German immigrants who had come to Central Texas and Mexico to farm and build breweries. In the Rio Grande Valley, Steve Jordan and Little Joe Hernández were popular, and Flaco Jiménez was the accordion king. The rhythms of Tex-Mex music are those of the polka, also adapted from the Germans, who in turn had borrowed the polka from the Czechs and Bohemians.

I remember the hot, sultry evenings when *corridos*—songs of love and death on the Texas-Mexican borderlands—reverberated out of cheap amplifiers from the local *cantinas* and wafted in through my bedroom window.

Corridos first became widely used along the South Texas/Mexican bor-der during the early conflict between Chicanos and Anglos. The *corridos* are usually about Mexican heroes who do valiant deeds against the Anglo oppressors. Pancho Villa's song, *"La cucaracha,"* is the most famous one. *Corridos* of John F. Kennedy and his death are still very popular in the Val-ley. Older Chicanos remember Lydia Mendoza, one of the great border *cor-rido* singers who was called *la Gloria de Tejas.* Her *"El tango negro,"* sung during the Great Depression, made her a singer of the people. The everpre-sent *corridos* narrated one hundred years of border history, bringing news of events as well as entertaining. These folk musicians and folk songs are our chief cultural mythmakers, and they made our hard lives seem bearable.

I grew up feeling ambivalent about our music. Country-western and 35 rock-and-roll had more status. In the 50s and 60s, for the slightly edu-cated and *agringado* Chicanos, there existed a sense of shame at being caught listening to our music. Yet I couldn't stop my feet from thumping to the music, could not stop humming the words, nor hide from myself the exhilaration I felt when I heard it.

There are more subtle ways that we internalize identification, especially in the forms of images and emotions. For me food and certain smells are tied to my identity, to my homeland. Woodsmoke curling up to an immense blue sky; woodsmoke perfuming my grandmother's clothes, her skin. The stench of cow manure and the yellow patches on the ground; the crack of a .22 rifle and the reek of cordite. Homemade white cheese sizzling in a pan, melting inside a folded *tortilla.* My sister Hilda's hot, spicy *menudo, chile colorado* making it deep red, pieces of *panza* and hom-iny floating on top. My brother Carito barbecuing *fajitas* in the backyard. Even now and 3,000 miles away, I can see my mother spicing the ground beef, pork and venison with *chile*. My mouth salivates at the thought of the hot steaming *tamales* I would be eating if I were home.

Si le preguntas a mi mamá, "¿Qué eres?"°

"Identity is the essential core of who we are as individuals, the conscious experience of the self inside."

—KAUFMAN[9]

Nosotros los Chicanos straddle the borderlands. On one side of us, we are constantly exposed to the Spanish of the Mexicans, on the other side we hear the Anglos' incessant clamoring so that we forget our language. Among ourselves we don't say *nosotros los americanos, o nosotros los españoles, o nosotros los hispanos*. We say *nosotros los mexicanos* (by *mexicanos* we do not mean citizens of Mexico; we do not mean a national identity, but a racial one). We distinguish between *mexicanos del otro lado* and *mexicanos de este lado*. Deep in our hearts we believe that being Mexican has nothing to do with which country one lives in. Being Mexican is a state of soul—not one of mind, not one of citizenship. Neither eagle nor serpent, but both. And like the ocean, neither animal respects borders.

Dime con quien andas y te diré quien eres.
(Tell me who your friends are and I'll tell you who you are.)

—MEXICAN SAYING

Si e preguntas a mi mamá, "¿Qué eres?" te dirá, *"Soy° mexicana."* My brothers and sister say the same. I sometimes will answer *"soy mexicana"* and at others will say *"soy Chicana" o "soy tejana."* But I identified as *"Raza"* before I ever identified as *"mexicana"* or "Chicana."

As a culture, we call ourselves Spanish when referring to ourselves as a linguistic group and when copping out. It is then that we forget our predominant Indian genes. We are 70 to 80% Indian.[10] We call ourselves Hispanic[11] or Spanish-American or Latin American or Latin when linking ourselves to other Spanish-speaking peoples of the Western hemisphere and when copping out. We call ourselves Mexican-American[12] to signify we are neither Mexican nor American, but more the noun "American" than the adjective "Mexican" (and when copping out).

Si le preguntas a mi mamá, "¿Qué eres?": If you ask my mom, "What are you?"
soy: I am.

Chicanos and other people of color suffer economically for not accul- 40 turating. This voluntary (yet forced) alienation makes for psychological conflict, a kind of dual identity—we don't identify with the Anglo-American cultural values and we don't totally identify with the Mexican cultural values. We are a synergy of two cultures with various degrees of Mexicanness or Angloness. I have so internalized the borderland conflict that sometimes I feel like one cancels out the other and we are zero, nothing, no one. *A veces no soy nada ni nadie. Pero hasta cuando no lo soy, lo soy.*

When not copping out, when we know we are more than nothing, we call ourselves Mexican, referring to race and ancestry; *mestizo* when affirming both our Indian and Spanish (but we hardly ever own our Black ancestry); Chicano when referring to a politically aware people born and/ or raised in the U.S.; *Raza* when referring to Chicanos; *tejanos* when we are Chicanos from Texas.

Chicanos did not know we were a people until 1965 when Cesar Chavez and the farmworkers united and *I Am Joaquín* was published and *la Raza Unida* party was formed in Texas. With that recognition, we became a distinct people. Something momentous happened to the Chicano soul—we became aware of our reality and acquired a name and a language (Chicano Spanish) that reflected that reality. Now that we had a name, some of the fragmented pieces began to fall together—who we were, what we were, how we had evolved. We began to get glimpses of what we might eventually become.

Yet the struggle of identities continues, the struggle of borders is our reality still. One day the inner struggle will cease and a true integration take place. In the meantime, *tenemos que hacerla lucha. ¿Quién está protegiendo los ranchos de mi gente? ¿Quién está tratando de cerrar la fisura entre la india y el blanco en nuestra sangre? El Chicano, sí, el Chicano que anda como un ladrón en su propia casa.*

Los Chicanos, how patient we seem, how very patient. There is the quiet of the Indian about us.[13] We know how to survive. When other races have given up their tongue, we've kept ours. We know what it is to live under the hammer blow of the dominant *norteamericano* culture. But more than we count the blows, we count the days the weeks the years the centuries the eons until the white laws and commerce and customs will rot in the deserts they've created, lie bleached. *Humildes* yet proud, *quietos* yet wild, *nosotros los mexicanos*-Chicanos will walk by the crumbling ashes as we go about our business. Stubborn, persevering, impenetrable as stone, yet possessing a malleability that renders us unbreakable, we, the *mestizas* and *mestizos,* will remain.

Notes

1. Ray Gwyn Smith, *Moorland is Cold Country*, unpublished book.

2. Irena Klepfisz, *"Di rayze aheym*/The Journey Home," in *The Tribe of Dina: A Jewish Women's Anthology*, Melanie Kaye/Kantrowitz and Irena Klepfisz, eds. (Montpelier, VT: Sinister Wisdom Books, 1986), 49.

3. R.C. Ortega, *Dialectología Del Barrio*, trans. Hortencia S. Alwan (Los Angeles, CA: R.C. Ortega Publisher & Bookseller, 1977), 132.

4. Eduardo Hernandéz-Chávez, Andrew D. Cohen, and Anthony F. Beltramo, *El Lenguaje de los Chicanos: Regional and Social Characteristics of Language Used By Mexican Americans* (Arlington, VA: Center for Applied Linguistics, 1975), 39.

5. Hernandéz-Chávez, xvii.

6. Irena Klepfisz, "Secular Jewish Identity: Yidishkayt in America," in *The Tribe of Dina*, Kaye/Kantrowitz and Klepfisz, eds., 43.

7. Melanie Kaye/Kantrowitz, "Sign," in *We Speak In Code: Poems and Other Writings* (Pittsburgh, PA: Motheroot Publications, Inc., 1980), 85.

8. Rodolfo Gonzales, *I Am Joaquín/Yo Soy Joaquín* (New York, NY: Bantam Books, 1972). It was first published in 1967.

9. Gershen Kaufman, *Shame: The Power of Caring* (Cambridge, MA: Schenkman Books, Inc., 1980), 68.

10. John R. Chávez, *The Lost Land: The Chicano Images of the Southwest* (Albuquerque, NM: University of New Mexico Press, 1984), 88–90.

11. "Hispanic" is derived from *Hispanis* (*España*, a name given to the Iberian Peninsula in ancient times when it was a part of the Roman Empire) and is a term designated by the U.S. government to make it easier to handle us on paper.

12. The Treaty of Guadalupe Hidalgo created the Mexican-American in 1848.

13. Anglos, in order to alleviate their guilt for dispossessing the Chicano, stressed the Spanish part of us and perpetrated the myth of the Spanish Southwest. We have accepted the fiction that we are Hispanic, that is Spanish, in order to accommodate ourselves to the dominant culture and its abhorrence of Indians. Chávez, 88–91.

Understanding the Text

1. Anzaldúa lists eight different languages that she speaks. What makes these languages different from one another, both in the features of the languages and in the ways Anzaldúa uses them?

2. What does Anzaldúa mean when she says that "ethnic identity is twin skin to linguistic identity" (par. 28)?

3. Though this essay weaves together many elements, including stories and poems, it also makes a strong argument. How would you summarize Anzaldúa's "thesis" in this piece?

Reflection and Response

4. Do you speak any of the non-English dialects Anzaldúa uses in this essay? What effect does your understanding, or lack of understanding, of her words have on you as a reader? Why do you think she chose to do some of her writing in a language that only some of her readers would understand?

5. Anzaldúa gives examples of words in Spanish, such as *chismosa* (gossip), that are applied to women and girls believed to be *mal criada* (poorly raised). These same words, she says, are never applied to men. Can you think of words, in English or any language you know, that tend to be used specifically for women or girls who talk too much, too loudly, and so on? In what other ways do our words encourage us to speak positively or negatively about certain traits in men and women?

6. Anzaldúa says that "often it is only with another Chicana *tejana* that [she] can talk freely" (par. 15). A Chicana tejana would share Anzaldúa's background and identity and thus likely have the most in common with her in terms of language. Think about your own background and identity, and what similarities in language (maybe a non-English language, maybe a regional or ethnic dialect, maybe slang or family language) you have with others who have a great deal in common with you. In what ways are you also able to "talk freely" with others like yourself?

Making Connections

7. In this chapter, both Lee Romney (p. 12) and Louise Erdrich (p. 18) mention the severe punishments that Native American children endured when they attempted to speak their non-English languages in the U.S. government-sponsored boarding schools of the late 1800s and early 1900s. Though Anzaldúa is talking about her experiences speaking Chicano Spanish in a more recent context, her perspective can help us to better understand how the children in such boarding schools might have felt. Based on Anzaldúa's essay, what can you conclude about why someone would not want to stop speaking their native language, or why it would hurt (not just physically but emotionally) to be forced to stop doing so?

8. Anzaldúa says that "Chicano Spanish is not incorrect, it is a living language" (par. 11). Robert MacNeil, in "English Belongs to Everybody," argues that "Change is inevitable in a living language" (p. 192). In what ways does Anzaldúa's essay show change to be a key part of the "living languages" she speaks? In what other readings from Chapter 3 of this text do you see change being important to language? Why is change necessary for a language to "live"?

Social Variables

Susan Tamasi and Lamont Antieau

Susan Tamasi directs the Program in Linguistics at Emory College and conducts research on everyday people's attitudes toward language variation and dialects in the United States. Lamont Antieau is an independent language consultant and editor in North Carolina who is interested in the language of the Rocky Mountain region and of American popular music. Tamasi and Antieau put their shared interest in U.S. language varieties to work in their coauthored textbook *Language and Linguistic Diversity in the US: An Introduction* (2015), from which the following selection is taken. Here, Tamasi and Antieau focus on language variation that connects to the identity categories of age, gender, and sexuality. Note that, as the authors say at the beginning of this piece, language features connected to social identities tend to be "group preferential" — more likely to occur in a particular group of people — as opposed to "group exclusive," or only occurring in that particular group.

In this section, we present some of the research that has been done on the language use of several specific social groups. The study of linguistic features as they correlate to social groups raises several issues. First, the link between linguistic features and social groups can be viewed the same as the link between features and regional groups in that linguistic features are typically group preferential rather than group exclusive (Smith, 1985). In Chapter 5, we reported that while use of the variant *y'all* is strongly linked to the Southern United States, the South is not the only place in the US (let alone, the world) where speakers use *y'all*. Here, we advise readers to expect linguistic variants linked to social variables to behave in a similar way, given the fluidity of social categories, the membership of individual speakers in a variety of sometimes overlapping categories, and the ability for different groups to adopt linguistic variants and to discard them as they see fit.

Although society can be classified in numerous ways, we focus below on several areas that sociolinguists have actively conducted research on, for example age, gender, sexuality, and ethnicity. Due to the limitations of space, we can only briefly summarize some of the research that has been conducted in these areas here.

Language and Age

Sociolinguists are interested in the intersection of language and age as a key means for exploring linguistic variation and change as well as the connection between language and speaker identity. Simply stated, people of different ages tend to speak differently from one another. For example, older speakers often retain features that they acquired in their youth, but which are no longer being acquired by younger speakers in their communities; younger speakers often choose varieties that align them with their peers over those that are associated with their parents and other authority figures. Sociolinguists who work in this area generally distinguish age-related differences that are socially motivated from those that are caused by physiological changes in the bodies of speakers, such as the ossification of the larynx in elderly speakers and the change in voice, particularly in males, that accompanies puberty. This distinction allows them to focus on the core goals of sociolinguistics: understanding the processes of language variation and change and the connections between language and society.

It is important to note, however, that age is a complex social variable, and the use of the word age can be used in several ways: chronological age, which is the number of years since an individual's birth; biological age, which is the stage an individual is at in terms of physical maturation; and social age, which is linked to the reaching of various milestones, such as graduation or marriage (Eckert, 1998). Furthermore, these different ways of viewing age are not mutually exclusive. Some chronological ages serve as milestones, such as birthdays that mark the day an individual can obtain a driver's license, register for selective service, or be served a drink legally. Just as age is a complex variable, its influence on language use can also be difficult to discern. For instance, although many researchers are interested in using age as an indicator of language change, they are challenged in doing so by the phenomenon of age-grading, which refers to the use of linguistic forms "correlated with a particular time of life... [and] repeated in successive generations" (Chambers, 1995, p. 188). In the remainder of this section, we focus on a single life stage that is discussed at great length in the sociolinguistic literature: adolescence.

Because adolescence is such an important time for establishing iden- 5 tity and group membership, much of the linguistic research on adolescence has investigated how language is used in these processes. In a study of suburban Detroit high schools in the 1980s, two primary groups were found to operate within the schools: burnouts and jocks (Eckert, 1989). The jock network consisted of those students actively involved in athletics and school activities who had college aspirations and identified with the middle class, whereas the burnout network comprised students who participated in school only minimally, had no intention of attending college, and identified with the working class. The two networks varied linguistically in several respects, particularly in that burnouts selected nonstandard variants, which were popular features in the local dialect, rather than the standard norms that were imposed by the school body. As such, the burnouts were much more likely to participate in the Northern Cities Shift, and this adoption of a local speech norm showed that they belonged to the local community and that their intention was to remain there, while the jocks' use of standard variants served as evidence of their intentions to attend universities and take jobs that extended well beyond their local networks. In addition, Eckert found that burnouts were more likely than jocks to use multiple negation, which was apparently used to show that the speaker was tough and rebellious.

A more general way that adolescents show group membership is through the use of slang, that is, highly informal words or phrases, or, as Eble (2004, p. 376) defines it, "deliberate alternative vocabulary that sends social signals." Besides being informal, a key aspect of slang is that it is typically ephemeral, lasting no more than a generation, although occasionally slang from one generation is recycled by a later one. Slang is often used for taboo topics such as sex, drinking, and bodily functions such as vomiting and, in this way, it acts as euphemism or code. It can also be used to add variety or color to everyday language; for example, every generation seems to have its favorite slang terms that are used in place of the high-frequency terms *good* and *bad*. Slang must be constantly updated to remain effective, and while the use of slang in general is a constant, the specific words that are used comprise an ever-changing set of terms. As speakers grow older, they don't necessarily lose the slang they grew up with; however, they have less occasion to use it, and they are less likely to adopt new slang, as they enter the workplace and meet its demands of professional language use. The use of a younger generation's slang by adults can sometimes be used to humorous effect.

Adolescents and young adults have also been associated with several innovations that extend beyond the lexicon into the domains of syntax and discourse. For instance, the importance of narration as a genre in adolescent discourse has culminated in several options for dramatizing narratives (Eckert, 2004, p. 367). Among these options is a variety of quotatives, markers used to show reported speech or thought, as in the use of *like*, which is illustrated below (Romaine & Lange, 1991, p. 241):

Shane's *like*, "She's in Baltimore," and I'm *like*, "No, she's not," and Shane's *like*, "Yes, she is."

In their study, Romaine and Lange (1991, p. 251) found that speakers who used *like* in this way tended to be young and female, and also reported that its use, which had originated in the early 1980s, was apparently spreading. Currently, this use appears regularly in the speech of both males and females, and its use is even spreading to speakers of various

Box 1.1 Slayer Slang

Television and radio shows, as well as films, often feature interesting uses of language; however, few have garnered as much attention as the language of television's *Buffy the Vampire Slayer* (Whedon, 1997–2003). In particular, the lexicon of the television program, or "slayer slang," was noted, among other things, for its liberal use of particular word-formation processes. For instance, the dialogue of *Buffy* often included words that had been converted from one part of speech to another, for example a noun to a verb, with no change in the form of the word, a word-formation process called functional shift. Characters in *Buffy* employed functional shift quite liberally, as illustrated in the use of adjectives as nouns in quotations from the series (from Adams, 1999):

1. a. "Love makes you do the *wacky*."
   b. "Stop with the *crazy*. Go talk to Angel."
   c. "I was making with the *funny?*"

Additionally, characters in *Buffy* often added the suffix *-age* for a variety of functions, as in the following (from Adams, 1999):

2. a. "Sorry I'm late. I had to do some unscheduled *slayage*."
   b. "Hey, speaking of wowpotential, there's Oz over there. What are we thinking, any *sparkage*?"
   c. "It's, like, freeze frame. Willow *kissage*—but I'm not going to kiss you."

Partially as a response to the amount of attention the language of the show garnered, the creator of *Buffy*, Joss Whedon, wrote and directed an episode called "Hush" that aired during the fourth season of the series. In the episode, the residents of Buffy's town lose their ability to speak, leaving the characters unable to communicate vocally. Thus, the show was able to explore directly the importance of language in the characters' lives.

ages, although it is still most commonly associated with adolescents. At the same time, the use of *like* for other functions has increased as well, for example as a hedge° and a focus marker (Buchstaller, 2001; D'Arcy, 2005).

hedge: a word used to soften the certainty or forcefulness of an expression. *Like* is a hedge when it is used to mean "maybe," "about," or "I think."

Other forms that have taken on the function of a quotative are *all* and *be all*, as in the following examples (Rickford, Wasow, Zwicky, & Buchstaller, 2007, p. 14):

a. He's *all* "Let me see your license; is that your car?"

b. Our parents would always *be all* "Can't wait till those kids get to bed."

Quotative *all* apparently has its roots in the speech of adolescents, more specifically, adolescents in California in the early 1980s, and by the early 1990s it was the predominant quotative among high school students in the state; however, Tagliamonte (2012) reports that its popularity was apparently short-lived (p. 254), as it was eventually supplanted by other quotatives, old and new, including *like* (Rickford et al., 2007, p. 12).

Language and Gender

If newspaper columns, blogs, talk shows, *The New York Times* bestseller list, comedy sketches, and daily conversations are any indication, there is a great deal of general interest in the linguistic differences of women and men; in linguistics, these differences have been a topic of research for nearly a century. Perhaps the earliest discussion of gender-related differences in language use was presented in a chapter called "The Woman" by the linguist Otto Jespersen (1922). The work of Jespersen and subsequent research along the same lines has been criticized for applying a deficit approach to gender-related differences in language use. That is, it assumed the speech of men as the norm, and then, in areas in which the speech of women differed from that of the male model, it assessed women's speech as being deficient in that area, as well as deficient in general.

Fifty years later, in her groundbreaking work on the speech of women, 10 Lakoff (1975) used anecdotal evidence and her own intuitions to study different facets of women's speech, pointing out linguistic features at all levels of grammar that differentiated the speech of women from that of men. In particular, Lakoff focused on lexical differences, such as a higher use of certain adjectives of approval by women, including *lovely*, *charming*, and *divine*, and a more elaborate color terminology, but she also claimed that grammatical differences, including the use of a greater number of tag questions and "superpolite forms," differentiated the speech of the two sexes.

Despite some of her intuitions on the relationship of women's speech and specific linguistic features being generally supported by subsequent research, Lakoff's (1975) work was the target of various criticisms. In terms of methodology, for instance, scholars were skeptical of the findings because Lakoff had relied on her own observations and intuitions for her conclusions, rather than on systematically collected data. Critics also found fault in Lakoff's interpretation of the linguistic features favored by women as being emblematic of powerlessness (e.g., Holmes, 1990, 1995; Coates, 1993, 1996), and some pointed out that the power of these features varied according to who was using them. For instance, one of the features that Lakoff uses in her characterization of women's speech as powerless, namely, indirectness, is often used by some of the most powerful people in English-speaking society—whether male or female (Tannen, 1990, p. 225).

Several researchers replaced the deficit approach with a difference approach, not only in studies on gender, but in investigating other social factors and their influence on language use as well. Tannen (1990), for instance, views males and females as belonging to different subcultures, both of which have been shaped by society to adopt behaviors, including linguistic behaviors, appropriate for their respective cultures. The language that emerges from these socialization processes, according to Tannen (1990), is a rapport style for women that is primarily aimed at creating and maintaining relationships and a report style for men that is primarily concerned with communicating information and placing themselves within a social hierarchy.

Several linguistic trends that have been investigated recently have been linked primarily to the speech of women. One of these is creaky voice, a low, creaky vibration created by a slow movement of the vocal cords. While creaky voice (also known as vocal fry) was historically considered a voice disorder that, if used continually, could damage vocal cords, in recent years researchers have noted its occasional use in speakers with normal voice quality, particularly at the end of utterances (Wolk, Abdelli-Beruh, & Slavin, 2012). Studies of this feature in American English have noted its more frequent use by females, particularly college-aged women (e.g., Gottliebson, Lee, Weinrich, & Sanders, 2007), although more research needs to be done to confirm this finding. Use of the feature has also been noted among Latinos. For instance, Fought (2003) found the feature to be common in the Chicano English of Los Angeles, where it may have been borrowed from the Anglo community. Although Fought found the feature to be used by men and women, it was more common for women in her study, for both Anglo and Latina speakers. Mendoza-Denton (2011) discusses how the feature has been used in the media to project a Chicano gangster persona that has since been adopted by some real-life gang members. Creaky voice appears in varieties of English throughout the world; however, it is associated with different social groups in different places, suggesting that it is being used to project identity. Despite the recent attention creaky voice has garnered, however, it does not appear to be an entirely new phenomenon or one that only affects young people; in one of her studies, Fought (2003) describes its use by a Hispanic woman in her 50s, and Liberman (2011) points to its use by the movie star Mae West in a film from 1933.

Another relatively recent linguistic trend that has been linked to females is the use of uptalk, which features a high rising pattern of intonation in the final syllable or syllables of a statement; in an early article describing this phenomenon, Ching (1982) refers to it as applying "[t]he question intonation in assertions." Now detected in varieties of English around the world, it appears to have spread from the West Coast of the US, where it is associated with the speech of "Valley girls" in Southern California in the 1980s. The function of uptalk in conversation is uncertain: some scholars have argued that it encourages the addressee to participate in the conversation, while others have claimed that it signals to others that the speaker is not yet finished and thus discourages interruption. In a study of contestants on the television game show *Jeopardy*, Linneman (2013) found that uptalk was used more by white, young, female contestants on the show than by male contestants, with males using uptalk more on the show when surrounded by female contestants and in correcting female contestants after they responded incorrectly to a clue. Furthermore, Linneman (2013) also found that the greater success a man had on the show, the less likely he was to use uptalk, and the greater success that a woman had, the more likely she was to use it. However, while this study suggested that uptalk might indicate insecurity on the part of the speaker, other studies have suggested otherwise; for example, McLemore (1991) found that uptalk was used more by sorority sisters with greater seniority and power, and it was used less by newer pledges. Finally, an investigation by Liberman (2005) revealed that President George W. Bush used more uptalk in the speeches he made during the second term of his presidency than in his earlier speeches.

In language and gender research, two basic findings have emerged that 15 deserve special merit. One is that women tend to lead linguistic change (Labov, 1990). The discussion of quotative *like* in the previous section as a feature used predominately by young females before becoming more widespread supports this view. The other finding is the tendency for males to use nonstandard linguistic features more than females do, a finding that emerged from the study by Fischer (1958) on the variability of (ing) among schoolchildren that has often been found in gender-based studies since that time (e.g. Trudgill, 1972). Following up on the use of the (Iŋ°), Kiesling (1998) investigates how members of an American college fraternity index working-class cultural models through the variant [in] to present themselves as physically powerful.

Finally, it should be noted that research on language and gender, especially earlier research, has often discussed the categories of male and female as if each were homogeneous (Bucholtz, 2004, p. 417). Newer research has taken diversity among the genders into account (see Mendoza-Denton, 2008; Kiesling, 2009; Lanehart, 2009; Bucholtz, 2011). In particular, studies in this area have become more inclusive, with regard to the experiences of people of color and the LGBT community, rather than attention being focused on gender differences between white, middle-class, heterosexual speakers.

Box 1.2 Sexist Language

Language change often takes place over long periods of time, with speakers often being unaware that it is happening. The replacement of gendered labels referring to occupation with gender-neutral terms, however, has proceeded relatively quickly and was consciously done to reflect social changes that began in the 1960s. Hence, *steward* and *stewardess* became *flight attendant, waiter* and *waitress* became *server*, and *chairman* and *chairwoman* became *chairperson* or, simply, *chair.*

The issue of sexist language has also influenced pronoun usage, especially with regard to the use of the masculine pronoun for both genders, as promoted by Strunk and White, among others:

> The use of *he* as pronoun for nouns embracing both genders is a simple, practical convention rooted in the beginnings of the English language. He has lost all suggestion of maleness in these circumstances. . . . It has no pejorative connotations; it is never incorrect. (1979, p. 60)

Despite Strunk and White's assurances, however, many studies have shown generic *he* to have adverse effects. Martyna (1978) found it to have a cumulative effect on women, in that many of her subjects reported either picturing males when the pronoun was used or

---

ŋ: the consonant sound "ng." "(Iŋ)" and "the variant [in]" refers to the difference between, say, *running* and *runnin'*.

not reporting any imagery at all. Through experimentation, Gastil (1990) found that generic *he* in texts created a male bias in readers and, on the basis that the use of generic *he* "interferes with effective communication," suggests that alternative generic pronouns be used (pp. 639–640). Based on the findings of studies such as these, several existing pronouns and pronoun combinations have been used as generics. In addition to using generic *she* or alternating between *he* and *she*, writers have also used *he/she, s/he, one*, and *they* as generics. However, the use of each of these has presented issues in terms of clarity and formality.

Speakers of English are not the only people concerned with this issue. Recently, the *Swedish National Encyclopedia* admitted *hen* as a gender-neutral third-person pronoun in Swedish (complementing the masculine third-person nominative *han* and the feminine *hon*); however, this did not happen overnight. The word was first introduced by Swedish linguists in the 1960s and was then reintroduced in 1994 by the linguist Hans Karlgren, who suggested that the adoption of such a pronoun would eliminate the problematic use of the Swedish equivalent of *he/she* in writing (Rothschild, 2013). It will be interesting to see whether English and other languages follow the lead of Sweden and one day introduce their own truly gender-free pronouns.

Language and Sexual Orientation

An area of inquiry that has broadened in scope in recent years is the relationship between language use and sexual orientation. Early studies investigating folk beliefs that homosexual women simply thought and behaved like men, while homosexual men thought and behaved like women, found little linguistic evidence to support this position, at least with respect to those qualities that are commonly used to support their similarities, such as pitch (Gaudio, 1994; Zwicky, 1997). Recent research in this area supports the findings of earlier studies that the language use of the LGBT community, as well as its relationship to heteronormative° speech, is not as easily generalizable as folk beliefs would suggest.

Some researchers in this area have focused on how people observe linguistic features when trying to determine whether speakers are gay or straight. In addition to investigating how accurate people are when linking speech to sexuality, the research also examines the linguistic features

heteronormative: based on a view of heterosexuality as "normal" and an assumption that the terms *men* and *women* refer to heterosexual men and women.

people use to make these determinations and whether their attitudes concerning sexual orientation have an effect on their ability to determine an individual's sexuality through their speech. Some studies have found that evaluators listening to speech samples without visual cues can identify the sexual orientation of speakers with some success (e.g., Gaudio, 1994; Pierrehumbert, Bent, Munson, Bradlow, & Bailey, 2004; Munson, McDonald, DeBoe, & White, 2006), while others have found evaluators to be unreliable in their ability to perform this task (Smyth, Jacobs, & Rogers, 2003). Additionally, Gaudio (1994) found that while people in his study were successful at the identification task, there was uncertainty in the linguistic features that they used to make these determinations; Smyth et al. (2003) were also unable to find any clear-cut phonetic cues that were used to identify the sexual orientation of speakers.

In terms of production as opposed to perception, much research on variation in American English among members of the LGBT community has investigated phonetic differences in groups based on sexual orientation. Pierrehumbert et al. (2004) found that the speech of gay men was characterized by articulatory precision that resulted in an expanded vowel space° and strong diphthongization.° Several studies have been conducted on production of variants of (æ),° including one that found gay men produced a "retracted" variant, while heterosexual men produced a variant similar to the tense° [æ] of the Northern Cities Shift (Munson et al., 2006); investigators in this study also found that gay men and heterosexual men varied in their production of (s). In a linguistic study of a "diva" persona adopted by a gay man (Podesva, 2004), it was noted that exaggerations were a salient feature. Podesva's (2006) ethnographic study of phonetic variation among three gay men investigated the use of style shifting in the LGBT community

> "The language use of the LGBT community, as well as its relationship to heteronormative speech, is not as easily generalizable as folk beliefs would suggest."

expanded vowel space: a greater-than-average difference between vowel sounds, caused by making them further away from each other in the mouth. (Different vowels are made in different parts of the mouth; for instance, say "sit back" and notice how the first vowel is higher than the second.)
diphthongization: A diphthong is a combination of two vowel sounds. Diphthongization occurs when a single vowel sound is drawn out or "broken" into two or three, such as in some variations of the U.S. "Southern drawl" where *cat* might sound more like "cayut" or *hit* more like "hiyut."
æ: the vowel sound sometimes referred to as a "short *a*," as in *cat* or *pan*.
tense: A "tense" vowel is produced slightly higher in the mouth, while a "retracted" or "lax" one is produced slightly lower.

and ultimately showed that one man's use of one marker of gay speech, namely, pitch raising in declarative° utterances, was more frequent in conversational interactions with gay peers than in professional interactions. This finding is in accordance with the observations of some scholars that LGBT speech characteristics are more apparent in group interaction than in one-to-one interaction (Munson & Babel, 2007, p. 442).

Mann (2011) builds on language attitude research in folk dialectology [20] and social psychology to investigate people's perceptions of American English as it is used by gay males. He also adapts methodologies from social network theory to investigate how the individual attitudes of gay males toward Gay American English (GAE) and their use of it are influenced by their connectedness to several networks. Mann's results show that while speakers of GAE were assessed positively for characteristics associated with status (e.g., intelligence) and solidarity (e.g., friendliness), the results also showed GAE to be associated with "effeminacy," which was negatively evaluated by participants in the study. In light of these findings, Mann (2011) concluded that the use of GAE might hinder a speaker's chances of upward social mobility. Mann's data also show a positive correlation between attitudes toward and/or use of GAE and connectedness to LGBTQ networks and practices. Mann (2012) found that negative attitudes toward the use of GAE decrease the possibility that a speaker will use linguistic features associated with it and is, as a result, less likely to be perceived as gay than men who hold positive attitudes toward the use of GAE.

Box 1.3 Reclaimed Epithets

A linguistic issue with relevance to the LGBT community is the use of reclaimed epithets, which are terms of derision that are redefined, to some extent, as expressions of pride by members of the group they are intended to denigrate (Zwicky, 1997, p. 22). In the LGBT community, *dyke, faggot,* and *queer,* for example, have been reclaimed by some individuals and groups, although acceptable uses of these terms are highly dependent on context. As Zwicky (1997, p. 22) says, "The issue for all such lexical items is: For which speakers, in which contexts, and for which purposes has the word been reclaimed?" The LGBT community is not alone in reclaiming epithets, as observed in efforts to reclaim *bitch* and *slut* by feminists (Joreen, 1970; Wurtzel, 1999) as well as the n-word within the African American community.

---

declarative: in the form of a statement—as opposed to a question, where pitch raising is more common.

A participant in a 2011 New York City "SlutWalk." The SlutWalk movement fights sexual violence and victim blaming by asserting that provocative clothing or a sexually active lifestyle are never invitations to rape. Many SlutWalk messages reclaim the epithet *slut* and reframe it in a positive light. Critics of the SlutWalk movement claim that *slut* is too damaging a word, particularly when used toward black women, who have for centuries been targets of racist assumptions about their sexual availability.

Tony Savino/Getty Images

References

Adams, M. (1999). Slayer slang (part 2). *Verbatim, The Language Quarterly* 24(4): 1–7.

Bucholtz, M. (2004). Language, gender, and sexuality. In E. Finegan, & J.R. Rickford (Eds.) *Language in the U.S.A.: Themes for the twenty-first century* (pp. 410–429). Cambridge: Cambridge University Press.

Bucholtz, M. (2011). "It's different for guys": Gendered narratives of racial conflict among white California youth. *Discourse and Society* 22(4): 385–402.

Buchstaller, I. (2001). *He goes* and *I'm like*: The new quotatives re-visited. Paper presented at the 30th annual conference on *New Ways of Analyzing Variation* (NWAV 30), Raleigh, NC, October 11–14. Retrieved from www.ling.ed.ac. uk/~pgc/archive/2002/proc02/buchstaller02.pdf.

Chambers, J. (1995). *Sociolinguistic theory*. Oxford: Blackwell.

Ching, M. (1982). The question intonation in assertions. *American Speech* 57: 95–107.

Coates, J. (1993). No gap, lots of overlap: Turn-taking patterns in the talk of women friends. In D. Graddol, J. Maybin, & B. Stierer (Eds.) *Research language and literacy in social context* (pp. 177–192). Cleveland, OH: Multilingual Matters.

Coates, J. (1996). *Women talk: Conversation between women friends*. Oxford: Blackwell.

D'Arcy, A.F. (2005). Like: Syntax and development. (Unpublished doctoral dissertation), University of Toronto.

Eble, C. (2004). Slang. In E. Finegan, & J. Rickford (Eds.) *Language in the U.S.A.* (pp. 375–386). New York: Cambridge University Press.

Eckert, P. (1989). *Jocks and burnouts: Social categories and identity in the high school*. New York: Teachers College Press, Columbia University.

Eckert, P. (1998). Age as a sociolinguistic variable. In F. Coulmas (Ed.) *The handbook of sociolinguistics* (pp. 151–167). Oxford: Blackwell.

Eckert, P. (2004). Adolescent language. In E. Finegan, & J. Rickford (Eds.) *Language in the U.S.A.* (pp. 361–374). New York: Cambridge University Press.

Fischer, J. (1958). Social influences on the choice of a linguistic variant. *Word* 14: 47–56.

Fought, C. (2003). *Chicano English in context*. New York: Palgrave Macmillan.

Gastil, J. (1990). Generic pronouns and sexist language: The oxymoronic character of masculine generics. *Sex Roles* 23: 629–643.

Gaudio, R. (1994). Sounding gay: Pitch properties in the speech of gay and straight men. *American Speech* 69: 30–57.

Gottliebson, R.O., Lee, L., Weinrich, B., & Sanders, J. (2007). Voice problems of future speech- language pathologists. *Journal of Voice* 21: 699–704.

Holmes, J. (1990). Hedges and boosters in women's and men's speech. *Language & Communication* 10(3): 185–205.

Holmes, J. (1995). *Women, men and politeness*. London and New York: Longman.

Jespersen, O. (1922). *Language: Its nature, development and origin*. London: George Allen & Unwin.

Joreen (1970). The bitch manifesto. In S. Firestone and A. Koedt (Eds.) *Notes from the second year: Women's liberation: Major writings of the radical feminists*. Pamphlet.

Kiesling, S.F. (1998). Men's identities and sociolinguistic variation: The case of fraternity men. *Journal of Sociolinguistics* 2/1: 69–99.

Kiesling, S.F. (2009). Fraternity men: Variation and discourses of masculinity. In N. Coupland, & A. Jaworski (Eds.) *The new sociolinguistics reader* (pp. 187–200). Basingstoke: Palgrave Macmillan.

Labov, W. (1990). The intersection of sex and social class in the course of linguistic change. *Language Variation and Change* 2: 205–254.

Lakoff, R. (1975). *Language and women's place*. New York: Harper & Row.

Lanehart, S.L. (Ed.) (2009). African American women's language: Discourse, education, and identity. Newcastle: Cambridge Scholars Publishing.Liberman, M. (2005). Uptalk uptick? *Language Log*, December 15. Retrieved from http:// itre. cis.upenn.edu/~myl/languagelog/archives/002708.html.

Liberman, M. (2011). Vocal fry: "Creeping in" or "still here"? *Language Log*, December 12. Retrieved from http://languagelog.ldc.upenn.edu/nll/?p=3626.

Linneman, T.J. (2013). Gender in Jeopardy! Intonation variation on a television game show. *Gender & Society* 27: 82–105.

Mann, S.L. (2011). Gay American English: Language attitudes, language perceptions, and gay men's discourses of connectedness to family, LGBTQ networks, and the American South. (Unpublished doctoral dissertation), University of South Carolina, Columbia.

Mann, S.L. (2012). Speaker attitude as a predictive factor in listener perception of gay men's speech. *Journal of Language and Sexuality* 1: 206–230.

Martyna, W. (1978). What does "he" mean? Use of the generic masculine. *Journal of Communication* 28: 131–138.

McLemore, C. (1991). *The pragmatic interpretation of English intonation*. Austin, TX: University of Texas.

Mendoza-Denton, N. (2008). *Homegirls: Language and cultural practice among Latina youth gangs*. Malden, MA: Blackwell.

Mendoza-Denton, N. (2011). The semiotic hitchhiker's guide to creaky voice: Circulation and gendered hardcore in a Chicana/o gang persona. *Journal of Linguistic Anthropology* 21(2): 261–280.

Munson, B., & Babel, M. (2007). Loose lips and silver tongues, or projecting sexual orientation through speech. *Language and Linguistics Compass* 1(5): 416–449.

Munson, B., McDonald, E.C., DeBoe, N.L., & White, A.R. (2006). Acoustic and perceptual bases of judgments of women and men's sexual orientation from read speech. *Journal of Phonetics* 34: 202–240.

Pierrehumbert, J.B., Bent, T., Munson, B., Bradlow, A.R., & Bailey, J.M. (2004). The influence of sexual orientation on vowel production. *Journal of the Acoustical Society of America* 116: 1905–1908.

Podesva, R.J. (2004). On constructing social meaning with stop release bursts. Paper presented at Sociolinguistics Symposium 15, Newcastle upon Tyne, UK, April.

Podesva, R.J. (2006). Phonetic detail in sociolinguistic variation: Its linguistic significance and role in the construction of meaning. (Unpublished doctoral dissertation), Stanford University, Stanford, CA.

Rickford, J., Wasow, T., Zwicky, A., & Buchstaller, I. (2007). Intensive and quotative all: Something old, something new. *American Speech* 82(1): 3–31.

Romaine, S., & Lange, D. (1991). The use of like as a marker of reported speech and thought: A case of grammaticalization in progress. *American Speech* 66(3): 227–279.

Rothschild, N. (2013). Sweden's new gender-neutral pronoun: *Hen. Slate,* April 12. Retrieved from www.slate.com/articles/double_x/doublex/2012/04/hen_swe-den_s_new_gender_neutral_pronoun_causes_controversy_.html.

Smith, P.M. (1985). *Language, the sexes and society.* New York: Blackwell.

Smyth, R., Jacobs, G., & Rogers, H. (2003). Male voices and perceived sexual orientation: An experimental and theoretical approach. *Language in Society* 32(3): 329–350.

Strunk, W., & White, E.B. (1979). *The elements of style.* New York: Macmillan.

Tagliamonte, S. (2012). *Variationist sociolinguistics: Change, observation, interpretation.* Chichester: Wiley-Blackwell.

Tannen, D. (1990). *You just don't understand: Women and men in conversation.* New York: Ballantine Books.

Trudgill, P. (1972). Sex, covert prestige and linguistic change in the urban British English of Norwich. *Language in Society* 1: 179–195.

Whedon, J. (Producer) (1997–2003). *Buffy the vampire slayer,* 20th Century Fox Television.

Wolk, L., Abdelli-Beruh, N.B., & Slavin, D. (2012). Habitual use of vocal fry in young adult female speakers. *Journal of Voice* 26(3): e111–e116.

Wurtzel, E. (1999). *Bitch: In praise of difficult women.* New York: Anchor.

Zwicky, A.M. (1997). Two lavender issues for linguists. In A. Livia, & K. Hall (Eds.) *Queerly phrased: Language, gender, and sexuality* (pp. 21–34). New York: Oxford University Press.

Understanding the Text

1. According to Tamasi and Antieau, what are some of the reasons why "people of different ages tend to speak differently from one another" (par. 3)?

2. What is the difference between the deficit and difference approaches to understanding gender differences in language?

3. What are some of the discoveries recent research has made about the connections between sexual orientation and language?

Reflection and Response

4. As in the example of *Buffy the Vampire Slayer*, television shows and movies frequently both influence and are influenced by the language of young people. What are some examples of current slang that comes from or is reflected in television shows and movies?

5. As Tamasi and Antieau note, many studies of gender and sexuality in language are not necessarily about differences between how men and women or gay and straight people talk, but rather about how people *think* they talk — for instance, what someone might hear in a man's speech that would lead to the assumption that he is gay. Based on this article and your own reflections, why is it important to be aware of these sorts of assumptions?

6. When Tamasi and Antieau discuss reclaiming epithets, they note that "acceptable uses of these terms are highly dependent on context" (Box 1.3). In other words, just because a group has taken a word that was formerly used to insult them and made it a marker of pride among themselves, that doesn't mean that others outside the group are free to use the word, or even that everyone within the group supports its use. What do you think Tamasi and Antieau would say to a man who asks, "Why can't I call women *bitches*, if they can call each other that?" or a straight person who asks, "Why can't I use the word *fag* but gay men can?" What would you say?

Making Connections

7. Using Tamasi and Antieau's "Sexist Language" section (Box 1.2), and Mark Peters's article "He Said, Sheme Said" (p. 162), discuss how changing ideas of gender, including gender roles and gender identities, have influenced recent language changes.

8. Examine Tamasi and Antieau's "Language and Gender" section alongside Marybeth Seitz-Brown's "Young Women Shouldn't Have to Talk Like Men to Be Taken Seriously" (p. 92) and Douglas Quenqua's "They're, Like, Way Ahead of the Linguistic Currrrve" (p. 178). How do these three pieces show women's and men's speech to be more alike than the average person might think? How do they defend women's speech against assumptions that it is less confident or mature than men's speech?

From *Slang and Sociability: In-Group Language among College Students*

Connie Eble

Connie Eble is a professor of English linguistics at the University of North Carolina at Chapel Hill. She teaches a range of classes on the grammar and history of English, but her main research interests are the dialects of Louisiana and the slang of young adults. Her book *Slang and Sociability: In-Group Language among College Students* (1996) is an in-depth study of college student slang. In it, she catalogs the many slang terms used by college students toward the end of the twentieth century, traces a history of college slang back through U.S. history, and analyzes the functions of slang in forming identities and holding together social groups. In her analysis, Eble outlines general trends and principles that we can apply to the new slang terms continually arriving in our language.

Like buildings, household utensils, and decorative artwork, words are indicators of human culture. They even offer an advantage over physical objects, in that words can communicate information about the intangibles of life—about the thoughts, beliefs, and values of their users. Even though the Indo-Europeans of five thousand years ago cannot be identified by a trail of physical objects, in a well-known essay in *The American Heritage Dictionary*, Calvert Watkins is able to speculate about their culture by examining their words. Watkins writes, "Though by no means a perfect mirror, the lexicon of a language remains the single most effective way of approaching and understanding the culture of its speakers" (1992, 2084). This chapter traces the slang lexicon of American college students over the years as a way of coming to a better understanding of their culture.

Good evidence of the use of slang by American college students dates only from the mid-nineteenth century. However, the creative use of language by students in grumbling to one another about their lot in life and about those in authority over them must date in western Europe from the earliest days of the medieval universities. To keep check on ribald, quarrelsome, and blasphemous speech among students, college statutes mandated a combination of silence and the use of Latin (Rait 1912, 59). Perhaps one of the first items of college slang was *lupi* (wolves), "spies who reported students for using the vernacular instead of Latin" (108). Students undoubtedly did use the vernacular, or there would be no need for *lupi,* and most likely they developed slang in their own language too. The editor of a fifteenth-century Latin manuscript suggests that the

English phrase *ars lyke* (*arse lick*) masquerading as a gloss above a Latin word may be "a naughty schoolboy's graffiti" (Ross 1984, 142). Five hundred years later students still maintain unflattering descriptions for "one who curries favor," for example, *kiss-ass* or *brown noser*. But, because of the oral and ephemeral nature of slang vocabulary, a direct, unbroken line of descent from earlier usage cannot be taken for granted.

Our knowledge of college slang in the United States during the nineteenth century relies heavily on two sources, B. H. Hall's *College Words and Customs* (1856) and Lyman Bagg's *Four Years at Yale* (1871). Hall's work, the more valuable for linguistic information, is a five-hundred-page listing of words and customs and draws examples from British universities as well as from thirty-three U.S. colleges. *Four Years at Yale*, a memoir, contains a seven-page alphabetized list of words from the author's undergraduate years at Yale in the late 1860s. In addition, the novel *Student Life at Harvard* (1876) purports to "give a faithful picture of student life at Harvard University as it appeared to undergraduates there" during the 1860s. These three sources reveal a slang vocabulary concerned with campus landmarks, rivalry among the classes, making a fashionable appearance, eating and socializing, and studying as little as possible.

The campus landmark that inspired the largest number of slang synonyms was the "privy," called the *joe, minor [house], coal yard, temple,* and *number fifty* and *number forty-nine* at Harvard and *number ten* and *number 1001* at Wesleyan, Vermont, and Dartmouth. "To be absent from recitation or lecture" was to *bolt* or *cut.* "To fail completely" was to *flunk,* but "to fail partially" was to *fizzle.* At North Carolina in 1851, "to fail in recitation" was to *fess* (Dickinson 1951, 182). "To study hard" was to *dig, grind, grub,* or *pole,* and to study hard at the last minute was to *cram,* its noun form *cramination.* "Someone who curried favor with teachers or others for advantage" was a *bootlicker, pimp, piscatorian, toady,* or *supe.* Other items were *scrub* "poorly dressed, socially inferior man"; *beggars* "rivals"; *chum* "roommate"; *rough* "tease"; *rub* "give difficulty to"; and *squirt* "attempt at recitation." The use of a translation for recitation in Greek and Latin classes was commonplace, and the metaphor of riding a horse gave rise to *pony, horse, trot, taking a ride, riding a pony,* and others. Relatively few slang words for "drunk" are recorded in these sources, and almost no terms have sexual referents; these depictions of college life were all written for polite society.

By current standards, the mid-nineteenth-century college slang lexicon 5 is spare both in size and in meaning, reflecting a social reality: higher education was still rare. Most of the colleges were private or church affiliated and for young men. College students were younger then, usually entering at age fourteen or fifteen. Those who attended were ordinarily from privileged backgrounds or intended for the ministry. Even if they used slang to talk about sex and other delicate topics with their college chums, the norms of social interaction prevented their mentioning the topics or disclosing their slang in wider circles or, especially, writing such words down. As a rule, people then did not write about sex, even in personal letters and diaries.

During the 1880s and 1890s, college enrollments almost doubled. The number of colleges likewise increased, particularly public ones. Many were coeducational, admitting women as well as men. The children of small farmers, merchants, and immigrants now claimed seats in college classrooms. Public interest in college slang at that time is shown by the many short and usually anecdotal articles on the topic published in newspapers and magazines. *American Notes and Queries,* for example, in November 1889 carried a list of twenty slang expressions from Harvard and three weeks later a comparable list from Hampden Sydney College in Virginia. The cleverest item is *Hoi Barbaroi,* from Hampden Sydney, for "members of no fraternity." This Greek expression alludes both to the English word *barbarian* and to its source, the Greek word meaning "foreigner, one who is not Greek." In college social circles, fraternities and their members are called Greeks. One who is not Greek, then, is not a member of a fraternity—and by implication is also a barbarian.

In 1895 Willard C. Gore, Ph.M., of the University of Michigan undertook what I believe to be the first systematic and sizable study of American student slang at a single university.[1] In the spring and fall semesters of 1895, he asked two hundred second- and third-year students in a rhetoric course at the University of Michigan to collect and define current student slang that they heard or read. Anticipating my methodology by eighty years, he did not define slang for them but accepted an expression as slang "because it was so regarded by the students who handed it in" (1993 23). Gore submitted the list of about five hundred words and phrases to the vote of a class of sixty-five students. "A large number were unfamiliar to many. Very few, however, were regarded by any as having emerged from the slang stage" (23).

Gore's collection seems contemporary in many ways. About 10 percent of the entries refer to types of people still familiar on college campuses: a *blug* is "one who is very stylish"; *a little tin god on wheels* is "a superior person (said ironically)"; an *ice wagon* is "someone who is slow"; a *prune* is a "disagreeable and irritable person"; a *huckleberry* is a "sweet and agreeable person"; a *grind* is "someone who studies too much." Almost as many terms are evaluative adjectives: *chiselly* means "unpleasant, disagreeable"; *rank* means "unfair or arbitrary"; *skatey* means "ill-bred, vulgar, cheap"; *woozy* means "pleasant, delightful"; and *out of sight* means "first-rate, superior." Several are expressions of support, like *I should say* and *too utterly too too.* About one-fourth of the items refer to academic matters, like *flim* for "to cheat"; *con* for "to get the grade *condition*"; *tute* for "tutor"; *fruit* for "a lenient teacher"; *heathen* for "an unreasonable teacher"; and *crust the instructor* for "make a good recitation." However, unlike more recent collections, the 1895 Michigan list contains fewer than ten items each that refer to females or to overindulgence in alcohol, and words with sexual implications are almost entirely absent.

Within five years of Gore's study, Eugene Babbitt and fellow members of the New York branch of the American Dialect Society conducted the most ambitious national survey of American college slang to date. After a pilot study that circulated thirty words to several leading colleges for confirmation and additions, an expanded list of three hundred items was sent to "all the colleges and universities in the country, as well as to a number of secondary schools" (1900, 5). The results of responses from eighty-seven schools are reported in a thousand-item word list accompanied by a perceptive seventeen-page essay.[2] "College Slang and Phrases," published in 1900 in *Dialect Notes*, is the baseline for the historical study of twentieth-century U.S. college slang.

The content of American college slang evidenced by the national survey does not differ much from that of the University of Michigan alone. What is more interesting is that in broad categories the college slang of the turn of the century is comparable to that of the 1850s and 1860s.   10

The privy continues to be a source of linguistic diversion, inspiring additional slang synonyms like *bank, chamber of commerce, domus, Egypt, poet's corner*, and *prep chapel*, as well as *Jake* for men and *Ruth* for women.

Fully one-third of the items in the national survey refer to the persons, places, requirements, rituals, and difficulties that students encounter in their role as students. The time-honored *horse* metaphor for "using a translation" has elaborated into *animal, beast, bicycle,* and *wheel*. A "user of a translation" is a *jockey* or *equestrian*, and "a bookshelf for translations" is a *stable*. A *race course* is a "meeting of several students to prepare a pony," and a *racetrack* is the site of such a meeting. Some synonyms for "failing to attend class" are *adjourn, hook, skip, sneak,* and *snooke*. A *safety* is "a slip of paper handed to an instructor at the beginning of a recitation stating that the student is unprepared," and attendance at recitation under those circumstances is called a *dry cut*.

Particularly plentiful are words for performing in classroom recitation or on examinations, with more terms for failure than for success. Among the verbs for "to fail" are *bust, crash, croak, fall down, fall down under the table, fluke, pitch, slump,* and *smash*. On the other hand, "to recite perfectly" is to *bat, do it bright, curl, kill, paralyze the professor,* and *twist*. Students who recite though unprepared *cheek it, go on general principles, muscle,* or *make a stab*. If they "get through a recitation without aids," they *walk*, that is, they do not *ride the pony*. One who "surprises an instructor by answering all the questions" *staggers*. "A passing examination in every subject" is a *clean shave*.

There are several terms for using unfair means to pass examinations, for example, to *frog, rogue through,* or *shenannygag*. The various ingenious devices prepared for the purpose of cheating have their own names: *cribs, panoramas, rolls, skins,* and *winders*. A *winder*, for instance, is "a crib constructed of a long strip of paper rolled on two pencils." But more contemptible than cheating as a way to succeed academically is currying favor with a teacher or someone else in authority. A student who does this is said to *bootlick, chin, coax, drag, fish, suck,* or *swipe*.

The polite reserve noticed in the college slang dating from the 1850s 15 and 1860s is barely broken at the turn of the century. The slang still contains few terms for drinking, women, or groups discriminated against in society at large. For example, only about a dozen terms refer to drinking alcohol and a comparable total to Jews, Italians, and African Americans. Babbitt thinks that the lack of such terms shows that college students have not developed a distinctive vocabulary of their own for talking about these topics (11). It is possible that the use of offensive slang among students was much more limited and cautious a century ago when rules for behavior were stricter. However, it is also likely that terms considered common or vulgar in general conversation are underreported in Babbitt's collection. I imagine that both students and faculty of the Victorian era would have felt uncomfortable writing down and mailing lists of such words to the American Dialect Society even if they knew or used them.

Nonetheless, the small set of slang words and phrases that refer to women and to relationships between men and women do give a hint of the collegiate culture then. A female domestic employed in college dormitories rates almost as many names as does a female student, being called an *Amazon, grace,* or *Venus*, as well as the less lofty *sheet-slinger* and *kitchen mechanic*. Bird names are the standard in referring to a female student, for instance, *canary, hen, pullet,* and *quail*; and a female residence hall is a *hen coop/ranch/roost, quail roost,* or *jail*. Another term for "female student" is *calico* and its shortened derivative *calic*, which gives rise by synecdoche to *dry goods*. Synonyms for "pretty girl" include *geranium, peach,* and *peacherine*. Several terms mean "to call on, escort, or entertain a lady," including *buck, buzz, fuss, go double, pike, swing,* and *turf*. Keeping company with the opposite sex is viewed in the context of marriage: a *college widow* is "a girl whom new men meet from year to year but whom no one ever marries," and to *take a cottage course* is "to marry before graduation." Some words, though, imply less respectable types of relations between the sexes. A *birdie* is a "girl eager to make a man's acquaintance without introduction"; *bat, fruit, seed,* and *scrub* all refer to a "loose woman"; and *cat* means "to keep company with a bad woman."

The words *bitch* and *slut* are part of the American college slang around 1900, but they both refer to the queen in playing cards.

Babbitt's study in 1900 was the last major undertaking in the scholarly study of American college slang for seventy years, until Gary Underwood's project (1975) at the University of Arkansas from 1970 through 1972. Mencken's admirable chapter on slang (1963)—which documents the in-group vocabulary of such diverse groups as aviators, jazz musicians, railroad workers, and prisoners—gives college students short shrift. To be sure, over the years journalists have continued to keep the public up to date on the latest zany expressions from college campuses. And beginning in 1925, the journal *American Speech* frequently printed brief word lists from various campuses and served as the primary outlet for the publication of scholarly studies of college slang, like that of Dundes and Schonhorn in 1963. The short-lived periodical *Current Slang*, which was issued quarterly from the English Department of the University of South Dakota from summer 1966 through winter 1971, focused mainly on college slang, documenting the sudden burgeoning in the college lexicon of terms from African Americans and from the drug culture.

During the period from 1900 to 1970, the scholarly collection and analysis of American college slang was at best sporadic. However, in these scattered treatments can be seen traces of the major changes that transformed college slang and college culture by the 1970s. By 1926–27, slang at Kansas University depicted not only "loose women" but also women students as having sex appeal, with terms like *hot-sketch* and *mean-baby* (Pingry and Randolph 1928). University of Missouri slang of 1931 called a "chic, up-to-date coed" a *hot number* and "one who necks on a date" a *giraffe* (Carter 1931). The collection from Johns Hopkins published in 1932 includes slang in three areas barely evident in student slang from 1900. An African American was a *smoke* or an *eight ball*. An effeminate male was a *birdie, fag, fairy, fluter, pansy,* or *queer*. But it is in the area of sexual relations between males and females that the greatest increases occurred. A "loose woman" was a *bag, blimp,* or *piece*; and "a woman who is easily possessed" was a *cinch, pushover,* or *sex job*. A "sexually repressed male" was *horny*, and to "have wandering hands" was to *develop* or *explore*. "Women's breasts" were *big brown eyes*. To "kiss" was to *mug, muzzle,* or *smooch,* and to "copulate" was to *go the limit* (Kuethe 1932). By 1948 at North Texas Agricultural College students were talking about "perfume" as *rape fluid*; about "a girl who enjoys arousing a male" as a *p.t.* (from *prick teaser*); and about "experiencing an orgasm" as *losing one's rocks* (Jarnagin and Eikel 1948). In 1955, at Wayne State University, students had a slang term for marijuana, *pod* (White 1955).

After World War II, the GI Bill altered the collegiate population of the United States and set into motion changes in higher education that are still being felt today. During the 1950s and 1960s American institutions of higher learning relinquished the philosophy of in loco parentis under which they had functioned in a parental role toward students. As a consequence, many college regulations for controlling student behavior outside the classroom were eventually abandoned—such as dress codes, curfews, and mandatory attendance at chapel or assemblies.

By the time Gary Underwood collected his lexicon of 750 slang items 20 at the University of Arkansas, from 1970 to 1972, American college slang had taken on its current shape. For instance, in the Arkansas collection there are multiple synonyms for *drunk* and *vomit,* derogatory terms for minorities, explicit words for sex, words with sexual connotations for women, and numerous terms for drugs or derived from the drug culture. As a whole, the terms Underwood reports from Arkansas parallel in meaning and effect the terms in the University of North Carolina collection. Both collections show plainly that since the turn of the century drastic changes have taken place in what college students are willing to reveal about their talk with one another.

Many of the hundreds of items of North Carolina slang used as examples throughout this book suggest various facets of college culture in the late twentieth century. For instance, *bro, sister,* and *homeboy/homegirl/homey* are the primary kinship terms in the college lexicon—and also among the most frequently used nouns of address. This usage implies a speech community formed on peer relationships rather than on hierarchy. Another example is provided by admonitions like *get a life, get a job, get a real job,* and *get with the program* for instructing others to conform to the expectations that society holds for adults. These expressions show that, despite the need of college students to merit the favorable judgment of peers, it is ultimately the standards of the world of work beyond college that count. Other slang presented throughout this book confirms that the current college culture is firmly rooted in the general culture. Unlike an antilanguage, in which the lexicon is highly developed specifically in those areas that set the users apart from mainstream culture, college slang invests little in vocabulary pertaining to the users' status as scholars. Instead, the focus is on relationships with other students and on activities that reinforce those relationships. College student vocabulary about relationships echoes the discourse of American society at large. Ubiquitous popular discussion about openness and honesty in relationships, for example, is the context for college expressions like *DHC* "deep, heavy conversation," as in "I'm afraid that when my grades arrive, I'm in for some *DHC*," and *DTR* "defining the relationship," as in "It's time for John and me to have the DTR conversation." Current uneasiness about the changing role of women in society underlies college slang expressions like *PMS* "be agitated, annoyed," from premenstrual syndrome, which is reinterpreted as Putting Up with Men's Shit, and *WHAM* "a woman who harms men physically or emotionally," from Women Hate All Men, and its plural *WHAMS,* supposedly from Women Have All Men Scared. Increasing national fears about new immigrant groups are shown by *FOB* "Asian who has not yet learned American culture" from Fresh Off the Boat and by *Nuprin,* a joking reference to "Asians," from the brand name of pills for pain that are "small, yellow, and different."

The University of North Carolina "top forty" are the lexical items that were submitted by a total of thirty students or more during the period extending from fall 1972 through spring 1993.

Thirty-two of the forty fall into these nineteen categories:

"excellent": *sweet, killer, bad, cool, awesome*
"socially inept person": *dweeb, geek, turkey*
"drunk": *wasted, catch a buzz, trashed*
"relax": *chill (out), veg (out)*
"fads": *not!, word up*
"fraternity/sorority member": *bagger, Suzi*
"disregard": *bag, blow off*
"kiss passionately": *grub, hook (up)*
"attractive": *hot*
"attractive person": *fox/foxy*
"have a good time": *jam*
"do well": *ace*
"insult": *diss*
"leave": *book*
"fail": *flag*
"eat rapidly": *pig out*
"out of touch": *clueless*
"pursue for sex": *scope*
"worst situation": *the pits*

The remaining eight are *slide* "an easy course"; *crash* "to go to sleep"; *cheezy* "unattractive, out of favor"; *trip (out)* "have a bizarre experience"; *granola* "one who follows the lifestyle of the sixties"; *homeboy/homegirl/ homey* "friend"; *dude* "male, any person"; and *slack* "below standard." The meanings of these eight are not unusual or unexpected for slang; they simply do not fall into one of the categories of meaning [Elisa] Fiorenza identified as generating high-frequency synonyms.

Viewed by grammatical rather than by semantic categories, eleven of the top forty are nouns; eleven, adjectives; sixteen, verbs; and two, faddish interjections (*not!* and *word up*). Of the nouns, one means "an easy course" and one means "the worst situation." The remaining nine are types of people. *Dweeb, geek,* and *turkey* are the most negative, as these sorts permanently lack social skills. *Baggers* and *Suzis* are the privileged types who join social organizations whose membership is by invitation only. A *granola* is the type who has chosen not to change with the times. On the positive side, a *fox* is a beautiful, well-groomed, fashionable woman. *Homeboy* and its derivatives name "friends." *Dude* is neutral in connotation, as it can apply to virtually anyone.

Of the adjectives, the two for "drunk" are the passive participles *wasted* 25 and *trashed*. *Clueless* indicates that the referent is not consciously aware of communal knowledge, and *slack* applies to someone who does not meet prevailing standards. *Sweet, awesome, bad,* and *cool* are all-purpose positive assessments, and *cheezy* is an all-purpose negative one. *Hot* is a positive evaluation of physical attractiveness. *Killer* means either "excellent" or "terrible."

The sixteen verbs summarize what students do. On the high-energy end of the scale, they perform well (*ace*), have a good time (*jam*), have a bizarre experience (*trip [out]*), and engage in romantic pursuits (*scope, hook,* and *grub*). At the other end of the scale, they cease an activity or neglect a responsibility (*blow off, bag*) and

> "Slang vocabulary is like an irregularly blinking signal that discloses someone's location to those privy to the code. The signal is deliberate, limited, and intended for a select audience."

fail (*flag*). To maintain themselves physically, they eat (*pig out*), drink (*catch a buzz*), relax (*chill [out], veg [out]*), go to sleep (*crash*), and depart (*book*). Judgmentally, they criticize others (*diss*).

The forty most frequent lexical items imply a community of speakers concerned with relationships among people, particularly with judgments of acceptance or rejection. They divide almost evenly between terms with positive associations and connotations and those with negative ones. Those that convey negative judgments are rather mild. None of the most frequently submitted negative labels is as vivid, memorable, or offensive as low-frequency derogatory terms like sexist *hosebag,* racist *porch monkey,* and homophobic *fudge packer*. The sexual activity pictured in the top forty is the pursuit, not the consummation; although the collection has many graphic verbs that refer to the physical union of male and female, such as *bounce refrigerators* and *parallel park,* none was submitted frequently enough to make the top forty. Interestingly, the drinking terms focus on the unpleasant effects rather than on the convivial process. Only two of the top forty Carolina slang items give a hint that the users are students, *slide* and *flag*.

The narrow scope of this subset of college slang is actually a rather accurate reflection of the range of the corpus as a whole. The narrowness is, in part, a function of the fact that the vocabulary items are slang. Slang vocabulary is like an irregularly blinking signal that discloses someone's location to those privy to the code. The signal is deliberate, limited, and intended for a select audience. Slang vocabulary is likewise restricted; it does not give speakers the resources to talk about the full range of human experiences. One cannot go about the business of living using only slang. As a simple and blatant example, slang does not provide vocabulary for numbers, for personal pronouns, or for concepts of time such as before and after. The slang that college students use with one another is vocabulary for a special purpose. That purpose is sociability, a pleasurable sense of being in harmony with other people.

A 2016 *Sarah's Scribbles* comic, by Sarah Andersen.

Sarah Anderson/Go Comics/Andrews McMeel Syndication

The studies of anthropologist Michael Moffatt (1989) and folklorist Simon J. Bronner (1990) both verify the primacy of social relations and activities in the lives of recent American college students. It is not academic concerns that shape undergraduate college culture or college slang—it is human ones. College students put more of their time and youthful spiritedness into figuring out who they are in relationship to others, what they like and dislike, what they can and cannot do, and what they will and will not tolerate than in trying to figure out their textbooks, lectures, and professors.

It is also possible that recent generations of college students are cre- 30 ating, appropriating, and using more slang than their counterparts did a century ago. This may be in part because in the United States colloquial vocabulary and slang are generally more widely used now than in the nineteenth century. Lighter notes a stylistic shift toward the highly informal with the advent of writing intended for mass circulation early in the century. The mass media explosion that began then has provided the context for an increase in slang: "for the tone of all current mass media, spurred by the demands of competition, plunges on in the direction of the breezy, the startling, the tough-minded and terse—attitudes that slang is born to impart" (1994, xviii). Undoubtedly because of the influence of the mass media, a type of national slang that conveys attitudes rather than identity with a group, what Chapman calls "secondary slang," has become more noticeable (1986, xii). Thus students arrive at college with a lifelong exposure to slang and its social functions. What's more, when first-year students join their newly forming speech community on the first day of registration, they have already survived an important sociolinguistic testing ground. As Danesi (1994) shows, they are already veteran users of the social dialect of their high school and the cliques to which they belonged. Slang, then, is not among the new and threatening features of college life.

What is the future for American college slang? What cultural phenomena will be lauded, supported, stereotyped, made fun of, or condemned in the slang at the turn of the twenty-first century? Currently, the two greatest sources of influence on college slang and on the linguistic style of college students are African Americans and gays. In a recent independent studies research project, UNC-CH senior Kenneth Levine analyzed the expressive styles and self-identifying vocabulary of these two groups and found common needs manifesting themselves in similar ways linguistically. Several of the lexical items Levine identified had already turned up in North Carolina student slang, like the verb *read* "tell someone off" and *work someone's last nerve* "annoy exceedingly." College students who do not belong to these groups, and who do not care to belong to them, nonetheless find their verbal dexterity appealing and worthy of imitation. The influence of African Americans and gays on college slang will continue as long as members of the two groups remain popular in the arts and entertainment media and as the groups achieve more recognition on campus.

Early indications are that the national debate over the rights of minorities and disadvantaged groups, the issue of "political correctness," will manifest itself in interesting ways in college slang. More than any previous generation, students of the 1990s are the beneficiaries of textbooks, lectures, workshops, and conferences designed to analyze critically the assumptions and consequences of discrimination of all kinds. In their public and academic discourse, they can cite facts about differential wages for males and females, explain the high incidence of African American households without an adult male, and advocate the reasonableness of including gays in the military and women in the Roman Catholic priesthood. They have learned, and many believe what they have been taught. But in their casual discourse among friends, in the circles in which they vent their frustrations and express their opposition toward those they feel control their lives, the same students are uttering offensive, stereotypical slang referring to people unlike themselves whom they intellectually and morally support. This abandonment of political correctness among friends is perhaps a sign of trust in others, like telling a secret. It may also be a sign of the fear that in the increasing fragmentation of American society into groups demanding a fair share, they may wind up among the "have-nots."

Acquiring the kind of knowledge transmitted in books and classrooms is ultimately an individual experience and therefore potentially lonely. No longer apparent are the well-defined groups that were once a natural outgrowth of a rather simple academic system where everyone followed the same curriculum, had the same professors, and lived on the college grounds—and where the students were a fairly homogeneous lot. American college student bodies are now much more diversified in age, national and regional origin, race, ethnicity, social class, financial resources, and academic preparation. Institutions of higher learning are larger, with more bureaucracy than ever. As a result, contemporary college students must take greater personal responsibility for identifying and becoming a part of groups that can fulfill their needs for companionship during their college years. An increase in slang use in this would not be surprising.

I find myself in agreement with folklorist Simon Bronner, who studied the rituals, customs, legends, and jokes of college students in the 1970s and 1980s: "Students seek to strengthen their social identity, value system, and emotional growth, but find that the academic setting once noted for assisting this cultural passage has alienated rather than involved them. Increasingly students turn to one another for support, but struggle to create group harmony in a mass society stressing the uprooted, competitive individual" (1990, 239). A large part of that struggle for group harmony for college students is internecine verbal skirmishing; and the terms for negotiating the struggle are slang.

Notes

1. Although mentioned in Babbitt (1900) as "the most careful and complete" collection of the slang of a particular institution during the nineteenth century, Gore's twenty-nine-page collection with commentary was almost inaccessible until 1993, when Gerald Cohen reprinted it in *Comments on Etymology*—from a hand copy he made from a fragile original in the New York Public Library. If a history of American vernacular language is ever written, it will rely heavily on the careful work Cohen has done in tracking down, documenting, and publishing obscure sources like this one.

2. "College Words and Phrases" lists about one thousand items in the lexicon of American college students in 1900. Many of these, though undoubtedly part of the vocabulary of the academy, are not slang, for example, *alumni society, bursar, commencement, dean, faculty, regent,* and *thesis.* When I eliminate these, Babbitt's list contains slightly more than nine hundred items.

References

The American Heritage Dictionary of the English Language. 1992. 3d ed. Edited by Anne H. Soukhanov. Boston: Houghton Mifflin Co.

Babbitt, Eugene H. 1900. "College Words and Phrases." *Dialect Notes* 2:4–70.

Bagg, Lyman. 1871. *Four Years at Yale.* New Haven: C. C. Chatfield & Co.

Bronner, Simon J. 1990. *Piled Higher and Deeper: The Folklore of Campus Life.* Little Rock: August House Publishers.

Carter, Virginia. 1931. "University of Missouri Slang." *American Speech* 6:203–6.

Chapman, Robert L., ed. 1986. *New Dictionary of American Slang.* New York: Harper and Row.

Current Slang (Department of English, University of South Dakota). 1966–71. Vols. 1–6.

Danesi, Marcel. 1994. *Cool: The Signs and Meanings of Adolescence.* Toronto: University of Toronto Press.

Dickinson, M. B. 1951. "Words from the Diaries of North Carolina Students." *American Speech* 26:181–84.

Dundes, Alan, and Manuel R. Schonhorn. 1963. "Kansas University Slang: A New Generation." *American Speech* 38:164–77.

Fiorenza, Elisa. 1992. "A Statistical Analysis of Patterns of Slang Usage at the University of North Carolina at Chapel Hill from Fall 1976 to Fall 1991." Undergraduate honors thesis, Department of Statistics, University of North Carolina at Chapel Hill.

Gore, Willard C. 1993. "Student Slang." In *Contributions to Rhetorical Theory*, ed. Fred Newton Scott. 1896. Reprinted with index, ed. Gerald Cohen, in *Comments on Etymology* 22 (April): 1–47.

Hall, B. H. 1856. *College Words and Customs*. Cambridge, Mass.: J. Barlett.

Jarnagin, Bert, and Fred Eikel Jr. 1948. "North Texas Agricultural College Slang." *American Speech* 23:248–50.

Kuethe, J. Louis. 1932. "Johns Hopkins Jargon." *American Speech* 7:327–38.

Levine, Kenneth. 1995. "A Comparative Study of African American English and Gay Argot." Course paper, Special Studies 90, University of North Carolina at Chapel Hill.

Lighter, J. E. 1994. *Random House Historical Dictionary of American Slang*. Vol. 1, A–G. New York: Random House.

Mencken, H. L. 1963. *The American Language*. 4th ed., rev. Raven I. McDavid and David Maurer. New York: Knopf.

Moffatt, Michael. 1989. *Coming of Age in New Jersey: College and American Culture*. New Brunswick, N.J.: Rutgers University Press.

Pingry, Carl, and Vance Randolph. 1928. "Kansas University Slang." *American Speech* 3:218–21.

Rait, Robert S. 1912. *Life in the Medieval University*. Cambridge: Cambridge University Press.

Ross, Thomas J. 1984. "Taboo Words in the Fifteenth Century." In *Fifteenth Century Studies: Recent Essays*, ed. Robert F. Yeager, 137–60. Hamden, Conn.: Archon Books.

Student Life at Harvard. 1876. Boston: Lockwood, Brooks, and Co.

Underwood, Gary N. 1975. "Razorback Slang." *American Speech* 50:50–69.

White, William. 1955. "Wayne University Slang." *American Speech* 30:301–5.

Understanding the Text

1. What topics does Eble argue are most common in college student slang? Why are they so common?

2. How have changes in higher education, such as who attends college and how much of a "parental" role college administrators play, been reflected in the slang of students?

3. Eble notes that far fewer slang words for "vulgar" or "taboo" topics, like drinking or sex, were recorded in the time period between 1850 and 1900 than have been recorded in more recent decades. According to her analysis, what are some possible reasons for this?

Reflection and Response

4. According to Eble, what are some of the reasons that college slang is important to students, and what functions does it serve in their lives? How does her analysis compare with your own sense of what slang does for you and your peers?

5. Eble lists nineteen of the most common "meaning categories" for student slang from the early 1970s to the early 1990s, such as "excellent," "attractive person," and "worst situation," as identified by her undergraduate student Elisa Fiorenza (par. 23). Consider this list in reference to college slang today. Would you say these are still the most common concepts that college students use slang to discuss? What current slang words show the continued importance of these concepts in college students' lives? Do any current slang words show new priorities?

6. From your reading of Eble, how much of what she says about slang is particular to college students, and how much is applicable to young adults in general? What might you add or change in Eble's analysis if you were going to make similar claims about slang among young adults who don't attend college?

Making Connections

7. In the "Language and Age" segment of "Social Variables" (p. 43), Susan Tamasi and Lamont Antieau note that we can think about "social age" in terms of "milestones" that a person reaches throughout life. Based on what you've read from Eble, in what ways would you say that slang frames the start of college as a social milestone?

8. Eble notes that African American groups have been an especially strong influence on recent popular culture and therefore on college student slang. H. Samy Alim (p. 74) notes that Hip Hop Nation Language is rooted in African American Language, so it seems plausible that at least part of the influence Eble is talking about comes from hip hop music. Based on what Alim and Eble say about the values and priorities of hip hop and college language, what are some factors that might make the language of hip hop appealing to college students?

Hip Hop Nation Language

H. Samy Alim

H. Samy Alim is professor of education, anthropology and linguistics at Stanford University, where he serves as the faculty director for the Institute for Diversity in the Arts. He is the author of *Roc the Mic Right: The Language of Hip Hop Culture* (Routledge, 2006) and coeditor (with John Baugh) of *Talkin Black Talk: Language, Education, and Social Change* (Teachers College, 2007). Alim is interested in hip hop culture, particularly in how hip hop influences the identities and languages of youth. In this piece, excerpted from his chapter in the textbook *Language in the USA: Themes for the Twenty-First Century* (2004), Alim discusses the linguistic features of Hip Hop Nation Language (HHNL) such as its lexical features (vocabulary) and syntax (grammar). He also examines the values and attitudes that connect HHNL to its "sociopolitical matrix" — that is, what life is like, socially and politically, in urban areas, particularly for African Americans. As Alim shows us, HHNL has progressed from its roots in African American language traditions to become a distinctive form of language that carries its own regional variations.

Hip Hop Nation Language [HHNL]

My own research on Hip Hop Nation Language and hip hop culture in general has led to the streets, homes, cars, jeeps, clubs, stadiums, backstage, performances, hotels, religious centers, conferences and ciphers (highly competitive lyrical circles of rhymers) where hip hop lives—up inside the "actual lived experiences in the corrugated spaces that one finds reflected in the lyrical content of rap songs" (Spady, Dupres, and Lee 1995). The centrality of language to the HHN is evident in such song and album titles as the "New Rap Language" (Treacherous Three 1980), "Wordplay" (Bahamadia 1996), "Gangsta Vocabulary" (DJ Pooh 1997), "Project Talk" (Bobby Digital 1998), "Slang Editorial" (Cappadonna 1998), *Real Talk 2000* (Three-X-Krazy 2000), "Ebonics" (Big L 2000), *Country Grammar* (Nelly 2000), and *Project English* (Juvenile 2001). In numerous ethnographic interviews, I have found that language is a favorite topic of discussion in the HHN, and its members are willing to discuss it with great fervor—and to defend its use.

What do we mean by "Nation Language"? In exploring the development of nation language in Anglophone Caribbean poetry, Caribbean historian, poet, and literary and music critic Kamau Brathwaite (1984: 13) writes: "Nation language is the language which is influenced very strongly by the African model, the African aspect of our New World/Caribbean heritage. English it may be in terms of some of its lexical features. But in its contours, its rhythm and timbre, its sound explosions, it is not English."

Concerned with the literature of the Caribbean and the sociopolitical matrix within which it is created, Brathwaite used the term *nation language* in contrast to *dialect*. Familiar with the pejorative meanings of the term *dialect* in the folk linguistics of the people, he writes that while nation language can be considered both English and African at the same time, it is an English which is like a "howl, or a shout, or a machine-gun or the wind or a wave." Then he likened it to the blues. Surely, nation language is like hip hop (as rapper Raekwon spits his "machine-gun-rap" (1999)). HHNL is, like Brathwaite's description, new in one sense and ancient in another. It comprises elements of orality, total expression, and conversational modes (Brathwaite 1984).

Rapper Mystikal, known for having a unique, highly energetic rhyming style highlighted with lyrical sound explosions, provides a perfect example of Nation Language when he raps: "You know what time it is, nigga, and you know who the fuck this is/DAANNN-JAH!!! [Danger] DAANNN-JAH!!! [Danger]/Get on the FLO' [floor]!/The nigga right, yeaaahhHHH!"[1] (2000). Mystikal starts out speaking to his listener in a low, threatening growl, asserting his individuality ("you know who the fuck this is"), and then explodes as if sounding an alarm, letting everyone know that they have entered a dangerous verbal zone! "Get on the FLO'!" has a dual function—simultaneously warning listeners to lie down before the upcoming lyrical "DAANNN-JAH!" and directing them to get on the dance floor. When rapper Ludacris (2001) commands his listeners to "ROOOLLLL OUT!" and raps: "Oink, Oink, PIG! PIG! Do away with the POORRK-uh/Only silverwuurrr [silverware] I need's a steak knife and FOORRK-uh!" he stresses his words emphatically, compelling one to do as he says. In that brief example, he is in conversation with African American Muslim and Christian communities currently dialoguing about the eating of swine flesh (which Muslims consider unholy).

When we speak of *language*, we are defining the term in a sense that 5 is congruent with the HHN's "linguistic culture" (Schiffman 1996), and HHNL can be situated in the broader context of African American speech:

There is no single register of African American speech. And it's not words and intonations, it's a whole attitude about speech that has historical rooting. It's

---

[1] The transcription of HHNL into print often leaves a lot to be desired. I have attempted to reconstruct the verbal agility of these hip hop artists on the printed page, but, as Brathwaite (1984) admits, it is best for the reader to listen along to the music whenever possible (see discography).

not a phenomenon that you can isolate and reduce to linguistic characteristics. It has to do with the way a culture conceives of the people inside of that culture. It has to do with a whole complicated protocol of silences and speech, and how you use speech in ways other than directly to communicate information. And it has to do with, certainly, the experiences that the people in the speech situation bring into the encounter. What's fascinating to me about African American speech is its spontaneity, the requirement that you not only have a repertoire of vocabulary or syntactical devices/constructions, but you come prepared to do something in an attempt to meet the person on a level that both uses the language, mocks the language, and recreates the language. (Wideman 1976: 34)

On her single recording "Spontaneity" (1996), Philadelphia rapper Bahamadia validates Wideman's assertion. She raps about her "verbal expansion" in a stream of consciousness style: "Rip here be dizz like everybody's on it cause eternal verbal expansion keeps enhancin brain child's ability to like surpass a swarm of booty-ass-no-grass-roots-havin-ass MC's." The verbal architect constructs her rhymes by consciously stretching the limitations of the "standard" language. In describing her lyrical influences, she cites rappers Kool Keith of the Ultramagnetic MCs, De La Soul, and Organized Konfusion as "masters at what they do in that they explore the English language and they try to push the boundaries and go against the grains of it, you know what I mean?" (Spady and Alim 1999: xviii).

"It's a very active exchange," says Wideman (1976: 34). "But at the same time as I say that, the silences and the refusal to speak is just as much a part, in another way, of African American speech." Rapper Fearless of the group Nemesis exemplifies the point: envisioning rappers, including himself, among the great orators and leaders in the Black community, he says:

I always looked up to great orators like Martin Luther King, Malcolm X. Anybody who could ever stand up and persuade a group of young men or a nation . . . Just the way they were able to articulate. The way they emphasized their words. And the way they would use pauses. They would actually use silence powerfully . . . Just the way they made words cause feelings in you, you know what I'm saying? Just perpetuate thought within people, you know. (Spady and Alim 1999: xviii)

So *language* in HHNL obviously refers not only to the syntactic° constructions of the language but also to the many discursive° and communicative practices, the attitudes toward language, understanding the role of language in both binding/bonding community and seizing/smothering linguistic opponents, and language as concept (meaning clothes, facial expressions, body movements, and overall communication).

In addition to the above, HHNL can be characterized by ten tenets.

(1) HHNL is rooted in African American Language (AAL) and communicative practices (Spady 1991, Smitherman 1997, Yasin 1999). Linguistically, it is "the newest chapter in the African American book of folklore" (Rickford and Rickford 2000). It is a vehicle driven by the culture creators of hip hop, themselves organic members of the broader African American community. Thus HHNL both reflects and expands the African American Oral Tradition.

(2) HHNL is just one of the many language varieties used by African Americans.

(3) HHNL is widely spoken across the country, and used/borrowed and adapted/transformed by various ethnic groups inside and outside of the United States.

(4) HHNL is a language with its own grammar, lexicon, and phonology as well as unique communicative style and discursive modes. When an early hip hop group, The Treacherous Three, rhymed about a "New Rap Language" in 1980, they were well aware of the uniqueness of the language they were rappin in.

(5) HHNL is best viewed as the synergistic combination of speech, music, and literature. Yancy (1991) speaks of rap as "*musical literature* (or rhythmic-praxis discourse)." Henderson (1973) asserts that the Black poetry of the 1960s and 1970s is most distinctly Black when it derives its form from Black speech and Black music. HHNL is simultaneously the spoken, poetic, lyrical, and musical expression of the HHN.

(6) HHNL includes attitudes about language and language use (see Pharcyde dialogue below).

(7) HHNL is central to the identity and the act of envisioning an entity known as the HHN.

(8) HHNL exhibits regional variation (Morgan 2001a). For example, most members of the HHN recognize Master P's signature phrase, *Ya heeeaaard may?* ("You heard me?") as characteristic of a southern variety of HHNL. Even within regions, HHNL exhibits

---

syntactic: related to the structure of sentences.
discursive: related to language's function in its social contexts.

individual variation based on life experiences. For example, because California rapper Xzibit grew up in the hip hop saturated streets of Detroit, New Mexico and California, his HHNL is a syncretization of all these Hip Hop Nation Language varieties.

(9) The fundamental aspect of HHNL—and, to some, perhaps the most astonishing aspect—is that it is central to the lifeworlds of the members of the HHN and suitable and functional for all of their communicative needs.

(10) HHNL is inextricably linked with the sociopolitical circumstances that engulf the HHN. How does excessive police presence and brutality shift the discourse of the HHN? How do disproportionate incarceration rates and urban gentrification impact this community's language? As Spady (1993) writes: "Hip Hop culture [and language] mediates the corrosive discourse of the dominating society while at the same time it functions as a subterranean subversion . . . Volume is turned up to tune out the decadence of the dominant culture."

Rappers are insightful examiners of the sociopolitical matrix within which HHNL operates. Discussing the role of HHNL in hip hop lyrics, Houston's Scarface concludes that HHNL functions as a communal "code of communication" for the HHN:

It's a code of communication, too . . . Because we can understand each other when we're rapping. You know, if I'm saying, [in a nasal, mocking voice] "Well, my friend, I saw this guy who shot this other guy and . . ." I break that shit down for you and you say, "Goddamn, man! Them muthafuckas is going crazy out where this dude's from." You know what I'm saying? It's just totally different. It's just a code of communication to me. I'm letting my partner know what's going on. And anything White America can't control they call "gangsters." Shit! I get real. Politicians is gangsters, goddamn. The presidents is the gangsters because they have the power to change everything. That's a gangster to me. That's my definition of gangster. (Spady, Lee, and Alim 1999: 301)

Members of Tha Pharcyde actively debated the concept of HHNL:

BOOTY BROWN: There's more than just one definition for words! We talk in slang. We always talk basically in slang. We don't use the English dictionary for every sentence and every phrase that we talk!

PHARCYDE: No, there's a lot of words out of the words that you just said which all . . .

BOOTY BROWN: Yeah, but the way I'm talking is not the English language . . . We're not using that definition . . .

> We're making our own . . . Just like they use any other
> word as a slang, *my brotha!* Anything. I'm not really
> your brother. Me and your blood aren't the same, but
> I'm your brother because we're brothas. That's slang . . .
> We make up our *own* words. I mean, it depends whose
> definition you glorify, okay? That's what I'm saying.
> Whose definition are you glorifying? Because if you go
> by my definition of "Black," then I can say "a Black
> person." But if you go by the *Webster Dictionary's* . . .
> You have your own definition. It's your definition.
> (Spady, Lee, and Alim 1999: xix)

Sociolinguistically, so much is happening in the first exchange above.
The HHN continues to "flip the script" (reverse the power of the dominant culture). Scarface is reacting to the media's labeling of reality-based
rap lyrics as "gangster." By redefining gangster, he effectively turns the
tables on what he believes is an oppressive state. If the presidents have
the power to change everything, why ain't a damn thing changed?

In Tha Pharcyde conversation, when the *brotha* says the way he is talking
is not the English language, he is talking about much more than slang. He
asks pointedly, "Whose definition are you glorifying?" By making up your
own words, he attests, you are freeing yourself from linguistic colonization (Wa Thiongo 1992). In an effort to combat the capitalistic comodifica-
tion of hip hop culture, and to "unite and establish the common identity
of the HHN," KRS-One refined the definition of hip hop terms and produced a document known as "The Refinitions" (2000)—putting the power
of redefinition to action. KRS defines the language of hip hop culture as
"street language" and proposes that "Hiphoppas" speak an Advanced Street
Language, which includes "the correct pronunciation of one's native and
national language as it pertains to life in the inner-city." KRS is reversing
"standard" notions of correctness and appropriateness, realizing that the
HHN has distinct values and aesthetics that differ from the majority culture. Clearly, members of the HHN would agree that the use of AAL stems
"from a somewhat disseminated rejection of the life-styles, social patterns,
and thinking in general of the Euro-American sensibility," as the writer of
the first AAL dictionary outside of the Gullah area put it (Major 1970: 10).

The Relationship between HHNL and AAL: Lexicon, Syntax, and Phonology

*"Dangerous dialect/Dangerous dialect/I elect . . . to impress America." That's it,
that's what it was about . . . Dangerous dialect, dangerous wording, you know*

what I mean? "I elect," that I pick, you know. "To impress America." That's what I pick to impress America, that dangerous dialect, you know. (San Quinn, 2000, Alim and Spady, unpublished interview)

The relationship between HHNL and AAL is a familial one. Since hip 10 hop's culture creators are members of the broader African American community, the language that they use most often when communicating with each other is AAL. HHNL can be seen as the *submerged area* (Brathwaite 1984: 13) of AAL that is used within the HHN, particularly during hip hop centered cultural activities, but also during other playful, creative, artistic, and intimate settings. This conception of HHNL is broad enough to include the language of rap lyrics, album interludes, hip hop stage performances, and hip hop conversational discourse. African Americans are on the cutting edge of the sociolinguistic situation in the USA (as evidenced by abundant recent sociolinguistic research on the topic). HHNL, thus, is the cutting edge of the cutting edge.

A revised edition of the lexicon of "Black Talk" (Smitherman 1994, 2000) begins with a chapter entitled, "From Dead Presidents to the Benjamins." The term *dead presidents* (meaning "money" and referring to American notes with images of dead presidents) has been in use in the African American community since the 1930s. In the late 1990s, hip hop group dead prez both shortened the term and made explicit its multivariate meanings (within the revolutionary context of their rhymes and philosophy, they are surely hinting at assassination—a form of verbal subversion). The *benjamins* is a term from the late 1990s popularized by rapper Sean "Puffy" Combs (P. Diddy).

While several scholars and writers have produced work on the lexicon of AAL (Turner 1949, Major 1970, 1994, Anderson 1994, Smitherman 1994, 2000, Stavsky, Mozeson and Mozeson 1995, Dillard 1977, Holloway and Vass 1997), it is important to note that hip hop artists, as street linguists and lexicographers, have published several dictionaries of their own. Old school legend Fab Five Freddy (Braithwaite 1992, 1995) documented the "fresh fly flavor" of the words and phrases of the hip hop generation (in English and German). Atlanta's Goodie Mob and several other artists have published glossaries on the inside flaps of their album covers. Of course, as lexicographers hip hop artists are only continuing the tradition of Black musicians, for many jazz and bebop artists compiled their own glossaries, most notable among them Cab Calloway (1944), Babs Gonzales, and Dan Burley.

Vallejo rapper E-40 discusses the genesis of *E-40's Dictionary Book of Slang, vol. 1* (2003):

I feel that I am the ghetto. The majority of street slang . . . "It's all good." "Feel me." "Fo' shiiiiiziiie," all that shit come from 40. "What's up, folks?" As a matter of fact, I'm writing my own dictionary book of slang right now . . . It's a street demand [for it]. Everywhere I go people be like, "Dude, you need to put out a dictionary. Let them know where all that shit come from," you know what I mean? (Spady, Lee, and Alim 1999: 290)

E-40 is credited with developing a highly individualized repertoire of slang words and phrases. If he were to say something like, "What's crackulatin, pimpin? I was choppin it up wit my playa-potna last night on my communicator—then we got to marinatin, you underdig—and I come to find out that the homie had so much fedi that he was tycoonin, I mean, pimpin on some real boss-status, you smell me?" not very many people would understand him. (*crackulating* = "happening," an extended form of *crackin*; *pimpin* is sometimes used as a noun to refer to a person, like "homie"; *choppin it up* = "making conversation"; *playa-potna* = "partner," "friend"; *communicator* = "cell phone"; *marinatin* = "a conversation where participants are reasoning on a subject"; *underdig* = "understand"; *fedi* = "money"; *tycoonin* = "being a successful entrepreneur"; *pimpin* = "being financially wealthy"; *boss-status* = "managing things like a CEO"; *you smell me?* = "you feel me?" or, "you understand me?")

In HHNL, *pimp* refers not only to someone who solicits clients for a prostitute; it has several other meanings. One could be *pimpin a Lex* ("driving a Lexus while looking flashy"), suffering from *record company pimpin* ("the means by which record companies take advantage of young Black artists lacking knowledge of the music industry") or engaging in *parking lot pimpin* ("hanging around the parking lot after large gatherings"). As we also saw above, *pimpin* can also refer generally to an individual, or specifically to one who sports a flashy lifestyle. The word *politickin* can refer to the act of speaking about political subjects relevant to the Black community, simply holding a conversation, or trying to develop a relationship with a female. One might catch *frostbite* or get *goosebumps* from all of the *ice* they got on (*ice* = "diamonds"). In the HHN, *rocks* can be a girl's best friend ("diamonds") or a community's silent killer ("crack cocaine"), while *to rock* can mean "to liven up a party," "to wear a fashionable article of clothing," or "to have sexual intercourse."

> "Given the fluidity of HHNL, speakers take a lot of pride in being the originators and innovators of terms that are consumed by large numbers of speakers."

Given the fluidity of HHNL, speakers take a lot of pride in being 15 the originators and innovators of terms that are consumed by large numbers of speakers. Rappers, as members of distinct communities, also take pride in regional lexicon. For instance, the term *jawn* emerged in the Philadelphia hip hop community. *Jawn* is what can be called a context-dependent substitute noun—a noun that substitutes for any other noun, with its definition so fluid that its meaning depends entirely upon context. For instance, you can say, *Oh, that's da jawn!* for *da bomb!* if you think something is superb; "Did you see that *jawn?*" for "female" when an attractive female walks by; "I like that new Beanie *jawn*" for "song," when the song is played on the radio, and so on. Recently, Philadelphia's Roots have handed out T-shirts with "JAWN" written on the front, advocating the use of the distinctive Philly hip hop term. Placed in a broader context, the meaning of the distinct lexicon of HHNL can be nicely summed up: "Slick lexicon is hip-hop's Magna Carta, establishing the rights of its disciples to speak loudly but privately, to tell America about herself in a language that leaves her puzzled" (Rickford and Rickford 2000: 86).

Several scholars have written that the syntax of HHNL is essentially the same as that of AAL (Remes 1991, Smitherman 1997, 2000, Morgan 1999, Spady and Alim 1999, Yasin 1999, Rickford and Rickford 2000, Morgan 2001b). This is true. We must also examine the syntax of HHNL closely enough to elucidate how the language users are behaving both within and beyond the boundaries of AAL syntax. What is happening syntactically when Method Man gets on the air and proclaims, "Broadcasting live from the Apocalypse, it be I, John Blazzzazzziiinnnyyyyy!" What is happening when Jubwa of Soul Plantation writes in his autobiography: "Jubwa be the dope me, freestylin' to the beat deep cover" (cited in Alim 2001a). An important question is, How does HHNL confirm our knowledge of AAL syntax—and how does it challenge that knowledge?

Probably the most oft-studied feature of AAL is *habitual* or *invariant be.*° Early studies of AAL syntax (Labov et al. 1968, Wolfram 1969, Fasold 1972) noted the uniqueness of this feature and were in agreement that it was used for recurring actions (*We be clubbin on Saturdays*) and could not be used in finite contexts (*She be the teacher*). Building upon this research, we see that HHNL provides numerous examples of what I call *be3* or the "equative copula"° in AAL (Alim 2001b). Some examples of this construction (Noun Phrase *be* Noun Phrase) follow:

I be the truth.—Philadelphia's Beanie Sigel

Dr. Dre be the name.—Compton's Dr. Dre

---

habitual or **invariant be**: the use of *be* to indicate an action that is habitual or recurring. Alim's example, "We be clubbin on Saturdays," then, implies that the same activity occurs every Saturday.

equative copula: similar to *habitual be,* but *be* indicates a constant state of being rather than a habitual action. (*Copula* is a linguistic term for the English verb *to be.*)

This beat be the beat for the street. — New York's Busta Rhymes

Brooklyn be the place where I served them thangs. — New York's Jay-Z

I be that insane nigga from the psycho ward. — Staten Island's Method Man

These are but a few of countless examples in the corpus of hip hop lyrics, but this equative copula construction can also be found in everyday conversation, as in these examples:

We be them Bay boys. — Bay Area's Mac Mall in a conversation with James G. Spady

It [marijuana] be that good stuff. — Caller on the local Bay Area radio station

You know we be some baaad brothas. — Philadelphia speaker in conversation

It is possible that speakers of AAL have begun using this form only recently and that AAL has thus changed. Alternatively, the form may always have been present in the language but escaped the notice of investigators. Certainly it is present in the writings of Black Arts Movement poets of the 1960s and 1970s, most notably in Sonia Sanchez's *We Be Word Sorcerers.* We also find the form being cited in one linguistic study of Black street speech (*They be the real troublemakers; Leo be the one to tell it like it is*) (Baugh 1983). It is possible that members of the HHN, with their extraordinary linguistic consciousness and their emphasis on stretching the limits of language, have made this form much more acceptable by using it frequently (Alim 2004).

The HHN's linguistic consciousness refers to HHNL speakers' conscious [20] use of language to construct identity. Addressing the divergence of AAL from standard English, Smitherman and Baugh (2002: 20) write:

Graffiti writers of Hip Hop Culture were probably the coiners of the term "phat" (meaning excellent, great, superb) . . . although "phat" is spelled in obvious contrast to "fat," the former confirms that those who use it know that "ph" is pronounced like "f." In other words, those who first wrote "phat" diverged from standard English as a direct result of their awareness of standard English: the divergence was not by chance linguistic error. There is no singular explanation to account for linguistic divergence, but Hip Hop Culture suggests that matters of personal identity play a significant role.

This conscious linguistic behavior deals with matters of spelling and phonemic° awareness. (See Morgan 2001a and Olivo 2001 on "spelling ideology.") One case — one of the more controversial uses of language in

---

phonemic: related to *phonemes*, the basic units of sound in a language. "Spelling and phonemic awareness" is an awareness of how changing one letter or sound within a word changes its meaning, as in the case of *cat* and *bat*.

hip hop culture—is the term *nigga*. The HHN realized that this word had various positive in-group meanings and pejorative out-group meanings, and thus felt the need to reflect the culturally specific meanings with a new spelling (*nigger* becomes "nigga"). A *nigga* is your "main man," or "one of your close companions," your "homie." Recently the term has been generalized to refer to any male (one may even hear something like, "No, I was talkin about Johnny, you know, the white nigga with the hair") although it usually refers to a Black male. Demonstrating hip hop's affinity for acronyms, Tupac Shakur transformed the racial slur into the ultimate positive ideal for young Black males—Never Ignorant Getting Goals Accomplished.

As with the highlighting of regional vocabulary, HHNL speakers intentionally highlight regional differences in pronunciation by processes such as vowel lengthening and syllabic stress (Morgan 2001b). When Bay Area rappers JT the Bigga Figga and Mac Mall announced the resurgence of the Bay Area to the national hip hop scene with "Game Recognize Game" (1993), they did so using a distinctive feature of Bay Area pronunciation. The Bay Area anthem's chorus repeated this line three times: "Game recognize game in the Bay, man (mane)." *Man* was pronounced "mane" to accentuate this Bay Area pronunciation feature. Also, as fellow Bay Area rapper B-Legit rhymes about slang, he does so using the same feature to stress his Bay Area linguistic origins: "You can tell from my slang I'm from the Bay, mane" (2000).

When Nelly and the St. Lunatics "busted" onto the hip hop scene, they were among the first rappers to represent St. Louis, Missouri on a national scale. Language was an essential part of establishing their identity in a fiercely competitive world of hip hop culture. For example, in a single by the St. Lunatics featuring Nelly they emphasize every word that rhymes with "urrrr" to highlight a well-known (and sometimes stigmatized) aspect of southern/midwest pronunciation (here → *hurrrr*; care → *currrr*; there → *thurrrr*; air → *urrr* and so on). By intentionally highlighting linguistic features associated with their city (and other southern cities), they established their tenacity through language as if to say, "We have arrived."

Nelly and the St. Lunatics are conscious not only of their pronunciation, but also of their syntax. On his platinum single "Country Grammar" (2000), Nelly proclaims, "My gramma bees Ebonics." Clearly, HHNL speakers vary their grammar consciously. An analysis of copula variation in the speech and the lyrics of hip hop artists concluded that higher levels of copula absence in the artists' lyrics represented the construction of a street conscious identity—where the speaker makes a linguistic-cultural connection to the streets, the locus of the hip hop world (Alim 2002). John Rickford has suggested (in a conference comment made in 2001) that the use of creole syntactic and phonological° features by many rappers supports the ability of HHNL speakers to manipulate their grammar consciously. Like San Quinn (see opening quote in this section) HHNL speakers elect dialects to demonstrate their high degree of linguistic consciousness and in order to construct a street-conscious identity.

References

Alim, H. Samy, ed. 2001a. *Hip Hop Culture: Language, Literature, Literacy and the Lives of Black Youth*. Special issue of *The Black Arts Quarterly*. Committee on Black Performing Arts: Stanford University.

2001b. "I Be the Truth: Divergence, Recreolization, and the 'New' Equative Copula in African American Language." Paper presented at NWAV 30, Raleigh, North Carolina, October.

2002. "Street Conscious Copula Variation in the Hip Hop Nation," *American Speech* 77: 288–304.

2004. *You Know My Steez: An Ethnographic and Sociolinguistic Study of Styleshifting in a Black American Speech Community*. Durham, NC: Duke University Press.

Anderson, Monica. 1994. *Black English Vernacular (From "Ain't" to "Yo Mama": the Words Politically Correct Americans Should Know)*. Highland City, FL: Rainbow Books.

Baugh, John. 1983. *Black Street Speech: Its History, Structure, and Survival*. Austin, TX: University of Texas Press.

Braithwaite, Fred. (Fab Five Freddy). 1992. *Fresh Fly Flavor: Words and Phrases of the Hip-Hop Generation*. Stamford, CT: Longmeadow Press.

Braithwaite, Fred. 1995. *Hip Hop Slang: English-Deutsch*. Frankfurt am Main, Eichborn.

Brathwaite, Kamau. 1984. *History of the Voice: The Development of Nation Language in Anglophone Caribbean Poetry*. London: New Beacon Books.

Calloway, Cab. 1944. *Hepster's Dictionary: Language of Jive*. Republished as an appendix to Calloway's autobiography, *Of Minnie the Moocher and Me*. 1976. New York: Thomas Y. Crowell.

Dillard, J. L. 1977. *Lexicon of Black English*. New York: Seabury.

Fasold, Ralph. 1972. *Tense Marking in Black English: A Linguistic and Social Analysis*. Washington, DC: Center for Applied Linguistics.

Henderson, Stephen. 1973. *Understanding the New Black Poetry: Black Speech and Black Music as Poetic References*. New York: William Morrow.

Holloway, Joseph E. and Winifred K. Vass. 1997. *The African Heritage of American English*. Bloomington: University of Indiana Press.

phonological: related to speech sounds (an adjective form of phonology, the study of speech sounds).

KRS-One. 2000. "The First Overstanding: Refinitions." The Temple of Hip Hop Kulture.

Labov, William, Paul Cohen, Clarence Robins, and John Lewis. 1968. *A Study of the Nonstandard English of Negro and Puerto Rican Speakers in New York City.* Report on Co-operative Research Project 3288. New York: Columbia University.

Major, Clarence. 1970 [1994]. *Juba to Jive: A Dictionary of African American Slang.* New York and London: Penguin.

Morgan, Aswan. 1999. 'Why They Say What Dey Be Sayin': An Examination of Hip-Hop Content and Language.' Paper submitted for LING 073, *Introduction to African American Vernacular English.* Stanford University.

Morgan, Marcyliena. 2001a. "Reading Dialect and Grammatical Shout-Outs in Hip Hop." Paper presented at the Linguistic Society of America Convention. Washington, DC, January.

2001b. " 'Nuthin' But a G Thang': Grammar and Language Ideology in Hip Hop Identity." In *Sociocultural and Historical Contexts of African American Vernacular English,* ed. Sonja L. Lanehard. Amsterdam: John Benjamins. Pp. 187–210.

Olivo, Warren. 2001. "Phat Lines: Spelling Conventions in Rap Music," *Written Language and Literacy* 4(1): 67–85.

Rickford, John and Russell Rickford. 2000. *Spoken Soul: The Story of Black English.* New York: John Wiley.

San Quinn. Personal interview with H. Samy Alim and James G. Spady, November 2000.

Schiffman, Harold. 1996. *Linguistic Culture and Language Policy.* London and New York: Routledge.

Smitherman, Geneva. 1994 [2000]. *Black Talk: Words and Phrases from the Hood to the Amen Corner.* Boston and New York: Houghton Mifflin.

1997. " 'The Chain Remain the Same': Communicative Practices in the Hip-Hop Nation," *Journal of Black Studies,* September.

2000. *Talkin That Talk: Language, Culture and Education in African America.* London and New York: Routledge.

Smitherman, Geneva and John Baugh. 2002. "The Shot Heard from Ann Arbor: Language Research and Public Policy in African America." *Howard Journal of Communication* 13: 5–24.

Spady, James G. 1993. " 'IMA PUT MY THING DOWN': Afro-American Expressive Culture and the Hip Hop Community," *TYANABA: Revue de la Société d'Anthropologie,* December.

Spady, James G., and H. Samy Alim. 1999. "Street Conscious Rap: Modes of Being." In *Street Conscious Rap.* Philadelphia: Black History Museum/Umum Loh Publishers.

Spady, James G., and Joseph D. Eure, eds. 1991. *Nation Conscious Rap: the Hip Hop Vision.* New York/Philadelphia: PC International Press/Black History Museum.

Spady, James G., Stefan Dupres, and Charles G. Lee. 1995. *Twisted Tales in the Hip Hop Streets of Philly.* Philadelphia: Black History Museum/Umum Loh Publishers.

Spady, James G., Charles G. Lee, and H. Samy Alim. 1999. *Street Conscious Rap.* Philadelphia: Black History Museum/Umum Loh Publishers.

Stavsky, Lois, Isaac Mozeson, and Dani Reyes Mozeson. 1995. *A 2 Z: the Book of Rap and Hip-Hop Slang.* New York: Boulevard Books.

Turner, Lorenzo. 1949. *Africanisms in the Gullah Dialect.* Chicago: University of Chicago Press.

Wa Thiongo, Ngugi. 1992. *Moving the Center: the Struggle for Cultural Freedom.* London: Heinemann.

Wideman, John. 1976. "Frame and Dialect: the Evolution of the Black Voice in American Literature," *American Poetry Review* 5(5): 34–37.

Wolfram, Walter. 1969. *A Sociolinguistic Description of Detroit Negro Speech.* Washington, DC: Center for Applied Linguistics.

Yancy, George. 1991. "Rapese." Cited in Spady and Eure, eds.

Yasin, Jon. 1999. "Rap in the African-American Music Tradition: Cultural Assertion and Continuity." In *Race and Ideology: Language, Symbolism, and Popular Culture,* ed. Arthur Spears. Detroit: Wayne State University Press.

Discography

Bahamadia. 1996. *Kollage.* EMI Records.

Big L. 2000. *The Big Picture.* Priority Records.

DJ Pooh. 1997. *Bad Newz Travels Fast.* Da Bomb/Big Beat/Atlantic Records.

JT the Bigga Figga. 1993. *Playaz N the Game.* Get Low Recordz.

Juvenile. 2001. *Project English.* Universal Records.

Nelly. 2000. *Country Grammar.* Universal Records.

Three X Krazy. 2000. *Real Talk 2000.* DU BA Records.

Treacherous Three (Kool Moe Dee, LA Sunshine, Special K and DJ Easy Lee). 1980. *New Rap Language.* Enjoy Records.

Understanding the Text

1. Summarize the fundamental linguistic features of Hip Hop Nation Language: What is unique about its grammar, vocabulary, and pronunciation?
2. What are some of the "attitudes toward language" found in the Hip Hop Nation?
3. How are HHNL and African American Language related?

Reflection and Response

4. Consider Alim's points in connection to the theme of language and identity. How does HHNL help to solidify and reflect an identity for its speakers?

5. Alim writes most of this piece in what could be called a formal academic English, but there are moments where he uses HHNL, such as his spelling in the phrase "the uniqueness of the language they were rappin in" (par. 8) or his grammar in the question "If the presidents have the power to change everything, why ain't a damn thing changed?" (par. 8). Why do you think he does this? How does it support the points he is making about HHNL?

Making Connections

6. Locate the lyrics to a hip hop song of your choice and use Alim's article to analyze them. Where do you see the grammar, vocabulary, pronunciation, or spelling of HHNL at work? How about the attitudes and sociopolitical contexts that Alim describes?

7. Consider Alim's discussion of the word *nigga* in relation to Susan Tamasi and Lamont Antieau's discussion, in "Social Variables" (p. 43), of reclaimed epithets. In what ways does Alim's description of HHNL speakers' use of the term exemplify what Tamasi and Antieau say about reclaimed epithets being "expressions of pride" (Box 1.3)? If you like, supplement your discussion by considering examples of the word's use in other hip hop songs.

2 How Does Language Affect How Others Perceive Us?

Writing and speech are meant to provoke reactions. When we have something to say, we want others to hear that message. Sometimes, though, people react not only to what someone is saying but also to how it is said. We notice when someone's language is different from ours, and many times we perceive that difference as indicating something about a person's identity, personality, or intelligence. We decide that someone "sounds," for example, unintelligent, professional, or rude. In this way, certain features of a person's language or dialect can lead others to pass judgment on them.

The selections in Chapter 1 illuminated the connections between language and identity. In this chapter, we explore the ways in which opinions of a language variety are influenced by preexisting assumptions about the sorts of people who tend to speak that variety. For example, as Marybeth Seitz-Brown explains, women, and particularly young women, are often viewed as less authoritative because of certain features of their speech. Given the prevalence of features like *uptalk* in the speech of people other than young women, though, Seitz-Brown contends that our assumptions about credibility and confidence have more to do with prejudice against young women than with anything about their speech itself.

Likewise, as Dennis Preston explains, people in the United States tend to harbor opinions of the country's regional dialects — those ways of speaking that are unique to a particular area of the country. People tend to have particularly negative opinions of Southern speech and New York speech; both Southerners and their speech are perceived as unintelligent, while both New Yorkers and their speech are perceived as rude. Building on the research of Preston and others, researchers Cheryl Boucher, Georgina Hammock, Selina McLaughlin, and Kelsey Henry confirm that even Southerners themselves find a speaker with a Southern accent less sophisticated and less professional.

In addition to regional dialects, dialects associated with particular racial and ethnic groups are a common target for judgment. Carmen Fought illuminates the complex perceptions of whiteness in language, showing that white speech is typically viewed positively, as intelligent and professional, but can also be perceived negatively in circumstances where being "too white" (or too formal) is inappropriate. Black speech, meanwhile, is more likely to face consistently negative perceptions. John McWhorter asserts that "Black English will always sound to most people like mistakes" (p. 126), a perception that persists despite the fact that, as Rusty Barrett illustrates, Black English has among the clearest rules and logic of any dialect of English.

There are also many interesting complexities in the judgments surrounding speech and sexuality. Kathryn Campbell-Kibler investigates which features of men's speech make listeners most likely to decide they "sound gay" (regardless of whether the men actually identify as gay). "Sounding gay" can affect how other aspects of one's speech are perceived, too. For instance, when a man is perceived to have a lisp, he will be perceived as less competent, unless other aspects of his speech make the listener hear him as gay, in which case he will fit the stereotype of the "smart, effeminate gay man" (p. 154).

As you read the articles in this chapter, keep in mind that everything here is about perception. There is nothing about any sound, word, or grammatical structure that makes it inherently better or more intelligent than another; judgments like these only become accepted because people have created and agreed to them. Have you made some of these assumptions without even realizing it?

Young Women Shouldn't Have to Talk Like Men to Be Taken Seriously

Marybeth Seitz-Brown

In December 2014, Marybeth Seitz-Brown, then the communications coordinator for Columbia University's Students Active for Ending Rape (SAFER) organization, gave an interview about survivors of sexual assault on the National Public Radio program *All Things Considered*. While much of the response she received praised her work, a notable minority of the feedback criticized her use of *uptalk*, claiming that it interfered with her authority and credibility. In this column from *Slate* (December 16, 2014), Seitz-Brown, who has a B.A. in linguistics from Columbia, uses her linguistic training to confront such criticisms of young women's speech.

If you're a young woman, you've probably been told there's something wrong with your voice.

It seems like there are always new features of women's speech that need to be corrected, be it uptalk,[1] vocal fry,[2] higher pitch,[3] swoopy[4] intonation (believe it or not, that's the technical linguistic term), using discourse markers like "like,"[5] or simply speaking too much.[6] One woman even made a movie[7] just to tell young women all the things they should change about their voices.

And I've been told the same thing. Last week, I gave an interview on NPR, and while most of the reactions were overwhelmingly positive, I also received several messages suggesting I change my voice so that people will take me seriously. Why? Well, I uptalk. But I'm not ashamed of it, and no one else should be either.

Uptalk, in case you've missed several years of media frenzy, is using a rising intonation at the end of a phrase or sentence. What's the matter with that? Well, that rising intonation is similar (although not identical) to how any English speaker sounds when asking a question, so to some people it sounds as if uptalkers are speaking only in questions, and are thus not very confident.

Or so they tell young women. But the funny thing is, uptalk isn't actually just used by the young and female. When you're on the lookout for it, you'll hear uptalk from people of many demographics. Yet I've never heard anyone condemn New Zealanders' speech for not being authoritative or confident enough, despite their rampant use of uptalk at all ages and genders.[8] I also hear many men, including former President George W. Bush,[9] using uptalk, and have yet to hear any of them be chastised for not sounding authoritative enough. In fact, there's no conclusive evidence[10] that women even use uptalk more than men.

But even if women *did* uptalk more than men, we've all heard enough uptalk to know that its rising intonation doesn't indicate a question. No one's actually confused. So why should anyone have a problem with it? The thing is, this pastime of critiquing women's speech is not limited to American English speakers. It's easy to find these attitudes in any culture that devalues femininity and women. In Belfast English,[11] stereotypical women's speech falls at the end of a sentence, while men's speech rises before it plateaus—basically, the men are uptalking. And yet Belfast women's speech is still perceived as more expressive or emotional, showing that it's not about their actual intonation at all: It's about whose mouth the speech is coming from. (In fact, vocal fry leads to a lower-pitched voice, essentially the opposite of uptalk, and yet somehow that's bad when young women do it too.[12])

> "It's not about their actual intonation at all: It's about whose mouth the speech is coming from."

And that's definitely not the only study, and it's not just gender. It's race,[13] it's class, it's sexuality,[14] it's geographic location,[15] it's many other factors.[16] But linguists have *never* been able to show anything intrinsically good or bad, authoritative or unconfident, desirable or grating about any kind of pitch, inflection, or vocal quality. Instead, we ascribe those qualities to speech based on who's articulating it. Think Black English sounds uneducated? That's probably because you have some racist notions about black people. Does a Southern accent sound unintelligent to you? Their vowels aren't to blame—it's our stereotypes about people from the South. Think that uptalk makes women sound less authoritative? Maybe that's because women are constantly robbed of agency and authority, and we view anything they do or say as less powerful.

The thing is, I actually believe that the people—mainly women, actually—who were messaging me about my uptalk sincerely wanted to help me reach a wider (read: male) audience. Some listeners said my rising intonation made me sound unsure of my information, others said my voice distracted listeners from my insights, still others said that I sounded too emotional and unconfident. I even had one older woman claiming to be an "English communication expert" offer to give me free vocal coaching.

And I get it. I owe a lot to these women who came before me, and I understand that they may not have had much choice in the matter when they were my age. After all, employers admit to actively punishing[17] workers who use uptalk, and many women, especially women of color, simply can't afford *not* to change their voice in order to gain respect. But just because sexism exists doesn't mean that the sexists are right about it: Women shouldn't have to wear pantsuits to be treated like human beings, and we shouldn't have to contort our voices to sound masculine (but not too masculine!) to make people hear us.

I really do appreciate these listeners' concerns, but the notion that my uptalk means I was unsure of what I said is not only wrong, it's misogynistic. It implies that if women just spoke like men, our ideas would be valuable. If women just spoke like men, sexist listeners would magically understand us, and we would be taken seriously. But the problem is not with feminized qualities, of speech or otherwise, the problem is that our culture pathologizes feminine traits as something to be ashamed of or apologize for.

I believe we can do better than that. We can evaluate the merits of an idea based on the soundness of its reasoning, not the pitch range in which it's articulated. We can reject the knee-jerk habit of dismissing people for the sound of their voices without actually hearing what they have to say. And—rather than telling women to talk like men or shut up—we can encourage each other to celebrate the different rises and falls, the creaks and quakes that make up our voices.

Notes

1. Green, Emma. "A Female Senator Explains Why Uptalk Is Part of Women's 'Nature.'" *The Atlantic,* 16 January 2014, www.theatlantic.com/politics/archive/2014/01/a-female-senator-explains-why-uptalk-is-part-of-womens-nature/283107/.

2. Khazan, Olga. "Vocal Fry May Hurt Women's Job Prospects." *The Atlantic,* 29 May 2014, www.theatlantic.com/business/archive/2014/05/employers-look-down-on-women-with-vocal-fry/371811/.

3. Simmons-Duffin, Selena. "VIDEO: Talking While Female." *NPR,* 24 October 2014, www.npr.org/sections/health-shots/2014/10/24/357584372/video-what-women-get-flak-for-when-they-talk.

4. Ryan, Erin Gloria. "Are Women's High-Pitched Ladyvoices Holding Them Back?" *Jezebel,* 16 November 2011, jezebel.com/5859882/are-womens-high-pitched-ladyvoices-holding-them-back/.

5. Jacobs, Ryan. "The Functions of 'Um,' 'Like,' 'You Know.'" *Pacific Standard,* 15 May 2014, psmag.com/the-functions-of-um-like-you-know-da2dc447953.

6. Marcotte, Amanda. "Women Don't Talk More Than Men, So Why Do People Believe That They Do?" *XX Factor,* Slate, 22 February 2013, www.slate.com/blogs/xx_factor/2013/02/22/do_women_talk_more_the_answer_is_no_but_the_belief_persists_despite_the.html.

7. Grose, Jessica. "Why Is Lake Bell Dissing Women's Voices?" *XX Factor,* Slate, 9 August 2013, www.slate.com/blogs/xx_factor/2013/08/09/lake_bell_s_in_a_world_is_a_movie_about_women_in_the_voiceover_ world_so.html.

8. "10 Theories on How Uptalk Originated." *BBC News Magazine,* 19 August 2014, www.bbc.com/news/magazine-28785865.

9. Liberman, Mark. "Uptalk Uptick?" *Language Log,* 15 December 2005, itre.cis.upenn.edu/~myl/languagelog/archives/002708.html.

10. Hoffman, Jan. "Overturning the Myth of Valley Girl Speak." *The New York Times,* 23 December 2013, nyti.ms/1cxCMEh.

11. Lowry, Orla. "Belfast Intonation and Speaker Gender." *Journal of English Linguistics,* vol. 39, no. 3, 2011, pp. 209–32. doi: 10.1177/0075424210380053.

12. Hess, Amanda. "Why Old Men Find Young Women's Voices So Annoying." *XX Factor,* Slate, 7 January 2013, www.slate.com/blogs/xx_factor/2013/01/07/vocal_fry_and_valley_girls_why_old_men_find_young_women_s_voices_so_annoying.html.

13. Hudley, Anne H. Charity. "Which Language You Speak Has Nothing to Do with How Smart You Are." *Lexicon Valley,* Slate, 14 October 2014, www.slate.com/blogs/lexicon_valley/2014/10/14/english_variation_not_related_to_intelligence_code_switching_and_other_ways.html.

14. Bigham, D. S. "Sounding Gay, Punk, or Jock: What Language Says about Your Social Group." *Lexicon Valley,* Slate, 24 November 2014, www.slate.com/blogs/lexicon_valley/2014/11/24/sounding_gay_punk_or_jock_what_your_language_says_about_your_social_identity.html.

15. McCulloch, Gretchen. "7 of the Best Dialect Quizzes." *Lexicon Valley,* Slate, 7 July 2014, www.slate.com/blogs/lexicon_valley/2014/07/07/_7_best_dialect_quizzes_is_your_accent_american_british_canadian_australian.html.

16. McCulloch, Gretchen. "Why Do You Think You're Right about Language? You're Not." *Lexicon Valley,* Slate, 30 May 2014, www.slate.com/blogs/lexicon_valley/2014/05/30/arguing_over_language_everyone_has_an_idiolect_standard_english_prescriptivism.html.

17. Dallett, Lydia. "This Communication Quirk Could Cost You a Promotion." *Business Insider,* 24 January 2014, www.businessinsider.com/how-uptalk-could-cost-you-a-promotion-2014-1.

Understanding the Text

1. What is *uptalk*, and why is it believed to make someone sound less credible or certain?

2. What proof does Seitz-Brown have that uptalk is not in itself feminine or unconfident?

Reflection and Response

3. Seitz-Brown gives a list of speech features for which women are criticized, including not just uptalk but also a higher pitch, talking "too much," and use of the word *like*. Just as she shows uptalk to be equally common in women and men, might some of these other features be just as common in men? What proof can you think of?

4. Consider the idea that women's speech is full of problems needing correction. What are some ways this idea spreads? Think of some examples of its reinforcement from broader cultural experience (media, education, etc.) and/or your individual experience.

Making Connections

5. Seitz-Brown argues that negative opinions of the speech of women, African Americans, and Southerners derive from negative opinions of those types of people (par. 7). Using one or more of the other readings in this chapter, provide support for her point.

6. In "They're, Like, Way Ahead of the Linguistic Currrrve," Douglas Quenqua quotes linguist Penny Eckert's statement that "A lot of these really flamboyant things you hear [in young women's language] are cute, and girls are supposed to be cute" (p. 178). Explain how you think Seitz-Brown would respond to this statement, using specific points from her article.

Some Plain Facts about Americans and Their Language

Dennis Preston

Dennis Preston is Regents Professor of English at Oklahoma State University. Having retired from Michigan State University in 2008, he now directs OSU's RODEO (Research on the Dialects of English in Oklahoma) program, which studies the many different dialects spoken in Oklahoma. Preston has spent decades studying the regional dialects of the United States and investigating everyday people's ideas and opinions about language. He provides a glimpse into these "linguistic folk beliefs" in the article below, originally published in the Winter 2000 issue of the journal *American Speech*.

The belief that some varieties of a language are not as good as others runs so deep that one might say it is the major preoccupation of Americans with their language. It is a belief nearly universally attached to minorities, rural people, and the less well-educated, and it extends even to well-educated speakers of some regional varieties. Evidence for this belief comes from what real people, not professional linguists, believe about language variety. Consider what one Michigan speaker has to say about the South:

[mimics Southern speech] As y'all know, I came up from Texas when I was about twenty-one. And I talked like this. Probably not so bad, but I talked like this; you know I said thiyus ['this'] and thayut ['that'] and all those things. And I had to learn reeeal [elongated vowel] fast how to talk like a Northerner. 'Cause if I talked like this people'd think I'm the dumbest shit around.

Next, consider New York City, which fares no better, even in self-evaluation, as shown in one example collected by William Labov in the mid-1960s:

Bill's college alumni group—we have a party once a month in Philadelphia. Well, now I know them about two years and every time we're there—at a wedding, at a party, a shower—they say, if someone new is in the group: "Listen to Jo Ann talk!" I sit there and I babble on, and they say "Doesn't she have a ridiculous accent!" and "It's so New Yorkish and all!"

I have bolstered these informal assessments with quantitative° studies.In one, nearly 150 people from southeastern Michigan (of European American ethnicity, of both sexes, and of all ages and social classes) rated

quantitative: based on statistical or mathematical data.

(on a scale of 1 to 10) the degree of "correctness" of English spoken in the 50 states, Washington, D.C., and New York City. Figure 1 shows the average scores of this task.

These responses immediately confirm what every American knows—the least correct English is spoken in the South and New York City (and nearby New Jersey). Michiganders give their home state a ranking in the 8 range, the only area so rewarded. They believe that they do not speak a dialect at all. Another task asks the same Michiganders to draw on a blank map of the United States where they think the various dialect areas of the United States are and label them.

From such hand-drawn maps is derived the generalized map in figure 2. This map shows not only where Michigan respondents draw lines for the dialect areas of the United States but also how many respondents drew a boundary around each one. Note the percentage of Michigan respondents who drew a South—94% (138/147). Even the home area is registered as a separate speech region by only 61% (90/147). The third most frequently drawn area is, not surprisingly, the area which contains New York City (54%, 80/147).

These Michiganders seem, therefore, to hear dialect differences on the 5 basis of their evaluation of the correctness of areas. The linguistic South, the area perceived most consistently as incorrect, quite simply *exists* as a linguistic area for these respondents more than any other area.

Michiganders are not unique; in other areas where this work has been done, a South is always drawn by the highest percentage of respondents—South

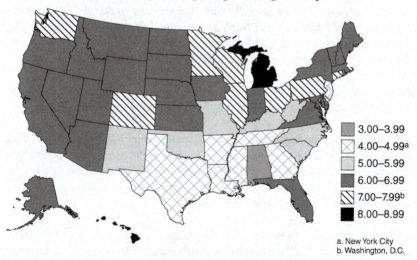

3.00–3.99
4.00–4.99[a]
5.00–5.99
6.00–6.99
7.00–7.99[b]
8.00–8.99

a. New York City
b. Washington, D.C.

FIGURE 1

Mean Scores of the Rankings for "Correct English" of the Fifty States, Washington, D.C., and New York City by Southeastern Michigan Respondents (1 = "worst English"; 10 = "best English")

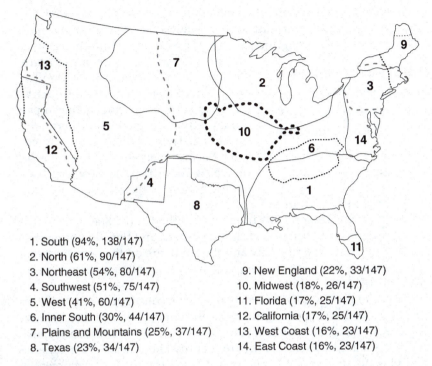

1. South (94%, 138/147)
2. North (61%, 90/147)
3. Northeast (54%, 80/147)
4. Southwest (51%, 75/147)
5. West (41%, 60/147)
6. Inner South (30%, 44/147)
7. Plains and Mountains (25%, 37/147)
8. Texas (23%, 34/147)
9. New England (22%, 33/147)
10. Midwest (18%, 26/147)
11. Florida (17%, 25/147)
12. California (17%, 25/147)
13. West Coast (16%, 23/147)
14. East Coast (16%, 23/147)

FIGURE 2

Generalized Map of 147 Michigan Respondents' Idea of the Dialect Areas of the United States

Carolina 94%, New York City 92%, western New York 100%, southern Indiana 86%, Oregon 92%, and Hawaii 94%. Also important to these respondents is the other place where they believe bad English is spoken. A Northeast (a small area with a focus in New York City) or New York City itself figures very high in the percentages—South Carolina 46%, New York City itself 64%, western New York 45%, southern Indiana 51%, Oregon 75%, and Hawaii 57%, nearly all of these second-place scores (after the South).

What about a quantitative analysis of Southerners' views of the correct-ness issue? In ratings by 36 Auburn University students (principally from Alabama with a few from Georgia and South Carolina), New York City fares even worse than in the Michigan ratings; it is the only area to fall in the 3 range. Other ratings for correctness, however, show none of the strength and certainty of the Michigan opinions. Michigan respondents consider their speech the best and steadily assign lower ratings the farther south a state is. Southerners pretty clearly suffer from what linguists would call *linguistic insecurity*.° They do not rate themselves at the top of the heap, as Michiganders do, and they appear to associate "correct English" with some official or national status (Washington, D.C.).

If Southerners don't find their own speech correct, can they find anything redeeming about it? Just as Michiganders found their variety "most correct" (i.e., 8), these principally Alabama students find theirs "most pleasant" (also 8). As one moves north, a steady disapproval of the "friendly" aspects of speech (its "solidarity" aspects) emerges, leaving Michigan part of a pretty inhospitable northern area, itself a 4. There is one thing, however, that Michiganders and Alabamians agree on. New York City (and New Jersey) are at the bottom of the scale for both "correctness" and "pleasantness."

> "These responses immediately confirm what every American knows—the least correct English is spoken in the South and New York City (and nearby New Jersey)."

In summary, respondents from all over the United States agree that some regions speak better English than others, and they do not hesitate to indicate that New York City and the South are on the bottom of that pile, but prejudiced-against groups themselves seem to rate their varieties high on solidarity factors.

I believe these studies of perception have contributed not only to a better understanding of our linguistic attitudes but also to the cognitive maps real people have of linguistic facts. Coupled with other perceptual tests (ordinary speakers' abilities to identify and imitate other varieties and their awareness of different specific aspects of linguistic differentiation), linguistic folk belief is also a big player in our general understanding of linguistic variation and change in America and is likely to become more important as globalization makes the drawing of both geographic and cognitive maps more challenging.

10

linguistic insecurity: anxiety about the less-standard features of one's language.

Understanding the Text

1. According to Preston's data, what areas of the country are believed to have the most and least "correct" language? What do people from those areas think of their own speech?

2. When asked to circle regions on a U.S. map where people have a distinctly different way of talking, which areas do Preston's participants most often circle? Why does he suspect that people tend to be more aware of these particular regions' ways of talking?

Reflection and Response

3. According to Preston's study, to what extent do people tend to consider the language in your state "correct"? Why is this, based on his explanation or your own interpretation? How would you respond?

4. Would you say that language "pleasantness" is important to people in your state? What features of sound, word choice, or grammar make language "pleasant," in your opinion?

Making Connections

5. The ratings of "correctness" and "pleasantness" given in this article are not based on any objective fact but rather on people's opinions. Use this reading and at least one of the others in Chapter 2 to explain how people's opinions of language can have real-life consequences.

6. Use Rosina Lippi-Green's "Standard (American) English" (p. 212) to supplement Preston's discussion of "correctness." Based on both these articles, why do we tend to see so much agreement among U.S. residents as to which parts of the country speak most and least correctly? What kinds of biases color our judgments of what is "correct"?

Perceptions of Competency as a Function of Accent

Cheryl Boucher,
Georgina Hammock,
Selina McLaughlin,
and Kelsey Henry

The article below, originally published in the Spring 2013 issue of the *Psi Chi Journal of Psychological Research*, investigates how speakers with Southern and non-Southern accents are perceived differently. At the time the article was written, Cheryl Boucher, Selina McLaughlin, and Kelsey Henry were M.A. students in psychology; they are now professional psychologists. Georgina Hammock, a social psychology professor at Georgia Regents University, was their faculty adviser. As a traditionally structured scholarly research article, this piece is divided into several parts, each with its own purpose: The abstract summarizes the purpose and findings of the research; the introduction and literature review section gives background on the topic, summarizes previous research, and provides the researchers' hypothesis; the method section explains how the experiment was done; the results section describes the data collected; and the discussion section explains how we can interpret the data and what questions remain to be answered.

ABSTRACT. Verbal communication provides explicit cues about groups and individuals (Lambert, Hodgson, Gardner, & Fillenbaum, 1960). Accented speech reflects individuals' characteristics such as race, biological sex, social class, and education and functions to categorize individuals according to group membership from which stereotyped evaluations may arise (Riches & Foddy, 1989). Specifically, regional dialects elicit evaluative judgments based on preconceived stereotypes associated with a geographical region (Schenck-Hamlin, 1978). The distinctiveness of the Southern region, due in part to perceptions of its nonstandard dialect, has been consistently established in linguistic and folk dialectology research (Fridland, 2008; Fridland & Bartlett, 2006; Preston, 1993). Based on these findings, the current study evaluated the effect of the Southern accent on perceptions of speaker competency. Regional accent (i.e., Southern and neutral[1]) was systematically varied in audio taped instructions presented to participants. We expected that participants would

---

[1]The "neutral" accent in this study refers to the type of accent used by most national news anchors. All speech is accented; we are referring to what might be recognized as a standard mid-western accent that does not clearly reflect a particular region or speech group.

evaluate the neutral speaker's abilities more positively than the Southerner. As predicted, participants viewed the neutral accented speaker as more competent (e.g., grammatically correct, effective instructor, professional manner) than the Southerner.

Research on the formation of stereotyped evaluations has generated a plethora of empirically derived theories that offer insight into the many nuances of social interaction (Billig & Tajfel, 1973; Jussim, Coleman, & Lerch, 1987; Tajfel, Billig, Bundy, & Flament, 1971). By expanding the scope of social stereotyping to include the influence of regional dialects as a determinant of evaluative perceptions, researchers have consistently established the effect of dialect on accuracy of group identification and categorization of accented speakers' group membership (Ellis, 1967; Gardner & Taylor, 1968; Lambert et al., 1960; Miller, 1975; Riches & Foddy, 1989; Strongman & Woosley, 1967; Vorster & Proctor, 1976). The present study extends previous findings of evaluations of various American accents by investigating stereotypes of a Southern regional accent.

One area noted for its distinct accent is the southeastern region of the United States. The Southern stereotype reflects the region's unique distinctiveness characterized by exclusive "regional types" (Reed, 1986) that are both positive and negative. The *Dictionary of American Regional English* (Hall, 2002) identifies *redneck* and the *American Heritage College Dictionary* (Picket et al., 2002) identifies *bubba* as slang terms synonymous with people from the South. Both derogatory characterizations connote educational and intellectual inferiority. Moreover, Hartigan (2003, p. 96) argues that slurs associated with poor rural Whites (i.e., *hillbilly*, *redneck*, and *white trash*) exist within a racial construct that partially emanates from perceived "rural versus urban identity and the relative degrees of education vs. backwardness." Stigma associated with the South also emerges from studies evaluating geographical and dialectical region distinctiveness on perceptions of regional attributes.

Sociolinguistic research focusing on dialectical mapping (Preston, 1993) substantiates the Southern region's uniqueness. Participants in these studies consistently identified the accurate geographical boundaries of the Southern and Northern divide more often than other geographical regions. Participant evaluations for language correctness produced lower ratings for the distinctive characteristics of the Southern accent than non-Southern accents. These participants labeled all regional speech areas, except for the South, in positive terms (i.e., standard, regular, normal, or everyday). Further supporting the potent influence of accent on evaluative judgments, Southern participants rated their own regional accent lower on language correctness and education measures than they did a non-Southern accent (Fridland, 2008; Fridland & Bartlett, 2006; Fridland, Bartlett, & Kreuz, 2005).

The well-documented history of the Southern stereotype operates along 5 a continuum that highlights the disparate range of characteristics associated with the admired Southern gentlemen and the backward redneck (Bernstein, 2000; Reed, 1986). Although many of the common Southern pejoratives have a distant historical connotation (Hartigan, 2003), mass media continue to strengthen the stereotype's negative aspects through exploitation of the inferior Southerner (Cooke-Jackson & Hansen, 2008). For example, in 2003 a major television network cancelled pilot programming for a modern "hillbilly" reality show in response to pressure from hundreds of businesses, private and public organizations, and 44 members of the House of Representatives (Center for Rural Strategies, 2003). In fact, Senator Robert Byrd repudiated the program's overt representation and perpetuation of the Southern stereotype (Congressional Record, 2003). Such widespread concern with programming subject matter reflects the persuasive power of both the regional stereotype and media's portrayal of the Southerner. Moreover, according to Van Dijk (1987), mass media represent a major source of content for everyday communication and, therefore, act as an agent of attitude formation. Further establishing the entrenched position of the Southern stereotype, Reed (1986) argues that a distinct and unique regional classification, unlike any other social categorization, emanates from historical, literary, and media representations of the Southerner.

Although linguistic research on Southern speech (Fridland, 2008; Fridland & Bartlett, 2006; Fridland et al., 2005) adds support for Reed's (1986) Southern regional typology, these findings emerged in the context of a repeated list of words that was synthesized to accentuate distinctive Southern and Northern vowel variations inherent in each accent. In other words, participants evaluated how Southern each word sounded and made judgments about the degree of correctness and education level of the speaker based on characteristics associated with each region. The current study is designed as a conceptual replication of Fridland and Fridland et al.'s work in that we intended to explore how a Southerner and a speaker without a discernable accent are evaluated when delivering an identical audio presentation. In order to avoid additional confounds arising from differences in individuals' vocal characteristics and message content, we employed a modified version of Lambert et al.'s (1960) matched-guise technique in conjunction with a scripted neutral message. The matched-guise technique° is designed such that a target

matched-guise technique: a method in which the same person speaks identical words in two different dialects so that researchers can investigate listeners' attitudes toward the dialects.

speaker produces multiple verbal presentations using different accents. To this end, we hypothesized that a Southern accented speaker would be evaluated as less competent than a speaker with a neutral accent when explaining how to download music from a compact disc to an iPod.

Method

Participants

Twenty-one men and 43 women were recruited from a moderately sized Southeastern university. The number of participants was slightly lower than the 69 participants suggested by the power analysis. The study was advertised in psychology classes and through the university's electronic recruiting system. Participants volunteered for this study and received required course credit or extra credit depending on their instructors' policies as compensation for participation. Participants ranged in age from 18 to 39 ($M = 21.72$, $SD = 5.15$). Approximately 54% described themselves as White, 25% as Black, and 13% classified themselves as "other." Eighty-three percent of participants described themselves as Southerners as defined by being raised in a Southern state. Thirteen participants in the neutral condition incorrectly answered the manipulation check evaluating perception of the speaker's accent (i.e., Where do you think Zack is from?) resulting in the exclusion of their data. Although the excluded participants represent a large percentage of the neutral condition, the accent effect remained significant after the data was removed. Analyses reflect data from the remaining 51 participants.

Design

The design was a randomized two group experimental design. Groups comprised of a maximum of 10 participants listened to an audio recording and completed questionnaires. The type of accent was manipulated so that approximately half of the participants were exposed to a person using a Southern accent and half were exposed to a more neutral accent. After excluding data from 13 participants in the neutral condition, the remaining 18 participants comprised the neutral condition and 31 participants made up the Southern condition. Participants were similar in characteristics (i.e., sex, age, race, state where raised) across both conditions with slightly more non-Southerners ($n = 6$) in the neutral condition than the Southern condition ($n = 2$).

Materials

Participants received questionnaire packets instructing them to rate the speaker Zack on 8 competency traits: reliable source of information, grammatically correct, unknowledgeable about the subject matter, effective instructor, persuasive presenter, unprofessional manner, articulate speaker, and unsophisticated demeanor. All competencies, even if phrased negatively, were rated on a 5-point scale ranging from 1 to 5 with the highest rating indicating a more positive evaluation (i.e., *very professional*) and the lowest rating reflecting a more negative evaluation (i.e., *very unprofessional*). The competency measure created for this study was used to explore perceptions on each of the eight characteristics associated with the quality and effectiveness of a speaker delivering an instructional audio presentation. In this study, competency items produced a Cronbach's alpha° of .80. Due to the matched guise of the speaker by which voice characteristics did not vary, it is expected that any differences in competency ratings for the Southern and neutral speaker can be attributed to the manipulation of accent. Participants also answered comprehension questions regarding the presentation content in order to bolster the cover story. Finally, participants disclosed personal information in response to questions about sex, age, and race/ethnicity, and state in which they were raised.

Procedure

Upon participants' arrival we explained the study's purported purpose 10
evaluating the effects of verbal versus written stimuli on comprehension. Having obtained IRB° approval for use of deception, we employed a cover story in order to elicit genuine responses from participants. Participants were told that they were assigned to the verbal condition, which consisted of an audio recording rather than a written transcript. Advised that participation was voluntary, participants read and signed the informed consent form indicating their voluntary participation. At this point, we randomly assigned participants to one of two possible conditions, Southern or neutral accent. Based on a modified version of Lambert et al.'s (1960) matched-guise technique, the same speaker read an identical set of instructions in both the Southern accent, characterized by the long-syllable drawl, and the neutral accent lacking specific regional distinctiveness. The speaker was a White man born and raised in the Southern United States who spoke in a Southern and neutral accent. Based on previous research investigating perceptions of male and female voices, common sex stereotypes underlie evaluative judgments based on speakers' sex (Linek, Gerjets, & Scheiter, 2010). Participants in Nass, Moon,

Cronbach's alpha: a statistical measurement of a test's or scale's reliability.
IRB: Institutional Review Board, the committee at each university responsible for ensuring that experiments are done ethically and with minimal risk to the participants.

and Green's (1997) study judged computerized female voices more competent in love and relationship issues than male voices and male voices more competent in computer knowledge than females voices. Therefore, by employing a man to deliver a computer related message, we increased the salience of accent and minimized potential confounds of speaker sex or message content. Vocal tone and pauses remained consistent in both guises, such that the speaker's voice differed only in accent. After instructing participants to listen quietly, the audio presentation was played. The recorded message for both the Southern and the neutral accented speaker was 1 min in duration and identical in content—instructions for downloading music from a CD to an iPod.

Following the audio presentation, participants received questionnaire packets that included written directions on how to proceed. Upon completion of the questionnaires, we debriefed the participants regarding the true nature of the study. In addition to the formal questionnaires, immediately following the debriefing session, we asked participants what they thought about the speaker, where they thought he was from, and the reasoning in support of their perceptions. After the informal discussion, we thanked and dismissed the participants.

Results

Correlational analysis of the relationships between the dependent variables° revealed statistically significant° correlations (*r*'s ranged from .05 to .70). Therefore, a multivariate analysis of variance (MANOVA) was used to analyze the responses to the evaluation items on the questionnaire. An alpha level of .05 was adopted for all analyses. Preliminary analyses were conducted to determine if the MANOVA° assumptions were met. Box's *M* test was used to determine whether variances were homogeneous. The test suggested no violation of this assumption.

As predicted, the MANOVA conducted on the competency variables revealed a significant main effect for the independent variable, accent, $F(8, 40) = 7.96$, $p = .00$, $\eta_p^2 = .61$. Subsequent univariate tests indicated that accent influenced perceptions of the speaker on five of the eight

dependent variables: In a study, the independent variables are the conditions created by the researcher (here, absence or presence of a Southern accent), and the dependent variables are the outcomes (here, the participant ratings such as "reliable source of information" and "effective instructor").
statistically significant: when mathematical calculation shows that the relationship between variables is strong enough to have been caused by something other than random chance.
MANOVA: an in-depth statistical test to determine the strength of relationships between variables.

Table 1   Univariate Effect: Significant Main Effects of Accent

			Southern[a]	Neutral	
Accent	$F(1, 47)$	p	M (SD)	M (SD)	η_p^2
Reliable Source of Information	.00	.99	3.98 (0.89)	4.41 (0.72)	.00
Grammatically Correct	10.07	.00	3.42 (0.99)	4.28 (0.75)	.13
Unknowledgeable About Subject Matter	.04	.84	1.69 (0.88)	1.62 (1.16)	.00
Effective Instructor	8.16	.01	3.74 (0.89)	4.44 (0.70)	.19
Persuasive Presenter	1.17	.29	3.50 (1.11)	3.92 (0.87)	.03
Unprofessional Manner	8.72	.01	3.26 (1.00)	4.22 (1.26)	.08
Articulate Speaker	54.59	.00	2.61 (1.12)	4.67 (0.49)	.55
Unsophisticated Demeanor	17.70	.00	2.87 (0.92)	4.06 (1.00)	.23

[a] Greater means indicate a more positive evaluation.

competency items excluding reliable source of information, unknowledgeable about the subject matter, and persuasive presenter. Participants perceived the non-Southerner as a more effective instructor and articulate speaker than the Southerner. Further, although the script was identical for both accent types, participants rated the neutral speaker more grammatically correct with a more professional manner and sophisticated demeanor than the Southerner. See Table 1 for univariate statistics including means, standard deviations, and effect sizes.

Discussion

We predicted a more negative evaluation of the Southern accented speaker than the neutral accented speaker due to pervasive stereotyped attitudes that consistently emerge in evaluative judgments of Southerners in previous research. As hypothesized, participants viewed the Southern speaker as less competent than the non-Southerner. This result becomes even more interesting when considering 83% of participants self-identified as Southern but stereotyped their ingroup member more negatively than the non-Southerner. Similarly, Tennessee participants in Fridland and Bartlett's (2006) research evaluated the Southern dialect more negatively than they did other regional dialects. These findings further point to the powerful effect of the Southern accent in eliciting stereotyped perceptions. Indeed, the effect size associated with accent was very large ($\eta_p^2 = .61$).

Perhaps the most surprising result is the non-Southerner sounded 15 more grammatically correct than the Southerner even though within each speaker guise the script was identical in wording. For example, instead of using the Southern pronoun variant "y'all" both speakers used the standard grammatical form "you." Is it possible that participants in the Southern condition perceived the speaker's words differently due to their expectations of how Southerners sound? Exactly what words participants perceived the Southerner to say cannot be ascertained from the current study but presents an interesting subject for further investigation.

Future research should address several limitations encountered in this study. First, the neutral speaker may have been erroneously associated with the research team. Following the debriefing session, several participants in the neutral condition who believed the speaker was from the South suggested the speaker was a member of the research team. Perhaps these participants assumed the neutral speaker to be a Southerner because of their perceived association between the speaker and the Southern university in which the study occurred. Some participants may have evaluated the neutral speaker based on the presumed relationship with the researchers rather than the speaker's voice. Therefore, disclosing more detailed information differentiating the speaker from the research team should alleviate this problem. Additionally, because stereotypes may vary between Southern rural and Southern urban accents, which may further reflect social class perceptions (Eckert, 2004; Luhman, 1990), the speaker's accent should ideally depict less distinctive social status characteristics while maintaining a strong Southern quality.

The speaker in the current study spoke with a Southern rural accent in order to ensure a strong manipulation. While the accent manipulation check confirmed that all the participants in the Southern condition identified the speaker as Southern, the rural accent may have prompted stereotypical thinking associated with economically deprived regions historically known for underperforming schools (MDC Inc., 2004). Indeed, Hartigan (2003) pointed out that one common distinction made between rural and urban regions reflects notions of the uneducated and educated Southerner, respectively. The negative evaluations in the current study may have been elicited because participants perceived the rural Southerner as uneducated. Therefore, the speaker's accent should ideally depict less distinctive rural characteristics associated with lower socioeconomic status. Future research should also focus on more realistic encounters as opposed to the scripted speech used in this study that may not generalize to more natural, spontaneous conversation styles. The scope of this study pertained to limited aspects related to perceptions of a Southern accented speaker amongst a small sample of college students. However, these results, taken with previous findings, warrant further investigation as opportunities to interact with diverse accented individuals continue to increase due to rapidly advancing digital communication technologies.

This study's results pertain to global communication dynamics and its impact on social and business networking in which electronic voice interaction may, in some cases, be as prevalent as face-to-face encounters. When initial contacts occur via electronic means, first impressions based on speech characteristics, such as accent, likely result in perceptions of group membership within a geographical region. If individuals hold prejudices about a particular regional accented group, akin to Reed's (1986) distinct regional typology, stereotyped evaluations may follow.

Due to burgeoning communication technologies, dialects and accents extend beyond geographical boundaries at a greater rate than before the digital age. However, despite negative Southern stereotypes, some Southerners gained prestige and renown such as the 15 Southern American Presidents (The White House, n.d.). Perhaps these presidential candidates' exceptional educational achievements, prominent social status, or other sociodemographic characteristics exceeded and violated stereotypical assumptions about Southerners' inferior standing. Although complex processes beyond the scope of this study's design affect perceptions of presidential candidates differently than a single exposure to a Southern speaker, an important question remains. Do Southerners with less prestigious status than elected presidents have the ability to escape negative stereotypes associated with their accent?

> "Do Southerners with less prestigious status than elected presidents have the ability to escape negative stereotypes associated with their accent?"

This question not only pertains to Southerners but individuals with other 20 nonstandard accents whether regional or foreign. In their study investigating ethnicity, nonstandard English accents, and employability, Carlson and McHenry (2006) found that nonstandard accented speakers (i.e., African American Vernacular English, Spanish and Asian influenced English) received lower status and employability ratings than standard American English speakers, regardless of speaker ethnicity. These authors suggested that individuals with a nonstandard accent who seek employment should avail themselves of speech modification therapies in order to become bidialectical. Amid the current milieu of diversity and pluralism awareness campaigns in employment and educational settings, the suggestion to modify an inherently unique characteristic indelibly linked to one's culture, ethnicity, and geographical region seems antiquated. As early as 1990, Reed lamented the rising trend of university courses designed to train out

Southern accents based on the assumption that standard American English speech provides more opportunity for success. According to Matsuda (1991), an attorney who argued in the 9th Circuit Court of Appeals for the protection of accented individuals from discriminatory hiring practices, "accent discrimination" remains alive and well.

While Reed (1990) spoke of intolerance for Southern accents and Matsuda (1991) of foreign accent discrimination, both argued that true cultural diversity necessarily includes linguistic pluralism as dialect and accent reveals place of origin. Similarly, O'Hara (2007) suggested that regionalism may be one of the remaining acceptable "isms" left intact despite mounting societal efforts to expunge many forms of repugnant discriminatory behavior. As a teacher educator on the subject of diversity in educational settings, O'Hara (2007) provided an informative perspective on strategies to overcome dialect discrimination and regionalism within the classroom. Based on her qualitative study in which teacher interns read about and responded to region and dialect based biases, O'Hara concluded that one of the most important endeavors for future educators is to provide a safe learning environment in which students are made aware of negative biases and regional stereotypes. In this way, educators would expose regional and accent discrimination as a form of bigotry such that these behaviors would be added to the long list of unacceptable discriminatory practices.

References

Bernstein, C. G. (2000). Misrepresenting the American South. *American Speech, 75,* 339–342.

Billig, M. G., & Tajfel, H. (1973). Social categorization and similarity in intergroup behaviour. *European Journal of Social Psychology, 3,* 27–52. doi: 10.1002/ejsp.2420030103

Center for Rural Strategies. (2003, March 19). Press release: 44 members of Congress sign letter opposing series. Retrieved from http://www.ruralstrategies.org/press-release-44-members-congress-sign-letter-opposing-series

Carlson, H. K, & McHenry, M. A. (2006). Effect of accent and dialect on employability. *Journal of Employment Counseling, 43,* 70–83.

Congressional Record (2003). Statement of Sen. Byrd (149 Cong. Rec. 112, S9989). Washington, DC: U.S. Government Printing Office.

Cooke-Jackson, A., & Hansen, E. K. (2008). Appalachian culture and reality TV: The ethical dilemma of stereotyping others. *Journal of Mass Media Ethics, 23,* 183–200. doi: 10.1080/08900520802221946

Eckert, P. (2004). Variation and a sense of place. In C. Fought (Ed.), *Sociolinguistic variation: Critical reflections* (pp. 107–118). New York, NY: Oxford University Press.

Ellis, D. S. (1967). Speech and social status in America. *Social Forces, 45,* 431–437. doi: 10.2307/2575202

Fridlard, V. (2008). Regional differences in perceiving vowel tokens on Southerness, education, and pleasantness ratings. *Language Variation and Change, 20,* 67–83. doi: 10.1017/S0954394508000069

Fridland, V., & Bartlett, K. (2006). Correctness, pleasantness, and degree of difference ratings across regions. *American Speech, 81,* 358–386. doi: 10.1215/00031283-2006-025

Fridland, V., Bartlett, K., & Kreuz, R. (2005). Making sense of variation: Pleasantness and education ratings of Southern vowel variants. *American Speech, 80,* 366–387. doi: 10.1215/00031283-80-4-366

Gardner, R. C., & Taylor, D. M. (1968). Ethnic stereotypes: Their effects on person perception. *Canadian Journal of Psychology, 22,* 267–276. doi: 10.1037/h0082767

Hall, J. H. (Ed.). (2002). *Dictionary of American regional English* (Vol. 4, pp. 531–532). Cambridge, MA: Belknap Press of Harvard University Press.

Hartigan, J. (2003). Who are these white people?: "Whitetrash," "rednecks," and "hillbillies" as marked racial subjects. In A. W. Doane & E. Bonilla-Silva (Eds.), *White out: The continuing significance of racism* (pp. 95–111). New York, NY: Routledge.

Jussim, L., Coleman, L. M., & Lerch, L. (1987). The nature of stereotypes: A comparison and integration of three theories. *Journal of Personality and Social Psychology, 52,* 536–546. doi: 10.1037/0022-3514.52.3.536

Lambert, W. E., Hodgson, R. C., Gardner, R. C., & Fillenbaum, S. (1960). Evaluational reactions to spoken languages. *Journal of Abnormal and Social Psychology, 60,* 44–51. doi: 10.1037/h0044430

Linek, S. B., Gerjets, P., & Scheiter, K. (2010). The speaker/gender effect: Does the speaker's gender matter when presenting auditory text in multimedia messages? *Instructional Science, 38,* 503–521. doi: 10.1007/s11251-009-9115-8

Luhman, R. (1990). Appalachian English stereotypes: Language attitudes in Kentucky. *Language in Society, 19,* 331–348. doi: 10.1017/S0047404500014548

Matsuda, M. J. (1991). Voices of America: Accent, antidiscrimination law, and a jurisprudence for the last reconstruction. *Yale Law Journal, 100,* 1–74.

MDC Inc. (2004, May). The State of the South. Retrieved from http://www.mdcinc.org/resources/state-of-the-south

Miller, D. T. (1975). The effect of dialect and ethnicity on communicator effectiveness. *Speech Monographs, 42,* 69–74. doi: 10.1080/03637757509375878

Nass, C., Moon, Y., & Green, N. (1997). Are computers gender-neutral? Gender stereotypic responses to computers. *Journal of Applied Social Psychology, 27,* 864–876. doi: 10.1111/j.1559-1816.1997.tb00275.x

O'Hara, H. (2007). Regionalism and the classroom. *Multicultural Education, 14,* 55–58.

Picket, J. P., Pritchard, D. R., Leonesio, C., Fortson, B. W., Kleinedler, S. R., Pope, J. . . . Rivera, E. B. (Eds.). (2002). *The American heritage college dictionary* (4th ed., p. 186). Boston, MA: Houghton Mifflin.

Preston, D. R. (1993). Folk dialectology. In D. R. Preston (Ed.), *American dialect research* (pp. 333–377). Philadelphia, PA: John Benjamins.

Reed, J. S. (1986). *Southern folk, plain & fancy: Native White social types* (4–19). Athens, GA: University of Georgia Press.

Reed, J. S. (1990). *Whistling Dixie: Dispatches from the South.* Columbia, MO: University of Missouri Press.

Riches, P., & Foddy, M. (1989). Ethnic accent as a status cue. *Social Psychology Quarterly, 52,* 197–206. doi: 10.2307/2786714

Schenck-Hamlin, W. J. (1978). The effects of dialectical similarity, stereotyping, and message agreement on interpersonal perception. *Human Communications Research, 5,* 15–26. doi: 10.1111/j.1468-2958.1978.tb00619.x

Strongman, K. T. & Woosley, J. (1967). Stereotyped reactions to regional accents. *British Journal of Social & Clinical Psychology, 6,* 164–167.

Tajfel, H., Billig, M. G., Bundy, R. P., & Flament, C. (1971). Social categorization and intergroup behaviour. *European Journal of Social Psychology, 1,* 149–178.

Van Dijk, T. A. (1987). *Communicating racism: Ethnic prejudice in thought and talk* (pp. 40–44). Newbury Park, CA: Sage.

Vorster, J., & Proctor, L. (1976). Black attitudes to "white" languages in South Africa: A pilot study. *Journal of Psychology: Interdisciplinary and Applied, 92,* 103–108.

The White House. (n.d.). The presidents. Retrieved from http://www.whitehouse. gov/about/presidents

Understanding the Text

1. Describe the process by which the researchers investigated perceptions of Southern accents.

2. What did this study conclude regarding the differences in people's perceptions of speakers with Southern and non-Southern accents?

Reflection and Response

3. Although speakers read from identical scripts, the participants still ranked the non-Southern speaker as "more grammatically correct" than the Southerner (par. 13). Why might this be?

4. As noted in the methods section, the researchers did not tell participants the true research question until after they had finished the questionnaire. Instead of comparing Southern and non-Southern accents, participants thought the study was comparing written and oral instructions. Why do you think the researchers deceived participants in this way? In what ways do you think the results might have been different without the deception?

Making Connections

5. How do Boucher and her colleagues' results compare to Dennis Preston's study of the perceived correctness and pleasantness of Southern speech in "Some Plain Facts about Americans and Their Language" (p. 97)? How do they add to your understanding of Preston's study?

6. How do the methods used in this study compare to the ones used in Kathryn Campbell-Kibler's "Intersecting Variables and Perceived Sexual Orientation in Men" (p. 140)? What makes these sorts of methods effective for discovering people's ideologies about language?

Are White People Ethnic? Whiteness, Dominance, and Ethnicity

Carmen Fought

Carmen Fought, a professor of linguistics at Pitzer College in California, studies the connections between ethnicity and language, particularly among Spanish-English bilinguals and speakers of Chicano English. The reading below is an excerpt from her book *Language and Ethnicity* (Cambridge University Press, 2006), which examines the uses and perceptions of language among different ethnic and racial groups in the United States. In the excerpt, pulled from a chapter focused on whiteness, Fought shows how, with a few notable exceptions, language practices perceived as "good" are also often perceived as "white."

"[clear throat] Oh goodness! [clear throat]"
"What's the matter, Chance?"
*"[clear throat] I don't know, Schuyler. [clear throat] I have a scratchy sensation
I am not familiar with. [clear throat] I better schedule an MRI [clear throat]."*
—GEORGE LOPEZ DOING "WHITE" CHARACTERS, *RIGHT NOW RIGHT NOW*, 2001

Many people might look at the title of this chapter and find the question absurd. Of course white people are ethnic; there is no such thing as a lack of ethnicity, just as there is no such thing as a dialect without an "accent." Everything is relative, and being a member of the dominant group will certainly change one's day-to-day experience of ethnicity, but that does not mean that ethnicity is absent. Nonetheless, there is good evidence that being "white" is not just another ethnicity, one neutral side of a neat boundary that divides, e.g., "White–Black" or "White–Latino" or "Pakeha–Maori." In places where people of European descent are the dominant group (which includes a majority of the places for which we have sociolinguistic studies of ethnicity), such ethnic boundaries are never neutral, because the two sides are not equal in terms of political power or influence on the dominant ideology.

One of the repercussions of this difference, in practice, is that their own whiteness can be invisible to members of the dominant culture, as highlighted in the emerging field of whiteness studies within sociology and anthropology. Hill (1998), in her discussion of white public space, identifies a set of contexts in which white people are seen as "invisibly normal" while other groups are both visible and marginal. Similarly, Bell comments, "Pakeha [white New Zealanders] are the dominant ethnicity and culture within New Zealand, but we tend to be identified by default, by what we are not rather than what we are . . . not Maori, not Polynesian, not Australian, not British, not European" (1999:539). In their introduction to a special issue of the *Journal of Linguistic Anthropology* focusing on whiteness studies, Trechter and Bucholtz sum up this view: "[i]deologically, whiteness is usually absence, not presence: the absence of culture and color" (2001:5). (As a number of scholars have pointed out, however, whiteness is much less likely to be invisible to members of other groups.)

In the dominant US discourse, it is not unusual for people of European descent to view themselves as lacking ethnicity, either partly or completely. A European-American friend said to me recently, "I wish I were more ethnic," as though, for her, ethnicity existed along a continuum, as something of which you could have a greater or lesser quantity. I perceive something similar among my European-American students, many of whom borrow clothing or hairstyles from African or Indian cultures, a sense among them that they are culturally empty in some way, and need to borrow from other cultures to fill that gap. One of the things they borrow is language.

Even if we begin with the quite reasonable (to social scientists, at least) assumption that whiteness is a constructed ethnicity, like all ethnicities, *how* it is constructed must be viewed in the context of ideologies° about dominant ethnic groups. A number of questions relevant to this context must be addressed, particularly with respect to the role of language in the construction of white ethnic identity. To begin with, stereotypes of minority groups may be easy to locate in the culture, while stereotypes of the dominant group may be more hidden or subtle. What stereotypes, particularly linguistic ones, might be associated with dominant groups, such as European-Americans, and where can we locate them? Also, is it possible to distinguish elements that characterize some more general category such as "educated" or "middle class" from the specific racial category of "whiteness" with which these categories might be conflated in public discourse? Furthermore, if a dialect of the dominant group is treated by society as unmarked or neutral in some sense, how can that dialect serve as an expression of ethnicity? Finally, what are the consequences for members of other groups of using linguistic (and other) features associated with whiteness, a practice that might seem useful or necessary in a society where the dominant group sets the norms for public arenas such as the school system, government, multinational corporations, and so forth?

ideologies: collections of beliefs, usually shared by a group.

"Explorations of what it means to be 'white' must be interpreted as being not about some essential quality of individuals, but about the dominant ideologies of race in a particular culture at a particular moment in time."

As scholars in the area of whiteness studies are careful to emphasize, the experience of being white is not monolithic, any more than the experiences of members of other groups. In some countries, the racial label "white" can apply to both majority and minority ethnic groups. Canada is a setting of this type, and a great deal of sociolinguistic research has been done on Francophone and Anglophone Canadians (e.g., Poplack 1989, Heller 1992, Thibault and Sankoff 1993, Blondeau et al. 2002).[1] In addition, the same group can be classified as "white" or "not white" differently over time. There are numerous discussions, for example, of European immigrant groups to the USA in the nineteenth century, particularly Italians and Irish, and how these groups were reclassified historically in terms of race, becoming what Zelinsky (2001) calls "unhyphenated whites." Zack, in her discussion of mixed race and the construction of race generally, comments, "before the 1920s white Anglo-Saxon Americans believed that Italian, Irish, and Polish immigrants were distinct races. No one would suggest that now" (1993:165). Perhaps the most famous study of this process is Ignatiev's *How the Irish Became White* (1995), which looks at a single group in the USA over time, in a political and historical context. In addition, a number of studies (e.g., Brander Rasmussen et al. 2001) have pointed out that certain members of white communities, such as gay individuals or those from low socioeconomic groups, may not be accorded the same types of privileges as others. Therefore, explorations of what it means to be "white" must be interpreted as being not about some essential quality of individuals, but about the dominant ideologies of race in a particular culture at a particular moment in time, in the same way that all explorations of race must be interpreted.

The Social Correlates of Being White

In general, ideologies concerning the social correlates of being white that we find in the discourse of societies like the USA follow directly from the dominant social position of white speakers and the privileges that being the dominant ethnic group affords. Whiteness is often associated with the middle class, for example. In Urciuoli's (1996) study of working-class Puerto-Rican Americans in New York City, this theme emerged frequently among the speakers she talked to, who often saw becoming middle class as inextricably linked with becoming more white. One man articulated this view in the following way:

I'm doing this, I'm doing that. I'm gonna get to the middle class. What do I do with my skin color, do I go and dye my color? Do I go and dye my hair? Do I try to speak fluent English, use these sophisticated words? . . . [you] bring the same economic problems, the same racial problems, the same language problems. (1996:143)

The very first thing that strikes me about this excerpt is that the speaker mentions his own "language problems," and refers to them in other places, but it is clear from the excerpt that he is quite articulate and additionally commands a very standard variety of English. I will return to specifically language-related associations with whiteness below. But this serves as a good example of the association of whiteness with the middle class. Similarly, the African-American drag queens studied by Barrett (1999) often indexed white personas as part of performing female gender. One individual specifically referred to herself as a "white woman," and talked about a life of privilege, including shopping, lunch in restaurants, owning expensive jewelry, and so forth. Barrett points out that the term "white woman" when used in this way refers primarily to a class distinction rather than an ethnic distinction. In other words, the drag queens he studied indexed whiteness as a way of indexing a middle-class identity.

Whiteness is also often associated with education and/or intellectual orientation (Trechter and Bucholtz 2001). A Puerto-Rican American woman in the experimental part of Urciuoli's study, for example, who was asked to describe a speaker whose voice she heard on a tape, said, "she's white. She's very educated and chances are she could be a teacher" (1996:116). The listeners consistently linked educated-sounding voices to whiteness, although not all the speakers identified this way were in reality white. Similarly, Clark (2003) found that African-American high-school students identified a rhetorical style which he calls "abstract/speculative inquiry," and performed parodies of it in class, evoking "white linguistic stereotypes" among their interlocutors. Bucholtz (2001) also found an association of whiteness with a scientific register among European-American "nerd" teenagers in California. While all the ideologies discussed here can be dangerous in their social repercussions, this link between education and whiteness seems particularly pernicious in the message it sends to people of other ethnic groups (which I will discuss more below). A similar but slightly different pattern is the association of whiteness with rationality and calm. For example, the teenage

European-American boy in Bucholtz (1999) uses a narrative involving both himself and several African-American participants to index his whiteness. In this narrative, as Bucholtz notes, he constructs himself as "nonconfrontational, reasonable, and *white*" (1999:451). This ideology is also explored in the work of Kochman (1981).

One ideological pattern that seems a bit more complex, and does not follow directly from a social position of dominance, is that whiteness does not seem to be associated with masculinity. In the US racial ideology, which tends to dichotomize race as white versus black, for example, masculinity is more closely associated with "blackness." In the narrative from Bucholtz's (1999) study, mentioned above, when the narrator emphasizes his whiteness, he is consistently linked to homophobic and misogynistic challenges to his masculinity, but when he begins to borrow AAVE° features and introduces an interlocutor who links him symbolically to African-American culture, his masculinity (as portrayed in the narrative) is strengthened. Fordham and Ogbu (1986) found that the African-American high-school students in their study linked doing well in school not only with whiteness but also with homosexuality. Even the "white men can't jump" stereotype exploited in the movie of the same name seems to be an instance of this unphysical, unmasculine view of whiteness.

Finally, one key characteristic of the ideology of whiteness is that whiteness is "not cool," or "unhip" (and I use this latter term deliberately, with full knowledge of its African-American and ultimately African origins). For example, Bucholtz (2001) found that the youth culture in the California high school she studied associated coolness with the black students at the school. In contrast, the deliberately "uncool" stance taken by the nerd group was associated with being "too white." One consequence of this perspective is the constant borrowing of slang terms from AAVE into white varieties. As Smitherman points out, these terms are discarded by AAVE speakers once they move into the "white mainstream" (2000:61).

I have not attempted to differentiate systematically here between 10 ideologies held by communities of speakers who identify themselves as white and those that do not. In many cases there seems to be overlap, and the examples above come from studies of speakers of European-American ethnicity (e.g., Bucholtz 1999, Bucholtz 2001) as well as studies of other groups. However, it seems probable that ingroup and outgroup views will differ in some respects. I will be discussing some specifically outgroup views of whiteness below.

AAVE: African American Vernacular English.

The Linguistic Correlates of Being White

The ideologies associated with linguistic aspects of whiteness often correlate with the social aspects discussed above in predictable ways. Three basic perspectives on language and whiteness seem to be dominant in the communities that have been the focus of recent anthropological and sociolinguistic studies:

1. Anything standard is associated with white speakers; for example, speaking standard varieties of English (which may be hard to define, but play an important ideological role).

2. A level of standardness that is somehow beyond the "basic" level is associated with white speakers, e.g., superstandard grammatical forms (see Wolfram and Schilling-Estes 1998:12–13) or highly specialized vocabulary.

3. Stereotyped (often stigmatized) varieties associated with a particular geographic region are seen as "white" e.g., Valley Girl dialects, New York City dialects.

Not all ideas about language and whiteness fall clearly into one of these categories, but they do encompass many of the perspectives found in sociolinguistic studies of language and ethnicity.

The first perspective is the one presented in Ogbu's (1999) study of African-Americans in California; Ogbu comments that "both voluntary and involuntary minorities consider standard English to be 'White language' and a symbol of White identity" (1999:154). In general, the African-Americans in his study believed that white Americans spoke "proper or correct English" and black Americans spoke "slang English." Fordham and Ogbu (1986) list "speaking standard English" as one of the characteristics that the African-American students in their study associated with "acting white" (in fact, it is the first item that the authors list, although this may not be significant). The same perspective can be found in the Puerto-Rican American community studied experimentally by Urciuoli (1996). Many of the listeners in the experiment linked standard grammatical forms to whiteness. One commented of a speaker on the tape (who in fact was white), "she's white . . . Because she knew where to put the letters where they belong, her English, her grammar was so good" (1996:116). Another man in Urciuoli's study said about a white Jewish male speaker on the tape, "He used the proper English, like 'ran.' If a Hispanic person would say that, he would say 'run'" (1996:116). His comment makes clear not only that he associates Standard English with whiteness, but in addition that he does not feel a standard variety could also potentially be associated with other groups, such as Latino speakers.

In other cases, whiteness seems to be associated not with *any* standard linguistic forms but rather with those that count as somehow at the extremes of the standard. This includes what have been called super-standard forms (Wolfram and Schilling-Estes 1998, Bucholtz 2001) such as "to whom" or "It is I," and overly careful phonetic articulations.° It can also include lexical items that sound particularly technical or literary. This is the perspective on whiteness represented by the European-American "nerds" in Bucholtz's (2001) study, who use these sorts of features to construct identities that are seen by other European-Americans as "too white" in comparison with the language of their peers. The African-American students in Ogbu's study associated white speakers with, among other things, "a better vocabulary" (1999:163).

Lexical items also featured prominently in the ethnic characterizations of voices as white by participants in Urciuoli's (1996) experiment. About one speaker, listeners picked out words and phrases such as "rather" and "the new breed of sanitation" in classifying him as white. One listener said of the same person, "He talks English like a little bit of high-class, like when he says 'congestion'" (1996:115). Interestingly, the speaker being described is not white, but rather Puerto-Rican American. In another case: a listener gave this description of a woman (who was, in this case, white): "She's good, she is good . . . She's white, she's well-educated . . . very articulated, and she uses very very good words, like 'chronically'" (1996:115). What strikes me about this last example is not only the reference to certain lexical items, but also the very clear value judgments being expressed. The presumably white speaker is "good" and her words are also "good"; it seems highly probable that this listener has a corresponding "bad" category as well. This is language ideology at its most naked.

The final perspective on whiteness and language is in some ways the most interesting. It involves the association of whiteness with linguistic varieties that are regionally marked. The African-American students in Ogbu's (1999) study listed "valley talk" (presumably the stereotyped dialect that originated with California teenagers) as something they associated with white people. Similarly, a Korean-American boy from Chicago in Chun's (2001) study identified the Southern US item *y'all* as a white term that he felt he should resist using. This example illustrates the mismatch that can occur between perceptions of the language associated with a particular ethnicity and reality, since *y'all* is in fact used by people of many ethnicities in the South (as the two Texan Korean-Americans in Chun's study later point out). Another question that this example raises is how regional varieties can be associated with white

15

---

phonetic articulations: pronunciations.

ethnicity in places where the regional features are also shared by members of other groups. One answer appears to be that regional features may be parceled out, so that some features mark region, regardless of ethnicity (like *y'all*), and others are tied to a particular ethnicity. Wolfram and Schilling-Estes (1998:180) note with respect to the Southern US process of /ay/ monophthongization,° for example, that only European-Americans apply the process before voiceless consonants, so that, for instance, *tahm* for "time" is considered just Southern, but *raht* for "right" is associated specifically with white speakers.

The Consequences of "Sounding White"

Is it bad to sound white? Despite all the privileges accorded to being in the dominant group, the answer at some level seems to be yes. Of course, speakers from other ethnic groups know that commanding a standard variety is a prerequisite for certain types of occupations, succeeding in the educational system, and more. And attitudes in various communities certainly reflect this reality at some level, despite the association of standard varieties with white speech. So, for example, the parents in Ogbu's (1999) study often encouraged their children to learn Standard English as a way of "getting into the system" and "learning the game." However, these same parents talked openly about the negative repercussions of being perceived as "talking white." One adult speaker in the study, for example, says of African-American members of his community:

they would probably tend to be somewhat prejudicial of someone speaking very proper English, and they would probably make an assessment on that person's character as being "uppity" or . . . she is trying to be White, or something like that. (1999:170–1)

Similarly, Rickford gives the example of a black teenager in California who comments, "Over at my school . . . first time they catch you talkin' white, they'll never let it go" (1999:275). The most comprehensive study of this phenomenon is Fordham and Ogbu (1986), which looks in detail

---

/ay/ **monophthongization:** Monophthongization is the conversion of a diphthong (a combination of two vowel sounds) to a monophthong (a single vowel sound). The "long *i*" vowel sound, marked in the phonetic alphabet as /ay/, is pronounced outside the Southern United States by sliding from the "ah" sound (as in "fall") to the "ee" sound (as in "see"). (Try saying "tah-eem" a few times, faster each time, until you can hear the sound becoming a long *i*.) Many Southerners, on the other hand, pronounce "time" and other "long *i*" words without sliding into the "ee" sound, resulting in a pronunciation more like "tahm."

at the attitudes of African-American students, and ties attitudes about standard varieties and whiteness with difficulties in orienting towards success at school.

This critical view of sounding white occurs over and over in a number of different ethnic groups. For example, the Korean-Americans in Chun's (2001) study discuss the negative properties of sounding white, and express frustration about, among other things, Koreans adapting family names to a more Anglo-sounding phonetic form. The Puerto-Rican Americans in Urciuoli's (1996) study gave a long list of qualities associated with "acting white," and one of the most crucial ones was pretending not to know Spanish. They also mentioned trying to speak without "an accent," and anglicizing one's name as behaviors the community may view as undesirable. Interestingly, in Latino communities, "sounding white" may be seen as relevant to Spanish as well. One monolingual English speaker in Fought (2003) commented, "I have like a fear of speaking Spanish because I can't roll my r's and I don't want to sound like a white boy" (2003:203). I have focused here on the views of minority ethnic groups, but there are indications that this negative view of sounding white is sometimes shared by white speakers as well, as in Bucholtz's (2001) study of the "too white" nerds. Particularly in minority ethnic groups, though, these views set up a conflict for community members who want the privileges that speaking a standard variety affords, but do not want to be negatively sanctioned in the community for sounding white.

In an earlier chapter, I discussed some of the ways that one group, middle-class African-American adults, resolves this conflict, including using a variety that is grammatically standard but includes non-standard or at least ethnically marked phonological forms. A different strategy was used by the low-income African-American students in Ogbu's (1999) study. The high-achieving students in this study countered the accusations of whiteness they drew from peers because of doing well in school or speaking a standard variety by emphasizing other traits in constructing their identities. The most frequent traits these students played up were athletic ability and acting "crazy" or being a clown. These choices are interesting in light of the ideologies about the social correlates of whiteness discussed above. The students used physicality and craziness to contrast with the intellectual orientation and rationality associated with whiteness.

Note

1. Although I have chosen not to look at this particular issue here, a systematic study of differences between settings where there are perceived racial differences and those in which there are not would be fascinating, especially from the perspective of language and ethnicity.

References

Barrett, Rusty. 1999. Indexing polyphonous identity in the speech of African American drag queens. In Bucholtz et al. 1999, pp. 313–31.

Bell, Allan. 1999. Styling the other to define the self: a study in New Zealand identity making. *Journal of Sociolinguistics* 3(4):523–41.

Blondeau, Helene, Naomi Nagy, Gillian Sankoff, and Pierrette Thibault. 2002. La Couleur locale du français L2 des anglo-montréalais. (The local coloring of French as a second language of anglophone Montreal residents.) *Aile: Acquisition et Interaction en Langue Etrangère* 17:73–100.

Brander Rasmussen, Birgit, Irene J. Nexica, Eric Klinenberg, and Matt Wray, eds. 2001. *The Making and Unmaking of Whiteness.* Durham, NC: Duke University Press.

Bucholtz, Mary. 1999. You da man: narrating the racial other in the production of white masculinity. *Journal of Sociolinguistics* 3:443–60.

Bucholtz, Mary. 2001. The whiteness of nerds: superstandard English and racial markedness. *Journal of Linguistic Anthropology* 11:84–100.

Chun, Elaine. 2001. The construction of White, Black, and Korean American identities through African American Vernacular English. *Journal of Linguistic Anthropology* 11:52–64.

Clark, John Taggart. 2003. Abstract inquiry and the patrolling of black/white borders through linguistic stylization. In Harris and Rampton 2003, pp. 303–13.

Fordham, S. and J. Ogbu. 1986. Black students' school success: coping with the burden of acting white. *Urban Review* 18:176–206.

Fought, Carmen. 2003. *Chicano English in Context.* New York: Palgrave/Macmillan Press.

Heller, Monica. 1992. The politics of codeswitching and language choice. *Journal of Multilingual and Multicultural Development* 13:123–42.

Hill, Jane H. 1998. Language, race, and White public space. *American Anthropologist* 100:680–9.

Ignatiev, Noel. 1995. *How the Irish Became White.* New York: Routledge.

Kochman, Thomas. 1981. *Black and White Styles in Conflict.* Chicago: University of Chicago Press.

Ogbu, John U. 1999. Beyond language: Ebonics, proper English, and identity in a Black-American speech community. *American Educational Research Journal* 36:147–84.

Poplack, Shana. 1989. Language status and linguistic accommodation along a linguistic border/Statut de langue et accommodation langagière le long d'une frontière linguistique. *Travaux neuchâtelois de linguistique* 14:59–91.

Rickford, John. 1999. *African American Vernacular English: Features, Evolution, Educational Implications.* Malden, MA: Blackwell.

Smitherman, Geneva. 2000. *Talkin That Talk: Language, Culture, and Education in African America.* London and New York: Routledge.

Thibault, Pierrette and Gillian Sankoff. 1993. Varying facets of linguistic insecurity: toward a comparative analysis of attitudes and the French spoken by Franco- and Anglo-Montréalais/Diverses facettes de l'insécurité linguistique: vers une analyse comparative des attitudes et du français parlé par des Franco- et des Anglo-montréalais. *Cahiers de l'Institut de Linguistique de Louvain* 19:209–18.

Trechter, Sara and Mary Bucholtz. 2001. White noise: bringing language into whiteness studies. *Journal of Linguistic Anthropology* 11(1):3–21.

Urciuoli, Bonnie. 1996. *Exposing Prejudice: Puerto Rican Experiences of Language, Race, and Class.* Boulder, CO: Westview Press.

Wolfram, Walt and Natalie Schilling-Estes. 1998. *American English.* Malden, MA: Blackwell.

Zack, N. 1993. *Race and Mixed Race.* Philadelphia: Temple University Press.

Zelinsky, Wilbur. 2001. *The Enigma of Ethnicity: Another American Dilemma.* Iowa City: University of Iowa Press.

Understanding the Text

1. According to the studies Fought summarizes, what positive characteristics tend to be associated with whiteness and white speech?

2. In what circumstances can "sounding white" be a bad thing?

Reflection and Response

3. Fought states that "The ideologies associated with linguistic aspects of whiteness often correlate with the social aspects . . . in predictable ways" (par. 11). Analyze this statement based on the stereotypes Fought discusses. How are *social* stereotypes about who white people are (middle class, educated, not particularly masculine or "cool") connected to *linguistic* stereotypes about how they speak (standard and sometimes overly correct)? In what ways might these stereotypes reinforce each other and discourage people from seeing a fuller picture of white people and their speech?

4. Have you held or encountered the perception Fought discusses that white speech is the best or "standard" form of spoken English? Keeping in mind Fought's point that "ingroup and outgroup views will differ" (par. 10), in what ways do you feel your perceptions are affected by whether or not you identify as white?

Making Connections

5. Fought notes that, because white speech is often perceived as "uncool," white speech varieties often borrow slang terms from African American Vernacular English (par. 9). Since hip hop is one of the main places where African American slang is innovated and spread, consider Fought's point in relation to H. Samy Alim's discussion of Hip Hop Nation Language (p. 74). What attitudes and features of HHNL might appeal to white youth seeking to be "cool"?

6. Fought asserts that the perception of white speech as sounding better or more educated can have extremely negative effects for speakers of nonwhite varieties of English. How does John McWhorter's "Straight Talk" (p. 125) and/ or Rusty Barrett's "Rewarding Language" (p. 130) help illustrate her point?

Straight Talk: What Harry Reid Gets about Black English

John McWhorter

In a book about the 2008 presidential election (John Heilemann and Mark Halperin's *Game Change*, HarperCollins, 2010), U.S. Senator Harry Reid was quoted as saying that Barack Obama was politically successful in part because he had "no Negro dialect, unless he wanted to have one." When this remark became public, Reid issued an apology, which Obama immediately accepted, but discussion of the controversy continued. In the column below, from the February 4, 2010, issue of the *New Republic*, Columbia University English professor John McWhorter contributes his opinion to the discussion. McWhorter has published extensively about Black English; his most recent book, about common perceptions and misconceptions of Black English, is titled *Talking Back, Talking Black: Truths about America's Lingua Franca* (Bellevue, 2017).

To rake Harry Reid over the coals about his "no Negro dialect" comment will bring to mind the Biblical passage about trying to take a speck out of someone's eye when you've got a log in your own. Pretty much all of America, black and white, feels exactly the way Harry Reid does about the way black people talk—and they aren't even worried about saying it out loud.

First of all, we need not pretend that, by "Negro dialect," Reid meant the cartoon minstrel talk of "Amos 'n' Andy." After all, why would Reid, a rational human being under any analysis, be under the impression that any black person talks like Uncle Remus, much less be surprised that one of them does not? My guess is that he said "Negro" in a passing attempt to name Black English in a detached, professional way, randomly choosing a slightly arcane and outdated term—"Negro English" was what scholars called Black English until the early 1970s. Reid likely caught wind of that terminology—he's been around a while, after all.

Second: Yes, there is such a thing as Black English. Sometimes one hears a claim that Black English is the same as white Southern English. We must always beware of stereotyping and be open to the counterintuitive, but here is an instance where we can trust our senses: There is a "Black sound." It's not just youth slang; it's sentence patterns—*Why you ain't call me?* (not a white Southernism, notice)—and a "sound," such that you'd know Morgan Freeman was black even if he were reading the phone book. The combination is what we all feel—with uncanny accuracy even without seeing faces, as linguists have found — as "sounding black." Of course, not all blacks speak Black English or have The Sound, and those that do (which is most) do to varying extents. But they do. That's what Reid meant — we all know it, and it's OK to know it.

Third: Reid's comment suggests that he associates Black English with lack of polish and low intelligence. But, before we burn him in effigy for it, or ask, "What's *that* all about?" as if we don't know, let's admit that most Americans feel like Reid does. He wasn't being a benighted "racist" holdout; he was speaking as an ordinary American. We have caught him in nothing we don't, most of us, feel ourselves.

It's a love-hate relationship we have with black speech. On the one   5
hand, we associate it with emotional honesty, vernacular warmth, and sex — Marvin Gaye would not have had a hit with "Why Don't We Venture to Consummate Our Relationship?" or even "Let's Have Sex," instead of "Let's Get It On." Yet it's not a dialect — a sound — that we associate with explaining Greek verbs or cosines or engaging in complex reasoning. Black English sounds cool, and even hot, and maybe "sharp" — but note that sharp is what you call someone whom you wouldn't necessarily *expect* to be smart . . . and whom you don't actually think is all *that* smart.

That's a shame, because Black English is as systematic as standard English, and what we hear as "mistakes" are just variations, not denigrations. Try telling a French person that double negatives are "illogical" — South Central's *I ain't seen nobody* is Lyon's *Je n'ai vu personne.* The "unconjugated" *be* in a sentence like *Folks be tryin' it out* is used in a very particular way, to indicate habits rather than current events, making explicit something that standard English leaves to context.

But, in the real world, it's very hard to hear it that way. You can get a sense of it with linguistic training, or curling up with *Spoken Soul*, by Stanford's John Rickford, and *African American English*, by University of Massachusetts Amherst's Lisa Green, but, otherwise, Black English will always sound to most people like mistakes, in all of its warmth. We also feel this way about Southern "hick" grammar — race is not the only factor here. In both cases, we spontaneously demote a dialect born in illiteracy. It's a weird intersection: Unlettered speech is not "broken." The most "primitive" societies' languages are the ones that are the most complicated; often, the backwater dialects of a language are harder than the standard. Out in the sticks in Bulgaria, there are often three ways to say *the* instead of one.

> "Black English is as systematic as standard English, and what we hear as 'mistakes' are just variations, not denigrations."

Of course, that's all very nice, but real life is that Harry Reid hears black speech as lowly. Yet so do black people, as often as not. In 1996 and 1997, during the Oakland controversy over whether Black English should be used in classrooms as a transition to standard English, black people were laughing as loud as anyone at the idea that "Ebonics" is "a language." Or, over the transom recently, I got a copy of a presentation that James Meredith, who was the first black person admitted to the University of Mississippi and caught hell for it physically and emotionally, has given to young black audiences. In his introduction, Meredith spells it out:

Most people in this room use a lot of Black English and a little Proper English.

Anyone who wants to become an intellectual giant must learn and use a lot of Proper English and as little Black English as possible.

I am not going to argue with anyone about the matter. You can do what you want to do.

However, I will tell you that anyone who continues to use a lot of Black English will never become an intellectual giant.

So Meredith would surely hear it as a plus that Obama has no trace of what a man of his years likely has been known to call, in all seriousness, Negro dialect.

Fourth: Reid's feelings about Black English are likely couched in a thoroughly compassionate position. Here's a guess, based on what I have heard countless people of all colors say: "Black people use bad grammar so much because they were brought here as slaves and denied education. The bad grammar holds on today because too many blacks still have bad schooling, and they pass it down the generations. They would be best off if society allowed them the education and opportunities to get rid of their bad grammar. It's not their fault."

There are all kinds of things that are off here, if we are inclined to 10 go pointy-headed. Humans can be bidialectal as well as bilingual and, therefore, can speak both standard and Black English—as Obama does, and as Reid acknowledged. Plus, the dialect is now felt by blacks as a cultural hallmark, amid a loving ambivalence about its "ungrammaticality." And so on—but most of this is for seminars. Back to, as always, real life. I know so very many black people who would agree with the above hypothetical quotation from Reid—many of them deeply dedicated in assorted ways to black uplift. Are they immoral? Do they hate their own people? No—upon which we can give Harry Reid a break.

Fifth: We have to really listen to what Reid said instead of getting carried away over the tangy, backward flavor of the one word "Negro." In mentioning that Obama doesn't speak in "dialect," Reid acknowledged something many blacks are hot and quick to point out: Not all black people use Black English. OK, they don't — and Reid knows. He didn't seem surprised that Obama can sound not black when he talks — he was just pointing out that Obama is part of the subset of blacks who can. He knows there is such a subset. Lesson learned.

Indeed, Reid implied that black dialect is less prestigious than standard, such that not speaking it made Obama more likely to become president. That is, he implied what we all think, too: Black English is, to the typical American ear, warm, honest — and mistaken. If that's wrong, OK — but since when are most Americans, including black ones, at all shy about dissing Black English? And who among us — including black people — thinks that someone with what I call a "black-cent," who occasionally pops up with double negatives and things like *aks*, could be elected president, whether it's fair or not? Reid, again, deserves no censure for what he said unless we're ready to censure ourselves, too.

Inevitably, there will be reminiscences of Joe Biden's comment about Obama being "articulate."° I'm less politic on that term, as applied to black people who have no reason not to be articulate. A recent favorite: Someone writing me a letter about one of my Teaching Company lectures on linguistics praised me for "enjoying yourself up there so confidently speaking standard English" — as if I have to take a deep breath and "wield" standard English and feel like I'm a pretty special fella for being able to, with my "native" ghetto inflections and expressions turning up in my speech when I'm tired.

But this isn't the same thing. Reid implied that Black English is lesser than standard English and that it's therefore good that Obama can speak without sounding black. This is not about whether black people have to sweat to speak standard English; it's about whether Black English is as good as standard English. Most of America, *black as well as white*, is at the exact same point in understanding vernacular speech and its proper evaluation as Reid is.

For which reason most of America should leave him alone about this 15 and move on.

Joe Biden's comment about Obama being "articulate": In early 2007, when both Biden and Obama were running for the Democratic presidential nomination, Biden described Obama to a *New York Observer* reporter as "the first mainstream African-American who is articulate and bright and clean and a nice-looking guy."

Understanding the Text

1. Why does McWhorter believe Americans should not condemn Harry Reid for his statement? If Reid is not to blame, who or what is?

2. What does McWhorter mean when he says we have "a love-hate relationship . . . with black speech" (par. 5)?

3. McWhorter references another controversial comment about Barack Obama's dialect, Joe Biden's praise of Obama for being "articulate" (par. 14). Why does he consider this comment worse than Reid's?

Reflection and Response

4. McWhorter expresses a number of conflicting ideas in this piece. For instance, he says that Black English is "systematic" and logical (par. 6), but that, "in the real world, it's very hard to hear it that way" (par. 7). He says that, in "real life," Black English is often seen as a result of poor education, even though, if we take a "pointy-headed" (a derogatory term for "intellectual") approach, we can see the cultural importance and heritage of the dialect (par. 10). Why do you think McWhorter holds such conflicting beliefs simultaneously? How do they align, or not, with your own views on Black English?

5. McWhorter expresses doubt that anyone who makes frequent use of Black English features like double negatives or *aks* could be elected president. Think of some examples of prominent public figures who are black. How strong are the Black English features of their speech? Do you see differences depending on what sorts of roles or jobs they have (say, politicians versus entertainers)? Do your examples support McWhorter's views?

Making Connections

6. McWhorter asserts that "variations" in dialect are often misinterpreted as "mistakes," as in the statement that "double negatives are 'illogical'" (par. 6). How would Rusty Barrett ("Rewarding Language," p. 130) argue against this view of double negatives? Use Barrett's article to explain why the use of double negatives in English is so widely believed to be illogical.

7. McWhorter claims that many of the general public's feelings about Black English's "warmth" and "mistakes" also apply to Southern speech (par. 7). Use Dennis Preston's "Some Plain Facts about Americans and Their Language" (p. 97) and/or Cheryl Boucher et al.'s "Perceptions of Competency as a Function of Accent" (p. 102) to provide support for McWhorter's point.

Rewarding Language: Language Ideology and Prescriptive Grammar

Rusty Barrett

Rusty Barrett is a linguistics professor at the University of Kentucky who studies a variety of social aspects of language. The excerpt below comes from his section of the coauthored book *Other People's English: Code-Meshing, Code-Switching, and African American Literacy* (Teachers College Press, 2014), which also includes sections by the teachers and scholars Vershawn Ashanti Young, Y'Shanda Young-Rivera, and Kim Brian Lovejoy. In this piece, Barrett challenges misconceptions about African American English, as well as other "undervalued" varieties of English, and encourages readers to develop a familiarity with its rules and logic.

First day I walk in the door, there she be, red-hot and hollering with the colic, fighting that bottle like it's a rotten turnip.

—KATHRYN STOCKETT, *THE HELP*

Like numerous sentences in Kathryn Stockett's *The Help*, the sentence above contains an example of what linguists call *invariant be,* a form of the verb "to be" that does not have "variant" forms such as *is, are,* or *am.* Although the use of invariant be is one of the features that distinguish African American English from other dialects of American English, it is obvious that the sentence above was not produced by a speaker of African American English. Although it would certainly be reasonable to say that Stockett's use of African American English is "wrong," the book has been extremely successful, spending months on the best-seller lists and being made into a major motion picture. Despite the fact that her African American English is inaccurate or incorrect, Stockett has definitely been rewarded for the quality of her writing. In other contexts, however, the use of African American English in writing is rarely rewarded. A child who writes in African American English in school is likely to be told that their writing is inappropriate for academic contexts, even when the child gets the grammar of African American English right. Why is a college-educated White woman rewarded for using African American English incorrectly in her writing, while an African American child who writes in perfectly correct African American English is likely to be reprimanded, corrected, or asked to switch it out for another more appropriate version of English?

All forms of human language are based on rules of grammar that children learn when they are very young (before they begin school). Like any other language (or dialect), African American English uses rules that determine when it is possible to use a form like invariant be.

In African American English, the use of invariant be marks habitual or repeated actions (*She be working all the time; She be in her office every day*), while actions in the regular present are marked without any form of *to be* (*She working today; She in her office now*). Actions that occurred in the past are marked by a conjugated form of

"Why is a college-educated White woman rewarded for using African American English incorrectly in her writing, while an African American child who writes in perfectly correct African American English is likely to be reprimanded?"

to be (*She was working yesterday; She was in her office this morning*). Following these rules of the grammar of African American English, a native speaker could say, *First day I walk in the door, there she <u>was</u>*, but it is highly unlikely that an actual speaker of African American English would ever say or write Stockett's sentence. This is because the sentence above violates the grammatical rules that speakers of African American English know. The first part of the sentence *First day I walk in the door* makes it clear that this action only occurred one time, while the use of *be* in the second part of the sentence clearly indicates that the action was repeated a number of times (as in *every time I walk in, there she be*). There are numerous examples of such sentences in *The Help: Today be Labor Day . . . He be dead . . . There be two white ladies talking,* and so on. From such examples, it is clear that Stockett does not know the grammar of African American English. In other words, she be getting it wrong all over the place.

Despite her persistent errors, however, some reviewers have praised Stockett for her authentic representation of African American speech. In her essay in the *Washington Post,* Sybil Steinberg (2009) writes "one of Stockett's accomplishments is reproducing African American vernacular. . . ." Thus Stockett is not alone in her misinformation about African American English grammar. This ignorance extends to her editors, the overwhelming majority of reviewers, numerous readers, and those working to adapt the novel into a screenplay. This is not surprising, as the grammar of African American English is rarely taught outside of specialized linguistics courses. Stockett's mistakes go largely unnoticed because people are unaware that the language she is trying to depict even *has* regular rule-governed grammar.

Understanding why Stockett's incorrect African American English 5 can be rewarded while the African American English of actual speakers can be denigrated requires an understanding of *language ideology,* or the dominant set of commonly held folk beliefs concerning language. Like the belief that African American English has no grammar (and is just "wrong"), language ideologies are not based on linguistic facts, but are primarily forms of social prejudice. This section discusses the linguistic facts that challenge the language ideologies that marginalize students who speak anything other than Standard English.

All Languages Are Based on Rules

The ignorance of African American English grammar that leads Stockett's incorrect grammar to go unnoticed results from the first belief we will consider, the belief that only Standard English has rules. But all varieties of all languages are based on rules. Even what we now are referring to as *code-meshing*, the combination of multiple dialects or languages in a single sentence, is based on rules. The ability to speak language is a basic part of being human, and all children are born with the ability to fully learn the rules of the language spoken around them. This genetic ability to acquire language is natural, like breathing or swallowing, and has nothing to do with intelligence or cognitive abilities. Regardless of their intellectual abilities, all children learn the grammatical rules of the language they hear around them. When children begin to write, they often continue to follow the rules of the language they have learned. "Errors" in writing are more likely to simply reflect different patterns of grammar that follow different sets of rules.

Linguists (like me) study the grammar that children learn regardless of what people think about that grammar (or the language ideologies involving that grammar). The approach of linguistics (often called *descriptive grammar*) is to study the rules that speakers know in order to understand both the ways in which grammar is organized in the human mind and the ways in which these rules interact with social and cultural factors. This differs from the approach to language typically taught in schools (called *prescriptive grammar*), which assumes that some forms of language are inherently superior to other varieties. From the prescriptive perspective, undervalued varieties are inappropriate for academic purposes and only one variety (the standard) is correct in professional and educational settings. The rules that people follow when they speak other varieties go largely ignored, as seen in the lack of awareness regarding the use of *be* in *The Help*.

When looking at language from a descriptive perspective, it is clear that all speakers of all languages follow rules. In order to avoid applying value judgments onto different ways of speaking, linguists avoid using terms like *wrong* or *incorrect,* and given the context of the present study, we might even extend this avoidance to using terms like *standard* and *nonstandard, appropriate* or *inappropriate,* because of their ranking connotations, suggesting languages can be superior or inferior. Instead, we use the concept of *grammatically* to distinguish between forms that follow the rules of a language and those that don't follow rules (forms that speakers would probably never produce). Thus forms that follow the rules are *grammatical* and those that break the rules are *ungrammatical* (linguists mark ungrammatical sentences with an asterisk).

The rules of any language (or dialect) determine which sentences are grammatical and which are ungrammatical. For many speakers in the South, for example, sentences with two modal auxiliaries like *I might could help you* or *I might should go home* are grammatical. However, there are rules governing the order of the auxiliaries, so that sentences like **I could might help you* or **I should might go* would be ungrammatical, and speakers wouldn't say them. Similarly, in the Midwest, *Are you coming with?* is grammatical while **Are you sitting with?* is ungrammatical (see Wolfram & Schilling-Estes, 1998). When linguists talk about the *rules* of language, they mean these patterns of (un)grammaticality.

Ideas about "Correct" Language Are Forms of Social Prejudice

Language ideologies, including ideas about prescriptive grammar, are 10 primarily about social stereotypes and have little to do with the actual structure of language that is seen as "incorrect." The exact same linguistic form may be considered "correct" in one "standard" language and "incorrect" in another. For example, the failure to pronounce [h] at the beginning of words is always "incorrect" in Standard British English ("Received Pronunciation"), but is always "correct" in Standard French. In American English, we find variation where the pronunciation of [h] is "correct" for some words (*house*) and "incorrect" for other words (*herb*). When an American pronounces *herb* without an initial [h] sound, it is considered correct even though the same pronunciation would be considered "incorrect" in Britain. Similarly, American English uses *gotten* as the past participle of *get* while British English uses *got*. Although many Americans would find a sentence like *Sue had got laundry supplies for Valentine's Day* before "incorrect," the sentence is "correct" for British English.

Consider the use of multiple negative markers in a single sentence (e.g., *I don't see no book*) in standard varieties of English and Spanish. In Standard English, more than one negative marker is "incorrect" while the rules of Spanish require multiple negators (e.g., *Yo no dije nada,* literally, "I didn't say nothing"). It cannot be the case that using more than

A 2013 *One Big Happy* comic, by Rick Detorie. Here, the character James displays his fluency in multiple dialects; notice how he can work effectively with both single and double negatives, and with both *ain't* and more "standard" conjugations of *to be*. Ruthie, meanwhile, does not realize that the sentences she judges "incorrect" and "correct" are identical in meaning and communicative effectiveness.
Go Comics/Creators Syndicate, Inc.

one negative marker is inherently inferior, as the Spanish pattern is more common among the world's languages and is generally seen as "correct" in languages other than English. Yet, when speakers of Chicano English use the type of negation found in Spanish (as in "He's not doing nothing"), it is considered "incorrect." Thus linguistic ideologies are arbitrary in that the same form may be "correct" in one language and "incorrect" in another. There is nothing inherently "right" or "wrong" about any given linguistic form. Rather, ideas about "right" and "wrong" are forms of social prejudice in which forms of language associated with marginalized speakers are typically "wrong" while the linguistic practices of social elites go unquestioned.

There are a number of linguistic studies that demonstrate that ideas about "correctness" are based on social prejudice rather than linguistic facts. For example, a number of studies have examined *reverse linguistic stereotyping,* in which assumptions about a speaker's identity distort the evaluation of that speaker's language (see Kang and Rubin, 2009 for a review). In one such study (Rubin 1992), students listened to the same recording (made by a White woman from Ohio) and were shown a picture of the supposed speaker. One group saw a White face and one group saw an Asian face. The students who saw the Asian face reported hearing an accent and had difficulty remembering what the speaker said (presumably because the speaker's accent made it difficult to follow what they were saying). Kang and Rubin (2009) found that listening comprehension drops by an average of 12% when students believe they were listening to a non-native speaker (even though they were actually listening to a native English speaker). This extends to writing, as teachers are more likely to find problems with a student's grammar if they believe they are reading something written by a minority child. So, prescriptive language ideology has little to do with language itself and everything to do with the social identity of language users.

Given that they are primarily forms of prejudice, it is not surprising that prescriptive language ideologies may have serious consequences for speakers of undervalued varieties. Children who speak undervalued varieties often find themselves in classrooms in which the language they know is deemed *wrong* or *inappropriate*. Even when answering correctly, these students are likely to be treated as if they are inappropriate simply because they answered in a different dialect. Speakers of undervalued varieties must continually monitor their own speech to match others' views of what is appropriate or acceptable in any given context.

The anxiety produced by being inappropriate simply because the rules of your language don't match those of your teacher continues even among successful students who go on to enroll in college. Several years ago, I was teaching introductory linguistics to a large lecture class at the University of Michigan. On the first day, as I explained the difference between prescriptive and descriptive linguistics, one of the students raised his hand and asked, "Does this mean we don't have to write proper on our exams?" I replied that it didn't matter what grammar students use because I was interested in what students knew rather than the dialect they happened to speak. That afternoon, the remaining 30 seats in the class filled and there were numerous students outside my office begging to get into the class. They were almost all African American or Middle Eastern American students who had heard rumors of a class where students weren't judged on their grammar. I was shocked by the number of students with anxieties about "proper grammar" strong enough to lead them to enroll in a course they weren't necessarily interested in simply because they knew they would not be judged on the basis of their dialect.

The anxiety of self-monitoring also extends beyond the classroom. 15 In conferences with teachers, job interviews, discussions with doctors or lawyers, and countless other daily interactions, speakers of undervalued varieties must watch not only what they say, but how they say it. Like other forms of prejudice, the idea that Standard English is inherently better than other dialects places an unfair burden on speakers of undervalued varieties, who must continually accommodate those who hold negative attitudes toward them and/or their dialects.

Good Writing Does Not Depend on "Correct" Grammar

Within prescriptive language ideology, prejudice against speakers of undervalued varieties often comes with arguments that only the standard variety is able to express nuanced meanings, encode logical thought, or produce good writing. Yet again, none of these beliefs has a valid basis in linguistic facts. All varieties of all languages are capable of expressing nuanced or subtle distinctions in meaning. Consider the case of invariant be. The Standard English sentence *She is working* could mean that she is working at this very moment or that she has a job and works regularly. This ambiguity does not occur in African American English, where these two meanings are expressed through different grammatical forms, *She working* (right now) and *She be working* (on a regular basis). Here, the meanings that are encoded in the grammar of African American English are certainly more nuanced than those found in Standard English.

Such patterns can be found in all undervalued varieties. For example, in my own English (from rural Arkansas), there is a distinction between *y'all's* (pronounced "yalz") and *y'alls'* (yalziz) that distinguishes individual and collective possession. Thus, if there are two books jointly owned by two individuals, I would use *y'all's books* to refer to the books that *y'all* own together. In contrast, if the two books are each owned separately by two individuals, I would use *y'alls'* to indicate that each of the two books belongs to a different one of *y'all*. This is a very subtle distinction that is easily expressed in my undervalued English, but requires a great deal of explanation to convey in Standard English. Thus it is not the case that Standard English is somehow more nuanced than other varieties.

The idea that Standard English is more "logical" than other varieties is equally problematic. In Standard English, verbs in the present tense are marked with a suffix +*s* if the subject is third-person singular (*he, she, it*). If the subject isn't third-person (*I, you, we, they*), there is no marking on the verb. Thus we have *I write*, but *She writes*. In terms of logic, the +*s* marker is highly illogical. Given that the subject noun (or pronoun) marks third person, the additional suffix on the verb adds no additional information to the meaning of a sentence. Thus the suffix in *writes* is entirely redundant and superfluous.

In terms of logic, it would be much more logical if the rules of Standard English didn't bother to add this additional suffix since it would always be obvious that the subject was third person without the suffix. Just as we don't get confused by having the same form of the verb in *I write* and in *you write*, we wouldn't be confused if we also used *she write*. In fact, this logical change in English can be observed in many undervalued varieties, where this +*s* suffix is optional (or doesn't occur at all), so that the verb doesn't change to mark third person (e.g., *I write, she write*).

All languages have forms that could be seen as more or less logical [20] when compared to those found in other languages. Verbs like *walk* that take regular forms across tenses (*walk, walked, have walked*) could be seen as more logical than verbs like *sing* (*sang, have sung*) or *be* (*am, is, are, was, were, have been*). The grammatical patterns across dialects do not suggest that any variety is somehow more logical than another.

The argument that good writing cannot occur except in Standard English does not hold water either. The use of multiple language varieties is a hallmark of American literature. Would it really make *Huckleberry Finn* a better book if it were written entirely in Standard English? Because language is closely tied to individual identity and personal experience, great writers know that the use of undervalued varieties is often the best way (if not the only way) to accurately convey specific ideas, experiences, and emotions.

Therefore, going back to our original example, it is also hard to imagine that *The Help* could have been written entirely in Standard English, although knowing the grammar of African American English would have, in my opinion, certainly helped. Good writing then emerges from a writer's ability to convey human experience, regardless of whether or not the language used to convey that experience is considered "right" or "wrong." Any approach to teaching writing that imposes a single type of grammar, regardless of whether that teacher says that such a grammar is more appropriate in this setting rather than that one, is bound to restrict students' ability to accurately express aspects of their identify and experience.

Conclusion

To summarize, all varieties of all languages have regular, rule-governed grammar. It doesn't make sense to assume that the rules of one variety are somehow inherently better than those found in some other variety. As all languages are basically equal in their regularity and their ability to convey complex thought, views about "right" and "wrong" forms of language are primarily forms of social prejudice, and this might rightly extend, as Young (2009) argues, to views about "appropriate" or "inappropriate" forms. We will see that there are also rules that govern the ways in which speakers/writers code-mesh, or combine multiple dialects or different languages. Just as with ideologies that denigrate undervalued varieties of English, beliefs that criticize speakers for moving between two dialects/languages can be seen primarily as forms of social prejudice with little basis in linguistic fact.

References

Kang, O., & Rubin, D. (2009). Reverse linguistic stereotyping: Measuring the effect of listener expectations on speech evaluation. *Journal of Language and Social Psychology, 28*(4), 441–456.

Rubin, D. L. (1992). Nonlanguage factors affecting undergraduates' judgments of nonnative English-speaking teaching assistants. *Research in Higher Education, 33*(4), 511–531.

Steinberg, S. (2009). Book review: *The help* by Kathryn Stockett. *The Washington Post.* Retrieved from http://www.washingtonpost.com/wpdyn/content/article/2009/03/31/AR2009033103552.html

Stockett, K. (2009). *The help.* New York: Putnam.

Wolfram, W., & Schilling-Estes, N. (1998). *American English: dialects and variation.* Malden, MA: Blackwell.

Young, V. A. (2009). "Nah, we straight": An argument against code-switching. *JAC, 29*(1/2), 49–76.

Understanding the Text

1. What are some of the rules of African American English that differ from the rules of Standard English?

2. How do the language ideologies Barrett describes explain the success of the book *The Help*, in spite of its incorrect use of African American English grammar?

3. How does a linguist's definition of *grammatical* differ from the typical definitions we might be used to?

Reflection and Response

4. Barrett asserts that all languages have rules, and all children grow up learning those rules. How would you describe the rules of a language you grew up speaking with your family or neighborhood friends? Were any of those rules different from the rules of a "standard" form?

5. Note Barrett's criticism of the use of terms such as *wrong*, *incorrect*, or even *nonstandard* to describe certain varieties of language (par. 8). Why do you think he prefers the term *undervalued*?

Making Connections

6. Barrett describes a study in which participants listening to a white person's speech heard an Asian accent if they were shown a picture of an Asian speaker. What does this say about how our expectations and prejudices influence what we hear? How might this study help explain the experiences of Amy Tan and her mother ("Mother Tongue," p. 24)?

7. Barrett claims that "Language ideologies, including ideas about prescriptive grammar, are primarily about social stereotypes" (par. 10). What evidence of

social stereotyping can you find in the examples of prescriptivist views that Robert MacNeil and William Cran include in "The Language Wars" (p. 201)?

8. Barrett asserts that "good writing" can be done in both standard and non-standard English, and many acclaimed writers do indeed use a variety of forms. Locate one of these two pairs of poems (all poems are readily available online):

- June Jordan: "1977: Poem for Miss Fannie Lou Hamer" and "It's Hard to Keep a Clean Shirt Clean"
- James Baldwin: "Some Days (For Paula)" and "The Giver (For Berdis)"

Which of the two poems in your pair shows more use of African American English grammar? What specific grammatical features do you note in that poem? How would you describe the differences in voice and feeling between the poem with more African American English grammar and the one with less?

Intersecting Variables and Perceived Sexual Orientation in Men

Kathryn Campbell-Kibler

Kathryn Campbell-Kibler, a sociolinguist at The Ohio State University, is interested in how specific features of language lead us to specific perceptions of people — for instance, how someone who says *runnin'* and *thinkin'*, as opposed to *running* and *thinking*, might be perceived as less formal or professional. This process, where something we see or hear in language points us to a particular assumption or interpretation, is called *indexicality* (think literally of an index in a book, where each entry points you somewhere else). Some of Campbell-Kibler's work, like the piece below (originally from the Spring 2011 issue of *American Speech*), looks at how indexicality works with issues of men's sexuality. What specific things do we hear in a man's speech, she inquires, that point our brains to the conclusion that he "sounds gay"? Note that, as with other readings in this chapter, Campbell-Kibler's focus is on perception rather than fact. She is not looking for the features that are most common in gay men's speech, but rather the features that most commonly make listeners assume someone is gay.

ABSTRACT. Sociolinguistic styles tie linguistic resources together into clusters and link them to social contexts of times, groups, places, and activities. Perceptions of masculinity and sexual orientation represent a well-studied area on sociolinguistic perception, offering many variables with potentially relevant social meanings. This study examines social perceptions of guises created by intersecting three masculinity-relevant variables: pitch, /s/-fronting or backing, and (ING). First, 110 online respondents provided descriptions and naturalness ratings of speech samples that were digitially modified to include the different variants; next, 175 respondents rated the speakers on six-point scales based on the terms "smart," "knowledgeable," "masculine," "gay," "friendly," "laid-back," "country," "educated," and "confident." The results showed that /s/-fronting carries strong social meaning across multiple speakers and other linguistic cues, making speakers sound less masculine, more gay and less competent. As documented elsewhere, use of the (ING) variants *-ing* and *-in* made speakers sound more or less competent, respectively. The combination of /s/-fronting and (ING), and, independently, /s/-backing, showed more complex effects, shifting relationships between multiple percepts. Taken together, these results provide some support for style-based sociolinguistic models, but also underline the need for more sophisticated statistical treatments of covariation in social perception.

Not everything has to have the same flavor, because style comes from mixing all of that up.

—STACEY LONDON, *WHAT NOT TO WEAR*

The concept of sociolinguistic style (in the sense of Arnold et al. 1993; Campbell-Kibler et al. 2006; Coupland 2007) refers to clusters of linguistic resources that combine to form a recognized whole, belonging to a social context, including extralinguistic resources like clothing, bodily hexis, and so on, as well as times, places, and physical and personal characteristics. Styles often require multiple resources to be recognized, but through the process of bricolage° (Hebdige 1979), individual resources or smaller clusters may be detached from their original style and deployed in a new context, thus incorporating social aspects of the original style into the performance.

To date, the majority of research on sociolinguistic style from this perspective has focused on linguistic production, noting instances where linguistic features with similar social characteristics co-occur (Arnold et al. 1993) or where features with independent meanings appear to be deliberately combined to create a meaningful package (Podesva 2006). Related to but independent of these questions about style in linguistic performance are questions about style in perception. Most fundamentally, is style a relevant construct for sociolinguistic perception; in other words, do listeners forming social images based on speech mentally tie certain cues to one another into sets? If this were the case, we might expect, for example, that some social effects only appear, or are enhanced, when multiple features appear together, as in clothing styles, where, say, a bowler can help to signify a mime, but only in the presence of other items. Alternatively, we might see effects triggered to the same degree by either or both of two features which function as carriers of a shared style. Once someone has donned a clown nose, wig, or shoes, the clown has been invoked: it does not gradually creep up as items are added.

Previous perceptual work has documented a tendency for linguistic features to contribute variably based on context (Campbell-Kibler 2007) and has shown that some social reactions may require multiple features

bricolage: generally, bringing together bits and pieces from a variety of places (sometimes compared to making a quilt). Hebdige uses the term specifically to talk about using these bits and pieces in a context different from the original.

to change (Levon 2007). The current study uses a social evaluation task to elicit listener perceptions of guises° representing four linguistic features with related social associations in the speech of four men similar in age and education but distinct in regional accent and other aspects of self-presentation. Two of the features, /s/-fronting and (ING), are independent social objects that do not require specific other correlates for social comprehensibility. In contrast, /s/-backing is more context-dependent, causing only a single ambiguous speaker to sound more "country," while the last feature, pitch change, though widely discussed, has little impact on perceptions. The results support the view that styles are not only formed by clusters of resources, but are also tied to clustered social meanings, which presents serious methodological challenges for the perceptual study of style.

Gay Speech

One of the most developed areas of sociolinguistic perception research, 5 the "gay speech" literature, has sought for more than 30 years to understand the acoustic cues that inspire listeners (both gay and straight) to identify a man's voice as gay-sounding and/or effeminate. Success in this endeavor has been uneven, but some acoustic areas, notably pitch or pitch range (Gaudio 1994; Smyth, Jacobs, and Rogers 2003), sibilant° production (Crist 1997; Linville 1998; Levon 2007), and vowel quality (Pierrehumbert et al. 2004; Munson and Zimmerman 2006), have been identified as potentially relevant. This pursuit has also come under critique, particularly for the sometimes essentialist° nature of the questions asked and the conclusions drawn (Kulick 2000). Despite the very real dangers of reifying° gay men's speech, the widespread phenomenon of speakers perceiving "gay accents" represents a perceptual question worthy of investigation independent of its relationship to the observed sociolinguistic behavior of self-identified gay men.

---

guises: In what is called a "matched guise test," linguistic researchers select a particular word, phrase, or longer passage, and then record that selection being spoken in several different ways (usually with distinctive characteristics of different dialects). Each different recorded version is called a *guise*. Asking listeners to rate one or more of the guises allows researchers to compare listener attitudes toward different dialects.
sibilant: a hissing sound made by pushing air through the teeth. In English, this category includes the sounds *s*, *sh*, and *z*.
essentialist: the idea that a particular thing has a single underlying truth made up of mandatory characteristics. In this case, an essentialist attitude toward gay speech would mean that there is one single way of "talking gay."
reifying: to make something seem real, often more real than it actually is.

David Thorpe, director of the documentary *Do I Sound Gay?*, pictured at the 2014 Toronto International Film Festival. *Do I Sound Gay?* explores the stereotype of the "gay voice" and the experience of living with a voice that "sounds gay."
Jeff Vespa/Getty Images

Much of the research on gay speech has sought direct connection between specific acoustic cues and actual or perceived sexual orientation. Podesva, Roberts, and Campbell-Kibler (2001) pointed out that gay men, like straight men, participate in different subcultures, leading to a range of linguistic performances that may be recognizable as gay, but also as young or old, mainstream or rebellious, and many other qualities. Linguistic cues are tied, not to sexual orientation, but to recognizable ways of being in the world—in other words, to styles. Sexual orientation merely represents one piece of information that may (or may not) be implicated in a stylistic performance.

Four features associated with sexual orientation and masculinity and amenable to large-scale automated manipulation were selected for the study: pitch, /s/-fronting, /s/-backing,[1] and (ING). Gaudio (1994) discusses the belief that gay men's pitch and pitch range differ from that of straight men, stemming from the expectation that gay men adopt linguistic patterns presumed to apply to women. It is true that pitch differs between men and women overall, in part due to physiology, and in part due to gendered linguistic choices adopted well before puberty (Sachs 1975). However, Gaudio rightly critiques the assumption that heterosexual men and women might represent a "real" form of masculinity or femininity, respectively, from which gay men and lesbians might diverge by "imitating" the other gender. Indeed, Gaudio's participants showed no use of pitch in their (largely accurate) assessments of which of his talkers were gay or straight, nor in any of their other social evaluations. Similarly, Smyth, Jacobs, and Rogers (2003) found no effect of pitch on perceptions of sexual orientation or gender. In both of these cases, pitch variation was examined as part of the naturally varying nature of voices across speakers. Levon (2007) looked at pitch more closely by manipulating the speech of two speakers (one gay and one straight) and found it to influence perceptions, but only when combined with manipulation of sibilant length.

Two features, /s/-fronting and backing, with a more neutral alternate, form a single variable in the study. /s/-fronting has received little attention, despite being the other widely known sound-based stereotype regarding the speech of gay men, to the extent that it is known as the "gay lisp." An exception is Van Borsel et al. (2009), who suggest a correlation in the speech of Dutch men between sexual orientation and fronted tokens of /s/ as coded by listeners, although Munson (2010) notes that this is not evidence that Dutch-speaking gay men produce fronted /s/ tokens at a greater frequency, given that listeners, familiar with the stereotype, may have misanalyzed the /s/ tokens under the influence of other acoustic cues. It does support an association between the feature and sexual orientation, whether in the speech of the talkers or the minds of the listeners. Other work has investigated sibilant length, including Levon (2007), as noted above, who found that shortening the sibilants of a gay-sounding male speaker decreased

---

/s/-fronting, /s/-backing: pronouncing the s sound with the tongue farther front or back in the mouth than average. A fronted s sounds a little more like a th and tends to be perceived as a "lisp"; a backed s sounds a little more like sh.

percepts of gayness only when combined also with flattened pitch range. Linville (1998) found correlations to actual and perceived sexual orientation based on both peak /s/ frequency and /s/ duration. Backing of /s/ and /z/ has not been discussed in relation to sexuality, although it has been tied to gendered styles in Glasgow (Stuart-Smith 2007). One of the speakers used in the present study had notable back /s/ production, apparently as part of a marked Southern and masculine style, inspiring the inclusion of this variable, to see what role his sibilant productions actually played in his style and how they would impact other styles.

The final variable is (ING), the alternation at the end of multisyllabic words between word-final [ɪn] or [ən], here referred to as *-in*, on the one hand, and [ɪŋ], here called *-ing*, on the other. This variable has primarily been studied with respect to social class and to formality, both concepts which bear complicated relationships to masculinity (Connell 1995). The first sociolinguistic study on (ING), Fischer (1958), explored its connection to masculinity, showing that not only were boys more likely to favor *-in* forms than the girls, but the (ING) use of individual boys differed. Specifically, a well-behaved boy tended to use more *-ing* tokens, while a "typical" boy (charming and badly behaved) favored *-in*. Subsequent work provided general, but not exceptionless, support for the claim that *-in* use is higher among men (Labov 1966; Trudgill 1974), but it was not until Kiesling (1998) that the issue of (ING) and differing types or styles of masculinity was revisited. Kiesling, examining language use in a fraternity, found that a particular style of rebellious working-class male identity was associated, not with greater *-in* use across the board, but with a refusal to decrease *-in* use in the more formal setting of the fraternity meeting.

All three of these variables were manipulated in the recorded 10 speech of four men from two different regions within the United States (California and North Carolina). Social evaluations of the guises were collected to examine whether and how the social impact of each variable changed when it was presented in combination with the variants of the other, in addition to the overall speech styles of the four men.

Methods

The stimuli for this study were adapted from those used in Campbell-Kibler (2007), in which clips of eight speakers were manipulated to create (ING) guises. The current study used the recordings of four male speakers, two from California and two from North Carolina, taken from informal interviews. Speakers returned for a second recording session, during which they produced alternate tokens° of -*in* and -*ing,* which were then spliced into excerpts of the original speech using Praat° to create matched pairs that differed only in tokens of (ING). In each of the 16 pairs, one contained only -*in* tokens and one contained only -*ing* tokens, all manipulated regardless of the (ING) use in the original utterance.

The recordings were then annotated to mark the /s/ and /z/ tokens, and three *s/z* pairs were prepared, representing mid /s/ production, noticeably fronted, and noticeably backed. The mid tokens were extracted from the recordings of one of the North Carolina speakers, who had in previous research been perceived neither as Southern nor as gay (Campbell-Kible 2007). The backed tokens were extracted from the speech of the other North Carolina speaker, Robert, whose /s/ production had already been a source of commentary. Finally, the fronted tokens were produced in the lab by a fellow linguist. Acoustic characteristics of the tokens are given in table 1. These tokens were then spliced in for every /s/ and /z/ token in every recording, after being manipulated to match the original in intensity and length.

The pitch manipulation created a "high pitch" variant by multiplying the pitch value at each point by 1.25, a value selected based on trial and error as the maximum manipulation that sounded natural. The primary effect was to raise the pitch, but the pitch variability was also slightly increased. The original intent had been to include pitch variability as an independent variable, but automatically widening these monotonic speech samples yielded results too bizarre to use. These manipulations of (ING) (two variants), /s/ and /z/ quality (three variants), and pitch (two levels) were applied to two excerpts for each of four speakers, giving a total of 96 individual recordings.

Response data were collected in two phases, both administered over the Internet. Participants were solicited through advertisements and announcements on Facebook and Craigslist. The first phase served as a pilot, to check the naturalness and believability of the manipulations and to generate descriptive words and phrases that listeners found relevant for these voices. Each listener heard a single recording from each of the four speakers and was asked to provide three descriptive words or phrases for each and to rate them on two six-point scales asking whether the clip sounded like a real person talking and about

---

tokens: individual instances of a particular language feature.
Praat: a software program for editing and analyzing speech.

Table 1 **Acoustic Values of /s/ and /z/ Tokens**

Token		CoG	Std. Dev.	Skew
Mid	/s/	5557	1456	0.036
	/z/	6751	2251	–1.673
Fronted	/s/	5226	4990	0.004
	/z/	943	2497	3.016
Backed	/s/	4050	1530	1.866
	/z/	3086	1857	0.713

the quality of the recording. One hundred and ten people participated from across the country (as well as a handful of international
participants).

Responses to the descriptive items were typically single words or short   15
phrases, with occasional longer responses. Competence assessments in
the descriptions were coded with positive mentions (e.g., knowledgeable, intelligent, thoughtful, smart, educated) assigned to 1, negative
mentions (not too smart/bright, uneducated, not literate, stupid, unintelligent) as –1, and responses which made no mention as 0. The other
common dimensions (gay, south, city, and country) were coded on a simple binary, "mention/no mention." These codings were analyzed using
mixed effect regression models (see below). Responses to the unnatural-
ness rating were checked to ensure that participants accepted the manipulations as believable speech. Overall they showed a mean of 2 (ranging
from 1, "real person talking," to 6, "synthetic or manipulated voice"),
with a standard deviation of 1.35. Means for each individual recording
were all under the midpoint of the scale.

The main phase of data collection likewise played listeners a single
clip from each of the four speakers, after completing a page with demographics questions. In this phase, participants were asked to rate each
speaker on nine different six-point scales, with terms drawn from those
produced in the first phase: "smart," "knowledgeable," "masculine,"
"gay," "friendly," "laid-back," "country," "educated," and "confident."
Of the 175 participants in this phase, 122 were women and 53 men, with
a mean age of 29 and a standard deviation of 12 years.

Results

Two main effects emerged in the data, between /s/-fronting and a per-
cept of being gay and less masculine and between (ING) and being
more or less smart and knowledgeable. At the same time, more complex

"Fronted /s/ emerged as the most salient cue in the study, robustly increasing perceptions of gayness and lowering perceptions of masculinity across the data."

relationships also emerged, between /s/-backing and sounding country, and between /s/-fronting, (ING), and the interrelationships between sexuality, competence, and masculinity.

Fronted /s/ emerged as the most salient cue in the study, robustly increasing perceptions of gayness and lowering perceptions of masculinity across the data. Guises with fronted /s/ and /z/ tokens were overwhelmingly heard as more gay than those with mid or backed tokens, receiving more instances of "gay" or synonymous terms in phase 1 of the study (23% fronted vs. 11% mid and 8% backed, $p < .001$) and higher ratings for gay in phase 2 (4.06 fronted vs. 2.75 mid and 2.90 backed, $p < .001$). Fronted guises were also rated as significantly less masculine than mid and backed guises (2.83 fronted vs. 3.54 mid and 3.49 backed, $p < .025$). Figure 1 shows that the effects on the phase 2 masculine and gay ratings by /s/ placement is relatively stable across each of the four speakers, despite variation in how masculine or gay each speaker sounded.

The strong effect of /s/-fronting may be due to its status as a sociolinguistic stereotype (Labov 1972), even a caricature, the "gay lisp." Listeners' conscious awareness of the feature is visible in responses to phase 1, with one participant entering the three responses: "first I thought he had a lisp," "then I realized he is gay," "not that there is anything wrong with

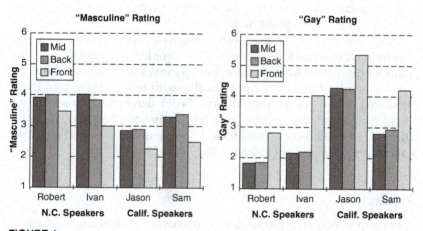

FIGURE 1

"Masculine" and "Gay" Ratings by Speaker and /s/ Placement

it." Such a well-known variable is presumably able to operate at both the conscious and unconscious levels and to be effective in a wider range of contexts.

Possibly due to the connection with lisping, /s/ fronting and backing 20 both emerged as an influence on competence. Speakers were heard as less smart/knowledgeable[2] in their fronted guises than either of the other two (p = .006), while both the fronted and backed guises caused the speakers to be perceived as less confident than the mid guises (p = .026 and p = .044, respectively).

The next main effect came from the impact of (ING) on perceptions of competence. Echoing previous work (Labov et al. 2006; Campbell-Kibler 2009), -ing guises decreased negative assessments of intelligence in both phase 1 responses, intriguingly while leaving positive assessments unaffected (-in: 15% positive, 8% negative; -ing: 14% positive, 2% negative; p = .008) and increased phase 2 ratings of smart/knowledgeable (3.63/3.77, p = .018).

These effects suggest that in some cases sociolinguistic resources have relatively stable relationships with primary meanings or closely related fields of meanings, which survive some degree of variation in speakers and linguistic context. At the same time, other results support more complex relationships, emerging only in the speech of some speakers or across multiple cues or implicating multiple percepts.

/s/-backing showed the expected connections to the South and the country, but did so less consistently, depending more on the context provided by both the speaker's other linguistic qualities and the task. In phase 1 responses concerning the speaker's origin, backed guises were significantly more likely than fronted guises to be described as from the South (30%/17%, p = .011) and less likely to be described as from a city (1%/8%, p = .015). Mid guises fell between the two, not significantly different from either. In the second phase, /s/ backing made only one of the speakers sound more country, specifically Ivan, the North Carolinian who was heard as less Southern (16% vs. 74% for the other Southerner,[3] interaction p = .002). As figure 2 shows, the Southern-sounding speaker, Robert, was consistently heard as country no matter his /s/ guise and the Californian speakers, Jason and Sam, were just as consistently heard as not country. Ivan's speech patterns, however, were ambiguous enough for the /s/-backing to have an effect. Unlike the fronting of /s/ and /z/ tokens, backing appears to be a less striking social influence, emerging with a clear social effect only in the limited situation of a single speaker.

The last result reported here is somewhat complex, involving the influence of linguistic variables — /s/-backing on the one hand and the

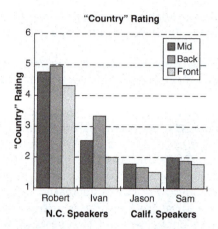

FIGURE 2
"Country" Ratings by Speaker and /s/
Placement

combination of /s/-fronting and -*ing* on the other—on the relationships between three percepts, namely sexual orientation, competence, and masculinity. This effect seems to emerge from linguistic features increasing the tendency of listeners to select particular combinations of these three qualities: "unintelligent, masculine, straight man" on the one hand and "intelligent, effeminate, gay man" on the other.

To contextualize this result, it is useful to first explain how factor structures behave and are treated in this analysis. As noted above, only one factor was used in analyzing the ratings data, because the factor structures were not otherwise consistent across the speakers. I suggest, however, that this lack of consistency is not due to general instability but to the structured, ideological nature of person perception. For example, all four speakers show a first factor consisting of competence qualities like smart and knowledgeable, as is frequently found in speech evaluation studies (Zahn and Hopper 1985). For three of the four speakers—Ivan, Jason, and Sam—this factor also has perceptions of "educated" assigned to it (loaded[4] greater than 0.7). The exception is Robert, the one speaker with the strong Southern accent (see Campbell-Kibler 2007), who, despite being heard as both educated and smart/knowledgeable, prompts listener reactions in which assessments of his education load only lightly with assessments of smart and knowledgeable (0.350). I suggest that these divergent factor structures occur due to ideologies about language and personalities, for example, that listeners are more willing to describe a Southern-accented man as simultaneously highly competent and not highly educated than they are a speaker without a Southern accent.

A similar pattern can be seen in the effect of /s/-backing and (ING) plus /s/-fronting. In the data overall, perceptions of the competence of the speakers and their masculinity show a moderate positive correlation° (0.37, $p < .001$), indicating that when assessing the masculinity of these speakers, the degree to which they seem competent matters (and/or vice versa). Likewise, overall masculinity and sexual orientation show a negative correlation, that is, the gayer a speaker is perceived as, the less masculine he is perceived to be (–0.48, $p < .001$), while sexual orientation and competence show no relationship. A complex interaction suggests that /s/-fronting and backing, (ING), and perceived sexual orientation mediate the relationship between these three percepts, specifically creating points at which competence ceases to correlate with masculinity. As figure 3 shows, the key result is that while competence and masculinity are positively correlated, this correlation disappears in two subsets of the data. In responses to guises containing backed /s/ and /z/ tokens, those listeners who perceived the speakers as straight (selecting 1 or 2 on the 6-point scale)[5] did not align competence and masculinity in their ratings ($r = 0.14$, $p = .149$; interaction $p = .013$). Even when assigning the lowest possible ratings for the qualities smart and educated, these listeners rated the backed guises with a mean rating of 4.00 on the masculinity scale (contrasted with 2.28 for the similarly low-competence reactions to other guises). While the backed guises are not seen as more or less masculine or competent overall, for those listeners specifically who rate them as straight-sounding and low-competence, this lack of intelligence is not the counter-masculine force that it is in other guises.

The second subset of the data in which the competence-masculinity connection is mitigated represents the other extreme: cases where guises with fronted /s/ and /z/ and -*ing* tokens are heard as gay ($r = 0.11$, $p = .486$; interaction $p = .008$). In these cases, the reduced connection results in a downgrading of masculinity at the high end of the competence scale; listeners who gave fronted /s/, -*ing* guises high ratings for gay and for smart and knowledgeable still rated these guises a mean of 2.00 on the masculinity scale (high competence reactions otherwise rated 3.98).

This loss of correlation suggests that in these cases the sociolinguistic variables do not contribute a meaning or even set of meanings, instead serving to constrain the most likely stylistic packages listeners perceive in the linguistic input. This constraint may apply to a simple dimension of meaning, increasing the likelihood that listeners will hear a style

---

correlation: how two variables are related. A *positive* correlation means that when one goes up, the other goes up; a *negative* correlation means that when one goes up, the other goes down.

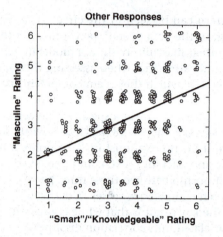

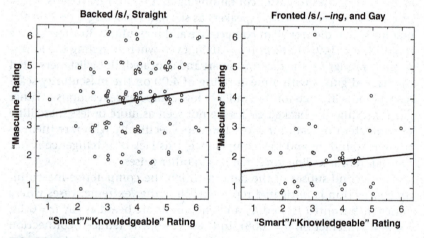

FIGURE 3

Perceived Masculinity against Perceived Competence.

Note: The datapoints have had jitter — small amounts of random noise — added to make visible the number of points at a given value.

they view as "not masculine" and reducing the chance they hear a style they would describe as "very masculine." But it may instead affect the interrelationships, increasing or decreasing the readings of, for example, "straight man, not very smart but very masculine," an assessment which comprised 3% of the reactions to the backed guises, but only 0.5% and 0% of the fronted and mid guises, respectively, or "gay man, really smart but not very masculine," representing 8% of the fronted guise reactions, but only 3% of mid and 2% of the backed guises.

Conclusions

Eckert (2008) proposed that sociolinguistic variation indexes fields of ideologically related social meanings. Different contextual elements, both linguistic and nonlinguistic, influence the particular meanings that emerge as relevant for a given speaker and listener. The results presented here support that view, but more specifically point to style as a way of understanding the sociolinguistic relationship (Coupland 2007). Indexical fields represent mappings between individual linguistic features and sets of related social concepts, within which a given indexical use may range. Styles allow for mappings between clusters of features and recognizable aggregates of social concepts, which are invoked as a set, including not only personal qualities or identity groups but also particular places, times, and ideological frameworks.

Sociolinguistic style may be better understood by drawing on other 30 stylistic realms in which practitioners are more overt in their semiotic analyses, for example, fashion. Some styles are enregistered (Agha 2003), that is to say defined within the culture at large, and circulate as pieces of cultural knowledge. A feather boa and a fringed, straight-seamed sleeveless dress combine to index the style "flapper," a style which carries personal associations of transgression, hedonism, and sexuality, behavioral associations like alcohol consumption and dancing, and contextual associations with a particular time and place. A given style invoked in a given situation is likely to have associations that may be either positively or negatively valenced in the new context, and speakers/wearers do not have control over the interpretations created, which depend not only on the stylistic production but on the knowledge, goals, and mood of the perceivers (Campbell-Kibler 2008). Nonetheless, individuals do attempt to invoke only aspects of a given style through the use of stylistic elements, in a process known as bricolage (Hebdige 1979).

Elements undergoing repeated bricolage become carriers of meaning in their own right, visible across a wide range of cofactors. Red stiletto-heeled women's shoes, for example, have developed into a standalone meaningful symbol, to the extent that it is possible to purchase keychains, t-shirts, mousepads, mugs, and the like, with the image of a red stiletto emblazoned on them, pieces which do not exist to any similar extent for stiletto shoes of other colors (although black stilettos have some representation). As a result of this process of detachment, these shoes have a strong and relatively consistent effect of a range of stylistic packages.

/s/-fronting and (ING) are both resources that have developed into what Labov (1972) refers to as stereotypes. Like red stilettos, /s/-fronting seems to function across a range of stylistic packages, indexing gayness and lack of masculinity on one hand and speech impediments and lowered competence on the other. (ING), as well documented elsewhere (Campbell-Kibler 2008; Eckert 2008) has a wide range of associations, but most often triggers perceptual responses regarding education, intelligence, and articulateness. Its effect is more subject to variation based on contextual features, however, making it a symbol that is meaningful but perhaps less heavy-handed than red stilettos, the blazer of the linguistic world.

A sensible treatment of style requires a process like bricolage to account for the emergence of individual resources. But it is the stylistic clusters that represent the heart of the theory, as a compelling tool for understanding sociolinguistic meanings that involve multiple cues. These stylistic packages may be enregistered, but they may also be less well-defined, clusters of characteristics that may be recognizable to some cultural agents but not others, or recognizable but not named. /s/-backing in the case of an ambiguously Southern speaker promotes a perception of him as "country" and shifts the relationship between competence, sexuality, and masculinity, by increasing perceptions of the complex style "masculine, unintelligent, straight man." Likewise, the combination of /s/-fronting and -*ing* seems to shift this same set of perceptual relationships, in part by promoting perception of the stylistic package "smart, effeminate gay man" — a familiar, though unnamed, character type in the U.S. popular landscape. The comedy troupe Second City has recently offered a named version known as "Sassy Gay Friend," a deliberate stereotype who sassily advises Shakespearean heroines and others regarding their love lives, perhaps a move toward greater enregisterment of this style.

While these more complex results are consistent with the notion of stylistic packages, their interpretation is made more challenging by the lack of reifications of the relevant styles. Without terminology to serve as landmarks, the multidimensional space of person perception quickly becomes too complex to definitively identify stylistic clusters on the basis of rating responses. The evaluation-based language attitudes literature has long assumed that the key aspects of evaluative data are found in their factor structures, assuming that a three-factor structure reveals that listeners assess competence, warmth, and dynamism and view these as independent and reflective of inherent models of person perception (Zahn and Hopper 1985). Zahn and Hopper (1985) note that the details of the specific terms assigned to factors like "competence" vary across studies. It is possible that variations in factor structure reflect real information about the social types entertained as possibilities by listeners. Given that these structures differ not only from study to study, but also from speaker to speaker and guise to guise, such differences in patterns of covariation may reflect patterns of social interpretation worth investigating. The results of the current study provide some support for a model of sociolinguistic perception that draws on stylistic clusters as key elements of the linguistic-social interface. More strongly, they support a move in sociolinguistic evaluation studies to better understand patterns of covarying perceived qualities and what they can tell us about sociolinguistic meaning.

Notes

1. In the manipulations, tokens of both /s/ and /z/ were altered. The terms /s/-fronting and /s/-backing are retained for ease of reference despite the inclusion of /z/ tokens in the features.

2. Four competence-related rating scales were included in the rating task of phase 2: "smart," "educated," "knowledgeable," and "confident," but due to the variety of factor structures visible across the different speakers (see discussion above), only "smart" and "knowledgeable" were well-motivated as factors across all the data. The effects reported here remain the same across the less motivated factors comprised of "smart," "knowledgeable," and "educated" and of all four responses.

3. See Campbell-Kibler (2007) for a more in-depth discussion of region perceptions of these stimuli.

4. Factor loadings are correlations between the input variable (like education) and a given factor. As correlations, they range on a scale from 0 to 1.

5. The assessment of sexual orientation was recast as a three-level factor: "straight" (ratings of 1 or 2), "mid" (3 or 4), and "gay" (5 or 6). The results described hold for the original numerical scale as well.

References

Agha, Asif. 2003. "The Social Life of Cultural Value." *Language and Communication* 23: 231–73.

Arnold, Jennifer, Renée Blake, Penelope Eckert, Melissa Iwai, Norma Mendoza-Denton, Carol Morgan, Livia Polanyi, Julie Solomon, and Tom Veatch (California Style Collective). 1993. "Variation and Personal/Group Style." Paper presented at the 22nd annual conference on New Ways of Analyzing Variation in English (NWAVE-22), Ottawa, Oct. 14–17.

Campbell-Kibler, Kathryn. 2007. "Accent, (ING), and the Social Logic of Listener Perceptions." *American Speech* 82: 32–64.

_____. 2008. "I'll Be the Judge of That: Diversity in Social Perceptions of (ING)." *Language in Society* 37: 637–59.

_____. 2009. "The Nature of Sociolinguistic Perception." *Language Variation and Change* 21: 135–56.

Campbell-Kibler, Kathryn, Penelope Eckert, Norma Mendoza-Denton, and Emma Moore (Half Moon Bay Style Collective). 2006. "The Elements of Style." Poster presented at the 35th annual conference on New Ways of Analyzing Variation (NWAV 35), Columbus, Ohio, Nov. 9–12. Available at http://www.ling.ohio-state.edu/~kbck/HMB_poster.pdf.

Connell, R. W. 1995. *Masculinities.* Berkeley: Univ. of California Press.

Coupland, Nikolas. 2007. *Style: Language Variation and Identity.* Cambridge: Cambridge Univ. Press.

Crist, Sean. 1997. "Duration of Onset Consonants in Gay Male Stereotyped Speech." In "Current Work in Linguistics," ed. Alexis Dimitriadis, Hikyoung Lee, Laura Siegel, Clarissa Surek-Clark, and Alexander Williams, 53–70. *University of Pennsylvania Working Papers in Linguistics* 4.3.

Eckert, Penelope. 2008. "Variation and the Indexical Field." *Journal of Sociolinguistics* 12: 453–76.

Fischer, John. 1958. "Social Influence of a Linguistic Variant." *Word* 14: 47–56.

Gaudio, Rudolf P. 1994. "Sounding Gay: Pitch Properties in the Speech of Gay and Straight Men." *American Speech* 69: 30–57.

Hebdige, Dick. 1979. *Subculture: The Meaning of Style.* London: Routledge.

Kiesling, Scott Fabius. 1998. "Men's Identities and Sociolinguistic Variation: The Case of Fraternity Men." *Journal of Sociolinguistics* 2: 69–99.

Kulick, Don. 2000. "Gay and Lesbian Language." *Annual Review of Anthropology* 29: 243–85.

Labov, William. 1966. *The Social Stratification of English in New York City.* Washington, D.C.: Center for Applied Linguistics.

_____. 1972. *Sociolinguistic Patterns.* Philadelphia: Univ. of Pennsylvania Press.

Labov, William, Sharon Ash, Maciej Baranowski, Naomi Nagy, Maya Ravindranath, and Tracy Weldon. 2006. "Listeners' Sensitivity to the Frequency of Sociolinguistic Variables." In "Papers from NWAV 34," ed. Michael L. Friesner and Maya Ravindranath, 105–29. *University of Pennsylvania Working Papers in Linguistics* 12.2.

Levon, Erez. 2007. "Sexuality in Context: Variation and the Sociolinguistic Perception of Identity." *Language in Society* 36: 533–54.

Linville, Sue Ellen. 1998. "Acoustic Correlates of Perceived versus Actual Sexual Orientation in Men's Speech." *Folia Phoniatrica et Logopaedica* 50: 35–48.

Munson, Benjamin. 2010. "Variation, Implied Pathology, Social Meaning, and the 'Gay Lisp': A Response to Van Borsel et al. (2009)." *Journal of Communication Disorders* 43: 1–5.

Munson, Benjamin, and Lindsey J. Zimmerman. 2006. "Perception of Sexual Orientation, Masculinity, and Femininity in Formant-Resynthesized Speech." Paper presented at the 35th annual conference on New Ways of Analyzing Variation (NWAV 35), Columbus, Ohio, Nov. 9–12.

Pierrehumbert, Janet B., Tessa Bent, Benjamin Munson, Ann R. Bradlow, and J. Michael Bailey. 2004. "The Influence of Sexual Orientation on Vowel Production." *Journal of the Acoustic Society of America* 116: 1905–8.

Podesva, Robert J. 2006. "Phonetic Detail in Sociolinguistic Variation." Ph.D. diss., Stanford Univ.

Podesva, Robert J., Sarah J. Roberts, and Kathryn Campbell-Kibler. 2001. "Sharing Resources and Indexing Meanings in the Production of Gay Styles." In *Language and Sexuality: Contesting Meaning in Theory and Practice,* ed. Kathryn Campbell-Kibler, Robert J. Podesva, Sarah J. Roberts, and Andrew Wong, 175–89. Stanford, Calif.: Center for the Study of Language and Information.

Sachs, Jennifer. 1975. "Cues to Identification of Sex in Children's Speech." In *Language and Sex: Difference and Dominance,* ed. Barrie Thorne and Nancy Henley, 152–77. Rowley, Mass.: Newbury House.

Smyth, Ron, Greg Jacobs, and Henry Rogers. 2003. "Male Voices and Perceived Sexual Orientation: An Experimental and Theoretical Approach." *Language in Society* 32: 329–50.

Stuart-Smith, Jane. 2007. "Empirical Evidence for Gendered Speech Production: /s/ in Glaswegian." In *Laboratory Phonology 9,* ed. Jennifer Cole and José Ignacio Hualde, 65–86. Berlin: Mouton de Gruyter.

Trudgill, Peter. 1974. *The Social Differentiation of English in Norwich.* Cambridge: Cambridge Univ. Press.

Van Borsel, John, Els De Bruyn, Evelien Lefebvre, Anouschka Sokoloff, Sophia De Ley, and Nele Baudonck. 2009. "The Prevalence of Lisping in Gay Men." *Journal of Communication Disorders* 42: 100–106.

Zahn, Christopher J., and Robert Hopper. 1985. "Measuring Language Attitudes: The Speech Evaluation Instrument." *Journal of Language and Social Psychology* 4: 113–23.

Understanding the Text

1. Explain what *style* refers to in sociolinguistics. How does this concept relate to the study of perceived sexual orientations?

2. What effect does the position of the /s/ sound (front, middle, or back) have on how likely a man is to be perceived as gay? On how likely he is to be perceived as masculine?

3. How do /s/ position and the use of *-ing* versus *-in* influence perceptions of a man's confidence and competence?

Reflection and Response

4. Campbell-Kibler mentions the "dangers of reifying gay men's speech" — in other words, the dangers of believing that there is indeed a "gay" way of talking (par. 5). Why might this belief be dangerous? How does Campbell-Kibler's research avoid contributing to this belief?

5. Campbell-Kibler notes two stylistic clusters into which study participants tended to file men's language: "unintelligent, masculine, straight man" and "intelligent, effeminate, gay man" (par. 24). Do you think these clusters of language traits connect to common stereotypes of men? What evidence can you see in popular culture for your answer?

Making Connections

6. In "Are White People Ethnic?," Carmen Fought notes that "whiteness does not seem to be associated with masculinity" (p. 118). After reading Campbell-Kibler, what ways do you see in which sexuality and regional dialect features (e.g., the /s/ backing of some Southerners) might either support or complicate Fought's statement?

7. Campbell-Kibler notes that the overall study data show a relationship between perceiving someone as masculine and perceiving them as competent. How do her findings help to explain some of the perceptions of women's speech described by Marybeth Seitz-Brown ("Young Women Shouldn't Have to Talk Like Men to Be Taken Seriously," p. 92)?

3

How Does Language Change (Whether We Like It or Not)?

anguages live alongside the people who speak them, almost as if they were living organisms themselves. They evolve over time, adapting to changes in the surrounding culture. It is a natural process, but not one that everyone celebrates, for changes in language can leave well-loved rules and standards behind and can introduce words and pronunciations that may be thought vulgar, sloppy, or overly trendy. In this chapter, we explore both some of the ways language changes and the attitudes people have toward that change.

We start with some specific examples of how cultural changes can spark language change. Mark Peters's "He Said, Sheme Said" addresses the English language's lack of a gender-neutral singular pronoun — a lack which, while a trouble spot for centuries, has become more acutely felt as contemporary society becomes more aware of nonbinary gender identities (those beyond simply male or female, such as intersex, genderqueer, or transmasculine/transfeminine). It may, Peters and the linguists he interviews suggest, finally be time to accept *they* as a singular pronoun.

Meanwhile, innovations in communication technologies are leading us to use language in new ways. For many of us who communicate in text messages and online settings, acronyms like *lol* and *omg* have become a regular, unremarkable feature of language. Mark Chatfield, in "OMG — It's the Textual Revolution," encourages us to look more closely at our use of acronyms so that we might see the complex meanings wrapped up in them. Naomi Baron, in "Are Digital Media Changing Language?," acknowledges that technology has led to some interesting surface changes in language, including not only the use of acronyms but also changes in spelling and punctuation. However, she argues that the truly significant changes are those that affect our *attitudes* toward language. For example, new communication technologies are encouraging us to take a more relaxed attitude toward language correctness, even as we assert more control over how we communicate.

Specific changes in cultural views or technology are not a prerequisite for language change. Humans continually change language as they use it — particularly, says Douglas Quenqua, young female humans. Quenqua's "They're, Like, Way Ahead of the Linguistic Currrrve" traces how young women tend to pioneer changes in the vocabulary and pronunciation of English, remaining innovative despite frequent criticism of their speech patterns. A particularly consistent source of language innovation, often associated with young people, is slang, and Edwin Battistella's "Slang as Bad Language" examines the reasons why the constant evolution of slang can elicit negative reactions.

Responses to language change differ widely. In "English Belongs to Everybody," Robert MacNeil applauds how English has evolved with society, refusing to follow the rules that some have attempted to impose upon it. Erin McKean, in "How Are Dictionaries Made?," explains that dictionary makers react to language change by watching and recording it as it happens. As MacNeil and William Cran explain in "The Language Wars," interest, and sometimes joy, in language variation and change represent one way of looking at language, an attitude known as *descriptivism*. The opposite view, *prescriptivism*, holds that we must do more with language than describe it; we must maintain a standard and correct any deviations from that standard.

But what is this standard that prescriptivists are trying to protect from change? Can we truly define it? Rosina Lippi-Green's "The Standard Language Myth" attempts to answer these questions via a tour of existing definitions, taken from authoritative sources like dictionaries as well as the opinions of laypeople.

Do we need to prescribe a correct way of using language and defend it against change, or can we be content to describe — and perhaps even delight in — change as it happens? See what you think after exploring the readings in this chapter.

He Said, Sheme Said

Mark Peters

Mark Peters is a language expert, with a PhD in English and membership in the American Dialect Society, as well as a humorist. Peters writes about language for sites and publications including *Slate* and *Visual Thesaurus*. His book-length works include *Idiot's Guides: Grammar and Style* (Alpha, 2014) and *Bullshit: A Lexicon* (Penguin Random House, 2015). Peters is also a regular contributor to "The Word," a language column in the *Boston Globe*, where the piece below was published on January 31, 2016. In this piece, Peters examines the growing need for a singular pronoun in English that, unlike *he* or *she*, does not specify a male or female gender. Is *they* already that pronoun?

English has a gender problem—but it's not a new problem. *He* and *she* (along with *his* and *her*) are perfectly functional singular pronouns, but they aren't much help when you need to discuss one person in a nongendered way. This old issue is newly relevant as transgender people and people without a primary gender demand words to match their lives. These days, *he* and *she* are less useful and less universal than ever.

It's likely *they* will be the permanent solution to this problem, since it's been used as singular for centuries and is getting more acceptance all the time—including being named 2015 Word of the Year by the American Dialect Society. One of the main factors in the success of *they* is that it doesn't look weird when you use it, unlike *ne, thon, ita,* and *hersh*—all real words suggested over the centuries as potential nonbinary pronouns. Though such words have all flopped, it's worth remembering these coinages that failed to fill the gap. They show that this issue (which feels so contemporary) is actually centuries old—and that people are quite creative when it comes to word-coining.

Much of the research on the quest for a gender-neutral singular pronoun has been conducted by Dennis Baron, professor of English and linguistics at the University of Illinois at Urbana-Champaign. Baron's recently updated paper, "The Words That Failed: A Chronology of Early Nonbinary Pronouns" (originally published in *American Speech* and currently available on his *Web of Language* site), tells the story of *le, hiser, sheme, ala, po,* and dozens of other words created to fill English's gender gap since 1792.

Such words haven't failed due to a lack of purpose or creativity. The oldest such coinage is *ou,* a dialect word that Scottish economist and philosopher James Anderson suggested elevating to standard English. Some coinages attempted to blend more familiar words: *hiser* is a union of *his* and *her* coined in 1850. In an 1868 letter to the *Boston Recorder*, a reader suggested terms that would today cause confusion among *Star Wars* fans: *han, hans,* and *hanself.* Of all the failed pronouns, Baron has a favorite: *ip,* coined by Emma Carleton in 1884. Though Baron finds *ip* adorable, he admits: "I would never use it other than to say it's cute."

Baron identifies three main reasons why the invented pronouns have 5 flopped. The first is that "You simply can't create and legislate language." Language changes by evolution, not declaration. As Baron says, "There's no mechanism for adoption" and "You can coin whatever you want"— but that doesn't mean anyone will use it, just as a bazillion commercials can't make the masses go to a movie.

While it's impossible to make any word successful by force of will, pronouns are an even tougher lexical nut to crack, as Gretchen McCulloch, a linguist and author of a forthcoming book on internet language, observes: "It's hard to make new pronouns catch on because pronouns are part of a small group of words called function words: short, common words that help stick other words together, like *the, of, and, a, that, to, my,* and so on. Pronouns and other function words do change sometimes—we used to have *thou/thee/you/ye,* for example, and now we just have *you*—but they change a lot less frequently than longer, more contentful words (like *selfie* or *facepalm*)."

The second reason such words have failed is that most invented pronouns look and sound bizarre, with unusual spellings and difficult pronunciations: Oddballs rarely do well in the Darwinian race to language success. This fact was pinpointed by Allen Metcalf, cofounder of the American Dialect Society Word of the Year event, who created the FUDGE scale to predict the success of words. FUDGE names five factors that influence a word's success: frequency of use, unobtrusiveness, diversity of users, generation of meanings and forms, and endurance of the concept. Most proposed nonbinary pronouns were used rarely by anyone and spawned few additional forms, but the real culprit is the U in FUDGE: Terms such as *zyhe, heesh, co,* and *mef* are all extremely obtrusive. When it comes to words, the sore thumbs don't catch on.

> "While it's impossible to make any word successful by force of will, pronouns are an even tougher lexical nut to crack."

The third reason no quirky coinage has succeeded is that no new word is necessary. As Michael Adams, Indiana University professor and author of *Slang: The People's Poetry* and *Slayer Slang: A Buffy the Vampire Slayer Lexicon,* puts it, "Why invent a new word when an old one will do?" Baron adds that, though *they* is newly relevant due to the increased profile of people with nonconforming gender, this word has been "simmering in the background (of English) for years and years." In fact, *they* has been used as singular since at least the 14th century; that history makes for a far more graceful adoption. McCullough adds, "If there's one thing that's even harder than getting an entire society to adopt a new pronoun, it's getting them to stop using a perfectly adequate gender-neutral pronoun in favor of a different one."

As for the objection that *they* and *their* must always be plural, Adams retorts, "The only people who need a new word to do the gender-neutral job are those who want a 'clean' system with no plurals acting like singulars, no masculines acting like feminines, as though one word can't serve two or more purposes—but every speaker knows *they* can. Most speakers prefer efficiency over logic."

Another question has accompanied the search for a nonbinary singular 10 pronoun: What to call these words? Often they've been described as common gender or gender neutral. When Baron first wrote his paper on such words, he used *epicene*, a word used to describe Greek and Latin words that can apply to either gender. These days, as awareness of nonbinary sexualities has increased, the word *nonbinary* has also attached itself to these words, taking the lead as the best current label.

But whatever you call words as different in form and success as *they* and *ip*, they're signs of the times and of something timeless—English ain't perfect, and people will keep trying to duct tape the holes. Though

Buttons worn by University of Kansas Libraries employees as part of the libraries' 2016 "You Belong Here" campaign. Increased awareness of nonbinary gender identities in recent years has led to increased opportunities to claim one's pronouns, including singular *they*.
Sarah Shepherd/AP Images

most attempts fail, you have to admire the persistent creativity and effort to represent more people. Promoting words like *thon* and approving singular *they* are really about accepting you and me.

Understanding the Text

1. Why is it more difficult to create new pronouns than it is to coin other sorts of new words?

2. What are some arguments for and against using *they* as a gender-neutral singular pronoun?

Reflection and Response

3. Peters notes that "awareness of nonbinary sexualities has increased" in recent years (par. 10). What are some examples of this increased awareness from popular culture or your personal experience?

4. What pronouns do you and the people around you use? If you or anyone you know uses *they* or another gender-neutral pronoun, what are their reasons for doing so?

Making Connections

5. As Peters mentions, linguist Dennis Baron is a prominent researcher on gender-neutral pronouns. Visit Baron's *Web of Language* blog (**https://illinois.edu/blog/view/25**) and search for *gender* or *pronouns*. Select a blog post to read and feel free to follow any links within it that interest you. What have you learned to supplement your understanding of gender-neutral pronouns?

6. Summarizing Baron, Peters notes that "Language changes by evolution, not declaration" (par. 5). What proof for this statement can you find in Robert MacNeil and William Cran's "The Language Wars" (p. 201) or Erin McKean's "How Are Dictionaries Made?" (p. 198)?

7. How does the discussion of prescriptivism and descriptivism in MacNeil and Cran's "The Language Wars" (p. 201) help explain the differing opinions as to whether *they* can be used as a singular pronoun?

OMG—It's the Textual Revolution

Tom Chatfield

Tom Chatfield is a writer and consultant with expertise in digital media and how we interact with it. He has been a writer and commentator for media organizations including the BBC and NPR. Among his six published books are *Netymology* (Quercus, 2013), which provides histories and definitions for one hundred key terms from the digital age, and *Fun Inc.* (Virgin, 2012), which looks at the role of video games in contemporary life. In this article, originally published in *New Scientist* on April 6, 2013, Chatfield encourages us to see the complexity within the seemingly simplified language of electronic communication.

The past few decades have seen a democratization of written language unprecedented in human history, driven by digital media. Thanks to more than 2 billion internet-linked computers and 6 billion cell phones in the world, we are all both authors and audiences—our daily discourse playing out via millions of words typed onto their screens.

For some, this is a process where "more" inexorably means "worse": a degeneration of written language into a shadow of former glories. Yet this misses much of the point. For alongside their loosening and cheapening of words, our young tools have combined the instant and the infinitely reproducible—and are steadily blurring the bounds between private utterance and public performance. It is a context within which even the most laughable-seeming simplicities conceal possibilities that demand our attention.

Consider the complexities lurking behind just six letters, in the form of two iconic contemporary initialisms: OMG (oh my God!) and LOL (laughing out loud). Both took up their official places in the Oxford English Dictionary in March 2011—but boast considerably longer pedigrees. OMG, for example, dates back to a 1917 letter from Admiral John Arbuthnot Fisher to Winston Churchill, in which the former exclaimed: "I hear that a new order of Knighthood is on the tapis—O.M.G. (Oh! My God!)—Shower it on the Admiralty!"

LOL, used to express amusement, is a rather younger coinage, dating to the pre-web bulletin board systems of the early 1980s. It is also, though, a more intriguing one, representing one of the earliest examples of a very particular trend of digital communications: self-dramatization.

As linguists such as David Crystal have observed, the phrase "laughing 5 out loud" is far from a straightforward description. Someone who types *LOL* or *lol* (the difference between upper and lower case signaling variations in intensity and formality) is rarely, if ever, literally laughing out loud. Rather, they are framing their words within a kind of stage direction: a present-tense commentary designed to communicate the conversational emotions that writing—outside the most elaborately crafted literary examples—cannot usually convey in the absence of a human voice and face.

It is a simple innovation that reflects a central contemporary fact. Typing onto screens is becoming a dominant driving force behind the evolution of language, and this has brought vast ingenuity to bear on turning typed language into a medium as efficiently dynamic as spoken language itself.

The force of this change is perhaps most evident in the fact that LOL has traveled in the opposite direction to normal language change, migrating not from spoken words to type, but from typing into speech. Usually pronounced to rhyme with *doll*, it features with increasing regularity in the talk of so-called digital natives°—a normalization echoing the older habit taught by web addresses of speaking punctuation out loud ("dot com" having long become a standard expression).

LOL is only the tip of this particular iceberg, of course, and its success in imparting emotional shading to rapidly typed exchanges has bred a remarkable proliferation of variations. To type *ROFL*

> "Because it is the briefest and most easily typed terms that are used most often, it is within just a handful of letters and characters that the most sophisticated layers of new meaning are gathering."

(rolling on the floor laughing) is, for example, to go one step beyond mere LOL-ing in both intensity and self-awareness; while to type *ROFLMAO* (rolling on the floor laughing my ass off) projects a state perhaps best described as highly amused irony.

Beyond these lie many hundreds of increasingly baroque versions, targeting particular groups, services, ideas and idiolects—and extending deep into the cultural mainstream. One of the best-selling dance music bands of recent years is called LMFAO (slightly too profane to spell out in full here). In a still more typing-centric move, there's even a British indie band whose name, ?, is pronounced "Alt-J" courtesy of a shortcut on the Apple keyboard used to produce the symbol for their name.

Pointlessly self-delighting as all this may appear, it shows a frantic evolutionary process in action. And it also points toward a central paradox of digital language: that, because it is the briefest and most easily typed terms that are used most often, it is within just a handful of letters and characters that the most sophisticated layers of new meaning are gathering. 10

digital natives: people who are comfortable and capable with technology, having grown up with it.

A 2014 *Zits* comic, by Jerry Scott and Jim Borgman. Contrary to Pierce's view that "We're doomed," is it possible that emoji, like initialisms, communicate more complex meanings than we realize?

Zits: © 2014 Zits Partnership Distributed by King Features Syndicate, Inc.

This is a minimalism with roots in one of the most unexpectedly versatile technologies of the modern era: the text message. Originally built into cell-phone networks as a testing facility for network operators, its initial success caught almost everyone by surprise—other than those young people who found in these precisely controlled few characters a perfectly minimal mode of interaction for an era of information overload.

Here, even one letter can carry an amazing burden of significance. On the more mischievous side of digital innovation, for example, there are those who follow an online philosophy of acting "for the lulz." Note the lower case letters and deliberate use of the "internet z"—a common typing error when typing the letter *s* fast that has, thanks to the primacy of the keyboard, become a way of subtly shifting meaning.

Together, the *z* ending and deliberate misspelling of *lol* as *lul* denote a subversive strand in online culture. As embodied in the name of the notorious hackers' collective, LulzSec (standing for "Lulz Security" and boasting the motto "the world's leaders in high-quality entertainment at your expense"), to do things "for the lulz" is to act in a spirit of anarchistic-bordering-on-nihilistic delight.

Language shifts like *lulz* represent what is technically known as "eye dialect": that is, a linguistic effect aimed at the eye rather than at the ear. It is a process that both increases the emotional nuances of communication and introduces a further layer of remove between words and meanings—something that, like so many things online, only yields its full sense if everyone involved knows the conventions being used.

All of which brings us back to the notion of performance, and its central 15 importance in online language. Ultimately, to type that I am "laughing out loud" is to signal my and my interlocutor's membership of a certain tribe. It is as much about acknowledging someone else's wit—or attempted wit—as signaling my own amusement. And it couches the entire exchange in a protective carapace of self-reference, ripe for augmentation and subversion.

Simplicity, here, sits above a complex arena of performance and layered perceptions—not the least of whose mysteries is the gulf between seemingly spontaneous words and the remote, anonymous business of typing them at a keyboard. Even if the "me" I vividly represent on screen resembles my true self—"I" remain an elaborate exercise in self-invention, conjured out of a performance crafted letter by letter.

Little wonder that some teenagers outsource the writing of crucial text messages and status updates to their most eloquent friends, or spend many hours selecting 140 characters perfectly pitched to sound spontaneous. No matter what the doomsayers may argue, we live in an age where mere handfuls of type mask the greatest verbal challenges of all.

Understanding the Text

1. What does Chatfield mean when he says that writing has undergone a "democratization" because of digital media (par. 1)?

2. What sorts of complexity does Chatfield see behind seemingly simple abbreviations like *lol*?

3. What does it mean to say that "performance" is "central . . . in online language" (par. 15)?

Reflection and Response

4. Chatfield notes that *lol* is "far . . . from . . . straightforward" because, when we say it, we are "rarely, if ever, literally laughing out loud" (par. 5) Would you say this is true of your own and others' use of *lol*? Why do we say this if we do not literally mean it?

5. Would you say that exaggeration or nonliteral phrasing is common in contemporary slang? Discuss some examples that support your opinion.

6. Chatfield mentions that some online language has found its way into speech, so that people will say *omg* out loud or pronounce *lol* as a word. What other examples of spoken abbreviations can you think of? Does using these acronyms in speech change their meaning in any way?

Making Connections

7. Chatfield claims that *lol* indicates "membership of a certain tribe" (par. 15). How does this compare to Connie Eble's description of slang in *Slang and Sociability* (p. 59) or Edwin Battistella's in "Slang as Bad Language" (p. 183)? Would you say that abbreviations such as *lol* and *omg* function like typical slang?

8. Chatfield calls online communication an "elaborate exercise in self-invention" (par. 16). How does Naomi Baron's argument in "Are Digital Media Changing Language?" (p. 170) support his point? Use both articles to describe and analyze the "self-invention" that you do in online communication.

Are Digital Media Changing Language?

Naomi S. Baron

Naomi S. Baron, a professor of linguistics at American University, researches the history and evolution of English language and literacy, particularly in relation to technology. Her eight books include the award-winning *Always On: Language in an Online and Mobile World* (Oxford University Press, 2008) and, most recently, *Words Onscreen: The Fate of Reading in a Digital World* (Oxford University Press, 2015). She published the article below in the journal *Educational Leadership* in 2009, at a time when teachers, parents, and society at large were quite anxious about the possibility that texting and instant messaging could damage young people's writing and reading skills. In response to such anxiety, Baron asserts that digital media's most profound effects on language — which are as evident today as when her article was written — concern our attitudes toward language and communication, rather than our use of acronyms and alternative spellings.

Are instant messaging and text messaging killing language? To hear what the popular media say, a handful of OMGs (oh my god) and smiley faces, along with a paucity of capital letters and punctuation marks, might be bringing English to its knees.

Although journalists tend to sensationalize the linguistic strangeness of "online lingo," quantitative analyses of instant messaging conversations and text messages reveal that abbreviations, acronyms, and even misspellings are comparatively infrequent, at least among college-age students. For example, in a study I did of college students' instant messaging conversations, out of 11,718 words, only 31 were "online lingo" abbreviations, and only 90 were acronyms (of which 76 were LOL). In a study of college students' text messaging, my colleague Rich Ling and I found a few more lexical shortenings; yet the grand total of clear abbreviations was only 47 out of 1,473 words, which is hardly overwhelming.

Yes, young people sometimes accidentally slip a btw (by the way) into a school essay. But a recent study by the Pew Internet and American Life Project confirms that middle school and high school students understand what kind of language is appropriate in what context (Lenhart, Smith, & Macgill, 2008). What's more, scholars of new media language, such as David Crystal and Beverly Plester, remind us that the new technologies encourage creativity, which can spill over into school writing (Crystal, 2008; Plester, Wood, & Bell, 2008).

Minor Shifts: Vocabulary and Sentence Mechanics

Those of us studying electronically mediated communication (language produced on computers or mobile phones) have been looking for evidence that mediated language is changing traditional speech and writing. To our surprise, the list of effects is relatively short. Here are my candidates:

Incorporation of a few acronyms into everyday language. These days you 5 sometimes hear students saying "brb" (be right back) to one another when they temporarily take their leave. I have also overheard "lol" (laughing out loud) in conversations among young people. However, these neologisms need to be put into perspective. Infusion of written acronyms into everyday speech is a common linguistic process—to wit, RSVP, AWOL, or ASAP. If a few more lexical shortenings make their way into general usage, that's nothing out of the ordinary.

Decreased certainly about when a string of words is a compound, a hyphenated word, or one word. This is a more nuanced proposition. Take the word *newspaper*. Should it be spelled *newspaper, news-paper,* or *news paper*? Obviously the first, you say. But historically, words tend to begin as separate pairings (*news* plus *paper*); gradually make their way to hyphenated forms (*news-paper*); and eventually, especially if they are high-frequency, become compounds (*newspaper*). The journey from *electronic mail* to *e-mail,* and, for many, to *email,* is a case in point.

Enter computers and the internet. If I write *news paper* (two words) in an e-mail, no one is likely to correct me, because on the internet no one is policing the grammar of the personal messages we construct. What's more, the two-word version handily passes spell-check (typically my students' criterion for correctness).

URL addresses for internet sites may also be affecting our notion of word breaks. URLs allow no spaces between words. To create a web page for selling beauty products, I need an address such as www.beautyproductsonline.com. It is easy to imagine *beauty products* crossing the line into *beauty products* in offline writing without many people giving the merger a second thought.

Diminished concern over spelling and punctuation. Spell-check, along with online search engines, may be convincing us that devoting energy to honing spelling skills is anachronistic. Even before you finish typing a word containing an error, spell-check often automatically corrects the word. Similarly, if you type a misspelled word (or phrase) into Google, chances are the search engine will land you pretty much at the same list of sites you would have reached had you been a finalist in the National Spelling Bee.

In the same vein, I am increasingly finding that my students have 10 little regard for apostrophes. (And as we know, URLs disallow punctuation marks.) My studies of college students' text messages show that "required" apostrophes (in a word such as *doesn't*) only appear about one-third of the time.

These effects on vocabulary and sentence mechanics are actually fairly minor. New words enter languages all the time. As for word separation, hyphenation, and spelling more generally, it helps to take the long view. A quick check of the *Oxford English Dictionary* reveals that lexical practices evolve, and yesterday's oddity may be today's norm — or vice versa.

In studying new media language, however, I've become convinced that more fundamental linguistic changes are afoot. The shifts I'm talking about are not in vocabulary, spelling, or punctuation, but in our *attitudes* toward language structure.

Attitude Shift 1: "Whatever"

Language is rule-governed behavior: That is, languages are constructed according to identifiable patterns that people follow. Native speakers have a mental template of these rules. Obviously linguistic rules have exceptions (the plural of *man* is *men*, not *mans*). And rules change over time. (Chaucer would have written "hath holpen" rather than "has helped.") However, we recognize exceptions — and change — by referencing our knowledge of rules currently shared within a language community.

By rules, I don't mean normative, prescriptive grammar — such edicts as, Don't end a sentence with a preposition. This arbitrary "rule" was concocted by 18th century self-appointed grammarians who took Latin, which has no word-final prepositions, as their model. Instead, I have in mind such rules as, Subjects and verbs need to agree in number — making a sentence like "Cookie Monster eat toast for breakfast" ungrammatical. If a language community adheres to the rule-governed model of language, its members will render consistent judgments about linguistic usage. Yes, we all make performance errors, but our rule-governed linguistic brains recognize, perhaps after the fact, that we have erred.

"Gradually, we have become less obsessed with correctness and more focused on tolerance and personal expression."

Since the 1960s, a constellation of 15 factors have combined to alter our sense of "good" language use (Baron, 2000). Revolutions in school pedagogy began replacing teacher-directed classrooms with peer review and activities designed to foster collaboration. The infamous red pen was now used more to encourage intellectual exploration than to correct sentence mechanics. Multiculturalism led us to encourage students not to be judgmental about their peers. No longer do we say that Li Po "talks strangely"; rather, she is an "English language learner." Instead of criticizing Bill from Appalachia (who says "Him and me went home"), we note that Bill speaks another dialect of English.

Gradually, we have become less obsessed with correctness and more focused on tolerance and personal expression. This shift, however admirable, has linguistic consequences. School is no longer necessarily a place to instill a sense that linguistic rules (or even linguistic consistency) matter.

Each year, I ask graduate students in my Structure of English class if it matters whether English continues to distinguish between the words *may* and *can* ("May I come in?" versus "Can I come in?"). Many of the students fail to see why anyone should care. The same laissez-faire attitude applies to distinguishing between the words *capital* and *capitol* (the first identifies the seat of state government, whereas the second refers to a building, such as the U.S. Capitol). Why not just ditch one and let the other do double duty?

My point is not to pass judgment. The issue is that attitudes toward linguistic "rules" have shifted. A wide swath of educated speakers of English (at least American English) simply don't worry about the niceties of such rules any more. One day it's *may*; the next day it's *can*. So what?

This attitude reminds me of spelling in Middle English, where you would often find the same word written half a dozen different ways, all on the same page. Standardized English spelling didn't become a reality until nearly the 18th century. By 1750, Lord Chesterfield famously warned his son that "orthography . . . is so absolutely necessary for a man of letters, or a gentleman, that one false spelling may fix a ridicule upon him for the rest of his life." Today, it is difficult to imagine anyone taking Chesterfield's admonition seriously. If spell-check doesn't catch the problem, whatever! Does spelling really matter, anyway?

The shift away from caring about language rules or consistency 20 predates new media language. It even predates personal computers. However, computer and mobile-phone technologies add fuel to the linguistic fire. An e-mail manual such as Constance Hale and Jessie Scanlon's *Wired Style* (1999) encourages writers to "celebrate subjectivity" (p. 9) and to "play with grammar and syntax. Appreciate unruliness" (p. 15). Scholars like David Crystal and Beverly Plester, as I noted earlier, highlight the creative potential of text messaging. We should not be surprised to find linguistic free spirits applying similar latitude to everyday speech and even to more formal writing.

Attitude Shift 2: Control

Besides amplifying the linguistic "whatever" attitude, computers and mobile phones are instrumental in a second attitudinal shift—a change in the degree to which we control our linguistic interactions.

Human communication has always involved varying amounts of control. If I see you coming down the street and don't wish to engage in conversation, I might cross to the other side and start window shopping. If you phone me and I don't like what you're saying, I can always hang up.

Contemporary online and mobile language technologies ratchet up the control options. On my instant messaging account, I can block you so you never get a message through. (I always appear to be offline, even though I'm busily instant messaging others.) I can multitask, talking with you on the phone while I search for a cheap airfare online or instant messaging you while I'm conducting half a dozen other online conversations.

Social networking sites offer additional forms of control. People exercise control in the way they design their pages: Staged photographs, exaggerated profiles, and padded friends lists enable online users to manipulate how others see them. In the words of one undergraduate, her Facebook page is "me on my best day."

These sites also enable users to maintain relationships with friends 25 without expending much effort. For example, young people commonly check up on their friends' activities by viewing their online photo albums or status reports, obviating the need for a phone call or e-mail, much less a face-to-face visit. One popular move is to post a Happy Birthday greeting on the Wall (a semi-public message board) of a friend's Facebook page without making real personal contact.

On mobile phones, caller ID informs us who's calling, so we can decide whether to answer. Sometimes when I'm meeting with students, their mobile phones ring. A quick glance at the screen, and then the phone is silenced and slipped into a pocket or backpack. "It's only Mom," they explain.

Another form of control on mobiles is deciding whether to talk or text. I might choose to send a text message rather than call to keep the communication short (meaning, "I don't want to get bogged down in a conversation in which I'm obligated to listen to what you have to say"). In cross-cultural research I conducted last year, more than one-third of the Swedish, U.S., and Italian university students I surveyed said "keeping the message short" was an important reason for texting rather than talking.

One inventive control technique is pretending to talk on your mobile phone when you see an acquaintance approaching—even someone you like—to avoid conversation. In my studies, 13 percent of U.S. students reported engaging in this behavior at least once a month. And 25 percent reported that they fiddled with text-based functions on their phones (such as checking old messages) to evade conversation with people they knew.

In each instance, technology enhances our ability to manipulate our communication with others. As the arsenal of control devices continues to grow, we increasingly come to see language not as an opportunity for interpersonal dialogue but as a system we can maneuver for individual gain.

Responding to Language Shifts

In thinking about the effects of new communication media on language, 30 we need to distinguish between "may fly" language (here today, gone tomorrow) and changes that are more substantial. If we care that a couple of new acronyms and alternative spellings could make their way into everyday spoken or written language (particularly when it comes to schoolwork), it actually is possible to just say no. Students already understand that particular styles of language are appropriate for one venue but not another (calling a teacher "Mr. Matthews" but using first names for friends). They understand (and probably even expect) reminders.

Responding to the linguistic "whatever" attitude is a more complex proposition. Parents and teachers need to understand that young people are not the only ones manifesting this attitudinal shift. One of my favorite examples is from the environmentalist and author Bill McKibben, who wrote this in praise of a book: "Go find a friend and tell them all about this fine book." We've all learned that a singular noun such as *friend* needs to be paired with a singular pronoun (here, *him* or *her*). Yet Simon and Schuster had no qualms about putting this blurb on a book jacket.

Depending on our pedagogical goals, we might choose to be linguistically hard-nosed (perhaps pluralizing the noun to *friends* and avoiding the gender question entirely). Or we might admit more casual spoken style into the classroom, following the general trend today for writing to reflect informal speech.

Before we despair that language is going to hell in a handcart, we should remember two lessons. First, normativeness in language goes through cycles, much like taste in music and politics. All is not lost. And second, regardless of the swings that language goes through, there is room for individual schools or teachers to set their own standards. Most schools have abandoned teaching handwriting, but a few have held their ground, to the good fortune of their students. Just so, if you choose to insist on written precision, students generally will follow your lead.

The issue of control is trickier, because it involves personal empowerment. Here the battles aren't about acronyms or noun-pronoun agreement but about such questions as, Should students be allowed to have mobile phones in school? or Is it the job of the school to teach online and mobile-device etiquette? These concerns rarely have easy solutions. However, by understanding that new language technologies have shifted our students' attitudes about who holds the power in linguistic exchange, we will be better prepared to understand their perspectives and to reach common ground.

References

Baron, N. (2000). *Alphabet to email: How written English evolved and where it's heading*. New York: Routledge.

Crystal, D. (2008). *Txtng: The gr8 db8*. Oxford, UK: Oxford University Press.

Hale, C., & Scanlon, J. (1999). *Wired style: Principles of English usage in the digital age*. New York: Broadway Books.

Lenhart, A., Smith, A., & Macgill, A. R. (2008). *Writing, technology, and teens*. Washington, DC: Pew Internet and American Life Project. Available: http://pewresearch.org/pubs/808/writing-technology-and-teens.

Plester, B., Wood, C., & Bell, V. (2008). Txt msg n school literacy: Does texting and knowledge of text abbreviations adversely affect children's literacy attainment? *Literacy*, 42(3), 137–144.

Understanding the Text

1. According to Baron, what sorts of "minor shifts" have happened to spelling and punctuation as a result of digital media?

2. What does Baron mean when she speaks of the "whatever" attitude toward language fostered by digital media?

3. As described by Baron, in what ways have digital media and electronic devices given us control over when and how we communicate?

Reflection and Response

4. Baron claims that "on the internet no one is policing the grammar of the personal messages we construct" (par. 7). Do you believe she is correct? Can you think of examples that contradict her statement?

5. Baron argues that schools no longer stress linguistic rules (par. 16). Do you agree? Why or why not?

6. Baron notes that changing attitudes toward language correctness did not start with contemporary digital media, but she asserts that such media "add fuel to the linguistic fire" (par. 20). Do you agree? Why or why not?

Making Connections

7. Baron asserts that we need not worry about minor changes to the mechanics of language because "lexical practices evolve, and yesterday's oddity may be today's norm — or vice versa" (par. 11). Use Erin McKean's "How Are Dictionaries Made?" (p. 198), Robert MacNeil's "English Belongs to Everybody" (p. 192), and/or Robert MacNeil and William Cran's "The Language Wars" (p. 201) to provide support for her point.

8. Baron dismisses teachers' fears that the spelling and mechanics of electronic communication will spill over into academic writing, stating, "Students already understand that particular styles of language are appropriate for one venue but not another" (par. 30). How do other writers' thoughts on the connections between academic and nonacademic writing support or complicate her view? Use one or more of these writings in your response: Kevin Roozen's "Writing Is a Social and Rhetorical Activity," (p. 224), Roozen's "Writing Is Linked to Identity" (p. 227), or Dan Berrett's "Students Come to College Thinking They've Mastered Writing" (p. 284).

They're, Like, Way Ahead of the Linguistic Currrrve

Douglas Quenqua

Douglas Quenqua is editor-in-chief of the online advertising and marketing industry publication *Campaign US*. In his career as a freelance journalist, he has been a frequent contributor to the *New York Times*, in which this article originally appeared on February 27, 2012. Here, Quenqua gathers perspectives from a number of prominent linguists on the topic of young women's contributions to language change. These perspectives show that although women are commonly believed to be linguistic innovators, many "feminine" language features are equally common in men.

From Valley Girls to the Kardashians, young women have long been mocked for the way they talk.

Whether it be uptalk (pronouncing statements as if they were questions? Like this?), creating slang words like *bitchin'* and *ridic*, or the incessant use of *like* as a conversation filler, vocal trends associated with young women are often seen as markers of immaturity or even stupidity.

Right?

But linguists—many of whom once promoted theories consistent with that attitude—now say such thinking is outmoded. Girls and women in their teens and 20s deserve credit for pioneering vocal trends and popular slang, they say, adding that young women use these embellishments in much more sophisticated ways than people tend to realize.

"A lot of these really flamboyant things you hear are cute, and girls 5 are supposed to be cute," said Penny Eckert, a professor of linguistics at Stanford University. "But they're not just using them because they're girls. They're using them to achieve some kind of interactional and stylistic end."

The latest linguistic curiosity to emerge from the petri dish of girl culture gained a burst of public recognition in December, when researchers from Long Island University published a paper about it in the *Journal of Voice*. Working with what they acknowledged was a very small sample—recorded speech from 34 women ages 18 to 25—the professors said they had found evidence of a new trend among female college students: a guttural fluttering of the vocal cords they called *vocal fry*.

A classic example of vocal fry, best described as a raspy or croaking sound injected (usually) at the end of a sentence, can be heard when Mae West says, "Why don't you come up sometime and see me," or, more recently on television, when Maya Rudolph mimics Maya Angelou on *Saturday Night Live.*

Not surprisingly, gadflies in cyberspace were quick to pounce on the study—or, more specifically, on the girls and women who are frying their words. "Are they trying to sound like Kesha or Britney Spears?" teased the *Huffington Post*, naming two pop stars who employ vocal fry while singing, although the study made no mention of them. "Very interesteeeaaaaaaaaang," said Gawker.com, mocking the lazy, drawn-out affect.

Do not scoff, says Nassima Abdelli-Beruh, a speech scientist at Long Island University and an author of the study. "They use this as a tool to convey something," she said. "You quickly realize that for them, it is as a cue."

> *"Girls and women in their teens and 20s deserve credit for pioneering vocal trends and popular slang."*

Other linguists not involved in the research also cautioned against 10 forming negative judgments.

"If women do something like uptalk or vocal fry, it's immediately interpreted as insecure, emotional or even stupid," said Carmen Fought, a professor of linguistics at Pitzer College in Claremont, Calif. "The truth is this: Young women take linguistic features and use them as power tools for building relationships."

The idea that young women serve as incubators of vocal trends for the culture at large has longstanding roots in linguistics. As Paris is to fashion, the thinking goes, so are young women to linguistic innovation.

"It's generally pretty well known that if you identify a sound change in progress, then young people will be leading old people," said Mark Liberman, a linguist at the University of Pennsylvania, "and women tend to be maybe half a generation ahead of males on average."

Less clear is why. Some linguists suggest that women are more sensitive to social interactions and hence more likely to adopt subtle vocal cues. Others say women use language to assert their power in a culture that, at least in days gone by, asked them to be sedate and decorous. Another theory is that young women are simply given more leeway by society to speak flamboyantly.

But the idea that vocal fads initiated by young women eventually 15 make their way into the general vernacular is well established. Witness, for example, the spread of uptalk, or "high-rising terminal."

Starting in America with the Valley Girls of the 1980s (after immigrating from Australia, evidently), uptalk became common among young women across the country by the 1990s.

In the past 20 years, uptalk has traveled "up the age range and across the gender boundary," said David Crystal, a longtime professor of linguistics who teaches at Bangor University in Wales. "I've heard grandfathers and grandmothers use it," he said. "I occasionally use it myself."

Even an American president has been known to uptalk. "George W. Bush used to do it from time to time," said Dr. Liberman, "and nobody ever said, 'Oh, that G.W.B. is so insecure, just like a young girl.' "

The same can be said for the word *like*, when used in a grammatically superfluous way or to add cadence to a sentence. (Because, like, people tend to talk this way when impersonating, like, teenage girls?) But in 2011, Dr. Liberman conducted an analysis of nearly 12,000 phone conversations recorded in 2003, and found that while young people tended to use *like* more often than older people, men used it more frequently than women.

And, actually? The use of *like* in a sentence, "apparently without 20 meaning or syntactic function, but possibly as emphasis," has made its way into the Webster's *New World College Dictionary*, Fourth Edition — this newspaper's reference Bible — where the example given is: "It's, like, hot." Anyone who has seen a television show featuring the Kardashian sisters will be more than familiar with this usage.

Like and uptalk often go hand in hand. Several studies have shown that uptalk can be used for any number of purposes, even to dominate a listener. In 1991, Cynthia McLemore, a linguist at the University of Pennsylvania, found that senior members of a Texas sorority used uptalk to make junior members feel obligated to carry out new tasks. ("We have a rush event this Thursday? And everyone needs to be there?")

Dr. Eckert of Stanford recalled a study by one of her students, a woman who worked at a Jamba Juice and tracked instances of uptalking customers. She found that by far the most common uptalkers were fathers of young women. For them, it was "a way of showing themselves to be friendly and not asserting power in the situation," she said.

Vocal fry, also known as creaky voice, has a long history with English speakers. Dr. Crystal, the British linguist, cited it as far back as 1964 as a way for British men to denote their superior social standing. In the United States, it has seemingly been gaining popularity among women since at least 2003, when Dr. Fought, the Pitzer College linguist, detected it among the female speakers of a Chicano dialect in California.

A 2005 study by Barry Pennock-Speck, a linguist at the University of Valencia in Spain, noted that actresses like Gwyneth Paltrow and Reese Witherspoon used creaky voice when portraying contemporary American characters (Ms. Paltrow used it in the movie "Shallow Hal," Ms. Witherspoon in "Legally Blonde"), but not British ones in period films (Ms. Paltrow in "Shakespeare in Love," Ms. Witherspoon in "The Importance of Being Earnest").

So what does the use of vocal fry denote? Like uptalk, women use it for 25 a variety of purposes. Ikuko Patricia Yuasa, a lecturer in linguistics at the University of California, Berkeley, called it a natural result of women's lowering their voices to sound more authoritative.

It can also be used to communicate disinterest, something teenage girls are notoriously fond of doing.

"It's a mode of vibration that happens when the vocal cords are relatively lax, when sublevel pressure is low," said Dr. Liberman. "So maybe some people use it when they're relaxed and even bored, not especially aroused or invested in what they're saying."

But "language changes very fast," said Dr. Eckert of Stanford, and most people—particularly adults—who try to divine the meaning of new forms used by young women are "almost sure to get it wrong."

"What may sound excessively 'girly' to me may sound smart, authoritative and strong to my students," she said.

Understanding the Text

1. What is *vocal fry*, and what negative stereotypes are associated with it?

2. How are perceptions of men who use vocal fry or uptalk different from perceptions of women who do the same?

Reflection and Response

3. Based on your experience and what you have observed in the media, to what degree do you think it is true that women lead linguistic change? Provide specific examples of what you have observed.

4. Quenqua lists several possible explanations for why young women would lead linguistic change: They may be more perceptive in social situations, they may use language to assert power because of their historical lack of physical power, or society may give them more leeway to speak "flamboyantly" (par. 14). Which of these explanations is most convincing to you and why?

5. Penny Eckert notes that there are generational differences in how speech features are perceived: Something like vocal fry might sound "girly" to older listeners, but "smart, authoritative and strong" to younger listeners (par. 29). How does vocal fry sound to you and why? Compare your impressions with those of a few peers and one or more people of a different generation.

Making Connections

6. Quenqua talks about several types of linguistic change that young women lead, including innovations in sound patterns and slang. How does Connie

Eble's discussion of the social functions of slang in *Slang and Sociability* (p. 59) help to explain why women might be innovators in this area?

7. Like Quenqua, Marybeth Seitz-Brown, in "Young Women Shouldn't Have to Talk Like Men to Be Taken Seriously" (p. 92), notes that men use stereotypically "feminine" speech features such as uptalk and *like* — in some cases as much as or more than women do. Use both authors, as well as your own reflection, to answer this question: If it is not true that women use such features more often than men, why are so many people under the impression that they do?

Slang as Bad Language

Edwin Battistella

Edwin Battistella is a professor of English linguistics and writing at Southern Oregon University. Throughout his career, Battistella has published over fifty articles and six books, most recently *Sorry about That: The Language of Public Apology* (Oxford University Press, 2014). The selection below is taken from his book *Bad Language: Are Some Words Better than Others?* (Oxford University Press, 2005). Battistella focuses here on historical and contemporary objections to slang, helping us to consider where these objections come from and why slang might not be all bad.

When I was growing up, the received wisdom among my college-bound peers in the New Jersey public schools was never to use slang expressions in writing and to avoid them in speaking in front of adults. In fact, the use of slang was something that teachers and parents commented on and attempted to discourage—it was a type of bad language seen as undignified and unintelligible. Nevertheless, such writers as Whitman, Twain, and Sandburg have seen slang as a source of inventiveness and vitality in the language. The term *slang* seems to have originated in the eighteenth century. The earliest *Oxford English Dictionary* citation for it dates from 1756, and early uses of slang associated it with the language of the criminal underworld.[1] Modern slang is broader and includes some vocabulary that shows familiarity with special activities both illicit and innocent, some that challenges authority and propriety (often through irony), and some that simply celebrates the inventiveness of language. Slang differs from colloquial language, from jargon, from regionalism, and from vogue usage, yet there is no easy mechanism for identifying it since other types of word formation use the same formal processes of affixation, clipping, metaphor, borrowing, and blending. Neologisms like *dot com* are hard to distinguish formally from slang usage like *dot bomb*; however, the distinction is apparent from the intended irony.

The difficulty of defining slang does not mean that no one has tried. Harold Wentworth and Stuart Flexner, in their *Dictionary of American Slang*, simply consider slang to refer to "a body of words accepted as intelligible, . . . but not accepted as good formal usage."[2] Other lexicographers are more specific, proposing such definitions as "A type of language especially occurring in casual and playful speech usually made up of short-lived coinages and figures of speech deliberately used in place

183

of standard terms for effects of raciness, humor, or irreverence."[3] This definition nevertheless requires further unpacking. Bethany Dumas and Jonathan Lightner, in their 1978 article "Is *Slang* a Word for Linguists?" suggest four characteristics for slang:

(1) Its presence will markedly lower, at least for the moment, the dignity of formal or serious speech or writing.

(2) Its use implies the user's special familiarity either with the referent or with that less satisfied or less responsible class of people who have such special familiarity and use the term.

(3) It is a taboo term in ordinary discourse with persons of higher social status or greater responsibility.

(4) It is used in place of the well-known conventional synonym, especially in order (a) to protect the user from the discomfort caused by the conventional item or (b) to protect the user from the discomfort or annoyance of further elaboration.[4]

These four characteristics—a lowering of seriousness, the presumption of familiarity with a topic or group, stigmatization in discourse with persons of higher status, and function as a shield for the user—help to elaborate the definition of slang. They also encapsulate both its social usefulness and its risks. Slang is used to create a kind of linguistic solidarity or status by identifying oneself with a group out of the mainstream or by setting oneself apart from conventional values through a style of toughness and ironic detachment.

Slang is often associated with adolescents and college students, groups making the transition into adulthood and thus negotiating new roles and identities. In her 1996 book *Slang and Sociability*, Connie Eble sees the key function of slang use among college students as that of establishing group identity and distinguishing student values from the values of those in authority. This function is consistent with the way in which slang borrows and adapts words from groups and topics perceived as falling outside of mainstream English. Eble's analysis of taped conversations among college students also reveals that slang is less commonly used among intimate friends but that the frequency of slang increases when someone new joins a close-knit group.[5] She suggests that students who are not especially close use slang to establish identity—their solidarity as students—while those who are already intimate friends have less need to demonstrate solidarity.

As noted earlier, creative writers have both recognized and exploited the vitality of slang—Carl Sandburg once commented that "Slang is language that rolls up its sleeves and spits in its hands."[6] Other writers, journalists, and teachers of academic writing have had a harder time dealing with slang, however, since their aim is often for a formal tone that addresses a hypothetical general audience. *The Associated Press Stylebook*, for example, recommends that journalists "in general, avoid slang, the highly informal language that is outside of conventional or standard usage."[7] And the *Harbrace Handbook* advises students that "On occasion, slang can be used effectively, even in formal writing. . . . But much slang is trite, tasteless, and inexact."[8] These guides hint at the relativity of slang usage but provide little help in understanding when slang might be effective. William Watt's 1957 *An American Rhetoric* is more helpful: Watt writes that "The trouble with slang is not, as many undergraduates assume, that it is always 'vulgar' or 'bad English.' The trouble is that much of it is (1) forced, (2) local, (3) overworked when alive, and (4) soon dead."[9] While the local currency of slang makes it attractive in speech, it can also make slang a distraction in formal writing.[10]

An understanding of the relativity of slang contrasts with folk attitudes   5 that see slang merely as bad English used by bad people. Jonathan Lightner remarks that in the eighteenth and early nineteenth centuries "slang was seen as both emerging from and sustaining an undisguised baseness of mind that must lead to the coarsening of both language and civilization."[11] The sentiments of Oliver Wendell Holmes, Sr., were typical. In an 1870 address to the Harvard University Phi Beta Kappa Society, Holmes asserted that "the use of *slang*, or cheap generic terms, as a substitute for differentiated specific expressions, is at once a sign and a cause of mental atrophy."[12] Lightner sees attitudes toward slang as beginning to shift in the last quarter of the nineteenth century as writers like Mark Twain incorporated it in popular writing to define sympathetic and unpretentious literary characters.[13] In addition, H. L. Mencken cites the influence of cartoonists, sports writers and news columnists, writing approvingly that "Slang originates in the efforts of ingenious individuals to make the language more pungent and picturesque."[14] Giving examples like *stiff, flat-foot, smoke-eater*, and *yes-man*, Mencken argues that slang provides new shades of meaning. Nevertheless, in the early twentieth century, we still find the prevailing attitude that slang implies too much familiarity with or interest in vices and rough behavior.[15] John Burnham notes that the early twentieth-century attitude was that "Nice children did not have anything to do with users of slang, who identified themselves by their words."

As slang usage has become less associated with criminal behavior and more the object of study by scholars and the popular press, objections have sometimes been treated as questions of communication rather than character and criminalization.[16] The supposed vagueness of slang is, in turn, linked to habits of mind. This linking is apparent in the comment of Holmes, cited earlier. It was apparent as well in the concern of James Greenough and George Lyman Kittredge in 1901 that slang has "no fixed meaning" and that it would "gradually reduce one's thought to the same ignorant level from which most slang proceeds."[17] A hundred years later we find essentially the same view expressed by writer Linda Hall, who complains that her students do not worry about precision, so they do not see most of their speech as needing to be taken seriously.[18] She argues, for example, that the use of *cool* to refer broadly to that which is fashionable (*a cool blouse*) or personable (*a cool teacher*) creates a vagueness that hinders communication.[19] But there

> "The argument that slang 'robs the language' and 'preys on vocabulary' misses the point that the living language is a marketplace of ideas, nuances, and images."

are many instances in which nonslang meanings are expansive as well. Consider the word *cup*, which can refer to a number of ounces, the container of a drink, or the drink itself (usually hot), a protective device for the male groin, or a size of brassiere or breast. The vagueness of *cup* is typically manageable through context and there is no reason to assume that the same is not the case for *cool* or to assume that slang reduces our abilities to make subtle distinctions vividly and effectively.

The argument is sometimes also made that slang is harmful to the language. For example, Jacques Barzun portrays slang as encroaching on the existing meanings of words. He writes that:

> *Far from injecting vigor into the upper layers of speech, the slang of today has managed to destroy or make doubtful more good words than it could make up for a long time. Whole series — from earlier* fairy *and* pansy *to* queer, *faggot,* adult, *and* gay — *have done nothing but rob the language of irreplaceable resources. Others, such as* ball, bomb, blow, screw *have been left uncertain in slang and unexpectedly embarrassing elsewhere. Nowadays, slang rather preys on the straight vocabulary than feeds it new blood; and the loss is made worse by the general abandonment of the educated of propriety in every sense of the term.*[20]

Barzun's objection focuses both on the character of slang users and on the effect of slang on the language, invoking the metaphors of theft and destruction. But his argument is far too general and ignores the fact that vocabulary changes to meet new needs and new shades of meaning.

In some cases change is driven by new technical, political, medical, or social developments (as with the borrowing of the name *spam* to refer to bulk electronic junk mail). In other cases the change is cultural, as when a group reexamines its identity (as in the recent reemergence of *queer* as an assertion of gay pride) or when social attitudes change. In some cases the change is market driven, as when the media and advertisers follow linguistic trends to position themselves with consumers (using superlative expressions like *phat*, for example). The argument that slang "robs the language" and "preys on vocabulary" misses the point that the living language is a marketplace of ideas, nuances, and images. Barzun's concern that slang makes words doubtful, uncertain, and potentially embarrassing for speakers not in the know is revealing, however. Slang does not so much rob the language of resources as it reduces the security of speakers like Barzun to assume that their norms can be used without fear of embarrassment or misunderstanding. In other words, slang requires speakers of one variety to adjust and accommodate to the norms of another. It is this challenge to assumed norms that places slang in the category of improper usage for some speakers. It is not the language that is destabilized by slang. What is destabilized is the assumption that mainstream norms are shared by everyone. And part of the pleasure of slang for its users is belonging to an in-group that excludes the conventional mainstream.

In attitudes toward slang, we continue to find a contest between those who view nonstandard language as a danger and those who see it as having contextual utility. Critics of slang have associated it with lower order speakers and character defects, with social impropriety and looseness by standard speakers, and with damage to the precision of the standard. Defenders, on the other hand, stress the inventiveness of slang, its role in stylistic vitality and identity, and the parallel between the creation of slang and other forms of neology. For descriptivists, the issue of slang usage, however, is one of social appropriateness and utility, not abiding propriety and defense of the standard against debasement by false coinage. As with coarse language, the relativist view is that effectiveness is the measure of good language. On this view, speakers and writers need the background and experience to decide when jocularity, familiarity, inventiveness, and local color are useful and when they are an impediment.

Notes

1. See Richard Bailey's *Nineteenth-Century English* and Farmer and Henley's *Slang and Its Analogues* for details.

2. Harold Wentworth and Stuart Berg Flexner, *Dictionary of American Slang* (New York: Thomas Y. Crowell, 1960), xvii.

3. *American Heritage Dictionary* (Springfield, MA: Merriam-Webster, 1997), 1279.

4. Bethany Dumas and Jonathan Lightner, "Is *Slang* a Word for Linguists?" *American Speech* 53.1 (1978), 14–16.

5. See Connie Eble, *Slang and Sociability: In-group Language among College Students* (Chapel Hill: University of North Carolina Press, 1996), 99–129.

6. The quote from Carl Sandburg is from the profile "Minstrel of America: Carl Sandburg," *New York Times*, Feb. 13, 1959, 21.

7. Norm Goldstein, ed., *The AP Stylebook and Libel Manual* (Reading, MA: Addison-Wesley, 1996), 191.

8. John Hodges, Mary Whitten, and Suzanne Webb, *The Harbrace College Handbook* (New York: Harcourt Brace, 1986), 198.

9. William Watt, *An American Rhetoric* (New York: Holt, 1957), 270.

10. For an example of the advice given to broadcasters, see Stuart Hyde's *Television and Radio Announcing*, 8th ed. (New York: Houghton Mifflin, 1998). Hyde also emphasizes the relativity of slang. He writes that "To some 'slang' means corrupted speech; to others it means a creative and effective use of language. Slang is condemned by language purists, but most of us use it without apology in some settings and contexts" (144). He adds that broadcast announcers should nevertheless be sensitive to the effective and ineffective use of nonstandard language: "Slang that might be appropriate in a commercial may be out of place in a newscast. Although sports announcers, talk-show hosts, and popular music announcers often use slang to good effect, it's usually avoided by news commentators and analysts" (147).

11. Jonathan Lightner, "Slang," *The Cambridge History of the English Language: 6, English in North America*, ed. John Algeo (Cambridge: Cambridge University Press, 2001), 227.

12. Oliver Wendell Holmes, Sr., "Mechanism in Thought and Morals," *Pages from an Old Volume of Life* (Boston: Houghton Mifflin, 1891), 275.

13. Lightner, 227. Among others, Lightner sees George Ade, Peter Dunne, Ring Lardner, and Jack London as influential.

14. H. L. Mencken, *The American Language* (New York: Knopf, 1937), 563.

15. John C. Burnham, *Bad Habits: Drinking, Smoking, Taking Drugs, Gambling, Sexual Misbehavior, and Swearing in American History* (New York: New York University Press, 1993), 215. Dennis Baron emphasizes the association of slang with linguistic disease, social poverty, and decay (*Grammar and Good Taste* [New Haven: Yale University Press, 1982], 216–17). An example of this in early twentieth-century psychological research can be found in Gladys Schwesinger's "Slang as an Indication of Character," *Journal of Applied Psychology* 10 (1926), 245–63. Schwesinger performed what she described as an attempt at "character detection and management" by surveying delinquents and nondelinquents for knowledge of slang terms.

16. An exception seems to be the characterization of African-American English, which is sometimes mischaracterized as "street slang" by commentators

reacting to both the 1979 King school decision and the 1996 Oakland School Board resolution, and an unsuccessful California Senate bill referred disapprovingly to school programs that "teach that slang is an appropriate alternative to correct English in some situations" (cited in John Baugh's *Beyond Ebonics* [New York: Oxford University Press, 1999], 79).

17. See James Bradstreet Greenough and George Lyman Kittredge, *Words and Their Way in English Speech* (New York: Macmillan, 1901), 73.

18. Linda Hall, "Coolspeak," *Hudson Review* (2002), 414.

19. For an analysis of the meaning and use of *cool* see Robert Moore's essay "We're Cool. Mom and Dad Are Swell: Basic Slang and Generational Shifts in Values," *American Speech* 79.1 (2004), 59–86.

20. Jacques Barzun, "What Are Mistakes and Why," in *A Word or Two before You Go. . . .* , 8–9. Barzun also suggests that slang ignores "the really working part of words drawn on" (6), citing *workaholic* and arguing that *–aholic* is being misused.

References

American Heritage Dictionary. Springfield, MA: Merriam-Webster, 1997.

Bailey, Richard. *Nineteenth-Century English*. Ann Arbor: University of Michigan Press, 1996.

Baron, Dennis. *Grammar and Good Taste: Reforming the American Language*. New Haven: Yale University Press, 1982.

Barzun, Jacques. "What Are Mistakes and Why." In *A Word or Two before You Go. . . .* , by Jacques Barzun (pp. 13–17). Middleton, CT: Wesleyan University Press, 1986.

Baugh, John. *Beyond Ebonics*. New York: Oxford University Press, 1999.

Burnham, John C. *Bad Habits: Drinking, Smoking, Taking Drugs, Gambling, Sexual Misbehavior, and Swearing in American History*. New York: New York University Press, 1993.

Bush, Douglas. "Polluting Our Language." *The American Scholar*, June 1972, 238–47.

Dumas, Bethany, and Jonathan Lightner. "Is *Slang* a Word for Linguists?" *American Speech* 53.1 (1978), 5–17.

Eble, Connie. *Slang and Sociability: In-group Language among College Students*. Chapel Hill: University of North Carolina Press, 1996.

Farmer, John, and William Ernest Henley. *A Dictionary of Slang*. New York: Wordsworth, 1987. 2 vols. (originally published as *Slang and Its Analogues*, 1890).

Goldstein, Norm (editor). *The AP Stylebook and Libel Manual*. 6th edition. Reading, MA: Addison-Wesley, 1996.

Greenough, James Bradstreet, and George Lyman Kittredge. *Words and Their Way in English Speech*. New York: Macmillan, 1901.

Hall, Robert A. *Leave Your Language Alone!* Ithaca, NY: Linguistica, 1950.

Hodges, John, Mary Whitten, and Suzanne Webb. *The Harbrace College Handbook.* 10th edition. New York: Harcourt Brace, 1986.

Holmes, Oliver Wendell, Sr. "Mechanism in Thought and Morals." In *Pages from an Old Volume of Life* (pp. 260–314). Boston: Houghton Mifflin, 1891.

Hyde, Stuart. *Television and Radio Announcing.* 8th edition. New York: Houghton Mifflin, 1998.

Lightner, Jonathan. "Slang." In *The Cambridge History of the English Language* vol. 6, *English in North America*, edited by John Algeo (pp. 219–52). Cambridge: Cambridge University Press, 2001.

Mencken, H. L. *The American Language: An Inquiry into the Development of English in the United States.* New York: Knopf, 1937.

"Minstrel of America: Carl Sandburg." *New York Times*, Feb. 13, 1959, 21.

Moore, Robert L. "We're Cool, Mom and Dad Are Swell: Basic Slang and Generational Shifts in Values. *American Speech* 79.1 (2004), 59–86.

Schwesinger, Gladys. "Slang as an Indication of Character." *Journal of Applied Psychology* 10 (1926), 245–63.

Watt, William. *An American Rhetoric.* New York: Holt, 1957.

Wentworth, Harold, and Stuart Berg Flexner. *Dictionary of American Slang.* New York: Thomas Y. Crowell, 1960.

Understanding the Text

1. What are some of the key characteristics of slang, according to the definitions Battistella cites?

2. How have attitudes toward English slang evolved over time, according to Battistella's description?

3. How does Battistella counter the criticism that slang creates a "vagueness that hinders communication" (par. 6)?

Reflection and Response

4. Paraphrasing Mencken, Battistella states that "slang provides new shades of meaning" (par. 5). Consider some of the slang words you have encountered recently, either in your own life or in popular culture. What words can you think of that provide more specific meanings than their dictionary counterparts, or that have meanings for which there is no formal term?

5. Battistella asserts, "It is not the language that is destabilized by slang. What is destabilized is the assumption that mainstream norms are shared by everyone" (par. 7). What does he mean, and do you think he is correct? Why?

Making Connections

6. Battistella notes that style manuals, such as the *Associated Press Stylebook* for journalists and the Harbrace family of handbooks for college students, tend to advise against the use of slang. Using Robert MacNeil and William Cran's "The Language Wars" (p. 201) and/or Rusty Barrett's "Rewarding Language" (p. 130), explain why this advice is common and what its advantages and disadvantages are. If your class uses a grammar handbook or other writing guide, consider including its perspective on slang here, too.

7. Battistella notes that slang can build "linguistic solidarity" (par. 2), allowing its users to establish a sense of group identity. Use examples from H. Samy Alim's "Hip Hop Nation Language" (p. 74) and/or Susan Tamasi and Lamont Antieau's "Social Variables" (p. 43) to support this point.

English Belongs to Everybody

Robert MacNeil

Robert MacNeil is a retired journalist and news anchor known for his coverage of the Kennedy assassination and Watergate hearings and for founding the award-winning *MacNeil/Lehrer NewsHour*, now called the *PBS NewsHour*. He has written a number of books, including analyses of language and politics, novels, and memoirs. In his memoir *Wordstruck* (Viking, 1989), he recalls developing his love for language and reading as a child and reflects on how that love has influenced his ideas about language. In the excerpt below, he reflects specifically on the versatility of the English language, which has grown and changed with time and always refused to conform to strict rules.

This is a time of widespread anxiety about the language. Some Americans fear that English will be engulfed or diluted by Spanish and want to make it the official language. There is anxiety about a crisis of illiteracy, or a crisis of semi-literacy among high school, even college, graduates. There is even anxiety that written English is on the way out. Gore Vidal expresses it elegantly in his introduction to Logan Pearsall Smith's *Trivia:*

As human society abandoned the oral tradition for the written text, the written culture is now being replaced by the audio visual one. . . . What is to become of that written language which was for two millennia wisdom's only mold?

Anxiety may have a perverse side effect: experts who wish to "save" the language may only discourage pleasure in it. Some are good-humored and tolerant of change, others intolerant and snobbish. Language reinforces feelings of social superiority or inferiority; it creates insiders and outsiders; it is a prop to vanity or a source of anxiety, and on both emotions the language snobs play. Yet the changes and the errors that irritate them are no different in kind from those which have shaped our language for centuries. As Hugh Kenner wrote of certain British critics in *The Sinking Island*, "They took note of language only when it annoyed them." Such people are killjoys: they turn others away from an interest in the language, inhibit their use of it, and turn pleasure off.

Change is inevitable in a living language and is responsible for much of the vitality of English; it has prospered and grown because it was able to accept and absorb change. . . .

As people evolve and do new things, their language will evolve too. They will find ways to describe the new things and their changed perspective will give them new ways of talking about the old things. For example, electric light switches created a brilliant metaphor for the oldest of human experiences, being *turned on* or *turned off*. To language conservatives those expressions still have a slangy, low ring to them; to others they are vivid, fresh-minted currency, very spendable, very *with it*.

That tolerance for change represents not only the dynamism of the 5 English-speaking peoples since the Elizabethans, but their deeply-rooted ideas of freedom as well. This was the idea of the Danish scholar Otto Jespersen, one of the great authorities on English. Writing in 1905, Jespersen said in his *Growth and Structure of the English Language:*

The French language is like the stiff French garden of Louis XIV, while the English is like an English park, which is laid out seemingly without any definite plan, and in which you are allowed to walk everywhere according to your own fancy without having to fear a stern keeper enforcing rigorous regulations. The English language would not have been what it is if the English had not been for centuries great respecters of the liberties of each individual and if everybody had not been free to strike out new paths for himself.

I like that idea and do not think it just coincidence. Consider that the same cultural soil, the Celtic-Roman-Saxon-Danish-Norman amalgam, which produced the English language also nourished the great principles of freedom and rights of man in the modern world. The first shoots sprang up in England and they grew stronger in America. Churchill called them "the joint inheritance of the English-speaking world." At the very core of those principles are popular consent and resistance to arbitrary authority; both are fundamental characteristics of our language. The English-speaking peoples have defeated all efforts to build fences around their language, to defer to an academy on what was permissible English and what not. They'll decide for themselves, thanks just the same.

Nothing better expresses resistance to arbitrary authority than the persistence of what grammarians have denounced for centuries as "errors." In the common speech of English-speaking peoples—Americans, Englishmen, Canadians, Australians, New Zealanders, and others—these usages persist, despite rising literacy and wider education. We hear them every day:

Double negative: "I don't want none of that."

Double comparative: "Don't make that any more heavier!" Wrong verb: "Will you learn me to read?"

The Kirkdale Sundial, in the wall of St. Gregory's Church in Kirkdale, North Yorkshire, England. Inscribed in approximately 1055, the words on the sundial provide a snapshot of the transition from Old English to Middle English. They also highlight the heritage of English as a "Celtic-Roman-Saxon-Danish-Norman amalgam," to borrow MacNeil's words. For instance, we can see Roman influence in the absence of spacing between words, while Danish is visible in the names, including "Orm Gamal" on the left and "Hawarth" and "Brand" in the middle.
Photo by Mike Carpenter

These "errors" have been with us for at least four hundred years, because you can find each of them in Shakespeare.

Double negative: In *Hamlet*, the King says:

Nor what he spake, though it lack'd form a little, Was not like madness.

Double comparative: In *Othello*, the Duke says:

Yet opinion . . . throws a more safer voice on you.

Wrong verb: In *Othello*, Desdemona says:

My life and education both do learn me how to respect you.

I find it very interesting that these forms will not go away and lie down. They were vigorous and acceptable in Shakespeare's time; they are far more vigorous today, although not acceptable as standard English. Regarded as error by grammarians, they are nevertheless in daily use all over the world by a hundred times the number of people who lived in Shakespeare's England.

It fascinates me that *axe*, meaning *ask*, so common in black American 10 English, is standard in Chaucer in all forms—*axe, axen, axed:* "and *axed* him if Troilus were there." Was that transmitted across six hundred years or simply reinvented?

English grew without a formal grammar. After the enormous creativity of Shakespeare and the other Elizabethans, seventeenth- and eighteenth-century critics thought the language was a mess, like an over-grown garden. They weeded it by imposing grammatical rules derived from tidier languages, chiefly Latin, whose precision and predictability they trusted. For three centuries, with some slippage here and there, their rules have held. Educators taught them and written English conformed. Today, English-language newspapers, magazines, and books everywhere broadly agree that correct English obeys these rules. Yet the wild varieties continue to threaten the garden of cultivated English and, by their num-bers, actually dominate everyday usage.

Non-standard English formerly knew its place in the social order. Characters in fiction were allowed to speak it occasionally. Hemingway believed that American literature really did not begin until Mark Twain, who outraged critics by reproducing the vernacular of characters like Huck Finn. Newspapers still clean up the grammar when they quote the ungrammatical, including politicians. The printed word, like Victorian morality, has often constituted a conspiracy of respectability.

People who spoke grammatically could be excused the illusion that their writ held sway, perhaps the way the Normans thought that French had conquered the language of the vanquished Anglo-Saxons. A genera-tion ago, people who considered themselves educated and well-spoken might have had only glancing contact with non-standard English, usually in a well-understood class, regional, or rural context.

It fascinates me how differently we all speak in different circumstances. We have levels of formality, as in our cloth-ing. There are very formal occasions, often requiring written English: the job application or the letter to the editor—the dark-suit, serious-tie language, with everything pressed and the lint brushed

"Our language is not the special private property of the language police, or grammarians, or teachers, or even great writers. The genius of English is that it has always been the tongue of the common people, literate or not."

off. There is our less formal out-in-the-world language—a more comfortable suit, but still respectable. There is language for close friends in the evenings, on weekends—blue-jeans-and-sweat-shirt language, when it's good to get the tie off. There is family language, even more relaxed, full of grammatical short cuts, family slang, echoes of old jokes that have become intimate shorthand—the language of pajamas and uncombed hair. Finally, there is the language with no clothes on; the talk of couples—murmurs, sighs, grunts—language at its least self-conscious, open, vulnerable, and primitive.

Broadcasting has democratized the publication of language, often at 15 its most informal, even undressed. Now the ears of the educated cannot escape the language of the masses. It surrounds them on the news, weather, sports, commercials, and the ever-proliferating talk and call-in shows.

This wider dissemination of popular speech may easily give purists the idea that the language is suddenly going to hell in this generation, and may explain the new paranoia about it.

It might also be argued that more Americans hear more correct, even beautiful, English on television than was ever heard before. Through television more models of good usage reach more American homes than was ever possible in other times. Television gives them lots of colloquial English, too, some awful, some creative, but that is not new.

Hidden in this is a simple fact: our language is not the special private property of the language police, or grammarians, or teachers, or even great writers. The genius of English is that it has always been the tongue of the common people, literate or not.

English belongs to everybody: the funny turn of phrase that pops into the mind of a farmer telling a story; or the traveling salesman's dirty joke; or the teenager saying, "Gag me with a spoon"; or the pop lyric—all contribute, are all as valid as the tortured image of the academic, or the line the poet sweats over for a week.

Through our collective language sense, some may be thought beauti- 20 ful and some ugly, some may live and some may die; but it is all English and it belongs to everyone—to those of us who wish to be careful with it and those who don't care.

Understanding the Text

1. What point is MacNeil making by providing examples of text from Shakespeare and Chaucer (pars. 8–10)?

2. According to MacNeil, what effects have broadcast media had on people's exposure to nonstandard or informal speech and their attitudes toward it?

Reflection and Response

3. MacNeil uses the example of the phrases *turned on* and *turned off* to show how changes in our lives and technology have created new language for us (par. 4). Does this point remain true today? What are some more recent developments in technology, industry, or media that have given us new language?

4. MacNeil notes that our language, like our clothing, can be dressed up or down depending on the formality of our surroundings (par. 14). Reflect on how his descriptions apply to your language. When do you speak your "suit-and-tie" language, and what does it sound or look like? How about your "pajamas and uncombed hair" language?

Making Connections

5. MacNeil asserts, "Language reinforces feelings of social superiority or inferiority; it creates insiders and outsiders" (par. 2). Using some combination of MacNeil and William Cran's "The Language Wars" (p. 201), Rusty Barrett's "Rewarding Language" (p. 130), and/or Connie Eble's *Slang and Sociability* (p. 56), expand on and support his assertion.

6. MacNeil speaks of English's "resistance to arbitrary authority" (par. 7). Draw on your reading of MacNeil and Cran's "The Language Wars" (p. 201) to describe the different responses that prescriptivists and descriptivists have to such resistance.

7. What examples of English's "resistance to . . . authority" can you find in Mark Peters's "He Said, Sheme Said" (p. 162) or Edwin Battistella's "Slang as Bad Language" (p. 183)?

How Are Dictionaries Made?

Erin McKean

Erin McKean is a lexicographer (dictionary maker) who runs the online dictionary *Wordnik*. She has been an editor of dictionaries at Oxford University Press and Scott Foresman, and she edited the journal *Verbatim: The Language Quarterly*. She has written several books about language, including *Totally Weird and Wonderful Words* (Oxford, 2006) and *That's Amore* (Walker and Company, 2007). In the piece below, originally published in *The 5-Minute Linguist* (Equinox, 2012), McKean shares her insider perspective on dictionary creation. Contrary to what you might imagine, the "science" of dictionary making is much less about telling us what is correct and much more about recording language change as it happens.

Think of our language as an immense glacier, a giant shining mass made of words instead of ice. Like a glacier, language usually changes very, very slowly, with occasional huge surges forward. The English language is moving—changing—very slowly, most of the time. Sure, there are sometimes surprising surges of new words, but most of the changes happen so slowly and gradually that they're almost imperceptible. A slightly different meaning here, a new ending on a word there—who notices? Well, lexicographers notice. Lexicographers keep track of language change and record it in the dictionaries they make—but they're always a step behind.

As recently as a few centuries ago it was possible for one very learned person to create a dictionary single-handedly. But these days virtually all dictionaries are built by whole teams of talented people. For each new dictionary, and each new edition of an existing dictionary, they collect huge amounts of written and spoken language—from newspapers, magazines, books, plays, movies, speeches, TV and radio shows, interviews and the internet—and sift them for evidence of how language is being used: what words haven't been seen before? What words are changing their meanings? What words are used only in particular ways? What are their histories, pronunciations, grammatical quirks and foibles?

If you think this makes lexicographers sound like scientists, you're exactly right. Most of them see their primary job as data collecting. They try to capture as accurate a picture as possible of how people actually use a language at a given point in time.

But a lot of people in the dictionary-buying public are uncomfortable with scientific neutrality when it comes to language. They don't want their dictionaries to describe how people actually write and speak. They believe that some language is right and some is wrong, period. And they think the lexicographer's job is to tell us which is which. They want prescriptive° dictionaries that omit vulgar language and condemn other words they disapprove of, like *irregardless* or *muchly*.

If you're one of those people, you'll be disappointed to learn that most 5 modern dictionaries are basically descriptive.° They don't prescribe what we ought to say or write; they tell us what people actually do. Like umpires, lexicographers don't make rules—they just call 'em the way they see 'em.

That doesn't mean that prescriptive views are completely left out. People's attitudes toward words are also a legitimate part of a dictionary. For example, the *New Oxford American Dictionary* doesn't forbid its readers to use the unlovely word *irregardless*, but it clearly notes that the word is "avoided by careful users of English." Because people no longer use words like *fletcherize* (meaning to chew each bite at least thirty-two times before you swallow), and because you don't talk the way people did in eighteenth-century Williamsburg, you know that language is always in flux. So if research finds a lot of good and careful writers using *irregardless*, or creating sentences like "Anybody could look it up if they wanted to"—using *they* where you might expect *he or she*—the dictionary can say with authority that it's becoming standard English—even if prescriptivists disapprove.

There's also a whole new category of dictionary—the online dictionary—where you can see word evidence as quickly as the lexicographers can, without waiting for it to make it through the editorial process. At Wordnik.com (a

> "Dictionary-makers put as good a map as possible into your hands, but devising a route is up to you."

site I founded), automated processes sift through billions of words to select sentences based on how well they represent the word you're interested in. The site allows users to leave comments, record pronunciations, tag words, and even see images from the online photo site Flickr.com. Purely crowd-sourced sites such as UrbanDictionary.com and Wiktionary.org let users put in their two cents, as well. The upside of all these sites is that they can show you much more information than a traditional dictionary, much faster (and Wordnik and Wiktionary also incorporate traditional dictionary information like parts of speech and synonyms). However, you need to use your own knowledge and employ your critical thinking skills to filter the information shown. For instance, if a word's usage is illustrated by plenty of sentences, but they're all from personal blogs, the word is likely considered more informal than one where all the sentences shown are from the *Wall Street Journal*.

prescriptive: an approach to language that "prescribes" behavior by insisting that there is a single "correct" way of using language.
descriptive: an approach to language that "describes" the full range of informal and formal language behavior without labeling any language better or worse.

So don't think of dictionaries as rulebooks. They're much more like maps. They show where things are in relation to each other and point out where the terrain is rough. And, like maps, dictionaries (especially online dictionaries) are constantly updated to show the changing topography of a language—not just with shiny new words (like *locavore* or *staycation* or *crowdsourced*) but new uses for old words (like *burn* meaning "record data on a compact disk") and even new parts of words (the suffix *-age* as in *signage* or *mopeage*—which is really just a funnier way of saying *moping*). Dictionary-makers put as good a map as possible into your hands, but devising a route is up to you.

Understanding the Text

1. According to McKean, how do lexicographers use media, such as newspapers, TV, and movies, in creating and updating dictionaries?
2. What differences exist between traditional dictionaries and online dictionaries? Consider issues like how long it takes a word to get into the dictionary, who is writing the definitions, and what sorts of information are offered about the words.

Reflection and Response

3. McKean notes that some people dislike the "scientific neutrality" of dictionary makers, and would prefer for dictionaries to tell us which language is "right" and which is "wrong" (par. 4). How do you view the role of dictionaries? Should they be more descriptive or prescriptive?
4. McKean mentions several kinds of language evolution that show up in dictionaries: new words, new definitions for existing words, and new uses for parts of words like suffixes (par. 8). Think of a few examples of these different types of change that have occurred in recent years. Would you expect them to be in the dictionary? (Feel free to check whether they are!)

Making Connections

5. Consider this statement from McKean: "If research finds a lot of good and careful writers using *irregardless*, or creating sentences like 'Anybody could look it up if they wanted to' — using *they* where you might expect *he or she* the dictionary can say with authority that it's becoming standard English — even if prescriptivists disapprove" (par. 6). Respond from the perspective of Rosina Lippi-Green in "The Standard Language Myth" (p. 212), and/or Jesse Sheidlower or John Simon, who are quoted in Robert MacNeil and William Cran's "The Language Wars" (p. 201).
6. McKean mentions several online dictionary sites, including Wiktionary.org, urbandictionary.com, and her own site, Wordnik.com. Visit one or two such sites and look at how each is described on its "About" page. Examine a few definitions to see who writes them, what information is included, and where any example sentences come from. What can you observe about the dictionary's goals and priorities? Is it important that definitions be correct, that many people get involved, or that the material be up-to-the-minute in currency? What would you be likely to use this dictionary for?

The Language Wars

Robert MacNeil and William Cran

In this piece, Robert MacNeil teams up with William Cran, who has been a television producer for over forty years and has produced over fifty documentaries and several major television series. MacNeil and Cran have worked together, with MacNeil as writer/host and Cran as writer/producer, on two television mini-series about the English language, *The Story of English* (1986) and *Do You Speak American?* (2004). The selection below comes from the book *Do You Speak American?*, which MacNeil and Cran coauthored as a companion to the TV series. In this chapter, they explain the differences between two contrasting views of language, prescriptivism and descriptivism. One caution in advance: Keep in mind as you read that prescriptivism and descriptivism describe *attitudes* toward language rather than ways of speaking. Just because a descriptivist finds slang acceptable, for instance, doesn't mean he or she necessarily uses it frequently.

What grammarians say should be has perhaps less influence on what shall be than even the more modest of them realize; usage evolves itself little disturbed by their likes and dislikes.

— H. W. FOWLER, *MODERN ENGLISH USAGE*[1]

For centuries there has been a struggle between those who want our language to obey strict rules and those willing to be guided by how people actually speak and write. The first, who want to *prescribe*, are known as *prescriptivists*, while those content to *describe* usage are called *descriptivists*. The war between the two camps has blazed up with particular belligerence in our times, as language issues engaged social conservatives and liberals and became a factor in the so-called culture wars. Away from that intellectual battleground, ordinary Americans can be either gloriously relaxed about their language or, to use the popular idiom, decidedly *uptight*.

A mild insecurity about language may be part of the American birthright, psychological residue from the one fiber in the colonial cord that was never quite severed. Language uneasiness is rife today, as generations of Americans leave high school much freer socially but without the linguistic confidence of earlier generations, who were better grounded in basic grammar. However informal and tolerant our society becomes, people know that the way they use language still matters. "Aside from a person's physical appearance, the first thing someone will be judged by is how he or she talks," says linguist Dennis Baron.[2]

Fear of such judgment may be feeding the free-floating anxiety that we have found, which manifests itself in adamant doctrines of correctness and the firm conviction that "other people" are ruining the language.

If you cringe when someone says *between you and I;* bristle at the word *hopefully;* detest *prioritize;* if you cherish the distinction between *disinterested* and *uninterested* and deplore their being treated as synonyms; if you wonder what's happened to education when you hear *criteria* used as a singular—then you are probably part of the large body of Americans who feel our language is in a state of serious decline. You may keep it to yourself or feel compelled to express your outrage at every opportunity. But the feelings are strong and very personal. You have the sense of being robbed of something precious to you, to the nation, to our basic cultural values, to your pleasure in knowing you are "correct," to your very sense of identity and where you belong in this society. You believe all of this is being wantonly destroyed by language barbarians among your fellow citizens, who, if you speak up, make you sound out of touch, hopelessly old-fashioned, and quaint in your concerns.

But are you justified in being so upset? Many Americans who also 5 care about the language don't agree with you. For example, Charles Harrington Elster, cohost of the radio program *A Way with Words* on KPBS, San Diego, believes our language "is thriving now probably more than at any time since the Elizabethans." He told the *San Diego Home/ Garden Lifestyles* magazine, "I think the language itself is in great shape and growing like Topsy."[3]

Let's begin with those who do think the language is going to hell in this generation. Perhaps the most outspoken is the essayist John Simon. Dapper, cultivated, and acerbic, a leather briefcase tucked under his arm, he is a familiar figure on Broadway as the theater critic for *New York* magazine.

Today, he sees the state of our language as "unhealthy, poor, sad, depressing, and probably fairly hopeless." Hopeless because he sees no improvement in the teaching of English in schools or colleges and "it's been my experience that there is no bottom and that one can always sink lower, or that the language can always disintegrate further."

Simon says all this with a slight lisp and the faintest trace of a foreign accent. But what really gives him away as someone who is not a native-born speaker of English is that his grammar, syntax, and pronunciation are, if anything, almost too polished and correct.

As a child in Yugoslavia, Simon spoke Serbo-Croatian, German, Hungarian, and French, and learned English only in high school. His family moved to the United States at the beginning of World War II, and Simon went on to earn a Harvard Ph.D. in English and comparative literature.

He believes that coming to a language late can be an advantage, because one brings better credentials, linguistic, cultural, and emotional.

Simon's own strong emotions about the state of American English 10 came to national attention in 1980 with his book *Paradigms Lost: Reflections on Literacy and Its Decline.* He wrote that language was "better" when he was a graduate student in the 1940s, when "people were not going around saying 'Come to dinner with Bill and I,' or 'hopefully it won't rain tomorrow.'"[4] To explain what started the language "on a downhill course," he offered a sweeping indictment of students, teachers, women, blacks, Hispanics, homosexuals, advertisers, television, and the permissive revolution of the sixties, which dealt education "four great body blows":

(1) the student rebellion of 1968, which, in essence, meant that students themselves became arbiters of what subjects were to be taught, and grammar, by jingo (or Ringo), was not one of them; (2) the notion that in a democratic society language must accommodate itself to the whims, idiosyncrasies, dialects, and sheer ignorance of underprivileged minorities, especially if these happened to be black, Hispanic, and, later on, female or homosexual; (3) the introduction by more and more incompetent English teachers, products of the new system . . . of ever fancier techniques of not teaching English, for which, if the methods involved new technologies and were couched in the appropriately impenetrable jargon, grants could readily be obtained; and (4) television — the non-language and aboriginal grammar of commercials, commentators, sports announcers, athletes, assorted celebrities, and just about everyone on that word-mongering and word-mangling medium, that sucks in victims far more perniciously than radio ever did.

In addition, Simon wrote, dictionaries were still relatively "prescriptivist," distinguishing between the correct and incorrect. "Descriptive (or structural) linguistics had not yet arrived—that statistical, populist, sociological approach, whose adherents claimed to be merely recording and describing the language as it was used by anyone and everyone, without imposing elitist judgments on it. Whatever came out of the untutored mouths and unsharpened pencil stubs of the people—sorry, The People—was held legitimate if not sacrosanct by those new lexicon artists."

Simon regarded the publication of *Webster's Third New International Dictionary* in 1961 as a "resounding victory" for descriptive linguistics and "seminally sinister" for its permissiveness. He attacked the "equally descriptive" *Random House Dictionary* and what he called the "amazingly permissive" *Supplements* to the *Oxford English Dictionary*.

Simon was not alone in hating the new *Webster's*. Many did because its editors had dropped the *colloquial* or *slang* labels people were used to. To Kenneth Wilson, a scholar who admired the new dictionary, "nearly everyone who didn't like the book came back to one devastating fault: the book was permissive: it did not tell the reader what was right. It included words and meanings that nice people shouldn't use." He added that "for many it was as though someone had rewritten the King James Version of the Bible or the *Book of Common Prayer* in words taken from the walls of the men's room."[5]

In joining the chorus against *Webster's Third*, John Simon had not just entered the raging "dictionary wars," but had thrown down a most provocative and elitist gauntlet. William Safire, the conservative-libertarian political columnist for the *New York Times*, said Simon made him feel like a "left-winger." In his column "On Language" for the newspaper's Sunday magazine, Safire called Simon "the Prince of Prescriptivists."[6]

In one of the most provocative statements in *Paradigms Lost*, Simon   15 presented an unapologetic defense of elitism:

Language, I think, belongs to two groups only: gifted individuals everywhere, who use it imaginatively; and the fellowship of men and women, wherever they are, who, without being particularly inventive, nevertheless endeavor to speak and write correctly. Language, however, does not belong to the illiterate or to bodies of people forming tendentious and propagandistic interest groups, determined to use it for what they (usually mistakenly) believe to be their advantage.[7]

The only salvation, Simon concluded, was "the eventual creation of an Academy of the Anglo-American Language." That idea had been around for about three hundred years—and consistently ignored. It was first proposed by Jonathan Swift, on the model of the French Academy, to dictate linguistic standards. His contemporary Daniel Defoe wanted to police the language to the extent that coining a new word would be a crime as grave as counterfeiting money. The English-speaking peoples shrugged that off, as they have all attempts to constrain their language sense. That is why there has been a natural or instinctive rebellion against rules from Latin grammar imposed on English during the seventeenth and eighteenth centuries because certain purists of the day thought our language had grown messy, like an unweeded garden, after the exuberance of Shakespeare and other Elizabethans. Instinctively, unless our high-school English teachers crouch over our shoulders, most Americans naturally say *It's me*, not *It is I*, they split infinitives, many use double negatives, and they end sentences with prepositions. . . .

Today, John Simon, aging gracefully with his Old World manners and faint accent, is a warrior unbowed, still willing to unsheathe his sword, as he did for us. Our conversation took place in the balcony of one of the Broadway theaters he frequents professionally, while, below, stagehands moved scenery for a new show, with the roar of New York traffic muted in the distance.

Simon believes American English has gotten worse in the quarter of a century since his book. "Our schools are not doing what they're supposed to do, they're not teaching us grammar or good usage. . . . Teachers in many cases don't know; and in any case they're lazy and they don't make enough corrections on papers." He went on to blame the media, political correctness, and descriptivist linguists, whom he called "a curse on their race, who of course think that what the people say is the law. I think a society in which the uneducated lead the educated by the nose is not a good society."

Jesse Sheidlower stands for all that John Simon hates. Sheidlower is the young Brooklyn-born American editor of the *Oxford English Dictionary* and a descriptivist linguist. Thin, bespectacled, wearing a dark suit and conservative tie, Sheidlower hardly looks like a champion of informality or permissiveness, yet he is the author of a scholarly book on the history of the word *fuck*. And he presides over the American contributions to a dictionary that embraces the most racy and up-to-the-minute expressions, if they have sufficient currency. Recent additions have included blamestorming, *churn rate*, and fistfuck. "We have a program at the *OED* devoted just to new words," he says. Apparently there is a group of editorial workers at the *OED* who do nothing but search for new words that have recently entered the language. Sheidlower gives the word *blog* as an example: "*Blog* is one of the newest, referring to Web logs or online journals, and all of the related terms, *blogging, blogger. Intranet* for an internet that's private to a company. We have older terms that missed out of the *OED* because they weren't paying that much attention to Americanisms. So, for example, the *disabled list* in baseball." Some others Sheidlower mentioned were *transgender* and *transgendered*, and *politically correct* words such as *lookism* and *sexism*. He noted, incidentally, that the term *politically correct* itself goes back to the late eighteenth century, where it is found in a Supreme Court decision. With our TV background, we noticed that the *OED* in 2003 adopted the word *magstripe*, meaning to apply a magnetic stripe to film to record sound, a term common in television since the 1960s.

Does Sheidlower believe that the language is being ruined by the 20 great informality of American life? "No, it's not being ruined at all," he says. "The language is what it is." Sheidlower does not like to talk about "mistakes or carelessness." He prefers to speak of "more informal usages." In Sheidlower's view, people have always spoken informally, but today this informal language is beginning to appear in printed form and publications, where it would never have been seen in the past.

Sheidlower denies Simon's charge that they are regarding as law whatever ordinary people say. "Absolutely untrue," he says. "In fact, it's still the case that what the *educated* say is the law, because a language feature used only by the uneducated would always be described as just that." What Sheidlower means is that his dictionary makes the distinction between what is accepted as correct usage and what is still seen as "slang" or "informal." Sheidlower is also an authority on slang, first as project editor, now as consultant to the authoritative *Historical Dictionary of American Slang*.

But dictionary references and usage notes do evolve. Take the common American expression *come clean*, to tell or confess everything, which originated in cant, or underworld jargon, and emerged as common slang in the 1920s. In 1987, even the *Random House Dictionary*, which Simon thought so permissive, labeled *come clean* as "slang," but by 2001, for the *New Oxford American Dictionary*, it had become merely "informal." By January 2004, the Associated Press deemed it acceptable for a news story about Pete Rose: "More than a year before he *came clean* publicly in his new autobiography, Pete Rose told a high school newspaper that he bet on baseball."

Sheidlower thinks that John Simon and others who believe that there is a serious decline in linguistic standards are "wrong and misguided," because "language change happens and there's nothing you can do about it."

To which Simon replies, "Maybe change is inevitable . . . , maybe dying from cancer is also inevitable, but I don't think we should help it along."

We met Sheidlower at the main branch of the New York Public Library, 25 at Fifth Avenue and Forty-second Street, where he often goes to look for new words and expressions. On that day he was examining magazines. "We try to find magazines that have words in them that we think are going to be of interest, and these can be in really any field out there." When we met him, he was looking at magazines related to tattooing, body piercing, and pop music: "There are terms for these different kinds of piercing and there are terms for different tattoos. *Blue Music* magazine has a lot of stuff about hip-hop, which has a big influence on the language."

When he finds a new word in one of these rather lurid magazines, does that mean that the dictionary will adopt, or recognize, the word? "No, not at all. For now it just means that we have an example in the database." The status of such a word begins to change when it makes a first appearance in a general-circulation magazine such as *Newsweek* or

New York: "And we start to think, Well, okay, this is a term that started off as a very restricted, subcultural thing, but now it's widespread." Sheidlower and his colleagues force themselves to read magazines whose interest is, to put it mildly, highly specialized, because this is where new words will initially appear. This process teaches the *OED*'s dictionary writers "something that we wouldn't know if all we read was *Newsweek.*"

To Simon's complaint that the dictionary is too "permissive," the editor responds that this is a common mistake: "The purpose of the *Oxford English Dictionary* is not to tell people how to use language. . . . Putting a word into the *OED* doesn't make it an official part of English, or an approved part of English. Our purpose is to show how the language is being used." No matter that some of these new words may be slang, may be obscene, may be ethnically offensive. "Our purpose is not to say . . . 'We can't put those words in, they're not good words.'"

Sheidlower says that written English in America has been evolving greatly over the last hundred years, and especially in the last thirty or forty. "Nowadays, if you look at even the most formal publications, things like *The New Yorker* or the *New York Times*, you will find a wide variety of colloquial or slangy language used even in news articles. People speak this way and want to reflect this in their writing. Written English has become much more informal than it ever used to be."

> "People have always spoken informally, but today this informal language is beginning to appear in printed form and publications, where it would never have been seen in the past."

Looking at the *New York Times* through Sheidlower's eyes did reveal the kind of language he described, with the stamp of contemporary informality and relaxed grammar. Some examples: "While the national *media is* roaring through Iowa" (accepting *media* as singular, which is now common); "But that process looked *like* it was going to take a year or two" (*like* in place of the *as if* or *as though* preferred by usage guides).[8]

These are the kinds of usage that annoy the prescriptivists like John 30 Simon, who took us through a list of his own pet peeves.

Like I said—"The word *as* has practically died out of English. It's *as I said*, not *like I said*. It's like underarm odor. I mean, you can live with it if the other person has it, but it's much nicer not to have to."

Media and *criteria*—"which are plural, but people don't know that because they haven't been taught properly and they think there's *a media* or *a criteria*, but there isn't. There's *a medium* and *a criterion.*"

It's not so big of a deal—"That's totally unnecessary and it's a sort of garbage word that just crept in there."

Masterful and *masterly*—"two very different words. A masterful person is a dominant, domineering person, but a masterly piece of work is masterly."

Between you and I—"which is all over the place, which Fowler called a   35 genteelism, because people think that *I* is better than *me*."

Disinterested and *uninterested*—"two very different words, and they should not be confused," the first meaning *unprejudiced*, the second *not interested*.

I'm trying to get something off of my parents—"Why the second *of*? I'm trying to jump off the roof, not off of the roof."

Who and *whom*—"Even the worthy *New York Times* gets that terribly wrong. It's not too bad if you say *who* for *whom*. But it's terrible if you say *whom* for *who*. *The man whom is my father*—that's ugly."

Hopefully—"There's the one where even the conservatives are beginning to give way. But it doesn't make any sense. I mean, *hopefully, mercifully*, anything that has -*fully* in it means that we need a vessel that is filled with this hope or this mercy. To say, *Hopefully it won't rain tomorrow*, who or what is filled with hope? Nothing. So you have to say, *I hope it won't rain tomorrow*. But you can say, *I enter a room hopefully*, because you are the vessel for that hopefulness."

Descriptivists see these changes as all part of the organic growth of   40 American English and of the language generally, as it has always grown. Thus the erosion of foreign plurals in words such as *media* and *criteria* is typical of the long development of English and is nothing to worry about. And *hopefully* is no different from *thankfully* or *mercifully*, which we have long accepted.

Modern computer technology, which makes it possible to scan and search through complete texts going back hundreds of years, casts a new light on this long-running debate: "We see that *hopefully* is not in fact very new, as people thought it was in the 1960s." Sheidlower. says. "It goes back hundreds of years, and it has been very common even in highly educated speech for much of that time. You find it in the twentieth century very commonly in academic journals."

Why, then, do people suddenly get so upset about it now?

Sheidlower: "Because they were told to be upset. Their teachers, you know, language conservatives, say that this is wrong and this is right, and they grow up thinking that, and often when there's no historical basis for it."

He instanced the "alleged distinction" between *masterly* and *masterful*. "This distinction never existed in language until Henry Fowler said it did in 1926. It was completely an invention. There is no basis for it whatsoever, but now people think that it is a real distinction and anyone who says this is wrong."

Sheidlower maintains that John Simon sees language through a kind of 45 middle- or upper-class prism, which means really taking an elitist view. He maintains that people like John Simon are actually complaining that linguists and dictionary writers are no longer focused exclusively on the language of top people: "When linguistic conservatives look at the way things were in the old days and say, 'Well, everything used to be very proper, and now we have all these bad words and people are being careless and so forth,' in fact people always used to be that way," Sheidlower says. "It's just that you didn't hear them, because the media would only report on the language of the educated upper middle class. Nowadays . . . we see the language of other groups, of other social groups, of other income levels in a way that we never used to. And the two world wars have had a very big effect on this. You take people from all sorts of different places and all sorts of different backgrounds and throw them together, and you have a tremendous blending of language that had a very big effect on how people speak."

That people are no longer bothering about the distinction between *uninterested* and *disinterested* "doesn't really matter in the long run," Sheidlower believes. "You can tell usually by context what the differences are. A very small number of words have distinctions like this. I don't think there's a distinction between *disinterested* and *uninterested*, which by the way is a very modern distinction. For most of the history of these two words they were used interchangeably, and only relatively recently did someone say *disinterested* means one thing and *uninterested* means another. You know, it doesn't really matter."

John Simon is perfectly happy to be called an elitist, regretting that it has become a pejorative word: "All it means is making good choices. And there is nothing wrong with making good choices: to eat at a good restaurant or a bad one, to drive a good car rather than a bad car. And, in the same way, to use words that are more correct, more precise, more correctly evocative of what you're trying to say. If that is elitist, well, perhaps it is, and in that case, I'm very happy to be an elitist. There is such a thing as beautiful behavior and ugly behavior, and that goes for language as well as for not breaking wind in public."

Does Simon think America no longer cares about language? "Yes, that's true. And, of course, it's the general devaluation. I mean, a society in which Maya Angelou can be thought to be a real poet of some importance is a doomed society. I mean, that is trash. . . . I think there ought to be some kind of public . . . protest against vulgarity, against bad usage, against bad manners, against the uneducated dictating to the educated.

It's not an easy proposition, I grant. It's a matter of standards. It's a matter of one aspiring to be a gentleman, for example, or a gentlewoman. And now one doesn't aspire to that anymore."

Notes

1. Fowler, p. 625.
2. Dennis Baron interview. Unless published works are cited, all quotations are from interviews by the authors for the PBS series *Do You Speak American?* © MacNeil-Lehrer Productions 2005.
3. Bill Manson, "Wordplay: Charles Harrington Elster at Home," *San Diego Home/ Garden Lifestyles* magazine, Nov. 2002.
4. Simon, p. xiv.
5. Wilson, pp. 12–13.
6. Safire, p. 226.
7. Simon, p. 24.
8. The two examples are from *New York Times*, Jan. 2, 2004, p. A12; Nov. 20, 2002, p. A18.

Bibliography

Fowler, H. W. *Modern English Usage*. 1926. Second ed. rev. and ed. by Sir Ernest Gowers. Oxford: Oxford University Press, 1965.

Safire, William. *What's the Good Word*. New York: Times Books, 1982.

Simon, John. *Paradigms Lost: Reflections on Literacy and Its Decline*. New York: Penguin Books, 1981.

Wilson, Kenneth G. *Rip Van Winkle's Return: Changes in American English, 1966–1986*. Hanover, N.H.: University Press of New England, 1987.

Understanding the Text

1. What does it mean to have a prescriptivist attitude toward language? What are some of the things prescriptivists believe?
2. What is a descriptivist view toward language? What are some of the things descriptivists believe?

Reflection and Response

3. How would you respond to Dennis Baron's statement that "Aside from a person's physical appearance, the first thing someone will be judged by is how he or she talks" (par. 2)? Can you recall a circumstance in which you or someone you know was the object of a snap judgment based on speaking style?

4. John Simon thinks today's English is "unhealthy, poor, sad, depressing, and probably fairly hopeless" (par. 7), while Charles Harrington Elster thinks it is "thriving now probably more than at any time since the Elizabethans" (par. 5). Why do you think two people can look at the same contemporary English language and have such different reactions? Which response do you tend to agree with?

5. While MacNeil and Cran never come out and tell us which side of the "language wars" they are on, they do show preference in subtler ways. When trying to determine the views of someone who is reporting a controversy or debate, you can ask questions like these: How likable or trustworthy do the sources used to present each side seem? What words are used to talk about each side? Is one side spoken about with words that have more positive connotations? Based on these and other observations, do you think that the authors of this piece side more with descriptivists or prescriptivists?

Making Connections

6. Recall Erin McKean's comment in "How Are Dictionaries Made?" about dictionaries being maps rather than rulebooks (p. 198). In what ways can we see Sheidlower as a mapmaker? How does he fight back against any idea that he should be producing rulebooks?

7. Sheidlower argues that prescriptivists like Simon are elitist because their standards are connected to the perspectives of higher socioeconomic classes. Looking at his points alongside those of Edwin Battistella in "Slang as Bad Language" (p. 183) and/or Rosina Lippi-Green in "The Standard Language Myth" (p. 212), explore the connections between language standards and social class.

8. Use your university library's website to access the *Oxford English Dictionary* online. On the dictionary's home page, you'll find a section of recent updates, including the newest words that have been added. Which of these words fit the pattern Sheidlower identifies, where they originally belonged to more restricted subcultures and now have come into more mainstream use?

The Standard Language Myth

Rosina Lippi-Green

Rosina Lippi-Green has a PhD in linguistics from Princeton University and works as an independent language scholar and consultant. She has published numerous articles in sociolinguistics as well as the book *English with an Accent* (Routledge, 2012), from which the selection below is taken. Lippi-Green is interested primarily in language ideology, or the underlying feelings and beliefs that people have about languages. One common component of language ideology is a belief that certain ways of speaking and writing are "better" or more "correct" than others, and that for any language, such as American English, there is one correct "standard." Here, Lippi-Green examines how that standard is defined and details some of the problems she sees with the definitions.

The Standard Language Myth

Non-linguists[1] are quite comfortable with the idea of a standard language, so much so that the average person is very willing to describe and define it, much in the same way that most people could draw a unicorn, or describe a being from *Star Trek*'s planet Vulcan, or tell us who King Arthur was and why he needed a Round Table. For the most part people will undertake describing any of these even though they know that the thing they are describing is imaginary. That is, your description of a unicorn would be a great deal like everybody else's, because the concept of a unicorn is a part of our shared cultural heritage. You picked up your mental image (a horse with a single pointed horn growing from its forehead) someplace along the line; most probably you don't remember when or where.

The same is true for what has been called, to this point, Standard American English. A comparison of published definitions for this term reveals some common themes. From *Pocket Fowler's Modern English Usage:*

Standard American English. The term has been variously defined and heavily politicized, but essentially it is the form of English that is most widely accepted and understood in an English-speaking country and tends to be based on the educated speech of a particular area . . . It is used in newspapers and broadcasting and is the form normally taught to learners of English.

A more recent definition from *Merriam-Webster's Dictionary* (2009), which proclaims itself *The Voice of Authority*:

Standard American English: the English that with respect to spelling, grammar, pronunciation, and vocabulary is substantially uniform though not devoid of regional differences, that is well established by usage in the formal and informal speech and writing of the educated, and that is widely recognized as acceptable wherever English is spoken and understood.[2]

Both definitions assume that the written and spoken language are equal, both in terms of how they are used, and how they should be used. *Merriam-Webster* sets spelling and pronunciation on common footing, and compounds this error by bringing in both formal and informal language use.

While the definitions make some room for regional differences, they make none at all for social ones, and in fact, they are quite definite about the social construction of the hypothetical standard: it is the language of the educated.

What is meant by "educated" is left unstated and neither are the implications explored anywhere else in the dictionary. People who are not educated—whoever they may be—are drawn into the definition by its final component: "Standard American English is acceptable wherever English is spoken and understood." The lexicographer assumes that those with lesser education will bow to the authority of those with more education, because that is what we are trained to do.

Cambridge Advanced Learner's Dictionary's (2009) definition is more 5 succinct, but it also draws on the idea of educated people as the source of acceptable English: "[The] language described as standard is the form of that language which is considered acceptable and correct by most educated users of it: Most announcers on the BBC speak Standard British English."

More specific information on exactly how the lexicographer draws on the language of the educated is provided by interviews with the pronunciation editor at *Merriam-Webster*, which followed from the dictionary's tenth edition. It falls to the pronunciation editor to decide which possible pronunciations are included in the dictionary, and how they are ordered. "Usage dictates acceptability," he is reported as saying. "There is no other non-arbitrary way to decide" (Nemy 1993).

In order to pin down usage, the editor listens to "talk shows, medical shows, interviews, news, commentary, the weather" (ibid.) on the radio and on television. The editorial preface to the dictionary is more specific about this procedure; the list of those who are consulted about pronunciation includes politicians, professors, curators, artists, musicians, doctors, engineers, preachers, activists, and journalists:

> *In truth, though, there can be no objective standard for correct pronunciation other than the usage of thoughtful and, in particular, educated speakers of English. Among such speakers one hears much variation in pronunciation . . . [our attempt is to] include all variants of a word that are used by educated speakers.* (Merriam-Webster 2009: 83)

The editors claim an objective standard (the language of the educated) and at the same time they acknowledge variation among educated speakers. This apparent inconsistency is resolved by the policy which includes *all variants* that are used by educated speakers. A close look at the pronunciations listed in the dictionary, however, indicates that this cannot be the case. An entry with three or more possible pronunciations is rare. If *Merriam-Webster's Dictionary* truly intends to include all pronunciations of the educated, then this definition of educated must be very narrow.

"Maybe there is no way to compile a dictionary which is truly descriptive in terms of pronunciation; maybe it is necessary to choose one social group to serve as a model. . . . But there is nothing objective about this practice."

The goal is to be representative, but how do the editors of the dictionary go about gathering a representative sample? If the primary source of data comes from broadcast media, then the sample is very shallow indeed. How many people appear regularly in a forum which is broadcast to a wider audience? The lesser educated, who by the dictionary definition must constitute the greatest number of native speakers of English, are rarely heard from.

Maybe there is no way to compile a dictionary which is truly descriptive in terms of pronunciation; maybe it is necessary to choose one social group to serve as a model. Perhaps there is even some rationale for using those with more education as this group. But there is nothing objective about this practice. It is the ordering of social groups in terms of who has authority to determine how language is best used.

The rationale for this ordering derives at least in part from the perceived superiority of the written language. Persons with more education are more exposed to the written language and literary traditions; they may, in simple terms, be better writers than those with less education. Why this should mean that their pronunciation and syntax 10 are somehow more informed, more genuine, more authoritative—that is never made clear.

Definitions of standard language supplied by people who do not edit dictionaries for a living echo many of the themes already established, but they sometimes become very specific. According to CompuServe (1995): *SAE° is . . .

- having your nouns and your verbs agree.
- the English legitimatized by wide usage and certified by expert consensus, as in a dictionary usage panel.
- the proper language my mother stressed from the time I was old enough to talk.
- one that few people would call either stilted or "low," delivered with a voice neither guttural nor strident, clearly enunciated but not priggish about it, with no one sound having a noticeably distinctive character. It is a non-regional speech but clearly and easily understood in all regions . . . Standard American English uses, in general, only one syllable per enunciated vowel so most accents from the South and West are not to the pattern.[3]

These references to the authority of educational institutions and unnamed experts correspond to the dictionary definitions in a fairly predictable way. Like the dictionary definitions, the written and spoken languages are being considered as one and the same thing. What is different about these personal definitions is the willingness to identify specific grammatical and phonological points which distinguish the hypothetical standard, and a highly emotional and personal element in the definitions. People feel strongly about language and will defend it: "In extreme cases . . . the tone is quasi-religious, even apocalyptic . . . The ideological basis of the most extreme complaints . . . is authoritarian and, seemingly, transcendental" (Milroy 1999: 20).

The most extreme ideological definitions of standard language come from those who make a living promoting the concept. Writers like Edwin Newman, John Simon and James Kilpatrick have published extensively on how English should be spoken and written. They do not address the source of their authority directly; that is taken for granted. They assume you will grant them authority because they demand it, and because it has always been granted. These men, and other men and women like them,

---

*SAE: Linguists typically use an asterisk (*) prior to an example that would not occur in the language. (For example, an English speaker would say *the red car*, not *red the car*.) By using an asterisk here, then, Lippi-Green is emphasizing her argument that Standard American English (SAE) is not real.

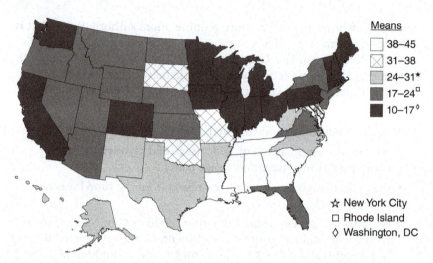

FIGURE 1 Ratings of the fifty states, New York City, and Washington, DC, for language "correctness" on a scale of 1 to 52 (lowest = "best") by seventy-six young, first- and second-year, white undergraduates from Southern Indiana.
Courtesy Dennis Preston

have made careers for themselves as prescriptivists because they meet a demand they created.

The social domain of the standard has been established: it is the language of the educated, in particular those who have achieved a high level of skill with the written language (the lack of logic here will be discussed later) or those who control the written or broadcast media. However, this attempt at a simple definition of *SAE begins to falter when language variation over space is added to the mix.

Dennis Preston has compiled a body of empirical studies in which he has quantified and summarized non-linguists' beliefs about the geographic distribution of a standard language. In "Where they speak correct English," he asked 76 young white natives of Southern Indiana to rank all 50 states as well as New York City and Washington, DC. The best English was 1, and the worst, 52. Figure 1 provides Preston's visual representation of the means for the respondents' rankings.

If a high level of education is a primary characteristic of the 15 hypothetical *SAE, then the opinions of these college students from Indiana would seem to provide relevant information about just where that language is spoken. Preston's analysis indicates that these informants found the most correct English in five areas: North Central (including their own speech); Mid-Atlantic (excluding New York City); New England; Colorado; and the West Coast. Standard deviations indicated that the students are most consistent in their positive evaluation in the case of Michigan, Minnesota and Wisconsin, with their agreement decreasing as they move Eastward through Ohio, Pennsylvania, Maryland, Delaware and finally Washington, DC (which showed little consistency in ranking with a standard deviation of 15.67). The worst standard deviation is for New York City. Preston hypothesizes this has to do with conflicting stereotypes about the city: from the center of culture to the center of crime.

Most interesting perhaps is the incredibly high level of consistency in the way his subjects found a lack of correct English in the South. Mississippi ranked last in terms of correct English and also was the most consistently ranked state. Preston takes the scores for the Southern states as "further proof of the salience of areas seen as nonstandard" (1989: 56).

From these various definitions, a picture begins to emerge. The hypothetical Standard is the language spoken and written by persons:

- with no regional accent;
- who reside in the Midwest, Far West or perhaps some parts of the Northeast (but never in the South);
- with more than average or superior education;
- who are themselves educators or broadcasters;
- who pay attention to speech, and are not sloppy in terms of pronunciation or grammar;
- who are easily understood by all;
- who enter into a consensus of other individuals like themselves about what is proper in language.

It seems that we want language to be geographically neutral, because we believe that this neutrality will bring with it a greater range of communication. The assumption, of course, is that the Midwest is neutral—at least, that is the way students in Indiana see it. Standard language ideology is responsible for the fact that a large percentage of students from other parts of the country agree with them.

We want language to be structured and rule-governed and clear. Something as important as language cannot be left to itself: normal people are not smart enough, not aware enough, to be in charge of their own language. There must be experts, persons in charge, structured authority. In the minds of the respondents, the areas of the country in which the hypothetical Standard is not spoken (the South, New York City), are the logical home of accent. From this assumption it follows that everybody else speaks the hypothetical Standard and thus, has no accent. A native of Mississippi or Brooklyn may have exactly the same educational background, intelligence, and point to make as their counterparts in Ohio and Colorado, but many believe that the accent must compromise the quality of the performance.

This mindset is set down quite clearly in the *Oxford English Dictionary* (1989):

[Accent is] The mode of utterance peculiar to an individual, locality, or nation, as "he has a slight accent, a strong provincial accent, an indisputably Irish, Scotch, American, French or German accent" . . . This utterance consists mainly in a prevailing quality of tone, or in a peculiar alteration of pitch, but may include mispronunciation of vowels or consonants, misplacing of stress, and misinflection of a sentence. The locality of a speaker is generally clearly marked by this kind of accent.

The judgmental tone is quite evident even without the heavily significant choice of *mispronunciation, misplacing,* and *misinflection.* It follows from this definition that there is a correct regional pronunciation, but it is not explicitly identified.

From a legal perspective, Matsuda notes the similarities between the construction of the hypothetical Standard, or English without an accent, on one hand, and hidden norms codified in our legal institutions, on the other:

As feminist theorists have pointed out, everyone has a gender, but the hidden norm in law is male. As critical race theorists have pointed out, everyone has a race, but the hidden norm in law is white. In any dyadic relationship, the two ends are equidistant from each other. If the parties are equal in power, we see them as equally different from each other. When the parties are in a relationship of domination and subordination we tend to say that the dominant is normal, and the subordinate is different from normal. And so it is with accent . . . People in power are perceived as speaking normal, unaccented English. Any speech that is different from that constructed norm is called an accent. (Matsuda 1991: 805)

The myth of standard language persists because it is carefully tended and propagated, with huge, almost universal success, so that language, the most fundamental of human socialization tools, becomes a commodity. This is the core of an ideology of standardization which empowers certain individuals and institutions to make these decisions and impose them on others.

Notes

1. Sociolinguists are still debating the parameters of such crucial terms as *prestige*, *education*, and *standard*: "Other[s] might share my sense of institutional frustration at how far sociolinguistics is from being able to present a consistent and persuasive set of principles and perspectives on [*SAE]" (Coupland 2000: 623). See also Milroy (2004) for a discussion of the importance of resolving these very basic matters.

2. The equivalent variety of British English will be referenced as *SBE.

3. These definitions were answers to queries posted to various CompuServe discussion forums in summer 1995 requesting personal definitions of *SAE. Answers came from adults in all parts of the country who provided answers with the knowledge that they would be used here in whole or part.

Bibliography

Coupland, N. (2000) Sociolinguistic Prevarication about "Standard English" (Review Article for Bex and Watts (Eds): *Standard English: The Widening Debate*). *Journal of Sociolinguistics* 4(4): 622–634.

Matsuda, M. J. (1991) Voices of America: Accent, Antidiscrimination Law, and a Jurisprudence for the Last Reconstruction. *Yale Law Journal* 100(5): 1329–2767.

Milroy, J. (1999) The Consequences of Standardisation in Descriptive Linguistics. In Bex, T. and Watts, R. J. (eds.) *Standard English: The Widening Debate*. London: Routledge, 16–39.

Milroy, L. (2004) Language Ideologies and Linguistic Change. In Fought, C. (ed.) *Sociolinguistic Variation: Critical Reflections*. Oxford: Oxford University Press, 161–177.

Nemy, E. (1993) At the Office with Brian Sietsema; Man of Many Words, Each One Overheard. *The New York Times*, July 22.

Preston, D.R. (1989) Standard English Spoken Here: The Geographical Loci of Linguistic Norms. In Ammon, U. (ed.) *Status and Function of Languages and Language Varieties*. Berlin: Walter De Gruyter, 324–354.

Understanding the Text

1. Why does Lippi-Green use the analogy of a unicorn to describe Standard English?

2. Why does Lippi-Green object to *Merriam-Webster*'s claim to include "*all variants* [of a word's pronunciation] that are used by educated speakers" (par. 7)?

Reflection and Response

3. Lippi-Green quotes several dictionary definitions of Standard English in her essay. What, in your opinion, is the typical reason someone would quote a dictionary definition? How is Lippi-Green's use of the quoted definitions different?

4. Lippi-Green quotes M. J. Matsuda's comment that "we tend to say that the dominant is normal, and the subordinate is different from normal" (par. 20). After reading Lippi-Green's piece, does it seem to you that labeling some language varieties "standard" and others "nonstandard" sets up some to be superior and others inferior?

Making Connections

5. How do you think Erin McKean ("How Are Dictionaries Made?," p. 198) would respond to Lippi-Green's suggestion that "Maybe there is no way to compile a dictionary which is truly prescriptive in terms of pronunciation" (par. 9)?

6. Lippi-Green lists John Simon, who is quoted extensively in Robert MacNeil and William Cran's "The Language Wars" (p. 201), as being among those who "make a living promoting" standard language and "assume . . . authority" on the subject (par. 12). Looking at this piece alongside MacNeil and Cran's, what parallels can you see between Lippi-Green's description of standard language ideology and Simon's promotion of prescriptivism?

4 | What Do We Do When We Write?

So far in this book, we have explored what our language does for us, what it says to others, and how we feel about its variation and evolution. Now, we take our exploration to the more specific focus of written language. Many of the same things that are true of language more broadly are true of writing: We write in ways that reflect our backgrounds and our goals. People make assumptions (some correct, some not) about us based on our writing. And people have strong opinions about what is right and wrong in writing.

As we move from looking at language in general to discussing writing specifically, we are also making a slight shift in academic discipline. While most of our reading until this point has been grounded in linguistics, we are now moving into the field of writing studies, also called rhetoric and composition. Scholars and enthusiasts in this field are interested in how people write, how people learn and teach writing, and how writing affects many facets of our lives. Most people who do writing studies research are also teachers of writing, which is why you will see some of the authors here speaking directly to fellow teachers or making suggestions for working with students.

The pieces in the first half of this chapter consider the activity of writing in ways that connect to the language discussion we have had thus far. Kevin Roozen shows us how some of the social and identity components of language play out in writing, while Paul Kei Matsuda advocates close attention to how variation in our languages and dialects creates variation in our writing. Next, Peter Elbow considers how "typical" writing differs from "typical" spoken language, but also encourages us to see the many ways that speaking and writing can be similar. Through reading these authors, we begin to see how writing shares the complexity inherent in all language. It is not enough to simply write "correctly"; we must negotiate identities and social connections, navigate a range of situations, and understand rules and standards that vary by context and change over time.

photo: Ganchev Anatolii / Shutterstock

The second half of the chapter looks at how we get ourselves in the mental and physical place necessary to do this negotiating. Susan Wyche looks at the importance of rituals in writers' processes, showing how physical factors like time and location can influence our ability to write. Complementing the physical strategies discussed by Wyche, Mike Rose's "Rigid Rules, Inflexible Plans, and the Stifling of Language" examines the mental strategies writers develop for tackling writing assignments. Rose exposes how those strategies can sometimes include overly strict rules that lead to writer's block. Finally, student writer Carie Gauthier adds another mental strategy in the form of metaphor, showing how the ways we think about our writing can influence the effectiveness of our processes.

As you read this chapter, then, consider how your thinking about language can translate to thinking about writing, and begin pondering the full complexity of what you are doing when you write.

Writing Is a Social and Rhetorical Activity

Kevin Roozen

This reading and the two that follow come from Linda Adler-Kassner and Elizabeth Wardle's edited collection *Naming What We Know: Threshold Concepts in Writing Studies* (Utah State University Press, 2015), which introduces key ideas for college students who are new to the field of writing studies. Many different scholars contributed to the book. Kevin Roozen, the author of the piece below, is associate professor of writing and rhetoric and director of First-Year Composition at the University of Central Florida. In this selection, he encourages us to think about how our writing incorporates the influences and participation of other people — much more than we might realize when sitting alone at the computer.

It is common for us to talk about writing in terms of the particular text we are working on. Consider, for example, how often writers describe what they are doing by saying "I am writing an email" or "I'm writing a report" or "I'm writing a note." These shorthand descriptions tend to collapse the activity of writing into the act of a single writer inscribing a text. In doing so, they obscure two foundational and closely related notions of writing: writers are engaged in the work of making meaning for particular audiences and purposes, and writers are always connected to other people.

Writers are always doing the rhetorical work of addressing the needs and interests of a particular audience, even if unconsciously. The technical writers at a pharmaceutical company work to provide consumers of medications with information they need about dosages and potential side effects. The father writing a few comments on a birthday card to his daughter crafts statements intended to communicate his love for her. Sometimes, the audience for an act of writing might be the writer himself. A young man jotting in his diary, for example, might be documenting life events in order to better understand his feelings about them. A child scribbling a phrase on the palm of her hand might do so as a way of reminding herself to feed the family pets, clean her room, or finish her homework. Writing, then, is always an attempt to address the needs of an audience.

In working to accomplish their purposes and address an audience's needs, writers draw upon many other people. No matter how isolated a writer may seem as she sits at her computer, types on the touchpad of her smartphone, or makes notes on a legal pad, she is always drawing upon the ideas and experiences of countless others. The technical writers at a pharmaceutical company draw collaboratively upon the ideas of others they work with as they read their colleagues' earlier versions of the information that will appear on the label. They also connect themselves to others as they engage with the laws about their products written by legislatures and the decisions of lawsuits associated with medications that have been settled

"No matter how isolated a writer may seem as she sits at her computer, types on the touchpad of her smartphone, or makes notes on a legal pad, she is always drawing upon the ideas and experiences of countless others."

or may be pending. The father crafting birthday wishes to his daughter might recall and consciously or unconsciously restate comments that his own parents included on the birthday cards he received as a child. As I work to craft this explanation of writing as a social and rhetorical activity, I am implicitly and explicitly responding to and being influenced by the many people involved in this project, those with whom I have shared earlier drafts, and even those whose scholarship I have read over the past thirteen years.

Writing puts the writer in contact with other people, but the social nature of writing goes beyond the people writers draw upon and think about. It also encompasses the countless people who have shaped the genres, tools, artifacts, technologies, and places writers act with as they address the needs of their audiences. The genres of medication labels, birthday wishes, and diary entries writers use have undergone countless changes as they have been shaped by writers in various times and places. The technologies with which writers act—including computer hardware and software; the QWERTY keyboard; ballpoint pens and lead pencils; and legal pads, journals, and Post-It notes—have also been shaped by many people across time and place. All of these available means of persuasion we take up when we write have been shaped by and through the use of many others who have left their traces on and inform our uses of those tools, even if we are not aware of it.

Because it conflicts with the shorthand descriptions we use to talk   5
and think about writing, understanding writing as a social and rhetorical activity can be troublesome in its complexity. We say "I am writing an email" or "I am writing a note," suggesting that we are composing alone and with complete autonomy, when, in fact, writing can never be anything but a social and rhetorical act, connecting us to other people across time and space in an attempt to respond adequately to the needs of an audience.

While this concept may be troublesome, understanding it has a variety of benefits. If teachers can help students consider their potential audiences and purposes, they can better help them understand what makes a text effective or not, what it accomplishes, and what it falls short of accomplishing. Considering writing as rhetorical helps learners understand the needs of an audience, what the audience knows and does not know, why audience members might need certain kinds of information, what the audience finds persuasive (or not), and so on. Understanding the rhetorical work of writing is essential if writers are to make informed, productive decisions about which genres to employ, which languages to act with, which texts to reference, and so on. Recognizing the deeply social and rhetorical dimensions of writing can help administrators and other stakeholders make better decisions about curricula and assessment.

Understanding the Text

1. What is the "rhetorical work" of a writer? In what ways is this work social in nature?

2. In what ways are the genres and technologies we use in writing social?

Reflection and Response

3. Before reading this article, did you think of writing as a mostly solitary act? Why or why not? How has this article challenged or confirmed your assumptions?

4. Consider a recent piece of writing you did — formal or informal, in or out of school. Who was your audience, and how did the idea of that audience influence your decisions about your writing?

Making Connections

5. Roozen says that "the social nature of writing . . . encompasses the countless people who have shaped the genres, tools, artifacts, technologies, and places writers act with as they address the needs of their audiences" (par. 4). Might we consider language to be one of the socially shaped tools of a writer? Use Erin McKean's "How Are Dictionaries Made?" (p. 198) to explain how people shape language and how that language contributes to the social nature of writing.

6. Use evidence from Susan Wyche's "Time, Tools, and Talismans" (p. 240) to support Roozen's central assertion that "Writing Is a Social and Rhetorical Activity."

7. How do the conventions of academic writing, as described by Chris Thaiss and Terry Myers Zawacki in "What Is Academic Writing?" (p. 288) and/or Susan E. Schorn in "A Lot Like Us, but More So" (p. 294), show influence of what Roozen refers to as "the countless people who have shaped the genres" (par. 4)?

Writing Is Linked to Identity

Kevin Roozen

In another chapter from *Naming What We Know*, Kevin Roozen considers the connections between our writing and our identities. These connections are central to Roozen's own research, which examines how students develop as writers both in and out of school. As he shows here, and as we know from considering identity and language more broadly in Chapter 1, communicating with others entails constructing and conveying an image of our selves.

Common perceptions of writing tend to cast it as the act of encoding or inscribing ideas in written form. To view writing in this manner, though, overlooks the roles writing plays in the construction of self. Through writing, writers come to develop and perform identities in relation to the interests, beliefs, and values of the communities they engage with, understanding the possibilities for selfhood available in those communities. The act of writing, then, is not so much about using a particular set of skills as it is about becoming a particular kind of person, about developing a sense of who we are.

Our identities are the ongoing, continually under-construction product of our participation in a number of engagements, including those from our near and distant pasts and our potential futures. Given that our participation with our multiple communities involves acting with their texts, writing serves as a key means by which we act with and come to understand the subject matter, the kinds of language, the rhetorical moves, the genres, the media and technologies, and the writing processes and practices at play in our various sites of engagement, as well as the beliefs, values, and interests they reflect (see "Writing Is a Social and Rhetorical Activity," p. 224 in this book). Writing, then, functions as a key form of socialization as we learn to become members of academic disciplines, professions, religious groups, community organizations, political parties, families, and so on.

Writing also functions as a means of displaying our identities. Through the writing we do, we claim, challenge, perhaps even contest and resist, our alignment with the beliefs, interests, and values of the communities with which we engage. The extent to which we align ourselves with a particular community, for example, can be gauged

> "The act of writing . . . is not so much about using a particular set of skills as it is about becoming a particular kind of person, about developing a sense of who we are."

by the extent to which we are able and willing to use that community's language, make its rhetorical moves, act with its privileged texts, and participate in its writing processes and practices. As we develop identities aligned with the interests and values of the communities in which we participate, we become more comfortable making the rhetorical and generic moves privileged by those communities.

Understanding the identity work inherent in writing is important for many stakeholders. For teachers and learners, it foregrounds the need to approach writing not simply as a means of learning and using a set of skills, but rather as a means of engaging with the possibilities for selfhood available in a given community. It also means recognizing that the difficulties people have with writing are not necessarily due to a lack of intelligence or a diminished level of literacy but rather to whether they can see themselves as participants in a particular community. For administrators, this threshold concept highlights the demand for structuring the curriculum in ways that allow learners to develop a sense of what it means to become a member of an academic discipline and creating models of assessment that address learners' identity work. For researchers interested in literate activity, it underscores the importance of theoretical perspectives and methodological approaches that make visible the construction of self.

Understanding the Text

1. How does writing, and the communities in which we write, influence the identities we develop?

2. How do we display our identities through our writing?

Reflection and Response

3. Consider this statement from Roozen: "The extent to which we align ourselves with a particular community . . . can be gauged by the extent to which we are able and willing to use that community's language, make its rhetorical moves, act with its privileged texts, and participate in its writing processes and practices" (par. 3). Now, consider a community you are part of, such as a class, sport, church, family, social media site, or online fan community. What is that community's language? What are its texts? How does your use of language or writing show your membership in that community?

4. Roozen says that writing is less about "a particular set of skills" and more about "becoming a particular kind of person" (par. 1). Writing skills are often taught explicitly in school, but what are some of the ways that we develop "the beliefs, interests, and values" (par. 3) that we display in our writing?

Making Connections

5. In Chapter 1 of this book, we examined how spoken as well as written language is linked to identity. Connect Roozen's points in the above piece to this broader picture of language. Using Connie Eble's *Slang and Sociability* (p. 59), Louise Erdrich's "Two Languages in Mind, but Just One in the Heart" (p. 18), or another reading of your choice from Chapter 1, explain how language, to use Roozen's words about writing, helps us "develop and perform identities in relation to the interests, beliefs, and values of the communities [we] engage with" (par. 1).

6. Roozen says that "Writing . . . functions as a key form of socialization as we learn to become members of academic disciplines" (par. 2). Use Susan Schorn's "A Lot Like Us, but More So" (p. 294) or J. Paul Johnson and Ethan Krase's "Writing in the Disciplines" (p. 303) to elaborate on and support this point.

7. Roozen notes that "the difficulties people have with writing are not necessarily due to a lack of intelligence or a diminished level of literacy but rather to whether they can see themselves as participants in a particular community" (par. 4). How does this statement help explain the academic difficulties experienced by student writers Keith, in Anne Elrod Whitney's "'I Just Turned In What I Thought'" (p. 339), and/or Martha, in Mike Rose's "Rigid Rules, Inflexible Plans, and the Stifling of Language" (p. 253)?

Writing Involves the Negotiation of Language Differences

Paul Kei Matsuda

This last selection from *Naming What We Know* is by Paul Kei Matsuda, professor of English and director of Second Language Writing at Arizona State University. Matsuda's research looks mainly at second language writing; he has published extensively in linguistics and writing studies journals and edited over ten books on writing and language, most recently *Exploring Composition Studies*, coedited with Kelly Ritter (Utah State University Press, 2012). Here, Matsuda explains the effects on writing for the language differences we have been exploring in this book, and he reminds us why it is important to notice these effects.

All writing entails language—or more specifically, the internalized knowledge of words, phrases, and sentences and how they are put together to create meaning. This statement may seem obvious to some. Yet, language is often taken for granted in the discussion of writing, especially when writers and writing teachers assume that all writers share more or less the same intuitive knowledge of language structures and functions—a condition described by Paul Kei Matsuda as the "myth of linguistic homogeneity" (Matsuda 2006). In reality, however, the knowledge of language held by individual language users varies. No one is a perfect language user, and writers from distinct sociolinguistic contexts (i.e., regional, socioeconomic, ethnic) often come with noticeably different language features in their heads—and in their writing. Furthermore, in today's globalized world, where the audience for writing is increasingly multilingual and multinational, it is more important than ever to see the negotiation of language as an integral part of all writing activities.

As writers strive to use a shared code that allows for effective communication, it is important for all writers and readers to develop the awareness that we are all participating in the process of negotiating language differences. In any writing context, the audience will likely include translingual individuals—those who grew up using different varieties of the target language or another language altogether. For this reason, language features (e.g., vocabulary, idioms, sentence structures) as well as rhetorical features (e.g., persuasive appeals, cultural references and reader-writer positioning) that were once unmarked may need to be negotiated by writers and writing teachers. For instance, writers cannot assume that the phrase *to beat a dead horse* will be understood by all readers universally; to be effective, writers may need to consider embedding contextual clues or even building in some redundancies.

By the same token, readers and writing teachers cannot assume that what were once considered errors are indeed errors; they may reflect language practices perfectly acceptable in some parts of the world — or even in different parts of the same country. For example, including some Spanish words or phrases into sentences is perfectly acceptable for an audience of English-Spanish bilingual writers or users of English-Spanish contact varieties — as long as they do not violate the language rules shared by both users. For a mixed audience that includes non-Spanish users (which is often the case in international academic writing), writers may need to provide additional information (translation, footnote, etc.) in order to facilitate the rhetorical goal of writing (see "Writing Is a Social and Rhetorical Activity," p. 224 in this book).

> "In today's globalized world, where the audience for writing is increasingly multilingual and multinational, it is more important than ever to see the negotiation of language as an integral part of all writing activities."

This renewed realization about the changing nature of language and the presence of language differences has several implications. Teachers who use writing as part of their instruction must develop an understanding of the nature of language, principles of language development, and language features situated in various contexts of use. Such knowledge is especially important in facilitating the development of communicative competence (Bachman 1990) among writers who come from nondominant language backgrounds. Teachers also must become more aware of the fuzzy boundary between appropriate usage and inappropriate usage (i.e., errors) to help students understand when and how language differences become negotiable. To help students negotiate language differences successfully — including making principled decisions about whether or not to adopt dominant language practices — teachers must understand various strategies for negotiating language differences. Finally, teachers must help students understand the risks involved in negotiating language differences. Beyond the classroom, all writers today need to fully understand the diversity within a language as well as how languages continue to change.

References

Bachman, Lyle. 1990. *Fundamental Considerations in Language Testing.* Oxford: University of Oxford Press.

Matsuda, Paul Kei. 2006. "The Myth of Linguistic Homogeneity in U.S. College Composition." *College English* 68 (6): 637–51. http://dx.doi.org/10.2307/25472180.

Understanding the Text

1. What are some factors that cause people to have different understandings of language?

2. How does language difference affect our understanding of "error"?

Reflection and Response

3. In what ways is the audience for writing "increasingly multilingual and multinational" (par. 1)? How is this true in the college setting? How is it true in business settings after college?

4. How is your own unique linguistic profile displayed in your writing? Consider influences such as the languages you speak, your regional and social dialects, and your past educational experiences. How do these affect the language and rhetorical features in your writing?

Making Connections

5. Use Rusty Barrett's "Rewarding Language" (p. 130) and/or Robert MacNeil and William Cran's "The Language Wars" (p. 201) to provide support for Matsuda's assertion that "readers and writing teachers cannot assume that what were once considered errors are indeed errors" (par. 3).

6. How does Helen Fox's "Worldwide Strategies for Indirection" (p. 317) support Matsuda's call for more attention to global language differences in writing?

Speaking and Writing

Peter Elbow

Peter Elbow, professor emeritus of English at the University of Massachusetts Amherst, is a pioneer in the field of writing studies whose ideas and research have been influential for decades. He is known for his work on writing process and writing instruction, including the books *Writing without Teachers* (Oxford University Press, 1973) and *Writing with Power: Techniques for Mastering the Writing Process* (Oxford University Press, 1981). Connections between speech and writing have figured into much of Elbow's work, including this piece, excerpted from his most recent book, *Vernacular Eloquence: What Speech Can Bring to Writing* (Oxford University Press, 2012). Here, he considers whether written language is truly as different from spoken language as we often assume.

Speech and Writing as Different Linguistic Products

People commonly assume that the language that comes from people's fingers is not like the language that comes from their mouths. But linguists have shown that strictly considered, there is no real difference between them. That is, any kind of language is sometimes spoken and sometimes written. Linguists show the vast overlap by collecting huge *corpora*° of millions of strings of spoken and written language. When they jumble together all the strings, they find they can't usually identify which ones were spoken and which were written. That is, when we look at spoken and written language that was produced in a full range of human contexts and purposes, the dividing line between spoken and written pretty much disappears. The linguist Douglas Biber probably has more experience and authority than anyone else on this topic, and in a 2007 survey of all the research on speech and writing, he and Camilla Vasquez conclude as follows: "[T]here are few, if any, absolute linguistic differences between the [language that is produced by the] written and spoken modes . . ." (537; see also Biber *Variation*).

People tend to assume that writing is more formal than speaking, but that's not always the case. Some writing is more informal and "speech-like" than much speech (consider the writing people put in diaries or email). And some speech is more formal and writing-like than much writing (consider certain lectures, announcements, and interviews). "Nothing consistently differentiates all varieties of speaking [spoken language] from all varieties of writing [written language]" (Chafe *Discourse* 48).

corpora: plural of corpus, a large collection of samples of language (such as speeches, conversations, or publications) that linguists can analyze.

But after linguists have finished demolishing the distinction between spoken and written language, they turn around and start using it again—but in a more careful way. They recognize that it's useful to distinguish what they call *typical speech* and *typical writing*. That is, they distinguish between two common *kinds* or *genres* or *registers* of language: everyday conversational *spoken language* versus careful informational or expository prose or "essayist" *written language*.

Thus, I cut Biber and Vasquez off in mid-sentence when they were saying that there's no difference between spoken and written mode. They finish their sentence as follows: "[but] there are strong and systematic linguistic differences between the registers of conversation and written informational prose—not only in English, but in other languages as well" (15). And so, interestingly, the latest and most careful analysis supports the common naive assumption that of course speech tends to be more informal than writing (as long as we add the word *typical*).

Typical writing. To define this, Biber and Vasquez use the somewhat 5 vague phrase "careful written informational prose." This makes a large umbrella that covers many kinds of writing that are called for in different fields at different educational levels and in many nonschool settings, but it's an umbrella that most people recognize. (See Olson "From Utterance" for the term *essayist prose*—which is a bit narrower since it tends to imply an argument or claim of some sort.)

Typical speech. This is what linguists mean when they use the short-hand term *spoken language*. It's the language that people start speaking and internalizing from infancy. It's a language with complex and intricate grammatical rules—rules that we tend to master by around age four and usually obey without any awareness of them. This is the complex language that comes out of our mouths without planning when we have a thought or feeling to share. (But if we don't feel comfortable and safe, we may plan our words slowly and carefully and produce language that linguists would call "not typical speech.") It's also the language we usually use when we talk to ourselves inside our heads. This is the language I'll be referring to when I write about *speech* and *spoken language*. I'll often add the terms *easy* or *unplanned* or *uncareful* to emphasize that it's casual, everyday speech. I'm distinguishing typical everyday unplanned speech from the wide range of language that *can be* spoken.

Here are some of the differences that linguists find between what's in casual conversation and what's typical in careful expository writing. Careful writing is claimed in general to be

1. more structurally complex and elaborate than speech, indicated by features such as longer sentences . . .

2. more explicit than speech, in that it has complete idea units . . .

3. more decontextualized, or autonomous, than speech, so that it is less dependent on shared situation or background knowledge . . .

4. less personally involved than speech, more detached and abstract and suggesting more distance . . .

5. characterized by a higher concentration of new information than speech . . .

6. more deliberately organized and planned than speech . . . (I am summarizing from Biber *Variation* 47. At the end of each item, he cites multiple research as evidence of these generalizations.)

But remember: these differences disappear once we consider the full range of language that humans speak or write.

Speaking and Writing as Mental Activities

Consider some famous writers. Isocrates helped shape the earliest sense of written prose in the West, and like so many ancient "writers," he seldom physically *wrote*. He mostly dictated spoken words to a slave. (Dictation was a common practice through much of antiquity, but scholars think that Isocrates occasionally did put stylus to papyrus himself. See W. V. Harris.) Milton was blind when he wrote *Paradise Lost,* and dictated it to his daughter. People in modern offices have traditionally dictated letters for secretaries to type. And now we can buy voice-activated software and just talk and the computer turns our audible speech into visible writing.

When people dictate letters, essays, poems, or other texts they are mak-   10 ing noises with their mouths, but often they *experience* themselves *mentally* as writing. As they speak their words, they are mentally creating *written sentences* or *written lines of a poem.* They think about where the sentences begin and end; sometimes they speak the punctuation aloud (one of the options with voice-activated software). Should we say to Milton, "Face it, John, you didn't *write Paradise Lost,* you spoke it"? Can we imagine that Milton let his daughter decide where to end his lines and how to punctuate? These observations fit my own experience too. I've sometimes *written* by dictating into a tape recorder or into my computer for a secretary, or used voice-activated software as I've just described—*feeling* my words as written sentences and sometimes *seeing* them in my head, even saying my punctuation aloud. I've been *mentally writing.*

But this isn't the whole story. Sometimes as I engaged in this mental process of careful writing, I got frustrated and tangled up trying to speak "sentences"—indeed, correct sentences—trying to speak written words. Sometimes I just gave up and said to myself, "The heck with this. I'm just going to *talk*." So I just "let go" and stopped trying to "write." I stopped thinking of my words as parts of a sentence. This gave me a completely different mental experience of using language. When I had been trying to dictate writing, I often had to pause and decide on the right word. But when I let myself dictate by just talking and I got going in the process, I no longer had to pause and often didn't even choose my words. They just *came*—out of my mental sense of having something I wanted to say. In fact I often stopped having any awareness of the words coming out of my mouth *as words;* I just felt myself uttering *thoughts* or *meanings*. This different process produced an observably different product, different language. The words looked much more like casual speech.

So if we want an adequate understanding of how people use their mouths and hands for language (and if we want to understand borderline cases like dictation), we need to distinguish the *inner mental* process from the *outer physical* process. This distinction has been made by a prominent linguist, M. A. K. Halliday. When he discusses the obvious differences between casual speech and careful writing, what interests him are the inner, mental differences that usually accompany them. He uses the words *natural, un-self-monitored, flowing,* and *spontaneous* to describe the mental process we tend to use when we speak in casual safe conversation in real time without pausing or worrying. And he uses the terms *self-monitoring* and *controlled* and *self-conscious* to describe the more careful, deliberate, "choosing" mental process we tend to use for careful writing. In writing, we can pause as long as we want—ponder and change our minds—before deciding on a word or phrase or even a whole structure ("Spoken and Written" 66, 79).

By paying special attention to the mental dimension of how we produce language, Halliday shows that the mental and physical dimensions don't have to match each other. That is, as we speak with our mouths, we don't *always* natter along without pausing or choosing; we *sometimes* plan or rehearse or monitor our words (as in a job interview or dangerous argument). And as we write with our fingers, we don't *always* choose words with care; we *sometimes* put out language in an unplanned or unself-monitored or spontaneous way (as in some emailing, diary writing, and freewriting).

If it seems odd or unrealistic to talk about a *mental* language use that differs from a *physical* language use, I would insist that we see it every day in something quite ordinary: "talking" inside our heads. Most people comfortably recognize that they speak *mentally* inside their heads while *physically* saying nothing.

In future references to these two mental processes of generating 15 language, I will often allow myself some metaphors—imprecise of course, but helpful. I like to say that we have a choice between two mental *gears*: a "mental speaking gear" and a "mental writing gear"—and we can use either gear whether we are physically speaking or writing. For example, in a job interview, we might start out comfortably chit-chatting in our speaking gear. But then the interviewer says, "Now tell me why you consider yourself qualified for this job." Suddenly we have to downshift into our writing gear so we can use care in planning, choosing, and monitoring our words.

> "We have a choice between two mental *gears*: a 'mental speaking gear' and a 'mental writing gear' — and we can use either gear whether we are physically speaking or writing."

Conversely, when we are writing with our fingers—pausing and choosing words with care—we can decide to upshift into our speaking gear and let words roll out unplanned or unmonitored, sometimes almost of their own accord. We allow ourselves to write just as spontaneously and uncarefully as we often do in safe conversation. This fluent process is what occurs in freewriting. Freewriting is an exercise designed, among other things, to bump ourselves into the mental speaking gear as we write. It's not that freewriting yields exactly the language of talking. But it harnesses the essential *resource* of talking that I'm interested in here: unplanned words.

There's another metaphorical contrast that I find very helpful: *uttering* language (i.e., using the speaking gear) versus *constructing* language (using the writing gear). The word *utter* helps imply the mouth-based nonplanning spontaneous process we so often use in comfortable speaking. The words *construct* and *compose* imply the more careful hand-based mental process most people use when they consciously choose words and phrases. I often use this metaphor when I'm responding to student writing. I point to sentences that are particularly tangled and clogged and say something like this:

I found this sentence difficult and unpleasant to read. Notice how constructed *it is. You would never* utter *a sentence like this. I sensed that as you were writing it, you paused or interrupted yourself quite often to ponder which words or phrases to use—or how the grammar ought to go. You chose words, but you didn't then get them to follow the kind of comfortable clear sequence that is natural to your mouth. You haven't broken any grammar rules, but your words don't hang together. Try* uttering *your thought, and your sentences will be much clearer and more inviting for readers.*

The Continuum between the Speaking Gear and the Writing Gear

My metaphors, speaking gear versus writing gear or uttering versus constructing, imply a binary, either/or choice. In the physical realm we're pretty much stuck with a binary choice between using the mouth or the fingers; in a bike or car with gears, we're in one gear or another. But in the mental realm, we have a full spectrum or continuum between our inner writing gear and our inner speaking gear — uttering and constructing — between full spontaneity and full planning. Whether we are speaking or writing, we spend lots of time at intermediate points — partly planning and partly blurting. Our choice among mental "gears" is not digital but analogue. As Halliday put it, "[mental] speaking" and "[mental] writing" are "modal points on a continuum" ("Spoken and Written" 69). We sometimes sort-of monitor or "watch our language" but still go fast without much pausing or planning — or vice versa.

Still, activity along a busy gamut does not deny the reality of the terminal points at each end. For instance, in my dictating experience, I felt an abrupt change of mental gears from constructing to uttering when I stopped trying mentally to "write." Suddenly I could stop thinking about words and let my mind focus on meanings, and the words took care of themselves. I stopped being conscious of what a sentence was — where it started and ended and how to punctuate it. As a result, I could find more words without struggle. It's probably more accurate to say that I didn't so much decide to *engage* my speech gear as *disengage* my writing gear. It was my writing gear that was distracting me and inhibiting language — even inhibiting thinking. The same thing happens in writing when I'm struggling to figure out how to say what I intend and choose my words — and I get slower and more stuck in molasses. Suddenly I remember I can just freewrite, and so I let go and let words tumble out; I seem to be able to "utter" my way through my perplexities. The process may not yield precise thinking, but it gives me words that will *lead* me to precision. And amazingly enough, occasionally precision is just what I get from the nonplanning.

Works Cited

Biber, Douglas. *Variation across Speech and Writing.* New York: Cambridge University Press, 1988.

Biber, Douglas and Camilla Vásquez. "Writing and Speaking." In *Handbook of Research on Writing: History, Society, School, Individual, Text.* Ed. Charles Bazerman. Mahwah, NJ: Erlbaum, 2007. 535–548.

Chafe, Wallace L. *Discourse, Consciousness, and Time: The Flow and Displacement of Conscious Experience in Speaking and Writing.* Chicago: University of Chicago Press, 1994.

Halliday, M. A. K. "Spoken and Written Modes of Meaning." In *Comprehending Oral and Written Language*. Ed. Rosalind Horowitz and S. Jay Samuels. San Diego: Academic Press, 1987. 55–82.

Harris, William V. *Ancient Literacy*. Cambridge, MA: Harvard University Press, 1989.

Olson, David. "From Utterance to Text: The Bias of Language in Speech and Writing." *Harvard Educational Review* 47.3 (1977): 257–281.

Understanding the Text

1. How do linguists define "typical" speech and writing? What are some commonly understood differences between the two?

2. What does it mean to "distinguish the *inner mental* process" of speaking or writing "from the *outer physical* process" (par. 12)? Why does Elbow feel this distinction is necessary?

Reflection and Response

3. Look again at Elbow's list of features that linguists have identified in careful writing (par. 7). Now examine either Elbow's article or a recent piece of your own school writing. How do you see these features demonstrated in the writing?

4. Think of two specific examples from your own experience: one when you were speaking while carefully planning your words, and another when you were writing without planning or thinking much before you wrote (as Elbow describes in par. 13). Reflect on these examples using Elbow's concepts of physical versus mental speech and writing.

5. Do you freewrite at any point in the process of writing essays? If so, how do your mental state and your experience of using language during freewriting compare to the more carefully planned parts of your essay-writing process?

Making Connections

6. In "The Standard Language Myth" (p. 212), Rosina Lippi-Green criticizes dictionaries for "assum[ing] that the written and spoken language are equal" (p. 213). Based on the views of speech and writing Elbow demonstrates here, how might he respond to both this assumption by dictionary makers and Lippi-Green's criticism?

7. How might the "blockers" identified by Mike Rose in "Rigid Rules, Inflexible Plans, and the Stifling of Language" (p. 253) benefit from "shifting mental gears" between writing and speaking? What other advice might Elbow give them?

Time, Tools, and Talismans

Susan Wyche

Susan Wyche has extensive experience as both a writing teacher and a professional writer. She currently works with the administration of the University of Hawai'i Community Colleges overseeing grant-writing projects. In the past, she has been a writing researcher in charge of writing programs at Washington State University, Pullman, and California State University, Monterey Bay. In her research, she has examined the rituals that student writers incorporate into their writing processes. She discusses some of her findings in the piece below, from a collection of essays called *The Subject Is Writing* (Heinemann, 2006).

Famous writers have been known to do a lot of crazy things to help them write: Dame Edith Sitwell sought inspiration by lying in a coffin. George Sand wrote after making love. Friedrich Schiller sniffed rotten apples stashed under the lid of his desk. A hotel room furnished with a dictionary, a Bible, a deck of cards, and a bottle of sherry suits Maya Angelou. Fugitive writer Salman Rushdie carries a silver map of an unpartitioned India and Pakistan. Charles Dickens traveled with ceramic frogs.

Writers also mention less bizarre practices. They describe eating, drinking, pacing, rocking, sailing, driving a car or riding in a bus or train, taking a hot bath or shower, burning incense, listening to music, staring out windows, cleaning house, or wearing lucky clothes. What do these rituals do for writers? The explanations are as varied as the rituals themselves. Tolstoy believed that "the best thoughts most often come in the morning after waking, while still in bed, or during a walk." Sonia Sanchez says that she works at night because "at that time the house is quiet. The children are asleep. I've prepared for my classes . . . graded papers . . . answered letters. . . . [A]t a quarter to twelve all that stops . . . then my writing starts." Although interpretations differ, one need not read extensively in the journals, letters, essays, and interviews of writers to know that they consider rituals an essential component of their work.

Do these behaviors serve a purpose in the composing process? Are some practices more common than others? Do rituals make for better writers? Until recently, the answer was usually "No," but anthropologists and others who study the subject of consciousness now say that private rituals are used by individuals to selectively and temporarily shut out the daily world. Researchers in psychophysiology have observed that rhythmic activities that can be performed "mindlessly" alter brainwaves into a more relaxed, creative state. Walking, pacing, and some kinds of exercise have this effect. So does staring out windows, which some researchers now believe may actively trigger daydreaming rather than being a symptom of it. Although coffins and frogs are probably effective only in the personal psychology of a Sitwell or a Dickens, scientists at Yale have discovered that rotting apples produce a gas that suppresses panic—a reminder that we should be careful not to scoff too soon at writers' rituals.

I became interested in the subject of rituals after suffering through my master's thesis with a bad case of writer's block. When a counselor asked me to describe my work habits, I became aware of the condition under which I had chosen to work: at school in the afternoon (my worst time of day) in an office where I was constantly interrupted or at home (also in the afternoon) while my husband's band practiced in the living room. I answered the phone, made coffee, and tried to shut out mentally what the walls could not. As Tillie Olsen points out, writing under such conditions produces a "craziness of endurance" that silences the writer. After awhile, even when I wasn't interrupted, I'd create my own distractions by calling friends, scrounging food in the kitchen, or escaping the house to run errands.

At the counselor's prompting, I began looking for a protected place to   5
work—at first in the library and later at coffeeshops, where the conversational buzz and clatter of dishes provided consistent background noise. Somehow the interruptions in these places were less disruptive than those at home. I also began to pay attention to those moments when ideas bubbled up effortlessly, like on my walks to and from the university or while soaking in a hot bath late at night. I realized that ideas had always come in offbeat moments, but I had rarely been able to recapture them at "official" writing times. In the next three years, I gradually revamped my work habits and was able to face writing my doctoral dissertation, not with fear-producing blank pages, but pocketfuls of short passages scribbled in the heat of inspiration.

As a teacher of writing who works with unprepared students who are "at risk" in the university, I began to wonder what they did when they wrote. I knew there were times when they, too, became frustrated, blocked, and turned in work that did not represent their actual abilities. In spring 1990, I conducted a project with two writing classes in the Academic Skills Department at San Diego State University. I wanted to know

What rituals did students practice when they wrote for school?

What explanations would they offer for their practices?

Where did they get their best ideas?

What did they do when they blocked?

Were they aware of habits that sabotaged their composing processes?

The writing hut of Roald Dahl, author of popular children's novels such as *James and the Giant Peach* and *Charlie and the Chocolate Factory,* in Great Missenden, Buckinghamshire, England. The hut was the most distinctive component of Dahl's writing rituals. The hut's interior, including a replica of his writing chair in which visitors may sit, now resides in the Roald Dahl Museum.

Photo by Ian Cook/The LIFE Images Collection/Getty Images

Students filled out several pages of a questionnaire on their schedules, their rituals, and the amount of time they allocated for writing school assignments. Afterward, several met with me for follow-up interviews. In the following section, I present edited transcripts of three students who represented the range of responses I received.

Interviews

The first student, Adriana, provides a profile of work habits typical of other students in her class. She takes five classes, works twenty hours each week, and spends six to ten hours per week on homework:

I create a schedule for a day but if there's one particular thing I'm supposed to do, and I fall behind, I just throw it out. Sometimes I call my friends on the phone and tell them what I'm writing about in the essay, and they give me ideas.

Everything has to be clean and neat because if I see my clothes hanging everywhere, I can't study; I can't concentrate. So I have to straighten it up—everything—before I start.

I do most of my writing at night. Last night I stayed up till three o'clock. Before, I used to go to the public library, but it got too loud because of all these high school students jumping around. Now I work primarily at home.

Pacing gives me time to relax and jot down what I'm doing. I can't stay in one place, like for five hours and write a paper. I have to stand up, walk around, watch a little bit of TV and then start again. If my favorite program comes on I just have to watch it. Sometimes it's hard to do both—writing and TV.

To relax, I breathe deeply, stuff like that. I lay in my bed, looking at the ceiling. Nothing special. I work sitting down or lying down. I stare out a window. That's how I get my thoughts all together. I guess it helps, I find myself doing it a lot. I also have this one cassette with all piano solos by George Winston.

At times I put off working on an assignment until it's too late to do my best work, because I work better under pressure. If I start maybe a month before, I won't really concentrate. If I start three days before, then I'll get on it. If I have a month to do a project, and I sit down the week before, I'm not even thinking about it the other three weeks. Sometimes I work when I'm too exhausted, because I have a deadline to make. I've got to do it or fail the class.

I get my ideas sometimes right away, but most of the time it takes an hour to sit and think about it. I also get ideas from reading essays or from the person next to me. I'd ask what they're writing about, and sometimes I get some ideas. When I do go blank, I get frustrated—don't even know what I do. I think I just sit there and keep staring at my paper.

Adriana has difficulty creating and following through on self-made schedules. Her problems are further compounded by being unable to concentrate for extended periods of time; instead, she takes numerous breaks, including watching television. By her own account she begins drafts cold, using only the hour prior to drafting to give the paper serious thought.

Given all this, it is surprising to note how many beneficial rituals she practices. She cleans her workspace, paces, and breathes deeply to relax. She stares out windows to gather her thoughts and focuses her attention by listening to instrumental music. However, she mitigates the effect of these practices by placing herself under the pressure of imminent deadlines. It's no wonder that she becomes frustrated when she blocks. She has little time left for delays, and her coping strategy—to sit staring at the blank page—is more likely to create stress than to relieve it. The conditions she chooses would torpedo even a stronger writer's chance for success.

The second student, Marcia, also has five classes, averages eighteen hours each week at a job, and spends sixteen to twenty hours each week (twice as much as Adriana) on homework.

Usually I study in the evening. I start at seven or eight, and lately I've been finishing about one or two. I talk my paper over with my friends. I ask if it's OK to write on this, or I ask them to read it when I'm finished, to see if it's OK. I usually work in my room, sometimes on my bed or in the living room on the floor. For some reason, I can't do my homework on my desk. When I'm in the family room, I just lie down on the couch, and do my homework with my legs up on the table. I play the radio, sometimes I'll watch TV. If it's an interesting show, I'll continue working during the commercials.

I guess I'm just a procrastinator. I always tend to do my writing assignments at the last minute. Like when they give it to you, and they say, this is due a month later, I'll start on it a week before it's due. Sometimes when I'm thinking about a paper, I think, oh, I could write that in my paper, but when I come to writing it, I forget. I get distracted when I watch TV, or when there's people there and I say, OK, I won't do this now, I'll do it later when I'm by myself. Sometimes I'm on the phone or I go out. Then I end up not doing it, or starting late. When I was doing one assignment, I wrote it in about an hour.

If I block, I put it down for a while, or I ask somebody to read it, or do something else. Then I'll go back to it. When I block, I feel mad, yeah, frustrated. I don't cry. I just think, I hate writing, I hate writing. Why do I have to do this? That kind of stuff. Writing is not my subject.

Marcia writes in the evening, after a full day of work and school. Like Adriana, she describes herself as a procrastinator. She has no designated workspace and often seeks distraction in friends or television. Although Adriana describes using an hour to generate and organize her ideas, Marcia mentions no such practice. She doesn't write down ideas and often doesn't remember them when she is ready to draft the assignment. There are other clues to serious problems. Although help from peers can be useful, she seems overly reliant on her friends for ideas and approval. She looks to them to tell her whether her choice of subject is a good one, to help her when she blocks, and to tell her whether her draft is adequate. She spends very little time on the work and may not even finish if interrupted. Her frustration with writing is obvious; her rituals—what few she practices—sabotage her efforts.

The third student, Sam, represents a highly ritualistic writer. He is 10 enrolled in four classes, works twenty-five hours, and spends six to ten hours on homework.

I'm really into driving. When I drive I notice everything. Things like, Oh, that billboard wasn't like that yesterday. I notice if my car feels different. I'm constantly looking and thinking. What's going on? And so, when I have time to prepare for my paper, all the thought goes into that, from there.

In high school, my thoughts used to go down on microrecording. But I haven't used it since college. My batteries went dead. I do a little bit of performing stand-up comedy, so now I carry a little book for when I see something funny or some kind of story I want to keep. I've probably been through three of those books. I lose a lot of creative energy when I don't write things down.

My roommates and I lift weights every day. A lot of thoughts come from that. I don't like to sit. When I'm thinking, I pace. I do a lot of what you could call role playing. I think, if I come from here, then I gotta hit the next paragraph this way. I actually look this way, then turn the other way. I really get into my papers, I guess. I'm Italian, I talk with my hands. It's a way to release energy both physically and mentally.

Ideas come at different times. I've been known to write paragraphs on napkins at work. At home, I don't have a desk. I have my computer, which just sits on top of my dresser. I usually sit on my bed. A lot of times I lie down; a lot of times I'll stand up, just depends. I write in the afternoon, I feel a lot better than I do when I write at night. I look out a window and just write. But, when it comes to the mid hours, six o'clock, seven o'clock, there's too many things going on. I'm too jumpy, too hyper to concentrate then.

I'm a very procrastination kind of guy. If I had a paper due in two weeks, there would be a lot of afternoon writing, a lot of jotting down. I'd probably end up pulling it all together late one evening. You never know, that last week, I might come up with something more. But at all times, I'm actively thinking about it.

I never keep working on a problem once I've blocked. I feel this is useless. So, I'll stop, and a half hour later, it'll hit me. If I block at night, I'll stop for the rest of the night. If it's in the day, I'll try to get it again at night. I prefer a sleep period in between. Everybody believes in a fresh new day. A new outlook.

Like Adriana and Marcia, Sam considers himself a procrastinator. But unlike either of them, he actively makes use of the interim between assignments, noting down ideas, even writing entire sections if they take shape in his mind. Because he works better in the afternoon than late at night after he's put in a full day, he tries to schedule his work periods early. He seems to be a kinetic thinker—getting ideas in motion—and he takes advantage of that by allowing himself to pace and act out ideas rather than work at a desk. His interest in stand-up comedy has taught him to pay attention to the world around him, and this has become a source of material for his school assignments. In a way, Sam is always preparing to write. The result? He spends less time on his homework than Marcia and rarely experiences, as Adriana does, the frustration of being blocked.

I appreciated the candor of these and other students in responding to my questions but, as a teacher of writing, I was disheartened by many of the things I learned. Over half of the students surveyed spent fewer than ten hours per week on homework for a full schedule of classes, and three-quarters averaged twice as many hours on the job. The picture that emerged of their composing processes, from both statistics and interviews, was even bleaker. Few practiced rituals to help them write, most wrote under conditions hostile to concentration, and more than two-thirds admitted that procrastination regularly affected the quality of their work.

How Rituals Help

Rituals cannot create meaning where there is none—as anyone knows who has mumbled through prayers thinking of something else. But a knowledge of rituals can make a difference for students who want to make better use of the time they spend on writing. For one thing, rituals help writers pay attention to the conditions under which they choose to work. Some people think, for example, that fifteen minutes spent writing during TV commercial breaks is the equivalent of fifteen minutes of continuous, uninterrupted time. If they knew more about the nature of concentration—such as the destructive effect of interruptions on one's ability to retain and process information—they would recognize the difference. If they knew that language heard externally interferes with tasks requiring the production of inner speech, they would know that instrumental music or white noise (like the hum heard inside a car) might enhance their ability to write but that television or music with lyrics is likely to make work more difficult.

A knowledge of rituals can also encourage more effective use of the time spent on assignments. While many teachers consider two hours of homework a reasonable expectation for each hour in class, the students I talked to spent half that time and projects were typically written in one stressful sitting. Writing teacher Peter Elbow calls this "The Dangerous Method" and warns that it not only increases the pressure but depends for its success on a lack of any mishaps or mental blocks.

The problem with waiting until the last minute to write is that ideas rarely appear on demand. Instead, they come when listening to others, while reading or dreaming, or in the middle of other activities. Certain conditions stimulate their production, such as when a writer is relaxed and the mind is not strongly preoccupied with other matters. These moments may occur at particular periods of the day, for example, during "hypnagogic" states, the stage between waking and dreaming. Automatic, repetitive activity has a similar effect, which may be why writers 15 often mention the benefits of walking, pacing, or exercising of some kind. They learn to make use of those times by noting down ideas or combining naturally productive times with their scheduled writing time.

Having some ideas to start with is an advantage to the writer, but not enough in itself. Ideas seldom occur as full-blown concepts, complete with all of the details, order, and connections that are required for formal writing. More often, they begin as an image, sensation, key word or phrase, or a sketchy sense of shape and structure. Transforming these bits into a full-fledged piece—whether poem, essay, or short story—usually requires one or more periods of concentration. The term *concentration* means "to bring together, to converge, to meet in one point" and in reference to thinking, it refers to keeping one's attention and activity fixed on a single problem, however complex. For the kind of writing required at the college level, concentration is crucial.

Most of us know that it is hard to concentrate when we are tired, when interrupted or preoccupied, ill or under stress—thus we recognize, experientially, that writing requires the concerted effort of mind *and* body. Some people can concentrate under adverse conditions—they could work unfazed in the middle of a hurricane if they wanted to—but most of us aren't like that. Concentration comes naturally to a few things that we like to do or are vitally interested in—music, perhaps, or sports. The rest of the time, we juggle several things at once, like jotting down a shopping list while we watch TV or organizing the day ahead while we take a shower. Switching from this kind of divided or scattered mental activity to a state of concentration often generates resistance, especially when the task is unpleasant or formidable.

> "Some people can concentrate under adverse conditions — they could work unfazed in the middle of a hurricane if they wanted to — but most of us aren't like that."

Mihaly Csikszentmihalyi (1975), a psychologist at the University of Chicago, refers to this state of intense concentration as "flow," and from interviews with athletes, artists, and various professionals, theorizes that flow can only be achieved when a person is neither bored nor worried, but in control, possessing skills adequate to meet the challenge at hand. The key to achieving and maintaining flow is to balance one's skills against the challenge. "What counts," he says, "is the person's ability to restructure the environment so that it will allow flow to occur" (53).

Although rituals can take a bewildering number of forms, they help writers restructure their environment in one or more ways: clear the deck of competing preoccupations, protect from interruptions, encourage relaxation, reduce anxiety, and provide a structure (through established limitations of time) for dividing projects into manageable increments. This last use is especially important as writing assignments increase in length and complexity. The transition from the shorter assignment that can be completed in the space of two or three hours to an assignment that requires weeks of reading, research, and multiple drafts can be devastating to those who have conditioned themselves to write in only one, high-pressured session. In such cases, the writer needs strategies to help him or her overcome mental resistance and make good use of scheduled work-time.

Using Rituals

Because no two writers are alike, no formula for effective rituals exists. 20 Even the same writer may use different rituals for different projects, or for different stages of a project. One writer may need several rituals involving workspace, time, and repetitive activities; another may need only a favorite pen. Every writer must learn to pay attention to his or her own needs, the demands that must be juggled, the mental and biological rhythms of the day, and the spontaneous moments of inspiration. Here are some suggestions for establishing productive rituals:

1. Consider the times of the day in which you are most and least alert. Most people have two or three cycles each day. Note the times that are your best.

2. Identify those times and activities in which ideas naturally occur. These may include certain times of day (when waking up, for example), during physical activities, or when engaged in repetitive or automatic behaviors (driving a car or washing dishes). Carry a tape recorder, small notebook, or some means of recording your ideas as they occur.

3. Draw up a schedule of a typical week. Mark those hours that are already scheduled. Note those times that are left open that correspond with the times identified in items 1 and 2. These are the most effective times to schedule writing. If possible, plan to do your writing during these times instead of "at the last minute." Each semester, once I know when my classes meet, I draw up such a schedule and post it on my refrigerator. Although I can't always use my writing time to work on writing, the schedule serves as a constant reminder of my priorities.

4. Consider the amount of time that you are normally able to maintain concentration. Even experienced writers tend to work for no more than three or four hours a day. They may spend additional time reading, making notes, or editing a text, but these activities can tolerate more interruptions and can be performed at less-than-peak times. Remember, too, it sometimes takes time to achieve a full state of concentration—an hour may provide only fifteen to twenty minutes of productive time. Writing frequently for short periods of time may be best. Many writers advocate working a little bit every day because the frequency helps lessen the initial resistance to concentration.

5. Consider the conditions under which you work best. Do you need absolute silence or background noise? Does music help you to focus or does it distract you? Do you prefer to work alone or with other people around? Do you prefer certain kinds of pens, inks, or paper, or do you need access to a typewriter or computer? Do you work best when sitting, standing, or lying down? Does it help you to pace or rock in a rocking chair or prepare a pot of coffee? Do you prefer natural, incandescent, or fluorescent light? Is the temperature comfortable? Is this a place you can work without being interrupted? Identify these needs and assemble an environment in which you are most comfortable.

6. Cultivate rituals that help you focus. Many writers use meditational exercises, write personal letters, or read recreationally to relax and prime the inner voice with prose rhythms. Some writers eat and drink so as not to be bothered with physical distractions; others eat or drink while they work because the repetitive activity helps them stay focused. Some writers feel they are more mentally alert if they write when they are slightly hungry. Experiment with different rituals and choose what works best for you.

Once concentration is achieved, writers tend to lose awareness of their rituals, but when concentration lapses or writers become blocked, they may consciously use rituals to avoid frustration and regain concentration as quickly as possible. The rituals vary according to the writer, the situation, the task, and the cause of the interruption or block, but common practices suggest several options:

1. Take a short break from the work and return later. If pushed for time, a short break may be most efficient. The trick is to stay away long enough to let strong feelings that may sabotage the writing

subside, without letting one's focus shift too far away from the project overall. This is time to get something to drink, stretch out, or put the clothes in the dryer—activities that don't require one's full attention.

2. Shift attention to a different part of the same task and work on that. If you don't need to take a break, work on a section of the project with which you are not blocked. If you know, for example, that you plan to describe a personal experience later in the draft and you know what you want to say about it (even though you are not yet sure how that experience fits within the overall organization of the piece), go ahead and write it and set it aside for later.

3. Shift attention to a different task and return later. Other tasks can provide a break from the writing and, simultaneously, maintain the feeling of productivity; some professional writers juggle more than one writing project at a time for this very reason.

4. Switch to reading—notes or other texts—to stimulate new ideas and to help regain focus. If you are working from notes or research materials, sometimes browsing through them will remind you of things you wanted to say. If that doesn't work, try reading materials that are not related to your task. One student told me that he used articles in *Rolling Stone* to help him get into a "voice" that helped him write. If you are working on a computer and have lost your sense of direction ("What should I say next?"), printing out your work and reading that may also help you regain your flow of thoughts.

5. Talk to someone about the problem or, if no one is around, write about it. Writers frequently use a friend or family member to talk through their ideas aloud (notice how often family members are thanked in the acknowledgments of books); reading or talking to someone not only offers a respite, but may result in the needed breakthrough.

6. Take a longer break, one which involves physical activity, a full escape from the task, or a period of sleep. If the block seems impenetrable or if you are so angry and frustrated that a short break won't make any difference, then spend enough time away from the task that you can begin afresh. Get out of your workspace, go for a hike, see a movie, or spend an evening shooting pool. Intense physical workouts can burn off tension created by writing blocks. If you're tired, take a nap. Some people can work well when tired, and pulling an all-nighter is possible for them, but others are far better off

sleeping first and working later, even if that means waking up at 3:00 a.m. to write.

Coda

Writing this article has reminded me that knowing about rituals and making use of them are not always the same thing. Parts of this developed easily; others had to be teased out line by line. Ideas came while walking the dog, stoking the woodstove, taking hot baths, and discussing my work with others. After reading the last draft, my husband asked me how I intended to conclude. By discussing X, Y, and Z, I answered. I knew exactly what I wanted to say.

That was several nights ago, and today, I can't for the life of me remember what I said. If only I had thought to write it down.

Annotated Bibliography

The writers' rituals described here were gathered from a variety of sources—interviews, published diaries and letters, biographical and autobiographical materials—but anecdotes about rituals appear almost anytime writers discuss their writing processes. For further reading, see the Paris Review Interviews with Writers series, Tillie Olsen's *Silence,* or *Working It Out: 23 Women Writers, Artists, Scientists, and Scholars Talk about Their Lives and Work,* edited by Sara Ruddick and Pamela Daniels.

For further reading on writing and altered states of consciousness, see Csikszentmihalyi's *Beyond Boredom and Anxiety,* Richard Restak's *The Brain* (based on the PBS television series *The Brain*), and Diane Ackerman's *A Natural History of the Senses.* For an older but excellent introduction to the subject of psychophysiology see *Altered States of Consciousness,* edited by Charles T. Tart.

Although the subject of rituals is not a common one for most teachers of composition, a few have discussed the personal and idiosyncratic needs of writers. See especially several of the self-reflective articles in *Learning by Teaching* by Donald M. Murray, Peter Elbow's *Writing with Power,* and James Moffett's essay, "Writing Inner Speech, and Meditation," in *Coming on Center.*

Work Cited

Csikszentmihalyi, Mihaly (1975). *Beyond Boredom and Anxiety.* New York: Jossey-Bass.

Understanding the Text

1. What are some ways that rituals help writers to think differently about their writing?
2. What does it mean to say that rituals "help writers restructure their environment" (par. 19)?

Reflection and Response

3. Which of the three writers Wyche profiles do you identify with most? Explain what connections you see between that writer's process or struggles and your own.
4. What is your experience with concentration? What sorts of things are easier for you to concentrate on, and what sorts of things are harder to concentrate on? Do you agree with Wyche that we tend to truly concentrate only on our strongest interests (par. 17)?
5. Do you have rituals for your own writing? If so, what are they? If not, or if you want to add to or change your rituals, what ideas can you glean from Wyche's "suggestions for establishing productive rituals" (par. 20)?

Making Connections

6. Wyche lists some common rituals that can help people experiencing writer's block (par. 21). How do her suggestions support Mike Rose's analysis, in "Rigid Rules, Inflexible Plans, and the Stifling of Language" (p. 253), of why students experience writer's block?

7. Wyche notes that procrastination can cause trouble for writers because "ideas rarely appear on demand" (par. 15). Use Kevin Roozen's "Writing Is a Social and Rhetorical Activity" (p. 224) to explain the social reasons why ideas need time to develop.

Rigid Rules, Inflexible Plans, and the Stifling of Language

Mike Rose

Mike Rose, currently a faculty member in the UCLA Graduate School of Education and Information Studies, has a long history of advocating for student writers. In his forty years of scholarship, he has published eleven books and many more articles; his best-known book is *Lives on the Boundary: The Struggles and Achievements of America's Underprepared* (Penguin Books, 1989). He studies and writes about issues of access to higher education, particularly relating to the thinking, learning, and writing of students from underprivileged backgrounds. In the article below, originally published in 1980 in the journal *College Composition and Communication*, Rose focuses on the specific academic struggle of writer's block. As you will see, he finds that writer's block has nothing to do with writing ability but rather with the rules student writers create for themselves.

Ruth will labor over the first paragraph of an essay for hours. She'll write a sentence, then erase it. Try another, then scratch part of it out. Finally, as the evening winds on toward ten o'clock and Ruth, anxious about tomorrow's deadline, begins to wind into herself, she'll compose that first paragraph only to sit back and level her favorite exasperated interdiction at herself and her page: "No. You can't say that. You'll bore them to death."

Ruth is one of ten UCLA undergraduates with whom I discussed writer's block, that frustrating, self-defeating inability to generate the next line, the right phrase, the sentence that will release the flow of words once again. These ten people represented a fair cross-section of the UCLA student community: lower-middle-class to upper-middle-class backgrounds and high schools, third-world and Caucasian origins, biology to fine arts majors, C+ to A– grade point averages, enthusiastic to blasé attitudes toward school. They were set off from the community by the twin facts that all ten could write competently, and all were currently enrolled in at least one course that required a significant amount of writing. They were set off among themselves by the fact that five of them wrote with relative to enviable ease while the other five experienced moderate to nearly immobilizing writer's block. This blocking usually resulted in rushed, often late papers and resultant grades that did not truly reflect these students' writing ability. And then, of course, there were other less measurable but probably more serious results: a growing distrust of their abilities and an aversion toward the composing process itself.

What separated the five students who blocked from those who didn't? It wasn't skill; that was held fairly constant. The answer could have rested in the emotional realm — anxiety, fear of evaluation, insecurity, etc. Or perhaps blocking in some way resulted from variation in cognitive style. Perhaps, too, blocking originated in and typified a melding of emotion and cognition not unlike the relationship posited by Shapiro between neurotic feeling and neurotic thinking.[1] Each of these was possible. Extended clinical interviews and testing could have teased out the answer. But there was one answer that surfaced readily in brief explorations of these students' writing processes. It was not profoundly emotional, nor was it embedded in that still unclear construct of cognitive style. It was constant, surprising, almost amusing if its results weren't so troublesome, and, in the final analysis, obvious: the five students who experienced blocking were all operating either with writing rules or with planning strategies that impeded rather than enhanced the composing process. The five students who were not hampered by writer's block also utilized rules, but they were less rigid ones, and thus more appropriate to a complex process like writing. Also, the plans these non-blockers brought to the writing process were more functional, more flexible, more open to information from the outside.

> "The five students who were not hampered by writer's block also utilized rules, but they were less rigid ones, and thus more appropriate to a complex process like writing."

These observations are the result of one to three interviews with each student. I used recent notes, drafts, and finished compositions to direct and hone my questions. This procedure is admittedly non-experimental, certainly more clinical than scientific; still, it did lead to several inferences that lay the foundation for future, more rigorous investigation: (a) composing is a highly complex problem-solving process[2] and (b) certain disruptions of that process can be explained with cognitive psychology's problem-solving framework. Such investigation might include a study using "stimulated recall" techniques to validate or disconfirm these hunches. In such a study, blockers and non-blockers would write essays. Their activity would be videotaped and, immediately after writing, they would be shown their respective tapes and questioned about the rules, plans, and beliefs operating in their writing behavior. This procedure would bring us close to the composing process (the writers' recall is stimulated by their viewing the tape), yet would not interfere with actual composing.

In the next section I will introduce several key concepts in the problem- 5 solving literature. In section three I will let the students speak for themselves. Fourth, I will offer a cognitivist analysis of blockers' and non-blockers' grace or torpor. I will close with a brief note on treatment.

Selected Concepts in Problem Solving: Rules and Plans

As diverse as theories of problem solving are, they share certain basic assumptions and characteristics. Each posits an *introductory period* during which a problem is presented, and all theorists, from Behaviorist to Gestalt to Information Processing,° admit that certain aspects, stimuli, or "functions" of the problem must become or be made salient and attended to in certain ways if successful problem-solving processes are to be engaged. Theorists also believe that some conflict, some stress, some gap in information in these perceived "aspects" seems to trigger problem-solving behavior. Next comes a *processing period,* and for all the variance of opinion about this critical stage, theorists recognize the necessity of its existence—recognize that man, at the least, somehow "weighs" possible solutions as they are stumbled upon and, at the most, goes through an elaborate and sophisticated information-processing routine to achieve problem solution. Furthermore, theorists believe—to varying degrees—that past learning and the particular "set," direction, or orientation that the problem solver takes in dealing with past experience and present stimuli have critical bearing on the efficacy of the solution. Finally, all theorists admit to a *solution period,* an end-state of the process where "stress" and "search" terminate, an answer is attained, and a sense of completion or "closure" is experienced.

These are the gross similarities, and the framework they offer will be useful in understanding the problem-solving behavior of the students discussed in this paper. But since this paper is primarily concerned with the second stage of problem-solving operations, it would be most useful to focus this introduction on two critical constructs in the processing period: rules and plans.

Rules

Robert M. Gagné defines "rule" as "an inferred capability that enables the individual to respond to a class of stimulus situations with a class of performances."[3] Rules can be learned directly[4] or by inference through

from Behaviorist to Gestalt to Information Processing: a range of different schools of thought in the psychology of learning. The first attends to observable behavior, the second to the mind as a whole, and the third to mental processing of information.

experience.[5] But, in either case, most problem-solving theorists would affirm Gagné's dictum that "rules are probably the major organizing factor, and quite possibly the primary one, in intellectual functioning."[6] As Gagné implies, we wouldn't be able to function without rules; they guide response to the myriad stimuli that confront us daily, and might even be the central element in complex problem-solving behavior.

Dunker, Polya, and Miller, Galanter, and Pribram offer a very useful distinction between two general kinds of rules: algorithms and heuristics.[7] Algorithms are precise rules that will always result in a specific answer if applied to an appropriate problem. Most mathematical rules, for example, are algorithms. Functions are constant (e.g., pi), procedures are routine (squaring the radius), and outcomes are completely predictable. However, few day-to-day situations are mathematically circumscribed enough to warrant the application of algorithms. Most often we function with the aid of fairly general heuristics, or "rules of thumb," guidelines that allow varying degrees of flexibility when approaching problems. Rather than operating with algorithmic precision and certainty, we search, critically, through alternatives, using our heuristic as a divining rod—"if a math problem stumps you, try working backwards to solution"; "if the car won't start, check x, y, or z," and so forth. Heuristics won't allow the precision or the certitude afforded by algorithmic operations; heuristics can even be so "loose" as to be vague. But in a world where tasks and problems are rarely mathematically precise, heuristic rules become the most appropriate, the most functional rules available to us: "a heuristic does not guarantee the optimal solution or, indeed, any solution at all; rather, heuristics offer solutions that are good enough most of the time."[8]

Plans

People don't proceed through problem situations, in or out of a laboratory, without some set of internalized instructions to the self, some program, some course of action that, even roughly, takes goals and possible paths to that goal into consideration. Miller, Galanter, and Pribram have referred to this course of action as a plan: "A plan is any hierarchical process in the organism that can control the order in which a sequence of operations is to be performed" (p. 16). They name the fundamental plan in human problem-solving behavior the TOTE, with the initial T representing a *test* that matches a possible solution against the perceived end-goal of problem completion. O represents the clearance to *operate* if the comparison between solution and goal indicates that the solution is a sensible one. The second T represents a further, post-operation, *test* or comparison of solution with goal, and if the two mesh and problem solution is at hand the person *exits* (E) from problem-solving behavior. If the second test presents further discordance between solution and goal, a further solution is attempted in TOTE-fashion. Such plans can be both long-term and global and, as problem solving is underway, short-term and immediate.[9] Though the mechanicality of this information-processing model renders it simplistic and, possibly, unreal, the central notion of a plan and an operating procedure is an important one in problem-solving theory; it at least attempts to metaphorically explain what earlier cognitive psychologists could not—the mental procedures (see par. 6 in this selection.) underlying problem-solving behavior.

"Always Grab Your Audience" — The Blockers

In high school, *Ruth* was told and told again that a good essay always grabs a reader's attention immediately. Until you can make your essay do that, her teachers and textbooks putatively declaimed, there is no need to go on. For Ruth, this means that beginning bland and seeing what emerges as one generates prose is unacceptable. The beginning is everything. And what exactly is the audience seeking that reads this beginning? The rule, or Ruth's use of it, doesn't provide for such investigation. She has an edict with no determiners. Ruth operates with another rule that restricts her productions as well: if sentences aren't grammatically "correct," they aren't useful. This keeps Ruth from toying with ideas on paper, from the kind of linguistic play that often frees up the flow of prose. These two rules converge in a way that pretty effectively restricts Ruth's composing process.

The first two papers I received from *Laurel* were weeks overdue. Sections of them were well written; there were even moments of stylistic flair. But the papers were late and, overall, the prose seemed rushed. Furthermore, one paper included a paragraph on an issue that was never mentioned in the topic paragraph. This was the kind of mistake that someone with

A playful take on writer's block, from a 1995 Calvin and Hobbes comic by Bill Watterson.

Bill Watterson/Andrews McMeel Syndication

Laurel's apparent ability doesn't make. I asked her about this irrelevant passage. She knew very well that it didn't fit, but believed she had to include it to round out the paper. "You must always make three or more points in an essay. If the essay has less, then it's not strong." Laurel had been taught this rule both in high school and in her first college English class; no wonder, then, that she accepted its validity.

As opposed to Laurel, *Martha* possesses a whole arsenal of plans and rules with which to approach a humanities writing assignment, and, considering her background in biology, I wonder how many of them were formed out of the assumptions and procedures endemic to the physical sciences.[10] Martha will not put pen to first draft until she has spent up to two days generating an outline of remarkable complexity. I saw one of these outlines and it looked more like a diagram of protein synthesis or DNA structure than the timeworn pattern offered in composition textbooks. I must admit I was intrigued by the aura of process (vs. the static appearance of essay outlines) such diagrams offer, but for Martha these "outlines" only led to self-defeat: the outline would become so complex that all of its elements could never be included in a short essay. In other words, her plan locked her into the first stage of the composing process. Martha would struggle with the conversion of her outline into prose only to scrap the whole venture when deadlines passed and a paper had to be rushed together.

Martha's "rage for order" extends beyond the outlining process. She also believes that elements of a story or poem must evince a fairly linear structure and thematic clarity, or—perhaps bringing us closer to the issue—that analysis of a story or poem must provide the linearity or clarity that seems to be absent in the text. Martha, therefore, will bend the logic of her analysis to reason ambiguity out of existence. When I asked her about a strained paragraph in her paper on Camus' "The Guest," she said, "I didn't want to admit that it [the story's conclusion] was just hanging. I tried to force it into meaning."

Martha uses another rule, one that is not only problematical in itself, 15 but one that often clashes directly with the elaborate plan and obsessive rule above. She believes that humanities papers must scintillate with insight, must present an array of images, ideas, ironies gleaned from the literature under examination. A problem arises, of course, when Martha tries to incorporate her myriad "neat little things," often inherently unrelated, into a tightly structured, carefully sequenced essay. Plans and rules that govern the construction of impressionistic, associational prose would be appropriate to Martha's desire, but her composing process is heavily constrained by the non-impressionistic and non-associational. Put another way, the plans and rules that govern her exploration of text are not at all synchronous with the plans and rules she uses to discuss her exploration. It is interesting to note here, however, that as recently as three years ago Martha was absorbed in creative writing and was publishing poetry in high school magazines. Given what we know about the complex associational, often non-neatly-sequential nature of the poet's creative process, we can infer that Martha was either free of the plans and rules discussed earlier or they were not as intense. One wonders, as well, if the exposure to three years of university physical science either established or intensified Martha's concern with structure. Whatever the case, she now is hamstrung by conflicting rules when composing papers for the humanities.

Mike's difficulties, too, are rooted in a distortion of the problem-solving process. When the time of the week for the assignment of writing topics draws near, Mike begins to prepare material, strategies, and plans that he believes will be appropriate. If the assignment matches his expectations, he has done a good job of analyzing the professor's intentions. If the assignment *doesn't* match his expectations, however, he cannot easily shift approaches. He feels trapped inside his original plans, cannot generate alternatives, and blocks. As the deadline draws near, he will write something, forcing the assignment to fit his conceptual procrustean bed. Since Mike is a smart man, he will offer a good deal of information, but only some of it ends up being appropriate to the assignment. This entire situation is made all the worse when the time between assignment of topic and generation of product is attenuated further, as in an essay examination. Mike believes (correctly) that one must have a plan, a strategy of some sort in order to solve a problem. He further believes, however, that such a plan, once formulated, becomes an exact structural and substantive blueprint that cannot be violated. The plan offers no alternatives, no "sub-routines." So, whereas Ruth's, Laurel's, and some of Martha's difficulties seem to be rule-specific ("always catch your audience," "write grammatically"), Mike's troubles are more global. He may have strategies that are appropriate for various writing situations (e.g., "for this kind of political science assignment write a compare/contrast essay"), but his entire approach to formulating plans and carrying them through to problem solution is too mechanical. It is probable that Mike's behavior is governed by an explicitly learned or inferred rule: "Always try to 'psych out' a professor." But in this case this rule initiates a problem-solving procedure that is clearly dysfunctional.

While Ruth and Laurel use rules that impede their writing process and Mike utilizes a problem-solving procedure that hamstrings him, *Sylvia* has trouble deciding which of the many rules she possesses to use. Her problem can be characterized as cognitive perplexity: some of her rules are inappropriate, others are functional; some mesh nicely with her own definitions of good writing, others don't. She has multiple rules to invoke, multiple paths to follow, and that very complexity of choice virtually paralyzes her. More so than with the previous four students, there is probably a strong emotional dimension to Sylvia's blocking, but the cognitive difficulties are clear and perhaps modifiable.

Sylvia, somewhat like Ruth and Laurel, puts tremendous weight on the crafting of her first paragraph. If it is good, she believes the rest of the essay will be good. Therefore, she will spend up to five hours on the initial paragraph: "I won't go on until I get that first paragraph down." Clearly, this rule—or the strength of it—blocks Sylvia's production. This is one problem. Another is that Sylvia has other equally potent rules that she sees as separate, uncomplementary injunctions: one achieves "flow" in one's writing through the use of adequate transitions; one achieves substance to one's writing through the use of evidence. Sylvia perceives both rules to be "true," but several times followed one to the exclusion of the other. Furthermore, as I talked to Sylvia, many other rules, guidelines, definitions were offered, but none with conviction. While she *is* committed to one rule about initial paragraphs, and that rule is dysfunctional, she seems very uncertain about the weight and hierarchy of the remaining rules in her cognitive repertoire.

"If It Won't Fit My Work, I'll Change It"—The Non-Blockers

Dale, Ellen, Debbie, Susan, and Miles all write with the aid of rules. But their rules differ from blockers' rules in significant ways. If similar in content, they are expressed less absolutely—e.g., "*Try* to keep audience in mind." If dissimilar, they are still expressed less absolutely, more heuristically—e.g., "I can use as many ideas in my thesis paragraph as I need and then develop paragraphs for each idea." Our non-blockers do express some rules with firm assurance, but these tend to be simple injunctions that free up rather than restrict the composing process, e.g., "When stuck, write!" or "I'll write what I can." And finally, at least three of the students openly shun the very textbook rules that some blockers adhere to: e.g., "Rules like 'write only what you know about' just aren't true. I ignore those." These three, in effect, have formulated a further rule that expresses something like: "If a rule conflicts with what is sensible or with experience, reject it."

On the broader level of plans and strategies, these five students 20 also differ from at least three of the five blockers in that they all possess problem-solving plans that are quite functional. Interestingly, on first exploration these plans seem to be too broad or fluid to be useful and, in some cases, can barely be expressed with any precision. Ellen, for example, admits that she has a general "outline in [her] head about how a topic paragraph should look" but could not describe much about its structure. Susan also has a general plan to follow, but, if stymied, will quickly attempt to conceptualize the assignment in different ways: "If my original idea won't work, then I need to proceed differently." Whether or not these plans operate in TOTE-fashion, I can't say. But they do operate with the operate-test fluidity of TOTEs.

True, our non-blockers have their religiously adhered-to rules: e.g., "When stuck, write," and plans, "I couldn't imagine writing without this pattern," but as noted above, these are few and functional. Otherwise, these non-blockers operate with fluid, easily modified, even easily discarded rules and plans (Ellen: "I can throw things out") that are sometimes expressed with a vagueness that could almost be interpreted as ignorance. There lies the irony. Students that offer the least precise rules and plans have the least trouble composing. Perhaps this very lack of precision characterizes the functional composing plan. But perhaps this lack of precision simply masks habitually enacted alternatives and sub-routines. This is clearly an area that needs the illumination of further research.

And then there is feedback. At least three of the five non-blockers are an Information-Processor's dream. They get to know their audience, ask professors and T.A.s specific questions about assignments, bring half-finished products in for evaluation, etc. Like Ruth, they realize the importance of audience, but unlike her, they have specific strategies for obtaining and utilizing feedback. And this penchant for testing writing plans against the needs of the audience can lead to modification of rules and plans. Listen to Debbie:

In high school I was given a formula that stated that you must write a thesis paragraph with only three points in it, and then develop each of those points. When I hit college I was given longer assignments. That stuck me for a bit, but then I realized that I could use as many ideas in my thesis paragraph as I needed and then develop paragraphs for each one. I asked someone about this and then tried it. I didn't get any negative feedback, so I figured it was o.k.

Debbie's statement brings one last difference between our blockers and non-blockers into focus; it has been implied above, but needs specific formulation: the goals these people have, and the plans they generate to attain these goals, are quite mutable. Part of the mutability comes from the fluid way the goals and plans are conceived, and part of it arises from the effective impact of feedback on these goals and plans.

Analyzing Writer's Block

Algorithms Rather than Heuristics

In most cases, the rules our blockers use are not "wrong" or "incorrect"—it is good practice, for example, to "grab your audience with a catchy opening" or "craft a solid first paragraph before going on." The problem is that these rules seem to be followed as though they were algorithms, absolute dicta, rather than the loose heuristics that they were intended to be. Either through instruction, or the power of the textbook, or the predilections of some of our blockers for absolutes, or all three, these useful rules of thumb have been transformed into near-algorithmic urgencies. The result, to paraphrase Karl Dunker, is that these rules do not allow a flexible penetration into the nature of the problem. It is this transformation of heuristic into algorithm that contributes to the writer's block of Ruth and Laurel.

Questionable Heuristics Made Algorithmic

Whereas "grab your audience" could be a useful heuristic, "always make 25 three or more points in an essay" is a pretty questionable one. Any such rule, though probably taught to aid the writer who needs structure, ultimately transforms a highly fluid process like writing into a mechanical lockstep. As heuristics, such rules can be troublesome. As algorithms, they are simply incorrect.

Set

As with any problem-solving task, students approach writing assignments with a variety of orientations or sets. Some are functional, others are not. Martha and Jane (see footnote 10), coming out of the life sciences and social sciences respectively, bring certain methodological orientations with them—certain sets or "directions" that make composing for the humanities a difficult, sometimes confusing, task. In fact, this orientation may cause them to misperceive the task. Martha has formulated a planning strategy from her predisposition to see processes in terms of linear, interrelated steps in a system. Jane doesn't realize that she can revise the statement that "committed" her to the direction her essay has taken. Both of these students are stymied because of formative experiences associated with their majors—experiences, perhaps, that nicely reinforce our very strong tendency to organize experiences temporally.

The Plan That Is Not a Plan

If fluidity and multi-directionality are central to the nature of plans, then the plans that Mike formulates are not true plans at all but, rather, inflexible and static cognitive blueprints.[11] Put another way, Mike's "plans" represent a restricted "closed system" (vs. "open system") kind of thinking, where closed system thinking is defined as focusing on "a limited number of units or items, or members, and those properties of the members which are to be used are known to begin with and do not change as the thinking proceeds," and open system thinking is characterized by an "adventurous exploration of multiple alternatives with strategies that allow redirection once 'dead ends' are encountered."[12] Composing calls for open, even adventurous thinking, not for constrained, no-exit cognition.

Feedback

The above difficulties are made all the more problematic by the fact that they seem resistant to or isolated from corrective feedback. One of the most striking things about Dale, Debbie, and Miles is the ease with which they seek out, interpret, and apply feedback on their rules, plans, and productions. They "operate" and then they "test," and the testing is not only against some internalized goal, but against the requirements of external audience as well.

Too Many Rules—"Conceptual Conflict"

According to D. E. Berlyne, one of the primary forces that motivate problem-solving behavior is a curiosity that arises from conceptual conflict—the convergence of incompatible beliefs or ideas. In *Structure and Direction in Thinking*,[13] Berlyne presents six major types of conceptual conflict, the second of which he terms "perplexity":

This kind of conflict occurs when there are factors inclining the subject toward each of a set of mutually exclusive beliefs. (p. 257)

If one substitutes "rules" for "beliefs" in the above definition, perplexity becomes a useful notion here. Because perplexity is unpleasant, people are motivated to reduce it by problem-solving behavior that can result in "disequalization":

Degree of conflict will be reduced if either the number of competing . . . [rules] or their nearness to equality of strength is reduced. (p. 259)

But "disequalization" is not automatic. As I have suggested, Martha and Sylvia hold to rules that conflict, but their perplexity does *not* lead to curiosity and resultant problem-solving behavior. Their perplexity, contra Berlyne, leads to immobilization. Thus "disequalization" will have to be effected from without. The importance of each of, particularly, Sylvia's rules needs an evaluation that will aid her in rejecting some rules and balancing and sequencing others.

A Note on Treatment

Rather than get embroiled in a blocker's misery, the teacher or tutor might interview the student in order to build a writing history and profile: How much and what kind of writing was done in high school? What is the student's major? What kind of writing does it require? How does the student compose? Are there rough drafts or outlines available? By what rules does the student operate? How would he or she define "good" writing? etc. This sort of interview reveals an incredible amount of information about individual composing processes. Furthermore, it often reveals the rigid rule or the inflexible plan that may lie at the base of the student's writing problem. That was precisely what happened with the five blockers. And with Ruth, Laurel, and Martha (and Jane) what was revealed made virtually immediate remedy possible. Dysfunctional rules are easily replaced with or counter-balanced by functional ones if there is no emotional reason to hold onto that which simply doesn't work. Furthermore, students can be trained to select, to "know which rules are appropriate for which problems."[14] Mike's difficulties, perhaps because plans are more complex and pervasive than rules, took longer to correct. But inflexible plans, too, can be remedied by pointing out their dysfunctional qualities and by assisting the student in developing appropriate and flexible alternatives. Operating this way, I was successful with Mike. Sylvia's story, however, did not end as smoothly. Though I had three forty-five minute contacts with her, I was not able to appreciably alter her behavior. Berlyne's theory bore results with Martha but not with Sylvia. Her rules were in conflict, and perhaps that conflict was not exclusively cognitive. Her case keeps analyses like these honest; it reminds us that the cognitive often melds with, and can be overpowered by, the affective. So while Ruth, Laurel, Martha, and Mike could profit from tutorials that explore the rules and plans in their writing behavior, students like Sylvia may need more extended, more affectively oriented counseling sessions that blend the instructional with the psychodynamic.

Notes

1. David Shapiro, *Neurotic Styles* (New York: Basic Books, 1965).
2. Barbara Hayes-Ruth, a Rand cognitive psychologist, and I are currently developing an information-processing model of the composing process. A good deal of work has already been done by Linda Flower and John Hayes. I have just received—and recommend—their "Writing as Problem Solving" (paper presented at American Educational Research Association, April, 1979).

3. *The Conditions of Learning* (New York: Holt, Rinehart and Winston, 1970), p. 193.

4. E. James Archer, "The Psychological Nature of Concepts," in H. J. Klausmeier and C. W. Harris, eds., *Analysis of Concept Learning* (New York: Academic Press, 1966), pp. 37–44; David P. Ausubel, *The Psychology of Meaningful Verbal Behavior* (New York: Grune and Stratton, 1963); Robert M. Gagné, "Problem Solving," in Arthur W. Melton, ed., *Categories of Human Learning* (New York: Academic Press, 1964), pp. 293–317; George A. Miller, *Language and Communication* (New York: McGraw-Hill, 1951).

5. George Katona, *Organizing and Memorizing* (New York: Columbia Univ. Press, 1940); Roger N. Shepard, Carl I. Hovland, and Herbert M. Jenkins, "Learning and Memorization of Classifications," *Psychological Monographs*, 75, No. 13 (1961) (entire No. 517); Robert S. Woodworth, *Dynamics of Behavior* (New York: Henry Holt, 1958), chs. 10–12.

6. *The Conditions of Learning*, pp. 190–91.

7. Karl Dunker, "On Problem Solving," *Psychological Monographs*, 58, No. 5 (1945) (entire No. 270); George A. Polya, *How to Solve It* (Princeton: Princeton University Press, 1945); George A. Miller, Eugene Galanter, and Karl H. Pribram, *Plans and the Structure of Behavior* (New York: Henry Holt, 1960).

8. Lyle E. Bourne, Jr., Bruce R. Ekstrand, and Roger L. Dominowski, *The Psychology of Thinking* (Englewood Cliffs, N.J.: Prentice-Hall, 1971).

9. John R. Hayes, "Problem Topology and the Solution Process," in Carl P. Duncan, ed., *Thinking: Current Experimental Studies* (Philadelphia: Lippincott, 1967), pp. 167–81.

10. Jane, a student not discussed in this paper, was surprised to find out that a topic paragraph can be rewritten after a paper's conclusion to make that paragraph reflect what the essay truly contains. She had gotten so indoctrinated with Psychology's (her major) insistence that a hypothesis be formulated and then left untouched before an experiment begins that she thought revision of one's "major premise" was somehow illegal. She had formed a rule out of her exposure to social science methodology, and the rule was totally inappropriate for most writing situations.

11. Cf. "A plan is flexible if the order of execution of its parts can be easily interchanged without affecting the feasibility of the plan . . . the flexible planner might tend to think of lists of things he had to do; the inflexible planner would have his time planned like a sequence of cause-effect relations. The former could rearrange his lists to suit his opportunities, but the latter would be unable to strike while the iron was hot and would generally require considerable 'lead-time' before he could incorporate any alternative sub-plans" (Miller, Galanter, and Pribram, p. 120).

12. Frederic Bartlett, *Thinking* (New York: Basic Books, 1958), pp. 74–76.

13. *Structure and Direction in Thinking* (New York: John Wiley, 1965), p. 255.

14. John R. Flower and Linda Hayes, "Plans and the Cognitive Process of Writing," paper presented at the National Institute of Education Writing Conference, June 1977, p. 26.

Understanding the Text

1. What was the major difference between the "blockers" and the "non-blockers" among the students Rose studied?

2. According to Rose, what is the difference between a heuristic and an algorithm? Why is one more appropriate for writing than the other?

Reflection and Response

3. Which of the student writers in Rose's study do you identify with most? What about your writing process is similar to theirs?

4. Choose one of the "blockers" (Ruth, Laurel, Martha, Mike, or Sylvia) and describe what advice you would give them to get past their blocks, based on Rose's analysis and your own insights.

5. What rules do you have for your own writing process? Which of them are most helpful to you? Are any of them causing blocks for you, and if so, how might you alter them?

Making Connections

6. Using ideas from Peter Elbow's "Speaking and Writing" (p. 233) or Susan Wyche's "Time, Tools, and Talismans" (p. 240), explain why one of the "non-blockers'" rules — such as "I can use as many ideas in my thesis paragraph as I need" or "When stuck, write!" (par. 19) — is an effective one for student writers.

7. Rose proposes that one of the greatest difficulties for the "blockers" is that "they seem resistant to or isolated from corrective feedback" (par. 28). Use Kevin Roozen's ideas in "Writing Is a Social and Rhetorical Act" (p. 224) to explain why this situation would cause problems for a writer.

Metaphors in the Writing Process of Student Writers

Carie Gauthier

Carie Gauthier began her research into the potential of metaphor as an aid to writing instruction as an undergraduate English major at the University of Wisconsin Oshkosh. She presented her initial research at the 2013 National Conference on Undergraduate Research and published it, in the form of the article below, in the 2013 issue of the student journal *Oshkosh Scholar*. She has continued her metaphor research at Northern Illinois University, where she is now finishing a master of arts degree in English. For Gauthier, the metaphors students create to describe their writing processes provide a window into their understanding of the writing process and help to deepen that understanding. As we have seen elsewhere in this chapter, more productive understandings lead to more productive writing.

ABSTRACT. Research shows that metaphors are a useful instructional tool in the science classroom, and additional research shows that student understanding of the writing process impacts the quality of the students' final products. This article investigates the potential value of applying metaphors to writing instruction. I asked experienced and inexperienced student writers to describe their metaphors for the writing process and compared their responses. I found that inexperienced writers had rigid metaphors focused on a perfect product, whereas experienced writers had fluid metaphors focused on developing through writing. This difference shows an opportunity for development within the student-generated metaphors, which educators can use to guide students to more developed concepts of academic writing.

We talk about arguments as if they are war and we talk about life and love as journeys. In fact, we cannot talk about any of our abstract ideas without talking in metaphorical terms. When I say metaphor, I don't exactly mean the literary metaphor we all learn in grade school. I am talking about the metaphors that are built into our consciousness and that provide a foundation for our understanding of the way the world works.[1] Try to describe hate without metaphors and you may get something like "hate is an emotion that we feel toward each other." However, that definition does not accurately describe hate because you could put

267

companionship in place of *hate* and still be right. When you add meta-phor, you can say, "Hate is a powerful emotion of dislike that can color our actions and thoughts black with its strength." The second defini-tion uses the metaphors that feelings are weak/strong and that actions and thoughts have color. Emotions are abstract and must be explained in concrete terms, but these concrete terms are by nature metaphorical because the target knowledge is not concrete.

But what if the target knowledge is not abstract? Metaphors are used for explaining the extremes of the natural world as well. In science, we use metaphors to describe natural phenomena such as electrical currents and light refraction.[2] We use metaphorical activities in our classrooms like role play, model building, and cartoons to show how the world works. The use of these metaphors deepens student understanding and has been proven to be an effective tool to generate student engagement.[3] More engaged students are then better able to explain the knowledge they have gained through their participation in metaphorical activity. The writing process is also very complex, so it naturally follows that met-aphor can help us to understand it.

My research aims to show the potential of metaphor as an aid to writing instruction and learning. There are two theoretical contri-butions in my argument. The first applies metaphors, already used in teaching scientific concepts, to the teaching of writing. The second adds complexity to the aspect of cognitive writing theory, which studies the differences between skilled and unskilled writers. My research aims to support the use of metaphors for teaching while also focusing on skilled and unskilled student writers. My claim is that students vary in their abilities, and by encouraging them to create metaphors for their writing processes, we can help both students and teachers understand students' progress as writers.

The seeds of my study were planted in my senior seminar class 5 discussion about some of the ways in which my classmates and I, as expe-rienced writers, picture ourselves in relation to the writing process. Our discussion was prompted by an article written by Paul Prior and Jody Shipka that describes the ways in which the writing environment is social, complex, and layered. In their study, they asked writers to draw a picture of the environment in which they write. The drawings were detailed, and varied based on the understanding the respondents had of what writing entailed. Prior and Shipka conclude that the conceptual bases for writing are "interior worlds of sense and affect [that are] fundamental elements of writing."[4] Our discussion of the article generated metaphors that describe our understanding of the writing process. I created what would become a highly detailed metaphor about how writing is like knitting. I also started to wonder what metaphors other, less experienced, students use when they describe the writing process.

In this article, I will describe the two theoretical contributions of my argument and then illustrate them with a sample of students with different levels of writing skill. The students' metaphors show clear differences in writing process concepts, which support my theoretical point. I aim to show the ways in which metaphors provide a starting point for writers in the writing process and how those metaphors can then be used in the classroom.

Theoretical Discussion

Metaphors in Writing Instruction

Meaningful learning happens as a result of creating an analogy/metaphor and then developing it based on student understanding. As I will argue again later on, student-generated metaphors for writing can help students improve their understanding of the writing process. In turn, their deeper understanding can lead to improved writing.

To date, the use of metaphors for writing instruction has not been explored in detail; however, writing educators are aware that metaphor can be a useful tool for their own pedagogy. For example, VanDeWeghe talks about how becoming aware of and building his own metaphor for his classroom has affected student engagement. He claims, "As we understand our teaching, metaphorically, so do we extend the metaphor in more complex and often compelling ways."[5] He writes that his classroom is a story in which the students are both the readers and the characters. As the instructor, VanDeWeghe is the narrator and the author, and the meaning that is created depends on the engagement of his students and the ways in which he presents material.

Using this metaphor, he resisted the urge to interfere with the writing process of one of his students, Dan, who started using images in his journaling process. Instead of telling Dan that journaling was written, not drawn, VanDeWeghe watched to see what would happen. He discovered that Dan was more productive in his writing, and that the images were vital to helping his writing become clearer as he demonstrated deeper understanding. VanDeWeghe used his metaphor of classroom-as-story to view Dan's images as character development, not deviation from the assigned work. VanDeWeghe learned the importance that analogical

> "Student-generated metaphors for writing can help students improve their understanding of the writing process. In turn, their deeper understanding can lead to improved writing."

processes can have in the classroom, not only to enable educators to explain their ideas but also to allow room for students to develop their own understanding. Though VanDeWeghe used metaphor as a pedagogical tool for himself, he did not call his students' attention to their own work. In fact, the use of student-generated metaphors to teach writing has not yet been explored; however, the impact of student understanding of specific writing concepts, such as structure and content analysis, has been examined by cognitive theorists.

Smith, Campbell, and Brooker investigated why some student work 10 showed a complex thought process while other student writing was superficial. The researchers desired to "further theoretical analysis of students' underlying conceptual understandings of the essay writing process" by recording and then interviewing students of varying skill levels.[6] Students who wrote in what was described as a "unistructural" mode primarily focused on repeating facts that other scholars had reported. When asked about the criteria of organization, synthesis, and critical evaluation, students in this category withheld personal connections, opting to give textbook definitions instead. Smith, Campbell, and Brooker found that students who wrote "relational" essays included their personal opinions of synthesis and aimed to connect several ideas together in a nuanced manner. The relational writers felt that organization was structural, but that the information needed to flow together as well.[7] The students they interviewed described critical evaluation as "analyzing it, looking at what's good and what's bad about it."[8] Smith, Campbell, and Brooker, therefore, found that students' understanding of specific writing activities directly affected the quality of the work they created.

Similarly, Mike Rose examined students' understanding of the writing process in an effort to help students overcome writer's block. He reviewed the blocking patterns of students who got stuck in their writing and the strategies of students who were able to work through their blocks. He found that students who were unable to get past their blocks were adhering to writing rules that hindered them. Ironically, he cites composition teachers and writing textbooks as two of the sources of the students' problems.[9] For example, one student he worked with only had a general idea of what the paper would look like and indicated that, if her initial plan did not work, she would change it. In contrast, another student he worked with would only start writing after she had mapped out everything she wanted to say in incredibly complex diagrams. This need to outline in great detail left her with too much information to put into her short essay, and she would end up turning her work in late and unpolished. Rose was able to help students work past their blocks by showing them ways their concepts of writing were preventing them from writing.

Nancy Sommers built on the cognitive theorists above by comparing experienced (professional) and inexperienced (student) writers in different contexts. She analyzed the ways in which writers conceptualized revision, and found that inexperienced writers were more interested in the mechanics of their writing whereas experienced writers were concerned with the content of their writing. She used this difference to distinguish students' from professional writers' conceptualizations of revision. Though she makes a good point, she assumes that all students are equally inexperienced. Despite this assumption, Sommers' model is useful because she draws our attention to the clear differences in the conceptual approaches toward revision in each skill level. We can use this same model when we look at different skill levels within the student writer group. The conceptual differences between inexperienced and experienced writers are reminiscent of the work Smith, Campbell, and Brooker did with unistructural and relational writers, as well as what Rose did with writer's block. In my study, I will look at the differences in concepts of writing between experienced and inexperienced *student* writers.

My research into metaphor and its use in the classroom reveals an area of metaphor that can be applied to the teaching of the writing process. When used successfully, student concepts of writing, embodied as a metaphor, can be examined and compared as well as manipulated.

Study of Student Writers

In designing a study that would support my theoretical ideas regarding the use of student-generated metaphors as a tool for teaching writing, I decided to compare the metaphors of writers who are identified as basic writers and those who are writing tutors. Basic writers are typically students who are required to take a remedial writing course before they can take the first-year composition course. Writing tutors in this study are mostly English majors who identify themselves as good writers and were employed by the UW Oshkosh Writing Center during the semester of my study. The tutors enjoy the task of writing, have a desire to help others become better writers, and are sometimes asked for feedback outside of the Writing Center.

I started by creating a brief survey that asked the following: "Thinking 15 about the writing process in general, what metaphor/analogy fits how you approach writing? Describe or draw all parts that make up your metaphor." I also provided a condensed version of my own metaphor in which I tried to account for different aspects of the writing process without influencing the responses: "Writing is like knitting. The yarn is the words, the pattern is my knowledge, the needles are my physical environment, and the product is my completed essay. If I make a mistake, I can choose to undo everything and start over, or I can rework the stitches (sentences, etc.) until I am back on track with my pattern. It takes practice and can be time consuming, but anyone can learn how to knit (write) well. For some people, knitting/writing is a hobby; other people can market their product for a profit."

Once I had the initial responses, I looked for general patterns. I found that inexperienced writers were concerned with the final product and the right and wrong way of writing. They wanted a perfect paper and felt that there was an ideal that they could get to if they only tried hard enough. For example, they wrote that writing was like a perfect game, the perfect outfit, or beating a video game. These ideas were not exactly wrong, but they were limited. They focused on a goal of perfection that has a clear beginning and end. On the other hand, the writing tutors gave metaphors that were much more fluid and allowed for a variety of tasks and goals in their writing. They wrote that writing was like running errands, growing a tree, or cleaning. None of these tasks, especially the cleaning, is ever done. While there is always room for adding details, the tutors were more process-oriented. To help you see what I was seeing, I will provide some examples from each group.

Inexperienced Writers

Brian, one of the basic writers, wrote that writing is like a maze.[10] There are clear boundaries, and the goal is to navigate without deviating from the correct path. He is confined by the rules, and he wants to get to the end of his writing quickly. He said, "You are trying to get to the end of the maze by taking the right path right away" and "there are certain paths you can take that will help lead to the end the fastest." Brian gave little attention to the value that a wrong turn in a maze can have. The metaphor is good in that there is a learning process that occurs in it, but there is room to develop it in terms of genre study, scope, and complexity of the writing. Brian may need to be careful that the urge to reach the end as fast as possible does not interfere with developing ideas. A tutor or a teacher could suggest that a more complex maze would make a better metaphor here, where the path of writing changes based on what happens and where there may be more than one way out. This would effectively open the metaphor to possibilities that a traditional maze does not offer without removing the idea of the maze.

Experienced Writers

Charlotte, one of the writing tutors, wrote that writing is a dance. Her metaphor indicates her awareness of genre and the historical value of writing: "There are many different styles of dance . . . [and they] have evolved over a period of time." Each person dances a bit differently, but can choose to follow a particular style. Since everyone writes a little bit differently, it is more important to learn the steps and then apply your own flourish. The words are the bodily expression of writing, and she recognizes that they may not be perfect and may present challenges. She identified the social aspect of writing in dance partners and others who have influenced her dancing (instructors, peers, etc.). She also provided some specific examples of dances: "A Tango may be a passionate love letter" and "a Rhumba may be a persuasive essay." Her metaphor indicated the need for structure and topical knowledge, but she also felt that individual voice is important to writing. Charlotte's discussion of instructors and partners in her metaphor shows that she is conscious of the role audience can play. This awareness of audience does not show up in the samples from the basic writers.

Matching Metaphors

Some students from each writing group chose to use the same metaphor. These pairs of students had the same ideas about writing but differed in how they mapped their ideas. Their differences illustrate the underlying conceptual ideas each group has toward writing. This is where my theoretical point stands out the most, because these pairs of matching metaphors are the same on the surface but follow the same pattern as the metaphors I evaluated above.

Ashley, a writing tutor, and Catherine, a basic writer, both wrote that 20 writing is like a tree. Ashley's metaphor was about the process of planting and nurturing a tree. She starts with a seed and then makes sure that she is caring for it, giving it the things it needs to grow into a healthy tree. Her emphasis on the process of growing fits the tendency of the writing tutors to focus on the process of writing, not the product. She writes, "You should be proud of your plant and not forget about it . . . it will die if you do not continually return to it."

Catherine's metaphor, on the other hand, was about a fully grown tree with established roots. She outlined the physical parts of the paper—intro, body, and supporting points—in terms of the physical aspects of the tree. She writes, "The roots is [sic] the structure of the main topics . . . the main body is where you write out the main ideas. . . . The branches and twigs are the evidence and information to support the body." Her description of her metaphor is focused on the basic structural parts, and does not acknowledge that the ideas in the writing are vital to the development of the paper.

Similarly, Logan, a tutor, and Alexa, a basic writer, both felt that writing is like painting, and the general pattern of process vs. product continues here as well. Logan begins with an idea, and lets the process work toward creating a whole that "flows well." He also is aware that different goals require different methods. He explains, "Writing an essay is different from writing a poem . . . in the same way that painting is not the same as drawing." Though he does not go into detail about how exactly they are different, it is clear that his goal in writing is creating a whole, though it does not have to be a perfect whole. His words indicate significant revision "in hopes of creating a cohesive whole." At no point does he indicate that the goal is a perfect and complete final product.

On the other hand, Alexa wants a beautiful masterpiece. She wants to have a final product that is perfect all the way down to the details. Like Catherine, Alexa is also looking at the physical parts of the paper. She mentions examples, details, and the words themselves, while taking herself out of the creation. She writes, "To paint, you let the brush do the work, like letting your fingers type," and leaves the knowledge and ideas to her sources.

Multiple Metaphors

My study also revealed that student writers used multiple metaphors. Only the tutors shared multiple metaphors, and this shows an additional level of thought process that the basic writers did not have in their responses. In his article "Metaphors We Write By," Stephen Ritchie describes the value of having multiple metaphors for writing. He asserts, "The generation and application of alternative writing metaphors might guide researchers to take up new challenges in writing."[11] When he created and used more than one metaphor, the quality of his collaborative writing improved based on the metaphor he used and the project's goal. He found it easier to collaborate with other writers because he had a clear idea of his role, resulting in more concise writing.

It is possible that Kara, one of the tutors, was doing something similar, 25 and that the multiple metaphors she shared with me are a reflection of how she writes differently in various situations. She wrote about how writing is social and described writing as natural disasters in which people and ideas come together to rebuild in the aftermath. She also wrote that writing is a science experiment, in which some ideas float on the top of the water while others sink through a filter to settle at the bottom of the bottle. Her third metaphor was that writing is headgear in the sense that the ideas need to be pushed around before they can be straightened into a final product. Each metaphor is well suited to different goals in writing.

Harold also shared more than one metaphor for his response. He did not describe each one, but both metaphors show that he equated writing to discovery. The first, a puzzle, is crossed off with no additional detail, but it is not hard to see how a puzzle would fit the writing process. The one he describes in more detail confirms his focus on discovering through writing. He decided that writing is like a fossil because it starts with an interesting idea that he can then explore by digging around his ideas.

Metaphors in Action

After the basic writers created their metaphors, the writing tutors were able to use them in their tutoring sessions with the basic writers. One of the writing tutors, Clark, wrote that the metaphors "open[ed] a new line of communication with the writer." When his writers created the metaphors, not only could he use them as icebreakers, but he could then refer to the metaphors as he worked with his students. He identified ways in which the students were doing something they had described, and he also found ways in which his own metaphor about making banana bread helped build his students' understanding.

A few weeks after their initial responses, the inexperienced writers were given a brief self-reflective writing assignment (approximately one paragraph) in which they reevaluated their metaphors and described the impact their metaphors had on their writing. While some students were not yet ready to identify a change in their metaphors, a few writers did show a deeper understanding. One changed her metaphor from an onion to an eyeball. Her metaphor is still the same shape and idea, but it is much more complex. This change indicates that she was self-aware enough to know that her initial idea needed to be more intricate.

Another basic writer did not change her metaphor, but her words showed a more developed idea of writing. When Alexa, the basic writer mentioned above with the painting metaphor, revisited her metaphor, she indicated that she did not feel that her metaphor had changed. However, she also started to get at the same idea as Logan, the writing tutor mentioned above, and focused on a general goal rather than a perfect product. She revealed, "Focusing on the goal, question, idea will get the job done." Even though she is still looking for a final product, she no longer stresses perfection. This difference reveals that though she may not be aware of the small changes her metaphor underwent during the semester, there was a shift in understanding.

Conclusions

The use of metaphor in the classroom and in tutoring sessions works well 30 with teaching that is tailored to the student. Teachers have the experience and understanding that students are only beginning to develop. As in the science classroom, the awareness of metaphors in writing can provide a better level of understanding for students and educators alike, and it is our responsibility, as educators, to help our students build their understanding. Being aware of a student's metaphor can influence the strategies we use to teach them to become better writers.

In "Analogies and Conceptual Change," Dagher advocates the study of the conceptual change that analogy can provide for students. He adds, "The contribution of instructional analogies to conceptual change may be tacit, leading to small but substantive shifts in students' understanding of concepts."[12] This would fit with what I found in the metaphors given by the inexperienced writers and showed in the examples above, with the onion changing to an eyeball and the potential for the maze to become more elaborate. The goal in working with the students to develop their metaphors would not be to get the students to scrap their ideas but to provide a small change that could lead to more developed academic writing.

The act of writing in metaphorical terms allows students to develop more complex meanings, and can help support their move into more developed academic discourse. My work has already been used by the Writing Center tutors and basic writing students at UW Oshkosh. Further use of my work should aim to chart the change in understanding the writing process, as Dagher proposes.

The longer I thought about my metaphor, the more detail I was able to give it. Longitudinal and comparative studies could explore any differences in the quality of student writing through interviewing the students and evaluating their writing samples. I would strongly recommend that future work be carried out as ongoing research and not as a single-semester research study to allow the researcher time to track the growth in more detail and with a larger sample. A comparative study, meanwhile, could use different sections of the same class to track the impact the students' metaphors have on their writing by evaluating the end of semester writing provided by each section.

Additionally, following Rose's methodology, conducting interviews could provide an opportunity for teaching students to reconceptualize their writing. Lackoff and Johnson claim that metaphor "becomes a deeper reality when we act in terms of it."[13] If we can foster student awareness of writing, we can help students develop their views of writing. By helping students see what is limited in their initial metaphors and then helping them see the ways in which their metaphors can become more adaptable to the varied tasks in writing, we would be able to help students move from a maze with only one way out to a maze in which the walls can move and may contain ideas never seen before. What would be important would be recognizing that there is no "right way" to write a "perfect paper."

Notes

1. George Lackoff and Mark Johnson, *Metaphors We Live By* (Chicago: University of Chicago Press, 1980), 4–6.

2. Allan Harrison, "The Affective Dimension of Analogy: Student Interest Is More Than Just Interesting!" in *Metaphor and Analogy in Science Education,* ed. Peter J. Aubusson, Allan Harrison, and Stephen M. Ritchie (Dordrecht, Netherlands: Springer, 2006), 52–63.

3. Ibid. 59.

4. Paul Prior and Jody Shipka, "Chronotopic Lamination: Tracing the Contours of Literate Activity," in *Writing Selves/Writing Societies: Research from Activity Perspectives,* ed. Charles Bazerman and David Russell (Fort Collins, CO: WAC Clearinghouse, 2003), 180, http://wac.colostate.edu/books/selves_societies.

5. Rick VanDeWeghe, "Teaching Writing as a Story," *Journal of Teaching Writing* 20, nos. 1 & 2 (2002): 103, http://journals.iupui.edu/index.php/teachingwriting/article/view/1282/1235.

6. David Smith, Jennifer C. Campbell, and Ross Rrooker, "The Impact of Students' Approaches to Essay Writing on the Quality of Their Essays," *Assessment & Evaluation in Higher Education* 24, no. 3 (1999): 327, Professional Development Collection, EBSCOhost, doi: 10.1080/0260293990240306.

7. Ibid., 331.

8. Ibid., 332.

9. Mike Rose, "Rigid Rules, Inflexible Plans, and the Stifling of Language: A Cognitivist Analysis of Writer's Block," *College Composition and Communication* 31, no. 4 (1980): 389, JSTOR, http://www.jstor.org/stable/356589.

10. All student names are pseudonyms.

11. Stephen Ritchie, "Metaphors We Write By," in *Metaphor and Analogy in Science Education,* ed. Peter J. Aubusson, Allan Harrison, and Stephen M. Ritchie (Dordrecht, Netherlands: Springer, 2006), 177.

12. Zoubeida R. Dagher, "Does the Use of Analogies Contribute to Conceptual Change?" *Science Education* 78, no. 6 (1994): 601, Wiley Online Library, 2013 Full Collection, doi: 10.1002/sce.3730780605.

13. Lackoff and Johnson, *Metaphors We Live By,* 145.

Bibliography

Dagher, Zoubeida R. "Does the Use of Analogies Contribute to Conceptual Change?" *Science Education* 78, no. 6 (1994): 601–14. Wiley Online Library, 2013 Full Collection, doi: 10.1002/sce.3730780605.

Harrison, Allan G. "The Affective Dimension of Analogy: Student Interest Is More Than Just Interesting!" In *Metaphor and Analogy in Science Education,* edited by Peter J. Aubusson, Allan Harrison, and Stephen M. Ritchie, 52–63, Dordrecht, Netherlands: Springer, 2006.

Lackoff, George, and Mark Johnson. *Metaphors We Live By.* Chicago: University of Chicago Press, 1980.

Prior, Paul, and Jody Shipka. "Chronotopic Lamination: Tracing the Contours of Literate Activity." In *Writing Selves/Writing Societies: Research from Activity Perspectives,* edited by Charles Bazerman and David Russell, 180–238. Fort Collins, CO: WAC Clearinghouse, 2003. http://wac.colostate.edu/books/selves_societies.

Ritchie, Stephen M. "Metaphors We Write By." In *Metaphor and Analogy in Science Education,* edited by Peter J. Aubusson, Allan Harrison, and Stephen M. Ritchie, 177–86. Dordrecht, Netherlands: Springer, 2006.

Rose, Mike. "Rigid Rules, Inflexible Plans, and the Stifling of Language: A Cognitivist Analysis of Writer's Block." *College Composition and Communication* 31, no. 4 (1980): 389–401. JSTOR. http://www.jstor.org/stable/356589.

Smith, David, Jennifer Campbell, and Ross Brooker. "The Impact of Students' Approaches to Essay Writing on the Quality of Their Essays." *Assessment & Evaluation in Higher Education* 24, no. 3 (1999): 327–38. Professional Development Collection, EBSCOhost. doi: 10.1080/0260293990240306.

Sommers, Nancy. "Revision Strategies of Student Writers and Experienced Adult Writers." *College Composition and Communication* 31, no. 4 (1980): 378–88.

VanDeWeghe, Rick. "Teaching Writing as Story." *Journal of Teaching Writing* 20, nos. 1 & 2 (2002): 103–22. http://journals.iupui.edu/index.php/teachingwriting/article/view/1282/1235.

Understanding the Text

1. What are the general differences Gauthier found between the metaphors used by basic writers and those used by writing tutors?

2. In the "Matching Metaphors" section (pars. 19–23), how do the differences between Ashley and Catherine's metaphors, and between Logan and Alexa's metaphors, illustrate the general differences Gauthier found between experienced and inexperienced writers?

Reflection and Response

3. Following Gauthier's prompt, the survey question in paragraph 15, develop a metaphor for your own writing process. Try to explain as many parts of that metaphor as possible.

4. Reflect on what the metaphor you created in the previous question says about your writing attitudes and processes. What pressures are you putting on yourself? Do you see any ways that a slight change to your metaphor might be productive?

Making Connections

5. Develop a metaphor for the writing process of one of the student writers profiled by Mike Rose in "Rigid Rules, Inflexible Plans, and the Stifling of Language" (p. 253) or by Susan Wyche in "Time, Tools, and Talismans" (p. 240). How does this metaphor help to explain some of the problems the student is having or help to suggest alternative ways for the student to approach writing?

6. Use both Gauthier and Rose ("Rigid Rules, Inflexible Plans, and the Stifling of Language," p. 253) to explain why improving our writing requires improving how we think about our writing.

5

What Does It Mean to Write "Academically"?

I n this final chapter, we bring together the many different threads of this book to consider how the negotiation of differences and standards in writing and language plays out in the academic writing students are expected to do in college. While you are likely working with this book in a course intended to teach you the standards of academic writing, the selections in this chapter demonstrate that the characteristics of "academic" writing are as difficult to pin down as a definition of "standard" or "correct" language.

As Dan Berrett explains, while many first-year college students believe they have already learned what they need to know about writing, professors' assumptions about what constitutes successful "academic" writing are more complicated than most of these incoming students realize. Chris Thaiss and Terry Myers Zawacki note that although there are some common conventions for academic writing, there is no clear-cut definition, and many of the rules students hear for making their writing "formal" or "academic" — such as avoiding the use of the first person — do not apply in all contexts.

One reason it is difficult to come up with a universal definition of what makes writing "academic" is that standards differ across the disciplines — that is, different majors have different expectations for college-level writing. Susan E. Schorn, a writing program coordinator who works with instructors across the curriculum, notes that while some priorities — such as understanding the audience one is writing for — are shared among the disciplines, there are significant differences in the details of what is considered good writing. We get a closer look at some of these differences in J. Paul Johnson and Ethan Krase's case study of two student writers who, like many college students, find that they must develop new priorities for their writing once they begin taking classes in their majors, and that they must be versatile in adapting to different professors' expectations.

In fact, even seemingly universal rules for good academic writing are tied to their context. In the United States, most teachers and students in college settings have historically been white, U.S.-born, native speakers of English. As a result, the standards for college writing in the United States are tied to the rules of Standard English (which, as the readings in Chapters 2 and 3 have shown us, is rooted in white speech) and to what is considered to be effective written communication in mainstream white American culture. However, as Paul Kei Matsuda explains, it is not the case that all college students are native speakers of Standard English. Students coming from other parts of the world, such as those described by Helen Fox, come with their own standards for effective communication that are often at odds with those taught in the United States. And students from communities within the United States that speak undervalued dialects of English, such as the black students discussed by Vershawn Ashanti Young, may struggle with expectations that they should separate their "home" and "school" varieties of writing and language.

Given the great deal of variation in what is considered "correct" in academic writing, and the potential some of these standards have for excluding students from certain backgrounds, some scholars of composition advocate that writing teachers pay less attention to specific rules and more attention to fostering the "habits of mind" referenced in Berrett's article — the attitudes toward learning and writing that will benefit students in college. The final two readings in this chapter discuss some of these beneficial habits of mind. Nancy Sommers and Laura Saltz explain the importance for first-year students of taking a "novice" attitude toward writing, in which one is open to learning and making mistakes. Anne Elrod Whitney, meanwhile, describes the need for students to see themselves in conversation with the sources they use when writing.

As you read this final chapter, think about how you are envisioning the college writing tasks ahead of you. Where is there room for you to complicate your current ideas about "good" writing? Remember that academic writing is just one of our many ways of using language, so, as with the other language varieties and practices we have discussed throughout this book, we can expect academic writing to be more complex, to say more about us and our circumstances, and to have much more going on behind the scenes than we previously imagined.

Students Come to College Thinking They've Mastered Writing

Dan Berrett

Dan Berrett writes about issues in college-level teaching and curriculum as a senior reporter for the *Chronicle of Higher Education*, where this article was published on March 28, 2014. In his article, Berrett describes some preliminary findings from a survey of first-year writing teachers. These teachers had gathered their students' perspectives on the sorts of writing they do and how well prepared they felt for college-level writing. With the help of some of the prominent writing studies researchers running the survey, Berrett explains why these student perspectives are important.

Freshmen believe their skills are fully formed; professors say learning to write is a process.

Freshmen estimate that they write about 25 hours each week, and most believe that they arrived on their campus with college-level writing skills fully formed.

The findings, which suggest that students' notions about writing may not match professors' expectations, emerged from a series of conversations between students and faculty members in composition and writing on several campuses. The conversations were organized by the Conference on College Composition and Communication, the Two-Year College English Association, and the Council of Writing Program Administrators, all professional organizations for teachers of college writing.

The effort produced what its organizers called an "impressionistic" picture of incoming college students' expectations of and experiences with writing. The results, based on students' self-reported behavior and mediated through their professors, are not thought to be scientifically valid. But the information, collected in the fall by 63 professors teaching 2,200 students, still provides food for thought, the organizers said. The findings also clarify many students' assumptions about writing, which faculty members may want to shift as they adapt how they teach the subject.

"What we found really interesting is that students reported that they 5 spent a lot of time writing," said Linda Adler-Kassner, a professor of writing at the University of California at Santa Barbara and an author of draft recommendations based on the findings.

"They wrote in lots of places and for lots of purposes," said Ms. Adler-Kassner, who also directs the writing program at Santa Barbara.

"They're doing more than texting. They're really writing, and that's great."

Most of the faculty members said their students had told them that they spent less than half of those 25 hours writing for informal purposes. And about 20 percent of students reported that they wrote for the purposes of political or social change, including letters to policy makers, opinion pieces, scripts for videos with a social message, and online commentary.

Eighty percent of faculty members said "some," "most," or "all" of their students described feeling well prepared for writing in college. That result echoes recent findings from the annual Freshman Survey, produced by the Cooperative Institutional Research Program, which is part of the Higher Education Research Institute at the University of California at Los Angeles. Only about 15 percent of freshmen in that survey anticipated that they would need to be tutored in writing. In contrast, about half rated their writing skills above average.

Writing as Process

The writing instructors' survey also revealed key differences between what students assume about writing and what faculty members expect, which have implications for teaching.

Three years ago, many of the same professional organizations involved   10
in the survey staked out a scholarly consensus on the skills and intellectual attributes that students need to succeed as writers. The "Framework for Success in Postsecondary Writing" did not prescribe a set of practices. Instead, it described the habits of mind and experiences that students should have if they are to thrive academically. They include attributes like curiosity and flexibility, habits like persistence and metacognition, and knowledge of how to write for various audiences using different conventions.

"Writing processes are not linear," the authors of the "Framework" wrote. "Successful writers use different processes that vary over time and depend on the particular task."

The emphasis on writing as process was not shared by students.

"We get the very strong impression from the responses that writing is basically a performance," Ms. Adler-Kassner and her co-authors wrote in the draft recommendations. "It is as if they believe that they are expected to know everything about writing already, not to learn writing."

Professors tend to blame the focus on standardized tests during the elementary and secondary grades for many of the frustrations they feel in their classrooms. The differing attitudes about writing are another example. Some students told their professors that writing in high school was often framed as preparation for tests. Time to develop ideas or revise prose was often seen as a luxury, the students said.

Professors of writing should encourage risk taking and failure, said   15
Dominic F. DelliCarpini, a professor of English at York University of Pennsylvania and an author of the draft recommendations.

> "When students talk about being ready for college, they don't realize they'll continuously be learning to write."

"It's an almost infinitely perfectible art, and you're always dissatisfied with it," he said. "When students talk about being ready for college, they don't realize they'll continuously be learning to write."

Changing Norms

Emphasizing the revision and continuous improvement of one's writing reflects a change in instructional approach for many professors, the authors acknowledged.

"What we call writing really is changing in our minds as faculty," Mr. DelliCarpini said. Writing is increasingly seen as an act that should not be limited to formal exercises like term papers, essays, or research reports.

Faculty members say the craft is practiced often in various forms, like social media and other informal contexts. They also know that writing in social media carries benefits and risks, which has been discussed for years.

In contrast, he said, "what students call writing hasn't changed that   20
much."

Students also don't see formal academic and informal personal writing as connected. Less than 20 percent of students in the survey felt that writing on social networks and other informal contexts could help them become better writers.

Faculty members have themselves to blame, said Mr. DelliCarpini. "The firewall they've placed between social media and academic writing has been reinforced by what we've said. They hear Twitter and Facebook are ruining how they write."

Instead, he added, faculty members should talk about how the rhetorical mechanisms are similar and different.

Professors can also take steps in class to bridge their students' informal and formal writing. They can require students to write on class blogs or wikis, use Twitter and Facebook for academic purposes, and make public presentations of their academic writing.

Writing in informal ways provides an opportunity to practice the   25
craft, the scholars said, even if it means students are using nonacademic conventions.

"For any writer to be successful they have to learn the expectations," said Ms. Adler-Kassner, of Santa Barbara. "No type of writing is perfect for all contexts and audiences."

Understanding the Text

1. As reported by Berrett, how do the first-year students surveyed feel about their preparation for writing coming into college?

2. How much and what kinds of writing do the students surveyed report doing?

Reflection and Response

3. Professor Dominic DelliCarpini, an author of recommendations based on the survey, notes that writing in college "should not be limited to formal exercises like term papers, essays, or research reports" (par. 18). What other, more informal types of writing do you do in your classes? How are these helping you to improve as a writer and thinker?

4. Berrett explains that faculty members believe writing on social media can make students better academic writers. Consider how this might be so. How are you, for instance, adjusting to your audience or providing accepted forms of proof when writing in both social and academic contexts?

Making Connections

5. How do the student views summarized here compare to the ones described in Nancy Sommers and Laura Saltz's "Writing That Matters" (p. 335)? Think specifically about students' views on the purpose of academic writing and whether it is okay to fail and make mistakes.

6. Below is the full list of "habits of mind" from the "Framework for Success in Postsecondary Writing" that Berrett mentions in paragraph 10 (quoted from wpacouncil.org/framework).

   - Curiosity — the desire to know more about the world.
   - Openness — the willingness to consider new ways of being and thinking in the world.
   - Engagement — a sense of investment and involvement in learning.
   - Creativity — the ability to use novel approaches for generating, investigating, and representing ideas.
   - Persistence — the ability to sustain interest in and attention to short- and long-term projects.
   - Responsibility — the ability to take ownership of one's actions and understand the consequences of those actions for oneself and others.
   - Flexibility — the ability to adapt to situations, expectations, or demands.
   - Metacognition — the ability to reflect on one's own thinking as well as on the individual and cultural processes used to structure knowledge.

   How does this list compare with your own sense of what you are being asked to do in your writing classes? Which of these habits of mind strike you as most important for writing in college and why?

What Is Academic Writing? What Are Its Standards?

Chris Thaiss and Terry Myers Zawacki

Chris Thaiss is a professor of writing at the University of California, Davis, and Terry Myers Zawacki is a professor emerita at George Mason University. Both scholars specialize in Writing across the Curriculum, a movement within writing studies that examines how writing is done and taught in different disciplines throughout colleges and universities. Their book *Engaged Writers and Dynamic Disciplines: Research on the Academic Writing Life* (Heinemann, 2006), from which this excerpt is taken, reports the results of a four-year-long study of students and professors in a variety of majors. Thaiss and Zawacki use their findings to explain how professors across the curriculum define good academic writing and how students learn to meet the writing expectations of their majors. In the brief excerpt below, Thaiss and Zawacki introduce readers to the difficulty of defining academic writing.

A*cademic writing* is one of those terms that is often invoked, usually solemnly, as if everyone agreed on its meaning, and so is used imprecisely yet almost always for what the user regards as a precise purpose; for example, commonly by teachers in explaining what they want from students. For our purposes as researchers, we'll define *academic writing* broadly as any writing that fulfills a purpose of education in a college or university in the United States. For most teachers, the term implies student writing in response to an academic assignment, or professional writing that trained "academics" — teachers and researchers — do for publications read and conferences attended by other academics. In this second sense, "academic writing" may be related to other kinds of writing that educated people do, such as "writing for the workplace," but there are many kinds of workplace writing that would rarely be considered "academic"; indeed, as the research by Dias et al. indicates, the distinctions in audience and purpose between academic writing by students and writing for the workplace greatly outweigh any perceived similarities. The distinction is important, because the teacher who is assigned to prepare students for the kinds of assignments they're likely to receive in other classes should distinguish between the characteristics of truly academic writing and characteristics of writing in other venues.

Most textbooks used in introductory composition classes either attempt to define or imply a definition of academic writing, but most of these definitions are abstract and are not based in research. These writers may or may not consider differences in standards and expectations among disciplines and among teachers. Some texts do attempt the somewhat easier—but still problematic—task of defining standards and characteristics of writing in particular "disciplines" or groups of disciplines, for example, writing in the "social sciences," but these do not bring us closer to a workable definition of academic writing as a whole.

Further, scholarly writers with an interest in "alternatives" to supposed standards and conventions in academic writing will invoke it in various ways, thereby assuming a definition. A few of these writers have attempted explicit definitions—for example, Patricia Bizzell in her introductory essay in *ALT DIS.* As opposed to a careful statement such as Bizzell's, most of what a student is likely to receive about academic writing, especially in the informal atmosphere of the classroom, relies too much on a teacher's limited personal experience of particular classrooms or on commonplaces that have been passed down. For example, one common assertion about academic prose—"It avoids the use of the first person"—continues to be made in classroom after classroom, even though many teachers across disciplines routinely accept first-person writing, and journals in every field accept articles with more or less use of the first person.

There are exceptions to almost every principle an analyst can identify as a characteristic of academic writing. So what can we say with confidence about its characteristics, regardless of differences among disciplines and individual teachers? Our reading, observation, and research suggest the following:

1. *Clear evidence in writing that the writer(s) have been persistent openminded, and disciplined in study.*

A 1993 *Calvin and Hobbes* comic, in which Calvin displays a common tendency to assume that academic writing is defined primarily by formal language.
Bill Watterson/AMU Reprints.

The concept of the discipline—and of *discipline* without the *the*—is central to the university, because academics have learned so much respect for the difficulty of learning anything sufficiently deeply so that "new knowledge" can be contributed. What the academy hates is the dilettante, the person who flits whimsically from subject to subject, as momentary interests occupy him or her, and who assumes the qualifications—merely because of that interest—to pronounce on that subject of the moment. Whether they are reading student papers or evaluating journal articles, academics are invariably harsh toward any student or scholar who hasn't done the background reading, who isn't prepared to talk formally or off the cuff about the subject of the writing, and whose writing doesn't show careful attention to the objects of study and reflective thought about them. Of course, standards for fellow professionals and for introductory students differ monumentally, but even the most neophyte student will be penalized for shallow reading and for lack of careful thinking about the subject. Persistent, disciplined study can be shown as well in a personal narrative as in a lab report, so this first characteristic of academic writing is not restricted in style or voice, although disciplines and subfields of disciplines do vary in customary ways of thought and in traditional modes of expression.

2. *The dominance of reason over emotion or sensual perception.*

> "And I wonder anew at a discipline that asks its participants to dedicate their lives to its expansion, but that requires a kind of imperial objectivity, a gaze that sees but rarely feels."
>
> —MALEA POWELL, "LISTENING TO GHOSTS" (16)

In the Western academic tradition, the writer is an intellectual, a thinker, a user of reason. This identity doesn't mean that emotions or sensual stimuli are absent from academic writing: indeed, the natural sciences have always depended on acute sensate awareness, detection of subtle differences in appearance, fragrance, flavor, texture, sound, movement; moreover, the arts and humanities would not exist without the scholar's intense and highly articulated sensual appreciation. As for emotion, every discipline recognizes at the very least the importance of *passion* in the ability to dedicate oneself to research, acknowledged as often tedious. But in the academic universe the senses and emotions must always be subject to *control by reason.* Political thinkers, for example, may be motivated by their passion for a system of government, even by their anger at opponents, but the discipline of political science demands, as do all disciplines, that *writing* about these issues reveals the writer as a careful, fair student and analyst of competing positions. The sociologist may describe in passionate detail personal experience of poverty or family dislocation, but the *academic* writer must not stop with the appeal to emotion (what Aristotle called *pathos*); the responsible sociologist must step back, as it were, almost as if he or she were a separate person, and place that emotional, highly sensual experience in a *context* of the relevant experiences of others and of the history of academic analysis of the topic. The literary or art historian, to cite one more example, might write about, and describe in great sensual detail, work that was intended by its creators to be pornographic, but the academic writer must be able both to appreciate the sensual power of the work and step back from the sensations to evaluate the work rationally.

With students, perhaps the most common instruction by teachers in regard to the control by reason of emotion is to avoid "impressionism": merely expressing "feelings" or opinions. The various formulations of the principles of the "personal essay" (e.g., Newkirk, Heilker), a popular assignment in composition classes, all countenance the telling of "personal experience" narratives that include the expression of emotion, but all demand of the writer an analytical persona that reflects on and evaluates the narrative in some way. The "discipline" of which we speak is largely this ongoing process by which scholars learn through practice to cultivate both emotion and the senses and, necessarily, to subjugate them to reason. It's not coincidental that "discipline" has been associated so often in education with, as the *Oxford English Dictionary* notes, "mortification of the flesh," the scourging of the body that is an extreme form of the subjugation of the senses to reason that is basic to all academic discipline.

> "Newcomers to academia, such as undergraduate students, often feel that teachers' reactions to their writing are mysterious."

3. *An imagined reader who is coolly rational, reading for information, and intending to formulate a reasoned response.*

The academic writer may wish also to arouse the emotions to agreement or to sympathy, as well as to stimulate the senses to an enhanced perception, but the academic writer wants above all to inspire the intelligent reader's respect for his or her analytical ability. The writer imagines the reader looking for possible flaws in logic or interpretation, for possible gaps in research and observation, and so tries to anticipate the cool reader's objections and address them. When an analyst such as Bizzell, in the essay mentioned earlier, calls the writer's "persona" "argumentative, favoring debate," we should understand "argument" not as an explicit form; after all, there is much academic writing that appears benignly descriptive, not "argumentative" in the formal sense. But all academic writing is "argumentative" in its perception of a reader who may object or disagree — e.g., the teacher who may take off "points" or the fellow scholar who may sit on a review panel; the writer's effort to anticipate and allay these potential objections is also part of the broadly "argumentative" ethos.

While the three "standards" we have described for academic writing 5 might appear simple, they are devilishly hard to teach and even to observe in any given piece of writing. Would that the standards were as straightforward as "avoid the first person" or "use correct English" or "have a clear thesis." As our findings chapters will describe in detail, our informants tended to speak vaguely about what they regarded as "standards" and "conventions" in their fields, even though none of them had any hesitancy to say that they knew what the standards were. What their stories imply to us is that their knowledge of standards accrued over time, through coursework, reading, attempts to write and reactions to that writing; through regular talk with fellow students and fellow researchers and teachers. It's no wonder, given this gradual trajectory of initiation, that newcomers to academia, such as undergraduate students, often feel that teachers' reactions to their writing are mysterious, perhaps motivated by social and personality differences rather than by factors clearly attributable to academic quality.

Works Cited

Bizzell, Patricia. 2002. "Preface." In Schroeder, Fox and Bizzell, vii–x.

Dias, Patrick, Aviva Freedman, Peter Medway, and Anthony Paré. 1999. *Worlds Apart: Acting and Writing in Academic and Workplace Contexts*. Mahwah, NJ: Erlbaum.

Heilker, Paul. 1996. *The Essay: Theory and Pedagogy for an Active Form*. Urbana, IL: NCTE.

Newkirk, Thomas. 1989. *Critical Thinking and Writing: Reclaiming the Essay*. Urbana, IL: NCTE.

Powell, Malea. 2002. "Listening to Ghosts: An Alternative (Non)argument." In Schroeder, Fox and Bizzell, 11–22.

Schroeder, Christopher, Helen Fox, and Patricia Bizzell. 2002. *ALT DIS: Alternative Discourses and the Academy*. Portsmouth, NH: Boynton/Cook.

Understanding the Text

1. Summarize each of the three major characteristics of academic writing that Thaiss and Zawacki list in paragraph 4.

2. Why do Thaiss and Zawacki say that the standards for academic writing are not, and cannot be, "as straightforward as 'avoid the first person' or 'use correct English' or 'have a clear thesis'" (par. 5)?

Reflection and Response

3. "Undergraduate students," say Thaiss and Zawacki, "often feel that teachers' reactions to their writing are mysterious" (par. 5). Consider what your current teachers, or those in your recent past, have said about your writing. What do you tend to get praised or criticized for? Do some responses to your writing seem more "mysterious" to you than others? Describe one of the more mysterious responses.

4. Thaiss and Zawacki acknowledge that because the three standards they list are very abstract, they "are devilishly hard to teach and even to observe in any given piece of writing" (par. 5). What are some ways in which you may have been taught these standards without realizing it? Consider at least three rules for writing that have been given to you by past or current teachers, such as Thaiss and Zawacki's examples of "avoid the first person" and "have a clear thesis." How do these rules compare or contrast with the more abstract standards that Thaiss and Zawacki list?

Making Connections

5. How do Thaiss and Zawacki's three abstract standards compare to the "habits of mind" discussed by Dan Berrett in "Students Come to College Thinking They've Mastered Writing" (p. 284)?

6. Use Thaiss and Zawacki's piece along with Nancy Sommers and Laura Saltz's "Writing That Matters" (p. 335) to explain some of the reasons why first-year college students can have difficulty understanding their instructors' expectations for their writing.

A Lot Like Us, but More So: Listening to Writing Faculty across the Curriculum

Susan Schorn

Susan Schorn does a great deal of "listening to writing faculty across the curriculum." As senior program coordinator and curricular specialist for writing at the University of Texas at Austin's Center for Skills & Experience Flags, Schorn is responsible for helping instructors in all majors think about how to use writing in their classes. In the piece below, a chapter from Patrick Sullivan and Howard Tinberg's edited collection *What Is "College-Level" Writing?* (NCTE, 2006), Schorn describes what she learned when she surveyed instructors all across the university about their expectations for student writing in college. She compares their responses to one another and to the typical priorities expressed by writing teachers — the "us" referenced in the title.

The editors of this volume asked me a very specific question: "How, if at all, do standards of 'college-level' writing change if faculty from departments outside of English weigh in on the subject?" As an administrator in a university-wide, cross-disciplinary writing program, and a teacher of composition, I have a sort of catbird's seat from which to consider this question. Accordingly, I solicited opinions from some of the hundreds of instructors teaching Substantial Writing Component (SWC) courses at the University of Texas (UT) at Austin. The SWC program at UT Austin is decentralized, and although it is built around a very basic set of course requirements, it does not bind instructors to a single set of learning outcomes. Thus our teachers, in eleven colleges and schools across campus, represent a cross-section of definitions of college-level writing outside of English.

Taking Patrick Sullivan's essay in this volume as a starting point, I asked SWC instructors in a wide range of disciplines a number of questions, including:

- What is college-level writing?
- How does it differ from, say, high school writing?
- Can we define what college-level writing looks like? Should we do so?
- Can we define the purpose of college-level writing?

The responses I received indicate that writing instructors outside English share virtually all of our many concerns about student writing. Moreover, as a group, they share our disagreements over the content, purpose, and need for standards. In short, they are a lot like us, only more so. I see this as a good thing. My sense is that, rather than trying to reconcile these many definitions into a single standard, we can do more to improve student writing by looking for the reasons behind the definitions. In fact, when we look at the range of ideas about writing across disciplines, we may become more comfortable with the level of disagreement we find within our own field. Disciplines obviously have divergent goals, but college writing must meet all of those goals. The differences among disciplines demand a more dynamic set of writing standards that are adaptable, as we assume all writing should be, to purpose, audience, and occasion.

In response to my first two questions, a professor in the School of Business provided a detailed, five-point list of skills:

College-level writing should demonstrate the following:

- *High level of accuracy (grammar, punctuation, spelling)*
- *Discipline-relevant vocabulary (e.g., business students should be able to use economic, financial, and management vocabulary appropriately)*
- *Discipline-relevant style (e.g., business students should use business-related formats and structures for writing such as memos, letters, reports)*
- *Ability to clearly and concisely relay a message (appropriate use of topic sentences, highlighting, introductions/conclusions, etc.)*
- *Writing that meets the intended purpose (demonstrates an understanding of the audience and goals of the message) (Loescher)*

Compare this response to the more general (and more ambitious) standard laid out by a professor of economics:

The rough, first stab I can offer is: College-level writing succeeds in communicating college-level content. A written product (essay, paper, monograph, etc.) achieves the standard of college-level writing if it could reasonably be included among college-level readings, assigned to be read by a relevant class of college students with the expectation that it would contribute to the students' learning in a way and to an extent similar to what instructors expect of the readings they typically assign. (Trinque)

These instructors approach their definitions of college writing quite differently. One foregrounds correctness and the other stresses content.

They are representative of the range of responses I received. And yet, the two definitions are not mutually exclusive; indeed, the professors could actually be describing the same ideal piece of writing.

Moreover, the instructors I surveyed clearly appreciated the interplay of small- and large-scale issues as they tried to define college-level writing. A professor of history, for example, narrowed the difference between college and high school writing down to three seemingly minor, but to her, telling, points:

> *I get seniors who are still tightly wedded to the five-sentence paragraph, who think they will go to hell if they write "I," and who can't imagine that [the professor] might be really truly interested in what they actually think (because I'm asking them to write on historiographical matters that are unsolved). Those three problems seem most clearly to define the difference between college and [high school] writing. (Frazier)*

When she goes on to discuss the purpose of college writing, this professor reveals why these high school writing habits are so troublesome to her:

> *I teach a period of history (European Middle Ages and Renaissance) that attracts students with many pre-conceived ideas. I'm happy enough if I manage to help them overcome those prejudices and see the sources we read in order to write about them freshly. (Frazier)*

No doubt the preconceived ideas about history she wants her students to overcome are reinforced by their preconceived ideas about writing. The ability to write "freshly," to contribute new ideas and perspectives, requires thinking that isn't bound by counterintuitive rules. Here, the instructor is concerned about how an overemphasis on such rules unfits her students for college writing—a somewhat different perspective from that of the business professor. This concern may reflect the demands of her discipline, or her personal experiences as a teacher, or some combination of the two. Whatever the source, it is a valid concern, and it arises because she is trying to accomplish a reasonable and worthwhile goal: getting students to reconceive history.

"I get seniors who are still tightly wedded to the five-sentence paragraph, who think they will go to hell if they write 'I,' and who can't imagine that [the professor] might be really truly interested in what they actually think."

A professor in art history described the difference between high school 5 and college writing this way:

For me it has to do with level of research (deeper and more sophisticated—no encyclopedias, for example), quality of analysis (there has to be some at the very least and it has to demonstrate a broader knowledge of the subject than the paper can or should represent), and the presence of an actual argument. (Canning)

Surface error is not what comes first to the mind of this instructor (though, knowing her, I am sure it bothers her when she sees it). She is looking for research ability, analysis, and argument. In fact, she sounds a lot like a composition teacher to me!

None of these responses is likely to surprise a composition instructor. We know all the things mentioned by these teachers are important. We understand the professional pragmatism that motivates these instructors' goals. We might disagree with the business professor's emphasis on surface issues if we felt it impeded a student's development, but we would probably admit the importance of error-free writing in the workplace. None of these descriptions could, I think, be called unreasonable. The question is: Can they all simultaneously be "right"? Can all these definitions and expectations be made to live together in harmony?

I believe they can. The result may be inelegant—a palette of definitions for different majors and careers rather than a single, neat standard, perhaps—and the process itself will certainly be noisy, but involving faculty across disciplines in defining college writing has many benefits. Such a process broadens an institution's understanding of the purpose of writing and sharpens awareness of writing's myriad uses. Standards devised by a cross-disciplinary process are more thoroughly interrogated and better understood by all parties. Giving all instructors a voice in setting the standards gives them a stake in improving student writing.

The key, I believe, lies in looking at the goals and expectations these faculty members bring to writing instruction, and how they *mesh* with those of English and composition faculty. I use the term *mesh* carefully; rather than expecting faculty in various disciplines to share the exact writing goals and expectations of English faculty, we should collectively discover where our goals coincide, where they diverge, and why. This helps everyone concerned determine who bears responsibility for meeting various goals.

Of course, discussing standards with many instructors does not mean accepting or validating all those standards. At some point, consolidation is necessary or the approach becomes pointlessly reductive. If each individual instructor sets his or her own standards, there is nothing standard about them. But there is good reason for writing instructors to expend at least some energy in that direction. In any act of writing, the standards, for content, correctness, purpose, and so on, ultimately reside in a tacit agreement between writer and audience. If the standard, whatever it is, is not met, the reader either fails to understand or refuses to read the writing. Thus, developing any standard for college-level writing requires spectacular generalization of what is really a quite individual relationship.

It is less than ideal, but on some level necessary. Based on my work   10 with instructors across the curriculum, it seems eminently possible to work toward a comprehensive set of learning strands related to writing. These would admit the need for, and benefit of, different emphases among strands, and different levels of performance, in different disciplines, institutions, and situations. Such a set of standards, while perhaps not as easily explained to state legislatures as a single rubric, is far more reflective of how writing really happens.

Creating such standards is good for us as composition instructors because it makes us more aware of the needs of students in majors other than English. We serve these students better when we know the full trajectory of their writing development in college, rather than just the stages that we guide them through. The process is good for instructors outside our field because it makes them aware of what we do — and what we don't do. It helps them better understand what *they* contribute (or should contribute) to their students' writing and critical thinking skills.

Having spent so much of this essay discussing differences, I would like to close by examining a common thread among the responses I received. It became clear as I read these instructors' thoughts that they all shared one specific goal for student writing. It is a goal dear to composition teachers. For these instructors in other fields, the goal is intimately connected with both the ideal and the intensely practical facets of their disciplines. The instructor in the School of Business expressed it this way:

If I had to pick one thing that separates adult-level writing from adolescent-level writing, it is the ability to reflect the needs of the audience in your writing. To be able to empathize with the reader and present the material in a way they can best receive and comprehend it. As part of the college journey, the adolescent needs to learn to empathize on this level and to leave behind the self-centered focus of youth. (Loescher)

Now, this is the same professor who provided the five-point list of grammatical, disciplinary, and stylistic skills quoted earlier in this essay.

But she takes pains to say that the *one thing* that denotes "adult-level" writing, to her mind, is empathy with the audience. Not just *awareness* of the audience, but "the ability to reflect the needs of the audience" and "leave behind the self-centered focus" of the immature writer.

A teacher in the School of Nursing strikes a similar note in her response:

You have to write to a wide variety of people, both inside your institution and outside. . . . Most writers don't spend nearly enough time understanding the people to whom they'll be writing. (Johnson)

Not just knowing who your readers are, but *understanding them.* This is a call for empathy much like that voiced by the business professor. Both teachers are concerned with the *practical* need for such empathy. It is, to them, simply necessary to good communication. And good communication is necessary to succeed in both their respective fields.

Along similar lines, the professor of Germanic studies worried that her students are too focused on "figuring out" the audience's point of view. This concern at first seems to contradict those voiced in the previous quotations, but the reverse is actually true:

The difference with "high-school writing" seems to be (and this is someone talking who has grown up in another educational system) that the students tend to assume that there is one correct answer to each question and one correct way to write it down. What they want from me is the "formula" that they can use. What I am trying to teach them is to find their own voice: develop their own opinion as opposed to trying to figure out mine. This, however, also means that they have to prove their point. (Hafner)

This professor's emphasis on "finding" voice and "developing" opinion is telling. She has observed her students using her as a stand-in audience for their writing—a tactic we have all probably witnessed. Why go to the trouble of trying to visualize a hazy professional or public readership when the teacher with the grading pen makes such a convenient substitute? If the student writer can just decode the biases of the faux audience embodied in the professor, he or she need never learn to empathize with amorphous, multifaced, imagined audiences (admittedly, a difficult task for any writer). But if students follow this course, the professor notes, they lose the opportunity to interrogate their own views—the very reason many of us in composition stress audience awareness in the first place. They will never develop the ability to prove a point or defend their opinions to real-world readers. They will lack both audience awareness and self-awareness. And this, according to these instructors, is what will keep them from being college-level writers.

In the College of Communication, a professor responded to my   15
questions with his own list of desired student writing skills. But he too specifically mentions the writer's approach to audience as central to college-level writing:

The move from high-school-level to college-level writing is, to my mind, a move toward a much greater consciousness and self-consciousness concerning the role of writing. That is, on the one hand, college-level writing involves a greater appreciation for the located-ness of the sources used and the subjects talked about. . . . On the other hand, the student's own writing should demonstrate a sense of audience: Am I writing this for people who have seen this film or to introduce it to people who have not seen it? Am I analyzing a film's formal qualities or am I concerned with its reception by viewers? What are the preconceptions my audience is likely to hold toward this film, this genre, this country's films, and the like? How will I either work with those preconceptions or attempt to change them through my writing? (Siegenthaler)

Again we see the concern for self- and other-awareness. Note too that this professor not only wants students to ask questions about audience ("Am I writing this for people who have seen this film or to introduce it to people who have not seen it?"), but expects them to then actively adjust their writing, so that they may, as Ronald Lunsford puts it, "talk to people who see the world differently" (190): *How will I either work with those preconceptions or attempt to change them through my writing?* Students of this professor must embrace the possibility that opinion is changeable through open discussion. If they cannot admit this possibility then they can never develop the skills to change opinion. And furthermore, they will never develop the ability to rationally modify their own opinions, or even interrogate them at all. And thus, the instructor in me feels compelled to add, they will be unable to tell when their own opinions are being changed, perhaps even grossly manipulated, by others.

My respondents were striking in their persistent concern over the quality that Ronald Lunsford, in his essay, calls "attitude." Moreover, they see this quality as integral to the work of people in their respective professions. Clearly, a writerly attitude is not merely something we demand in English or composition. The need to talk to people who see the world differently, rather than simply yelling at them, is integral to all disciplines — even the "objective" sciences, the ever-so-pragmatic world of business, and the life-and-death world of health and medicine. This fact strikes me as a vindication of our focus, in composition, on the ability to question, reflect, persuade, and listen. All too often I have been faced with students who not only did not want to seriously consider a different viewpoint, but felt it was unfair of me to require them to do so. It is heartening to know that instructors in other disciplines will continue to emphasize this important skill, and work to teach it to our students. Anyone involved in that great struggle, I think, deserves to have his or her opinions about writing heard.

Works Cited

Canning, Charlotte. "RE: Questions on 'college-level' writing." E-mail to author. 21 June 2004.

Frazier, Alison. "RE: Questions on 'college-level' writing." E-mail to author. 16 June 2004.

Hafner, Susanne. "RE: Questions on 'college-level' writing." E-mail to author. 16 June 2004.

Johnson, Regina. "College Level Writing." E-mail to author. 15 Sept 2004.

Loescher, Kristie. "RE: Questions on 'college-level' writing." E-mail to author. 9 July 2004.

Lunsford, Ronald F. "From Attitude to Aptitude: Assuming the Stance of a College Writer." In *What Is "College-Level" Writing?*, Ed. Patrick Sullivan and Howard Tinberg. Urbana, IL: NCTE, 2006. 178–98.

Siegenthaler, Peter. "Questions on 'college-level' writing." E-mail to author. 28 June 2004.

Sullivan, Patrick. "An Essential Question: What Is 'College-Level' Writing?" In *What Is "College-Level" Writing?* Ed. Patrick Sullivan and Howard Tinberg. Urbana, IL: NCTE, 2006. 1–28.

Trinque, Brian, "Thoughts on 'college-level' writing." E-mail to author. 24 June 2004.

Understanding the Text

1. How would you summarize some of the main priorities instructors had when defining what college-level writing should do?

2. What sorts of differences do you see between instructors in different types of majors? Consider, for instance, how much emphasis they put on different facets of writing such as argumentation, research, or grammatical correctness.

3. How important do the instructors Schorn surveyed think considering one's audience or readers is in academic writing?

Reflection and Response

4. Consider the writing assignments you have done for classes other than this one. Have you found that instructors in different departments have different priorities for writing — expressed either in what they ask for in their assignments or in how they respond to and grade your writing?

5. What do you think of Schorn's statement, "All too often I have been faced with students who not only did not want to seriously consider a different viewpoint, but felt it was unfair of me to require them to do so" (par. 16)? Have you found college to be an environment where you are challenged to consider views different from your own? If so, how do you and your classmates feel about being challenged in this way?

Making Connections

6. Compare the statements made about college writing by the instructors Schorn surveyed to the general characteristics described by Chris Thaiss and Terry Myers Zawacki in "What Is Academic Writing? What Are Its Standards?" (p. 288). Which of these professors' ideas illustrate Thaiss and Zawacki's points?

7. Add your own data to Schorn's study. Choose an instructor other than the one for this writing class — perhaps someone in your major, if you have one picked out. Contact the instructor and inform him or her that, as a project for your writing class, you are exploring what teachers across the university think about academic writing and would like to ask a few questions via email or in person. Then, prepare a list of three to five questions: you might use Schorn's list in paragraph 2 or prepare some more specific questions such as "What general strengths or weaknesses do you tend to see in your students' writing?" or "When students write for a class assignment, whom should they consider their audience to be?" After interviewing your chosen instructor, write up a reflection in which you discuss the most interesting things he or she said and explain how they compare with the points made in Schorn's article.

Writing in the Disciplines: A Case Study of Two Writers

J. Paul Johnson and Ethan Krase

J. Paul Johnson and Ethan Krase are English professors at Winona State University. They have worked together to study how students adjust to writing expectations in different majors — surveying a group of students in their first year and working again with those same students in their senior years. In the excerpt below, from an article in a 2012 issue of the *Journal of Teaching Writing*, Johnson and Krase focus on two students, given the pseudonyms of Kate and Mary. This portion of the article discusses Kate's writing as a senior biology major and Mary's writing as a senior double major in TESOL (Teaching English to Speakers of Other Languages) and Spanish education.

Kate: "With More Knowledge and More Experience, I've Been Able to Make My Writing Better"

A Biology major concentrating in ecology and allied health, Kate completed courses in conservation, physics, anatomy, organismal diversity, biochemistry, biometry, and immunology during her senior year. As a consequence, the majority of Kate's writing takes place in laboratory-oriented classes, with reports following a fairly standard pattern of abstract, introduction, literature review, materials and methods, results, and discussion. Devoted to her field of study and fully engaged in its contents and conventions, Kate sees writing a lab report as an opportunity "to gain a better understanding of what you did in the experiment," and acknowledges its heuristic° value: "I always realize things I didn't realize when just doing the experiment." Almost every comment from Kate's interviews speaks positively to her understanding of writing as a means of learning and communicating that knowledge with others.

Also germane to Kate's positive attitude towards writing in her discipline is her professed fondness for creative writing. Even while disavowing its utility, she enjoyed composing a memoir in first-year composition (FYC), and an "Intro to Creative Writing" class, completed as a general-education elective in sophomore year, further sparked her interest in literary pursuits. Both before and since completing that course, Kate

---

heuristic: here, enabling self education and learning from experience. (This is an adjectival meaning of *heuristic*, as opposed to the noun meaning Mike Rose explains in "Rigid Rules, Inflexible Plans, and the Stifling of Language" in Chapter 4.)

continued to write creatively on her own. The conflict between literary and scientific prose may prove daunting to some students, but for Kate, the contrast has been illuminating: "I'm able to judge what the audience is going to know already and use that [to inform] my writing," she says. As Dias et al. observe, general writing competence may not transfer directly from one milieu to another, but selective skills such as syntactic and lexical sophistication are indeed "portable" from one task to the next (201). Her heavy load of science courses in her senior year precludes much creative output, but she understands well the distinctions she needs to observe when writing for one audience as opposed to another.

Writing in these senior-level science courses has also presented Kate with many opportunities to hone the research skills she had begun developing in FYC. Her work in FYC demonstrated a developing ability to locate and use authoritative sources to support claims; her report writing in her science courses now routinely employs the university's scientific databases to present medical and scientific research relevant to her current projects. Kate said she is now able to incorporate sources more appropriately in her writing: "I've been able to more subtly include research," she says.

Kate's reports cover such topics as brown trout population studies in local creeks and streams and the presence of microbial properties in various forms of garlic. By senior year, Kate has read and written so many of these lab reports that the structure of them has been fully inculcated. In a longitudinal case study of a science student, Christina Haas observed increasing rhetorical sophistication led to the student's eventual understanding of her reading and research as a part of an apprenticeship (66–69). Kate's growth is similar. Her own reports adroitly introduce each study, cite relevant literature, and describe the methodology and data with precision. In some instances, the lab report is additionally formatted to resemble a published journal article, with a byline and biography, columnar format, numbered tables and figures, and a keyword-searchable abstract. Requirements such as these help students see themselves in appropriate roles as apprentice writers-in-the-disciplines and familiarize them with the characteristics of the work they are expected, in these roles, to produce. Furthermore, an increased emphasis on presentation of student research at the university has helped create opportunities for Kate and many others to present their work in a public forum.

These laboratory-research reports are hardly the only types of writing 5 Kate produces in her senior year, but they are by far the most common and, as she has come to understand them, the most important. Thaiss and Zawacki, among others, cite the importance of faculty contextualizing their assignments, practices, and feedback, and Kate's instructors routinely provide detailed instructions for projects and emphasize the goals of reading and writing scientific literature. While Kate reports only infrequently discussing writing matters one-to-one with her professors, she has improved her work in at least a few distinct ways since FYC: through an emphasis on concision, the employment of what she calls the "objective style," an embrace of her instructors' "write-to-learn" philosophy, and careful revision and editing.

Early in FYC, Kate's work evidenced a demonstrable lack of concision, her sentences often meandering in search of a conclusion and individual paragraphs reaching (and sometimes crossing) a full page in length. Yet her final paper in FYC showed that she had made considerable progress in this area. By senior year, Kate's research reports in particular are models of concision. Assignment instructions often delimit stringent space requirements, emphasizing presenting what need be said "in as few words as possible." All that matters, Kate says, is "what you found, why it's important, and how you did it," not the "flowery details." Kate's reports evidence this economy on both a macro-level—where nothing is included that is not absolutely necessary to the description of the experiment—and on the micro-level, where each sentence is cut to eliminate any wordiness.

By senior year, the quantity and type of the writing she has done has also helped reinforce her understanding of what she calls the "objective style" of scientific reporting. Included among the tenets of this style are not only standard patterns of the broad section-level divisions, but within them, the relatively short, discrete, purposeful paragraphs; the unambiguous, precise use of diction; fairly strict commonplaces and conventions for the presentation of data, figures, and tables; and the general effacement of the writer. With vigilant sentence-level revision, Kate makes certain that her reports employ the style her intended readers expect.

It is interesting to witness too Kate's understanding of the *purpose* of these reports. Kate does not particularly expect each experiment to yield significant results, nor does the lack thereof impact negatively her care with her report-writing. In a circumstance where the results of a specific experiment prove to be insignificant, such as in her paper "The Effect of Garlic Variations on Growth of Staphylococcus Aureus" (antimicrobial properties were found in increments in all three variants of garlic—cloves, powder, and flakes—but not to any measurable degree of statistical significance), Kate's discussion section speculates intelligently on the possible flaws of the original hypothesis, the limitations of the research design, and the necessity of future studies. She has learned from her instructors that flaws in an experiment's design or execution do not warrant flaws in writing or presentation; conversely, accounting for what does not work in an experiment may instead require extra care to offer readers strong value in the report's discussion. Further, she notes, "writing out your thoughts is important because it makes you think differently about things"—an indication that Kate sees value in the process of writing-to-learn. In a number of important ways, then, Kate has taken on the discursive practices as well as the habits of mind that are requisites to professional scientific research.

Through all of her work in the major, Kate has become especially diligent at revision and vigilant about proofreading. She writes in other formats, for other audiences, to an extent—a letter to the family of a patient suffering hypertension for her immunology class, for instance—and in these and in all assignments she evidences care with the presentation of her work. From FYC, she learned to be particularly attentive to matters of coherence and concision, and she revises all of her work through multiple drafts and edits to economize as much as possible. This is work that Kate embraces—the revision, proofreading, and editing: "I notice when I read things out loud, I often change the wording or the order of a sentence." Some students see these tasks as unwelcome chores; others avoid them. But Kate continues to follow processes begun in FYC, reading every paper aloud, checking for grammar, spelling, and word choice before submission. Her meticulousness is just one indication of how she takes the writing projects in her field seriously and professionally.

For Kate, writing in the discipline has come to mean, first and foremost, a mastery of the scientific reporting style. Relatively constant practice in report writing has deeply ingrained in her both familiarity with, and respect for, its commonplaces and conventions. What others might see as a slavish obeisance to prescriptive rigidity, Kate sees as purposeful and communicative attention to readers' expectations. In addition, her creative tendencies, fostered largely outside her major field, present no obstacle to her learning, but instead help deepen her understanding of the conventions of her chosen field. "I feel confident in my abilities," Kate says. "With more knowledge and more experience, I've been able to make my writing better." From FYC to her advanced science courses, Kate has developed significantly as a writer, exhibiting an unfailingly positive attitude towards her writing, enjoying her creative pursuits, and managing her readers' expectations adroitly. 10

Mary: "I Don't Want to Be Like Every Other Writer Who Doesn't Take Chances"

By her junior year, Mary had earned herself All-American honors in her sport and settled into a double major in TESOL and Spanish Education. Having dabbled briefly with a more traditional (non-teaching) major in English, Mary completed the gateway course requirements there but then opted for a more "pragmatic" choice of a teaching major. But career pragmatism was not the only driving force behind her decision; her keen interest in applied linguistics, sparked in part by discussion and writing in FYC, helped motivate her work in TESOL as well as in her study of Spanish.

Anne Herrington and Marcia Curtis argue that writing development in the college years is not merely a cognitive matter but also an ethical and emotional one in which growth occurs at the intersection of the personal and the academic (357–58). For Mary, these intersections were many. In addition to the multiple and sometimes conflicting demands of intercollegiate athletics and a double major, she completed an internship on the university's common book project, where she selected, promoted, and presented a screening for a related film series and blogged about her reading. (One blog entry discusses her new commitment to vegetarianism, a topic she had explored in FYC and that was reinforced by her reading of the year's common book selection, a novel about the meat industry.) Study abroad in the summer between her junior and senior years helped her identify with the challenges faced by non-native speakers. This led her, in turn, to volunteer as a cultural exchange partner for the international student program and as a tutor for a native Korean-speaking local high-school student. These experiences fostered an even greater thirst for academic linguistic knowledge, so, to supplement her coursework in TESOL and Spanish, she completed a set of introductory and intermediate courses in Chinese. As an athlete, tutor, scholar, traveler, vegetarian, language-learner, and apprentice teacher, Mary pursued multiple connections between what she studied and what she lived.

Her writing in the two majors nonetheless presented various challenges, however, as Mary strove to learn disciplinary assumptions and conventions that frequently contrasted with one another. For Mary, having written in a wide diversity of genres through her sophomore and junior years proved helpful to her developing considerable stylistic nuance and generic° flexibility. Where some writers are vexed by transition from one genre, audience, or purpose to the next, Mary had worked on a considerable variety of projects large and small by senior year: not only the kinds of argument-based research papers she had practiced in FYC, but also literary analyses and explications (in English and Spanish), blog entries, and position papers, among others. By her senior year, most of the writing done in her advanced coursework was limited to teaching

---

generic: here, the adjective form of genre, which refers to a typical form of writing such as a research paper, lab report, memo, or résumé.

philosophy statements written for multiple education courses; lesson plans prepared for her methods courses; and research projects in applied linguistics for her TESOL courses, including annotated bibliographies, literature reviews, and case studies.

Of these three general categories of projects completed during senior year, Mary finds the least satisfaction in (and, perhaps, the greatest frustration with) teaching philosophy statements. Mary bristles at having to adopt the necessary "heartfelt" and "passionate" tone her professors require. "I've just learned pretty much to mimic the language of the texts I've read," she says. "Even if that's not exactly what I think or the exact way I would present information, I do it anyways just to get a good grade." Since Mary sees these essay requirements as a measure of students' motivation and commitment, values of her own that are already deeply-ingrained (as evidenced by her academic workload, intercollegiate athletics, and other extracurricular endeavors), these philosophy statements to her were little more than an exercise in giving her professors what they need. It is worth noting, though, that the essays she composed in response to these assignments adopt the requisite tone and articulate her philosophies in ways that any reader would find wholly convincing. Like the more successful students in Lee Ann Carroll's *Rehearsing New Roles: How College Students Develop as Writers,* Mary works to understand and respond to each new environment, to take on the new challenge, and provide what is asked for.

More pragmatic and purposeful to her needs are the lesson plans Mary 15 develops in methods classes. While these do not require skills in articulating a thesis or developing an argument, Mary finds them to help her "address specific standards and goals efficiently" and to provide useful practice in working with "instructional methods and assessment." Carefully organized and methodically presented, Mary's plans inventively integrate literary reading and media texts with state standards, precise outcomes, and student-centered pedagogies. A lesson plan on the *Arabian Nights,* for instance, designed for intermediate ESL students, focuses on reading comprehension with a number of active-learning strategies, doing so with careful display of all of the requisite components required by licensing agencies. It is perhaps not surprising that Mary sees the immediate value in such exercises in the semester preceding her student teaching: she knows that faced with what may be a crowded classroom of second-language learners, under the watchful eye of her supervising teacher, she will need to be able to plan

"Mary works to understand and respond to each new environment, to take on the new challenge, and provide what is asked for."

effective classroom activities with clear purpose, intentional design, and precisely-articulated outcomes. A "statement of teaching philosophy," though not unimportant, surely will matter less in her Monday morning ESL class.

In her TESOL courses, Mary frequently compiles annotated bibliographies, composes literature reviews, designs observational projects, and writes up case studies based on her research. For these, Mary employs APA documentation format (she had learned only MLA in FYC, but exhibited no difficulty with the transition). Her research work shows her to have developed significant competence and confidence in working within disciplinary convention. The sources employed are located in a small but functional set of university-provided databases: WilsonWeb, J-STOR, IdeaLibrary, Expanded Academic ASAP, and ScienceDirect, and they include both scholarly books from university presses as well as articles from periodicals like *Cognitive Psychology, Hispania, British Journal of Psychology, Social Cognition,* and *Brain and Language.* Mary's ability to navigate and employ these databases is perhaps the most noticeable feature of her senior-year writing, though it must be said that her advanced course of study presents with it a set of its own concepts and terms: *the Sapir-Whorf hypothesis, cross-cultural understandings, L1 interference, contralateral perception,* and *ethno-lingual relativity.* That in just a few years Mary can develop from a novice examination of euphemisms employed in the meat industry to an advanced study of memory storage and narrative recall in second-language composition is hardly unprecedented, but it is nonetheless worth remarking upon.

In their foreword to *Coming of Age: The Advanced Writing Curriculum,* Linda Shamoon et al. insist that advanced writing curricula should prepare students for "highly rhetorical participation in public life" (xv), a prospect for which Mary seems well situated. In her advanced coursework, Mary has developed the abilities to work fluently in varying genres (annotations, plans, cases, philosophy statements) and employ multiple modes of development (narration, exposition, comparison/contrast, definition argument). Perhaps in part because of the diversity of her own linguistic experience, in the classroom, as a tutor, and as a second-language learner abroad, she does not register differences between genres or modes as *obstacles,* but simply as *variables.* In a pragmatic sense, she does "what is necessary" for success in the given situation.

Mary describes nearly all of her interactions with her professors and classmates as successful ones, with professors providing explicit instructions and generally helpful feedback. Even when she experiences a less-than-optimal instructional experience, such as when in an Education course her professor gives every student the exact same feedback ("add more substance") or in a TESOL course her professor's instructions are unclear, her period of being "infuriated," as she says, does not negatively impact the ultimate quality of her work. On the surface, one might assume that the conventions of her two major fields, language and education, would have much in common, yet to her and to us, the differences between them are more stark—and Mary's ability to navigate them, more apparent.

Evident everywhere in Mary's senior-year work are strongly developed streaks of perfectionism and individualism. Acknowledging one of her weaknesses to be grammatical error, she assumes that she may still "make mistakes" in her writing and proofreads every piece of her own work carefully so as to address them. Three years earlier, Mary's FYC professor told her that awareness of conventions is critical to successful writing, a dictum that still motivates her to judge her own and others' work scrupulously. Perhaps her most noticeable trait as a writer, however, is her individualism, manifest in her drive to improve her work. Developing her skills—playing with alternative and unusual organizations, experimenting with different syntactic structures, and diligently incorporating disciplinary vocabulary into her growing lexicon—is crucial to her sense of self as a writer. "I don't want to be like every other writer who doesn't take chances," she says. "I want to write something new."

With a double major, a teaching licensure, intercollegiate athletics, and significant community service, Mary must navigate the varying discourse communities° of each of her academic disciplines. In addition, despite her very high level of accomplishment, not every one of her academic endeavors succeeds as intended: in her interviews, Mary pointed out her occasional disappointment with vague feedback and unclear instructions. Yet from FYC to her advanced work in multiple majors, she has developed as a writer in many remarkable ways, from her capability as a researcher and her fluency in multiple genres to her command of advanced linguistic concepts.

Works Cited

Carroll, Lee Ann. *Rehearsing New Roles: How College Students Develop as Writers.* Carbondale: Southern Illinois UP, 2002. Print.

Dias, Patrick, Aviva Freedman, Peter Medway, and Anthony Paré. *Worlds Apart: Acting and Writing in Academic and Workplace Contexts.* Mahwah: Erlbaum, 1999. Print.

---

discourse communities: communities (such as students in a specific major, members of a sorority or fraternity, or users of a specific social media site or online discussion board) that have shared expectations and norms for communication, including specialized vocabulary, common topics, and typical genres.

Haas, Christina. "Learning to Read Biology: One Student's Rhetorical Development in College." *Written Communication* 11.1 (1994): 43–84. Print.

Herrington, Anne, and Marcia Curtis. *Persons in Process: Four Stories of Writing and Personal Development in College.* Urbana: NCTE, 2000. Print.

Shamoon, Linda K., Rebecca Moore Howard, Sandra Jamieson, and Robert A. Schwegler, eds. *Coming of Age: The Advanced Writing Curriculum.* Portsmouth: Boynton/Cook, 2000. Print.

Thaiss, Chris, and Terry Myers Zawacki. *Engaged Writers and Dynamic Disciplines: Research on the Academic Writing Life.* Portsmouth: Boynton/Cook, 2006. Print.

Understanding the Text

1. What are the purposes and features of scientific writing, according to Kate?

2. Mary has written in many different genres. What has been the effect of this experience on her writing ability and her attitudes toward writing?

3. In what ways are Kate and Mary using skills they developed in their first-year composition classes for their writing in their majors? How have their skills improved beyond what they were doing in those early classes?

Reflection and Response

4. When Kate talks about her experience with creative writing, Johnson and Krase describe her as "disavowing its utility" to her major, since she does not do creative writing as a scientist (par. 2). Nonetheless, Kate likes and values creative writing. What types of writing do you do that are unlikely to be used in your major? Can you think of skills or ways of thinking that you are learning in the process of doing these types of writing?

5. We can see various examples of how Kate and Mary, as seniors in their majors, use habits they developed in their first-year composition classes. What strategies or advice have you learned in first-year writing that you think will be applicable to writing in your planned major?

Making Connections

6. In what ways do Kate and/or Mary display the writing abilities sought by the teachers interviewed in Susan E. Schorn's "A Lot Like Us, but More So" (p. 294)?

7. In what ways do Kate and/or Mary display the connections between formal or in-school writing and informal or out-of-school writing that are advocated in Dan Berrett's "Students Come to College Thinking They've Mastered Writing"?

The Image of College Students and the Myth of Linguistic Homogeneity

Paul Kei Matsuda

Matsuda's piece in Chapter 4, "Writing Involves the Negotiation of Language Differences" (p. 230), introduced us to the importance of attending to language difference in writing. In this selection, excerpted from his 2006 *College English* article "The Myth of Linguistic Homogeneity in U.S. College Composition," he applies his arguments to the specific context of academic writing. Arguing that all teachers make assumptions about who their students are and where they come from, Matsuda cautions college teachers about the dangers of assuming "linguistic homogeneity" — that is, assuming that all of their students have come to college with similar levels of skill in "standard" English.

Behind any pedagogy° is an image of prototypical students — the teacher's imagined audience. This image embodies a set of assumptions about who the students are, where they come from, where they are going, what they already know, what they need to know, and how best to teach them. It is not necessarily the concrete image of any individual student but an abstraction that comes from continual encounters with the dominant student population in local institutional° settings as well as the dominant disciplinary discourses. Images of students are not monolithic; just as teachers incorporate pedagogical practices from various and even conflicting perspectives, their images of students are multiple and complex, reflecting local institutional arrangements as well as the teaching philosophies and worldviews of individual teachers. Although there is no such thing as a generalized college composition student, overlaps in various teachers' images of students constitute a dominant image—a set of socially shared generalizations. Those generalizations in turn warrant the link between abstract disciplinary practices and concrete classroom practices.

Having a certain image of students is not problematic in itself; images of students are inevitable and even necessary. Without those images, discussing pedagogical issues across institutions would be impossible. An image of students becomes problematic when it inaccurately represents the actual student population in the classroom to the extent

---

pedagogy: a theory of or approach to teaching.
institutional: of an institution—in this case, a university.

that it inhibits the teacher's ability to recognize and address the presence of differences. Just as the assumption of whiteness as the colorless norm has rendered some students of color invisible in the discourse of composition studies (Prendergast 51), theoretical practices that do not recognize and challenge other inaccurate images reinforce the marginal status of those students by rendering them invisible in the professional discourse. At the same time, pedagogical practices based on an inaccurate image of students continue to alienate students who do not fit the image.

One of the persisting elements of the dominant image of students in English studies is the assumption that students are by default native speakers of a privileged variety° of English from the United States. Although the image of students as native speakers of privileged varieties of English is seldom articulated or defended—an indication that English-only is already taken for granted—it does surface from time to time in the work of those who are otherwise knowledgeable about issues of language and difference. A prime example is Patrick Hartwell's "Grammar, Grammars, and the Teaching of Grammar," a widely known critique of grammar instruction in the composition classroom. In his analysis of a grammar exercise, he writes that "[t]he rule, however valuable it may be for non-native speakers, is, for the most part, simply unusable for native speakers of the language" (116). While this is a reasonable claim, to argue against certain pedagogical strategies based on their relevance to native speakers seems to imply the assumption of the native-English-speaker norm. Hartwell also claims that "[n]ative speakers of English, regardless of dialect, show tacit mastery of the conventions of Standard English" (123), which seems to trivialize important structural differences between privileged varieties of U.S. English and many other domestic and international varieties of English.

Language issues are also inextricably tied to the goal of college composition, which is to help students become "better writers." Although definitions of what constitutes a better writer may vary, implicit in most teachers' definitions of "writing well" is the ability to produce English that is unmarked° in the eyes of teachers who are custodians of privileged varieties of English or, in more socially situated pedagogies, of an audience of native English speakers who would judge the writer's credibility or even intelligence on the basis of grammaticality. (As a practicing writing teacher, I do not claim to be immune to this charge.) Since any form of writing assessment—holistic, multiple-trait, or portfolio assessment—explicitly or implicitly includes language as one of the criteria, writing teachers regularly and inevitably engage in what Bonny Norton and Sue Starfield have termed "covert language

---

privileged variety: a form of English considered standard, mainstream, or correct.
unmarked: not different from the norm or what is expected.

assessment"° (292). As they point out, this practice is not problematic in itself, especially if language issues are deliberately and explicitly included in the assessment criteria *and* if students are receiving adequate instruction on language issues. In many composition classrooms, however, language issues beyond simple "grammar" correction are not addressed extensively even when the assessment of student texts is based at least partly on students' proficiency in the privileged variety of English. As Connors has pointed out, "the sentence [. . .] as an element of composition pedagogy is hardly mentioned today outside of textbooks" (97), and has become a "half-hidden and seldom-discussed classroom practice on the level of, say, vocabulary quizzes" (120). It is not unusual for teachers who are overwhelmed by the presence of language differences to tell students simply to "proofread more carefully" or to "go to the writing center"; those who are not native speakers of dominant varieties of English are thus being held accountable for what is not being taught.

The current practice might be appropriate if all students could 5 reasonably be expected to come to the composition classroom having already internalized a privileged variety of English — its grammar and the rhetorical practices associated with it. Such an expectation, however, does not accurately reflect the student population in today's college composition classrooms. In the 2003–04 academic year, there were 572,509 international students in U.S. colleges[1] (Institute of International Education, *Open Doors 2004*) most of whom came from countries where English is not the dominant language.° Although the number has declined slightly in recent years, international students are not likely to disappear from U.S. higher education any time soon. In fact, many institutions continue to recruit international students — because they bring foreign capital (at an out-of-state rate), increase visible ethnic diversity (which, unlike linguistic diversity, is highly valued), and enhance the international reputation of the institutions — even as they reduce or eliminate instructional support programs designed to help those students succeed (Dadak; Kubota and Abels).

In addition, there is a growing number of resident second-language writers who are permanent residents or citizens of the United States. Linda

---

covert language assessment: evaluating the *language* of a student's writing even when an assignment is only intended to evaluate the student's *understanding* of the subject they are writing about.
dominant language: the language spoken by the greatest number of a country's people.

---

[1] Editor's Note: The 2016 *Open Doors* report (**http://www.iie.org/Research-and-Insights/Open-Doors**) says that 1,044,000 international students studied in U.S. colleges during the 2015–16 academic year.

Harklau, Meryl Siegal, and Kay M. Losey estimate that there are at least 150,000 to 225,000 active learners of English graduating from U.S. high schools each year (2–3). These figures do not include an overwhelmingly large number of functional bilinguals — students who have a high level of proficiency in both English and another language spoken at home (Valdés) — or native speakers of traditionally underprivileged varieties of English, including what has come to be known as world Englishes.° The myth of linguistic homogeneity — the assumption that college students are by

> "The myth of linguistic homogeneity — the assumption that college students are by default native speakers of a privileged variety of English — is seriously out of sync with the sociolinguistic reality of today's U.S. higher education as well as of U.S. society at large."

default native speakers of a privileged variety of English—is seriously out of sync with the sociolinguistic reality of today's U.S. higher education as well as of U.S. society at large. This discrepancy is especially problematic considering the status of first-year composition as the only course that is required of virtually all college students in a country where, according to a 2000 U.S. Census, "more than one in six people five years of age and older reported speaking a language other than English at home" (Bayley 269).

Works Cited

Bayley, Robert. "Linguistic Diversity and English Language Acquisition." *Language in the USA: Themes for the Twenty-First Century.* Ed. Edward Finegan and John R. Rickford. Cambridge: Cambridge UP, 2004. 268–86.

Connors, Robert J. "The Erasure of the Sentence." *CCC* 52 (2000): 96–128.

Dadak, Angela. "No ESL Allowed: A Case of One College Writing Program's Practices." *Politics of Second Language Writing: In Search of the Promised Land.* Ed. Paul Kei Matsuda, Christina Ortmeier-Hooper, and Xiaoye You. West Lafayette, IN: Parlor, 2006.

Harklau, Linda, Meryl Siegal, and Kay M. Losey. "Linguistically Diverse Students and College Writing: What Is Equitable and Appropriate?" *Generation 1.5 Meets College Composition: Issues in the Teaching of Writing to U.S.-Educated Learners of ESL.* Ed. Linda Harklau, Kay M. Losey, and Meryl Siegal. Mahwah, NJ: Erlbaum, 1999. 1–14.

Hartwell, Patrick. "Grammar, Grammars, and the Teaching of Grammar." *College English* 47 (1985): 105–27.

world Englishes: unique local variants of English spoken outside of traditionally English-speaking countries. Examples include Singapore English, Indian English, and Ugandan English.

Institute of International Education. *Open Doors 2004*. New York: Institute of International Education, 2005.

Kubota, Ryuko, and Kimberly Abels. "Improving Institutional ESL/EAP Support for International Students: Seeking the Promised Land." *Politics of Second Language Writing: In Search of the Promised Land*. Ed. Paul Kei Matsuda, Christina Ortmeier-Hooper, and Xiaoye You. West Lafayette, IN: Parlor, 2006. 75–93.

Norton, Bonny, and Sue Starfield. "Covert Language Assessment in Academic Writing." *Language Testing* 14 (1997): 278–94.

Prendergast, Catherine. "Race: The Absent Presence in Composition Studies." *CCC* 50 (1998): 36–53.

Valdés, Guadalupe. "Bilingual Minorities and Language Issues in Writing: Toward Profession-wide Response to a New Challenge." *Written Communication* 9 (1992): 85–136.

Understanding the Text

1. Why does Matsuda claim that teachers need an "image of prototypical students" (par. 1) — that is, an assumption about who their students are? When does this image become a problem?

2. What proof does Matsuda provide that "linguistic homogeneity" does not exist in U.S. universities?

Reflection and Response

3. Discuss Matsuda's argument in the context of your own college environment. How linguistically homogenous or diverse are your college's classrooms? What do you think is the "image of prototypical students" held by your teachers, and to what degree do you and your classmates fit that image? Would you suggest any changes to teaching based on Matsuda's argument, or any adjustments to Matsuda's points based on your observations?

4. Matsuda makes a variety of claims about grammar instruction in paragraph 4, such as that teachers almost always include grammar among the features they grade for in student writing and that not all teachers are teaching grammar. How do his descriptions compare to your own experiences of grammar instruction in high school and college?

Making Connections

5. Compare Matsuda's ideas about a "generalized college composition student" to Rosina Lippi-Green's ideas about Standard English in "The Standard Language Myth" (p. 212). In what ways are such generalizations needed? In what ways are they dangerous?

6. Use Helen Fox's "Worldwide Strategies for Indirection" (p. 317) and Vershawn Ashanti Young's "The Problem of Linguistic Double Consciousness" (p. 325) to explain and support Matsuda's point that "pedagogical practices based on an inaccurate image of students continue to alienate students who do not fit the image" (par. 2).

Worldwide Strategies for Indirection

Helen Fox

Helen Fox has worked for decades on multicultural issues in education and on related issues of race and social justice. She is Lecturer Emerita of Social Theory and Practice at the Residential College of the University of Michigan, where she started the minor in peace and social justice. Her most recent book is titled *Their Highest Vocation: Social Justice and the Millennial Generation* (Peter Lang, 2012). The piece below is from Fox's book *Listening to the World: Cultural Issues in Academic Writing* (NCTE, 1994), which explores how U.S. standards for academic writing compare to writing and language practices worldwide. This excerpt describes one of the many challenges faced by international students adapting to U.S. academic writing.

Raj is sitting glumly in my office, staring at the fifth draft of a personal experience essay that he has titled "Problem Child." He hates this paper, he tells me. No matter what he does with it, it won't flow.

After living in the United States for a week, my sister-in-law admitted me in a nearby high school. My lack of knowledge and understanding of the English language caused me so much embarrassment and hardship in school that I wanted to go back to India. I had a hard time making friends here because of my language problems. At the end of my first year in school I had learned to speak fragmented English. I, however, was deficient in reading and comprehension. Music is a universal language.

"I don't know how to connect this last sentence," he tells me. But this is the least of his problems. Raj is having a terrible time understanding how to connect anything to a main point, to wind his thoughts around a central theme—"a point of tension," as his TA says in her notes on his paper. It's not a problem with logic. Within each section, each ministory, the connections are there:

One day I was in a library and I came across a book called "Introduction to Psychology." I read the preface and understood very little, however I did comprehend the notion that psychology dealt with people and their behavior. After reading the preface I became very interested in psychology because I wanted to learn how to make new friends. I learned from the psychology book that in order to make new friends with other people I needed to have something in common with them.

Raj and I have spent a lot of time talking about his life in order to find a central theme for this "self-analysis" paper. He seems to enjoy my questioning. "Did you always have trouble making friends, even in India?"

"Hm. Did I always have trouble making friends. I guess so, yes."

Raj is relaxed and smiling now, looking at me affectionately from behind his thick glasses. He may feel uncomfortable with his peers, but talking with family—brothers, cousins, nephews, aunts—is a passionately engaging activity in India, and his family is now far away.

"I never went out of the house much except for school," he continues. 5 "My parents encouraged me, but I didn't really feel like it." He smiles, thinking back to his home village. "I did go out once, though, on a holiday when everyone flies kites. We had so much fun that day—the kite went up so high it completely disappeared. You know, it's *very* hard to bring down a kite when it's up that high," he tells me earnestly. There is such enjoyment in his face as he remembers those days that I am reluctant to stop him, even though I'm feeling a little impatient. I had been expecting this story to be an example of how he was a loner, even in India, but Raj has gotten diverted into the mechanics of kite flying, losing the thread, losing the point of what he was saying.

I continue my questioning, trying to refocus his attention so that we can work on that elusive central theme. I am hoping to find out just how he might have been different from other children in the neighborhood, and where those differences might have come from. "What did the other kids do after school?"

"Just hung around," he says.

"At tea stalls? Sweet shops?" I am thinking back, remembering my days in India. Raj gives a half nod after each of these possibilities, smiling in my direction. "But wait a minute," I remember, "that doesn't sound right." Kids like Raj wouldn't have been allowed to just hang around with street kids at tea stalls.

"At other kids' houses?" I ask. "Yes," he agrees. His voice is assertive, positive now. My mind flashes back to my Peace Corps service in India, to my exasperation with friends who were reluctant to give me a "no" for an answer when they thought I really wanted to hear a "yes," regardless of my need for information. "Will the bus leave soon?" "Yes, yes, right away." Hours later, the bus, which has had a flat tire that my companions knew about all along, finally pulls out of the terminal. It's amazing how much can flash back in the spaces within a conversation.

So, of course, middle-class boys spend time after school at the homes 10 of their friends, not hanging around cheap tea stalls. I should have known this, since I have made much of the fact that I lived in India, but Raj is too polite to emphasize my mistake by contradicting me. Instead, he has subtly, deftly, and completely unconsciously guided my understanding by his tone of voice and body language, even while giving me information that would mislead me if I hadn't learned, by experience fraught with bewilderment and frustration, how to interpret it.

Even though he has always felt uncomfortable around his peers, Raj is skilled at using subtle forms of communication in social situations. And it seems to me that the ability to use these nonverbal methods for giving information, internalized in childhood and perfected over eighteen years of intense social activity with extended family, is at least part of what is causing Raj so much trouble in his paper. Indeed, these politeness strategies are only the beginning of his repertoire of indirection; he also has a strong tendency to give the listener contextual information, stories that may seem unrelated to any main point, but which are intended to give the listener the *feel* of the situation, the context within which people act and by which their actions are understood. The kite incident, even though exemplifying the opposite of what I had been looking for, is part of the picture of his childhood, his life in his home town on the other side of the world. For people whose culture teaches that they can know something best when they immerse themselves in it, when they can feel—and thus experience—the complexities of all the relationships among people, things, and events, such contextual information is rich in possibilities for understanding.[1]

But when Raj writes for the U.S. university, his audience finds such information beside the point, if not totally irrelevant. And his attempts to use these indirect communication strategies to fulfill his instructor's expectations that he build the story around a single point of tension create a sketchy series of unrelated incidents. His paper moves from his arrival in America to learning from a library book how to make new friends, to some background on the Top 40 (that they are songs played on the radio, that they are free for anyone to listen to, that most people listen to them "because most people aren't rich"), to some statistics on his home town in India, to the literacy and English skills of the farmers in the area, to Raj's own trouble making friends in his home town, to how he now tries to make friends through music.

When I look at the topics of these disconnected paragraphs, I realize that it might be possible to create a story line from them just as they are—a few transitional phrases, a few explicit statements of cause and effect, a little cut and paste—especially of "music is a universal language"—and all would be well. But what is both odd and telling is that

Raj—hard as he tries—doesn't get it. I have suggested several ways of linking the parts directly, shown him how to make those smooth connections. But although Raj knows exactly where the links should be and can identify disjunctions easily without my help, he seems not to be able to keep the central theme in his mind long enough to weave his examples and facts and stories around it.

By now, Raj has no hope that he will ever really "learn to write," as he puts it. All he wants to do is get through the semester. It's gotten so that he is waiting outside my office when I come in the morning, hoping to catch me for a few minutes without an appointment. He is so agitated sometimes that I worry about him. I remember what a graduate student from Chile told me about how it feels to try to do something in writing that is contrary to what everything inside you is telling you to do. "When I tried to go straight to the point," she said, "I was putting things down that I didn't want to put. Every time I got the thoughts that were natural to me, I had to look for other ones. It felt as though I was being aggressive to myself. I was really mad sometimes, because I felt as if something was going against me."

The tendency to communicate through subtle implication, which is 15 giving Raj such excruciating memories of his composition class, is shared by world majority students° from cultures on every continent.[2] I learned of a particularly surprising similarity the summer I was training young Japanese stock-market analysts who had been sent to the U.S. by their employer to improve their English and gain some understanding of American culture. Part of our plan had been to introduce them to the idea of the U.S. as a multicultural society with various lifestyle choices, and so one weekend we packed them off to Provincetown on Cape Cod with a group of graduate students from Côte d'Ivoire. The West Africans and the Japanese took to each other readily, and by the end of the weekend they had discovered some interesting similarities in their cultures, including a sophisticated formality; a preference for subtle, indirect strategies in conversation; a deference to age, rank, and wisdom; and the use of roundabout strategies to show politeness.

> "In my country, you don't say, 'Listen, I want to talk to you about this!' . . . If you want to talk to me about something and you already said it, why should I listen any further? I'm going!"

world majority students: a term Fox uses for students from places outside western Europe and North America. While they may be the minority in the United States, they represent a majority of the world's population.

"In my country, you don't say, 'Listen, I want to talk to you about this!'" said one of the Ivoirians, banging his fist on the table. "If you want to talk to me about something and you already said it, why should I listen any further? I'm going!" he said, getting up abruptly and walking to the door to emphasize his point. "You try to make a sort of suspense," he added, "and as we say: 'It brings appetite to the conversation,' you know? The person is thinking, 'What is he or she going to tell me?' And you really pull him to listen to you, you see? And finally you say it. And by the time you say it, you are also at the end of what you are going to say."

A Japanese student told of how her respectful conversational style had caused her to be treated rudely by one of her undergraduate advisers at an exclusive U.S. college, "I still remember the day I walked into his office and started explaining about my papers, my ideas, what I would like to do, and he just cut me off. 'Stop beating around the bush! This is America! I have five minutes for you!' I was behaving out of my politeness, not to get into the issue right away, giving him the background first."

"Giving the background first" is, I would suggest, not only an oral strategy used in polite Japanese conversation between student and teacher, but a common way of communicating in both speech and writing in cultures around the world . . . that place more value on subtlety and context. In cultures that value directness, it is assumed that the reader needs to be shown exactly how any background information is tied to the ideas that the author wants to get across. Not only do we require transitional words and phrases and a careful, logical ordering of information, but we expect reminders of our previous points from one paragraph to the next, as well as careful emphasis on words that show precise and explicit relationships between ideas. Of course, even within the U.S. university there are styles of writing which are not as direct or explicit as what composition instructors expect in a basic academic argument. Writers of literary criticism, for example, can take more liberties than those in, say, political science or psychology. Journal articles in social anthropology or women's studies are generally more abstract and ornamental than the straightforward prose of biology or chemistry, which strives for correctness, simplicity, and dispassionate reporting of concrete detail even at the expense of reader interest.[3] But even in the writing of the more abstract disciplines at the U.S. university, there is an underlying *tendency* to directness, to precise relationships between verbs and their subjects, to clear and relatively obvious transitions, to announcements of intent and summary statements.

This tendency to explain everything, to make points and transitions and beginnings and endings obvious is not, then, a natural feature of "good writing." It *seems* natural because it is based on a straightforward style of oral communication used in many everyday interactions that is nonetheless relatively rare outside of western° cultures. Though no style of communication is either completely explicit or completely implicit all of the time, in general it is fair to say that in western cultures, and especially in the U.S., children grow up with teachers, parents, and peers admonishing them to speak directly to the point and be relatively quick about it. "What are you driving at?" we ask when children digress. "Oh god, not another shaggy dog story!" "I don't get it." "Can you give me an example?" "So basically, what you're saying is. . . ." In "non western" cultures, however, children are taught from a very young age to present themselves and think about the world in quite different ways—myriad ways to be sure but, in general, ways that value subtlety.[4] Anthropologist Edward T. Hall (1976) draws a helpful distinction between high- and low-context cultural communication styles. In low-context cultures—mainly European, British, and U.S. mainstream—most of the information in the message must be made explicit, or, as I tell many world majority students, you need to talk to us the way you talk to a computer, leaving nothing to the imagination. In high-context cultures, on the other hand, much of the information in a message is not put into words at all, but is found, as Hall says, "either in the physical context or internalized in the person" (91). Like communication between twins who have grown up together, information transfer in high-context cultures relies on a good deal of a previous history of shared understanding and assumes that very little information is required, or even desired, for the audience to get the message.

These worldwide strategies of indirection—linguistic, rhetorical, 20 poetic, psychological—create a richness that to world majority students makes the spare, relentless logic of the western tradition seem meager in comparison. "When I read something written by an American it sounds so childish," confessed a graduate student from Chile. "It's because we don't see with these connections. It's just like: 'This is a watch, the watch is brown, da-da, da-da.' For us, that's funny. I think that for Americans, it must be funny, the way I describe things."

Notes

1. Anthropologist Richard A. Schweder notes in *Thinking through Cultures* (1991) that rich, contextual detail in personal and social description has been found by observers in Africa, Central America, the South Pacific, and Central Asia.

western: within North America, western Europe, or Australia (some definitions also include some or all of South America). "Nonwestern cultures" are ones outside of these areas.

The "context-dependent person," or "holist," is "convinced that objects and events are necessarily altered by the relations into which they enter [and thus] is theoretically primed to contextualize objects and events, and theoretically disinclined to appraise things *in vacuo,* in the abstract" (153).

For a discussion of digression in Hindi expository prose, see Kachru (1982), "Linguistics and Written Discourse in Particular Languages: Contrastive Studies: English and Hindi."

2. An important exception is African American communicative style, which is more direct, more "confrontational" even than white, mainstream U.S. culture. See Kochman (1981), *Black and White Styles in Conflict.*

3. See, for example, Day (1992), *Scientific English: A Guide for Scientists and Other Professionals;* Bazerman (1988), *Shaping Written Knowledge: The Genre and Activity of the Experimental Article in Science;* Maimon (1983), "Maps and Genres: Exploring Connections in the Arts and Sciences"; MacDonald (1987), "Problem Definition in Academic Writing"; Elbow (1991), "Reflections on Academic Discourse"; and McGann (1992), *Critical Thinking and Writing in the Disciplines.*

4. For an interesting discussion of how young children learn discourse strategies in Athabaskan culture, see Scollon and Scollon (1981), *Narrative, Literacy, and Face in Interethnic Communication.*

Works Cited

Bazerman, C. (1988). *Shaping written knowledge: The genre and activity of the experimental article in science.* Madison: University of Wisconsin Press.

Day, R. A. (1992). *Scientific English: A guide for scientists and other professionals.* Phoenix, AZ: Oryx Press.

Elbow, P. (1991, February). Reflections on academic discourse: How it relates to freshmen and colleagues. *College English, 53*(2), 135–155.

Hall, E. T. (1976). *Beyond culture.* Garden City, NY: Doubleday, Anchor Press.

Kachru, Y. (1982). Linguistics and written discourse in particular languages: Contrastive studies: English and Hindi. In *Annual Review of Applied Linguistics,* 50–77. Rowley, MA: Newbury House.

Kochman, T. (1981). *Black and white styles in conflict.* Chicago: University of Chicago Press.

MacDonald, S. P. (1987, March). Problem definition in academic writing. *College English, 49*(3), 315–331.

McGann, M. E. (1992). *Critical thinking and writing in the disciplines.* Boston: Allyn & Bacon.

Maimon, E. P. (1983). Maps and genres: Exploring connections in the arts and sciences. In W. Horner (Ed.), *Composition and literature: Bridging the gap.* Chicago: University of Chicago Press.

Schweder, R. A. (1991). *Thinking through cultures: Expeditions in cultural psychology.* Cambridge, MA: Harvard University Press.

Scollon, R., and Scolion, S. B. K. (1981). *Narrative, literacy, and face in interethnic communication.* Norwood, NJ: Ablex.

Understanding the Text

1. Why can the indirectness and politeness of students like Raj cause them problems with writing in a U.S. college context?

2. What are some characteristics of western writing that make it different from nonwestern writing?

3. What is the difference between a "high-context" and a "low-context" culture?

Reflection and Response

4. Consider the comparisons made by the international students quoted in this piece between features of conversation and writing in their countries of origin and standard U.S. styles. What, for example, is your reaction to the Ivoirian student's point that U.S. directness lacks the "suspense" necessary to make a conversation interesting (par. 16), or the Chilean student's opinion that American writing "sounds so childish" (par. 20)? How do you feel your response is influenced by the culture in which you grew up?

5. Fox compares a high-context culture, which she says "relies on a good deal of a previous history of shared understanding and assumes that very little information is required," to "communication between twins who have grown up together" (par. 19). This suggests that high-context can describe relationships between individuals as well as cultures. Do you have any relationships — perhaps with a sibling, best friend, or significant other — that you would call high-context? How does your understanding of audience needs when communicating an idea to that person differ from your understanding when writing in an academic context?

Making Connections

6. Examine the features of academic writing described in Chris Thaiss and Terry Myers Zawacki's "What Is Academic Writing?" (p. 288) and/or Susan E. Schorn's "A Lot Like Us, but More So" (p. 294). Now that you have read Fox's piece, which of these features can you identify as being specific to a more direct, western style of writing?

7. How do Fox's examples help to illustrate Kevin Roozen's points about the connections between our comfort with particular types of writing and our membership in the communities that do those types of writing ("Writing Is Linked to Identity," p. 227)?

The Problem of Linguistic Double Consciousness

Vershawn Ashanti Young

An associate professor of drama and speech communication at the University of Waterloo, Vershawn Ashanti Young has research and teaching interests that span theater, speech, English, and education. Young is perhaps best known for developing the concept of *code meshing*, which he defines in his 2009 *JAC* article "'Nah, We Straight': An Argument against Code Switching" as "the blending and concurrent use of [both standard and nonstandard] American English dialects in formal, discursive products, such as political speeches, student papers, and media interviews" (51). The piece below, excerpted from that article, explains the problems with a "code switching" approach in which educators require speakers of black English and other undervalued dialects to "switch" between using nonstandardized dialects at home and using Standard English at school.

It's a peculiar sensation, this double consciousness. . . . The history of the American Negro is the history of this strife—this longing . . . to merge his double self into a better and truer self.

—W.E.B. DU BOIS

Double-consciousness has a history and should not be manufactured in the composition classroom.

—CATHERINE PRENDERGAST

Linguistic integration is preferable to segregation.

—GERALD GRAFF

Seven years after the Supreme Court legalized racial segregation (*Plessey v. Ferguson*, 1896), upholding the right of individual states to restrict and prohibit black people's public (and private) interaction with whites, sociologist W.E.B. Du Bois published *Souls of Black Folks* (1903). *Souls* is an analysis and critique of the effects of Jim Crow on blacks in America. During this period when blacks were deemed a separate and inferior race in relation to whites, Du Bois used the term *double consciousness* to describe the psychological impact this judgment had on blacks. He borrows the term from medical terminology that was used to diagnose patients suffering from split-personality disorder. Du

Bois believed that legal segregation produced a similar, if metaphorical, mental disorder in blacks—racial schizophrenia.[1]

The doubling of one's racial self-consciousness is produced, he writes, from having to "always look at one's self through the eyes of others" (2), from being recognized as an American citizen while simultaneously being denied the rights of citizenship, from trying to reconcile how one's racial heritage justifies legal and social subordination not only to whites but to non-citizens residing in the United States (Thomas 58).[2] Du Bois's statement in the epigraph above illustrates blacks' "longing" to resolve double consciousness, "to merge his double self" (2), the American and black selves, into a unified identity that would be better than either could ever be alone, divided, unmerged.

Yet more than a century later blacks still contend with double consciousness, despite the fact that the Supreme Court reversed its earlier sanctioning of segregation with its 1954 decision in *Brown v. The Board of Education,* in Topeka, Kansas. What's so strange about the present circumstances of double consciousness is that it has been adopted and translated into an instructional strategy that is used, like legal segregation, to govern blacks' social interactions in public, paradoxically in an era where allegedly, as linguist John McWhorter opines, "racism is quickly receding" (266).

Double consciousness shows up in one of its most pronounced and pernicious forms in both the theory and practice of teaching oral and written communication to black students, where code switching is offered as the best strategy. Code switching is a strategy whereby black students are taught contrastive analysis—a method comparing black English to standard English so that they can learn to switch from one to the other in different settings. The description on the back of Wheeler and Swords' co-authored textbook reads: "The authors recommend teaching [black] students to recognize the grammatical differences between home speech and school speech so that they are then able to choose the language style most appropriate to the time, place, audience, and communicative purpose."

On the surface this instructional method sounds fair because it 5 appears to allow black students to have their racial identity and speak it too. Yet in truth, to teach students that the two language varieties cannot mix and must remain apart belies the claim of linguistic equality and replicates the same phony logic behind Jim Crow legislation—which held that the law recognized the equality of the races yet demanded their separation. Indeed, the arguments used to support code switching are startlingly and undeniably similar to those that were used to support racial separation.

Justice Billings Brown, who delivered the majority opinion in the case upholding segregation, wrote that the "assumption that the enforced separation of the two races stamps the colored race with a badge of inferiority" was a false and mistaken view. He continues: "If this be so, it is not by reason of anything found in act, but solely because the colored race chooses to put that construction upon it" (Thomas 33). In dispute of this notion, Justice Thurgood Marshall argued 58 years later in the case that opened the way for desegregation that "separate is inherently unequal." The badge of inferiority that was stamped upon blacks racially and that remains attached to black speech was and is not contrived by blacks. The evidence that they were considered racially inferior then for their speech now resides in their experience in school where, as Graff writes, they are "urged to use Black English on the streets and formal English in school while keeping these languages separate" (27). Graff believes code switching is a misguided approach and argues: "Linguistic integration is better than segregation" (27).

Similarly, literacy scholar Catherine Prendergast substantiates Graff's view in her study *Literacy and Racial Justice: The Politics of Learning after Brown v. The Board of Education* (2003), which uncovers the segregationist practices that still inform the instruction of black students. As she explains, educational institutions still constitute a "site of racial injustice in America" (2), making literacy teachers accomplices, often unwittingly, in the continuation of racial inequality.

Literacy and Racial Justice is a conceptual enlargement of Prendergast's earlier essay, "Race: The Absent Presence in Composition Studies," where she focuses on writing instruction at the college level and uses Du Bois's complaint about double consciousness to "describe the experience of domination and exclusion within a society which professes equality and integration" (39). While analyzing the writing of minority law professors (e.g., Derrick Bell, Richard Delgado, and Patricia Williams), she points out how, like Du Bois, their writing reflects double consciousness because they view themselves as residing both inside and outside the legal profession. Their two-ness doesn't stem from any insecurity on their parts, nor are they uncomfortable being lawyers. To the contrary, it arises from the way that everyday legal practices reflect a segregationist ideology, which recognizes the existence of minorities but often excludes their experience from legal discourse and decisions. Prendergast cautions writing teachers against imposing a segregationist logic on students by creating models of instruction, like code switching, out of double consciousness, which, as she puts it, "has a history and should not be manufactured in the composition classroom" (51).

Yet double consciousness is continually manufactured in writing classrooms. In fact, it's commonly reproduced at all levels of literacy instruction because so many educators, including many blacks, promote it. This is so even though double consciousness stems from the legacy of racism and generates the very racial schizophrenia Du Bois condemned. To be clear, educators who support code switching are not all conscious proponents of racism. Thus I am not suggesting that self-described anti-racist advocates of code switching are really intentional racists. Nevertheless, the inherent racism of code switching cannot be denied.

Racism is the belief that race is the primary determinant of human 10 traits and abilities and that the different behaviors and capacities among distinct groups of people (e.g., blacks and whites) produce a racial taxonomy: One group's behaviors are understood to be superior while another group's abilities are perceived as inferior. Although racism is slowly being unhinged by our current understanding that race is not a naturally occurring biological fact but is rather a social construction, advocates of code switching apply old-time racial thinking to their current understanding of culture and language.

If, as linguists propose, standard English arises primarily from the speech habits of middle- and upper-class whites, and students who speak black English are required to give up their variety and switch to standard English in public and in school, then students are simultaneously required to recognize the superiority of standard English and the people associated with it. The response that Wheeler, Swords and teachers who promote language changing provide to this perspective is that neither black English nor standard English is superior. They say both are equal; each has prestige in their respective, separate sites (standard English in school, black English at home). This reasoning reflects the false logic of equality that permitted people to support legal segregation. It's reasoning that doesn't hold up when the two varieties meet in the public domain or in "formal settings." Since black English is restricted in school and the mainstream public, it is, in effect, rendered inferior, even if it is euphemistically described by Wheeler and Swords as "appropriate for other settings, times, situations" (read: "ineffective" and "inappropriate" in formal communication[3]).

Therefore while many advocates of code switching also claim to be anti-racists who would never seek to reinstitute racial subordination, they nonetheless translate the racist logic of early twentieth century legal segregation into a linguistic logic that undergirds twenty-first century language instruction. Toni Cook, the outspoken member of the Oakland School Board who helped persuade other members "to unanimously support the nation's first education policy recognizing Ebonics as the 'primary language' of many students," personifies this paradox (Perry and Delpit 172). In an interview after the Oakland School Board's decision, Cook was asked: "Why don't children automatically know Standard English, since they hear it all the time on television and at school?" She responded:

African Americans whose economic status and exposure is closer to that of the Huxtables have the exposure to work with the youngsters and teach them about the "two-ness" of the world they're involved in. But some schools are located in very depressed areas, have a primary population of African Americans on a fixed income. They see very little, the young people are exposed to very little, and there isn't a whole lot of reason in the home—this is just my guess—to adopt the behavior of duality. (Perry and Delpit 176)

Cook's observation of the "two-ness of the world" apparently refers to the vestiges of segregation that blacks must still negotiate. It's illegal, of course, to restrict blacks from integration based on their "color." But it's currently legal to discriminate on the basis euphemistically called "the content of their character," which in this context is manifested by whether or not they talk black in public.

In Cook's view, blacks should develop a dual personality, acting and speaking one way with whites, another with blacks in recognition of "the two-ness of the world they're involved in." From this perspective, what's really wrong with code switching is that it seeks to transform double consciousness, the very product of racism, into a linguistic solution to racial discrimination. Thus the real irony of Cook's belief that black people should "adopt the behavior of duality" is that the very anti-racist, liberal-minded individuals who claim to oppose racial discrimination are the same ones who unconsciously perpetuate it. Instead of attacking racism, they attempt to teach black folks how to cope with it. As school retention rates and test scores indicate, they fail quite miserably at convincing the majority of black students to embrace double consciousness as a coping strategy, but succeed at allowing the residue of racism to remain.

Double consciousness and the related belief in the value of code switching are so widespread that both are unfortunately encouraged by even prominent black linguists John Russell Rickford and Geneva Smitherman—two admirable scholars, who tirelessly pursue racial justice and the validation of black English. *Spoken Soul: The Story of Black English,* a book Rickford co-authored with his son, journalist Russell John Rickford, and for which Smitherman wrote the foreword, ends with a section titled "The Double Self." This last section has only one chapter, "The Crucible of Identity." The Rickfords begin it with the same epigraph

Keegan-Michael Key in the role of Luther, President Obama's "anger translator," at the 2015 White House Correspondents' Association Gala. Elsewhere in the article from which this excerpt is taken, Young discusses Obama's ability to code mesh by including African American vernacular features in his otherwise fairly standardized English. Key's Luther could be seen as drawing attention to the limits of that meshing, since Luther uses not just angrier speech but also speech with more distinctively black characteristics. Luther, by saying what President Obama cannot, reinforces Young's assertion that African Americans are frequently expected to leave behind nonstandardized dialect features in public settings.

Getty Images

from Du Bois's *Souls* that I use above. And they close it with four strong "suggestions": (1) Accept black English as a language; (2) Reject linguistic shame; (3) Urge black youth to "become proficient in Standard English, *especially the black Standard English*" (229, emphasis added). And, the last suggestion is worth quoting at some length:

Don't ever shun or jeer a brother or sister because of the way he or she speaks. It is only when we have claimed both Spoken Soul and Standard English as our own, empowering our youth to appreciate and articulate each in their respective forums, *that we will have mastered the art of merging our double selves into a better and truer self. Remember: to become an accomplished pianist (jazz and classical), you've got to be able to work both the ebonies and the ivories. (229, emphasis added)*

Although they pursue very noble work in their book, Rickford and 15 Rickford end with a fallacious claim. They believe that code switching can help one master the art of merging linguistic double selves. But how can the meshing occur if each self is restricted to "their respective forums," each limited to its own environment? If the two languages are not used together, at the same time, in the same place, no merging will materialize. Really, how could one ever really learn to speak the "black Standard English" they say black youth must learn, the language that so many black leaders have used, the very product of code meshing, if we can't combine the dialects together?

Even their ending music metaphor is at odds with code switching and actually supports code meshing. For pianists don't use only white keys to perform classical music nor only the black ones to create jazz. Pianists use "both the ebonies and the ivories" all the time, in all cases, in classical, the blues, jazz, and hip hop to access a range of harmonic combinations and possibilities that make genres and styles of music. As the Rickfords themselves state in their introduction, to "abandon Spoken Soul and cleave only to Standard English is like proposing that we play only the white keys of a piano" (10). Their own comparison illustrates that the white keys, representing standard English, and the black keys, representing Spoken Soul, are always already co-existent. No music is created playing only white keys and none playing only black. To attempt to compose music or even speech for that matter using only one set of keys would mean consciously and strategically ignoring and avoiding the other set of keys. A sheer impossibility! Yet this is the very arduous feat that code switching depicts. Both sets of keys must be used simultaneously to compose music. Likewise, both dialects should be used to communicate in all sites.

> "Pianists don't use only white keys to perform classical music nor only the black ones to create jazz. Pianists use 'both the ebonies and the ivories' all the time, in all cases."

As a matter of fact, the Rickfords' *Spoken Soul* itself is a beautiful composition using both the black and white keys. Note these examples: (1) The title of their first chapter "What's Going On?" is adapted from black cultural discourse (Marvin Gaye's musical critique of the Vietnam War in the title song of his hit R & B album *What's Going On?* 1971); (2) In the second chapter where they discuss how various writers employ black English in literature, they write: "Charles Chesnutt and Alice Walker could have hung with [poet Stephen] Henderson" (15). Their use of "could have hung" follows the standard English grammatical formulation for the informal "hang out with," which in black English means to leisurely loiter around with a group of like-minded people. And (3) in the conclusion, they write that Spoken Soul should be embraced in order for blacks "to determine for ourselves what's good and what's bad, even what's *baaad*" (228). This use of "baaad" is a superlative expression meaning very amazing, the exact opposite of the standard English "bad." It signifies cultural triumph and strength, especially in the face of mainstream oppression (remember Melvin Van Peeble's film, *Sweet Sweetback's Baadasss Song*, 1971). These authors mix and mingle black English and standard dialect. They code mesh.

Smitherman's "Foreword" is even more exemplary in its meshing (as is most of her writing). Her two short pages are replete with meshings of black English and standard dialect, beginning with her opening statement: "It's been a long time coming, as the old song goes, but the change done come" (ix). In this sentence, like the Rickfords, she appeals to the black musical tradition to empower her rhetoric. The old song she refers to is Sam Cooke's posthumous hit single "A Change Is Gonna Come" (1964), which was a score often used to exemplify the 1960's civil rights movement. On the same page, she explains: "In writing that is rich and powerful — and funky and bold when it bees necessary — they dissect black writing and black speech . . ." (ix). Smitherman uses "bees," an emphasized version of the verb "be" from the grammar of AAE, instead of the standard verb form "is." And she later praises the Rickfords' effort to discuss language, culture, race, and American history and offers their example to others, by writing: "To get it right, you have to do what the Rickfords have done. You have to represent" (x). In AAE "represent" means to be an outstanding example. In this case, the Rickfords exemplify both careful scholarship and cultural critique, doing both while also using black English. They indeed did represent.

Supporting linguistic segregation is fundamentally at odds with the social justice work the Rickfords and Smitherman seek to accomplish and even contradicts their very own writing. So why would such erudite intellectuals back code switching? I have argued elsewhere that the most unlikely people accept code switching because American racial logic exaggerates the differences between black and white people, which leads to exaggerations between black and white languages. Exaggerated perceptions of racial difference lead the very people who would never accept the idea that black and white people are biologically different to zealously displace that difference onto a vision of black and white language (Young, "Your Average Nigga" and *Your Average Nigga*). It makes sense then that code switching takes place in the mind, is essentially ideological, and that code meshing is what happens in actual practice—because in reality the languages aren't so disparate after all. The ideology of code switching eclipses the wonderful code meshing that occurs in black people's speech and writing. And it's this pervasive ideology that needs to be critiqued.

Notes

1. For an extended discussion of Du Bois, double-consciousness and racial schizophrenia in the context of African American English, see Chapter 6, "To Be a Problem," in my *Your Average Nigga: Performing Race, Literacy, and Masculinity*. For more on double-consciousness as a synonym for schizophrenia, see the insightful analyses of Bruce, Jr., Early, and Wells.

2. Thomas explains that in *Plessey v. Ferguson* the only justice to oppose the decision based his dissent in part on what he considered to be a legal irony: that although Chinese immigrants were ineligible for U.S. citizenship, they were not subject to separate but equal laws, while black citizens were segregated.

3. It should be noted that Wheeler and Swords' discussion of language has to do with pitting one language variety against another. When describing how they settled on using the unraced terms "informal English versus formal English," they report they considered "*nonstandard versus standard*"; "*community English versus Standard English; Everyday English versus Standard*" (emphasis in original, 19–20).

Works Cited

Bruce, Dickson D., Jr. "W. E. B. Du Bois and the Dilemma of Race." *American Literary History* 7 (1995): 334–343.

Du Bois, W. E. B. *The Souls of Black Folk*. New York: Dover Thrift Edition, 1994.

Early, Gerald. *Lure and Loathing: Essays on Race, Identity, and the Ambivalence of Assimilation*. New York: Penguin, 1993.

Graff, Gerald. *Clueless in Academe: How Schooling Obscures the Life of the Mind*. New Haven: Yale UP, 2003.

McWhorter, John. *Losing the Race: Self-Sabotage in Black America*. New York: Free, 2001.

Perry, Theresa, and Lisa Delpit, eds. *The Real Ebonics Debate: Power, Language, and the Education of African-American Children*. Boston: Beacon, 1998.

Prendergast, Catherine. *Literacy and Racial Justice: The Politics of Learning after Brown v. Board of Education*. Carbondale: Southern Illinois UP, 2003.

——. "Race: The Absent Presence in Composition Studies." *College Composition and Communication* 50 (1998): 36–53.

Rickford, John Russell, and Russell John Rickford. *Spoken Soul: The Story of Black English*. New York: Wiley, 2000.

Smitherman, Geneva. Foreword. *Spoken Soul: The Story of Black English*. Ed. John Russell Rickford and Russell John Rickford. New York: Wiley, 2000. ix–x.

Thomas, Brook. *Plessy v. Ferguson: A Brief History with Documents*. Boston: Bedford/ St. Martin's, 1996.

Wells, Susan. "Discursive Mobility and Double Consciousness in S. Weir Mitchell and W. E. B. Du Bois." *Philosophy and Rhetoric* 35 (2002): 120–137.

Wheeler, Rebecca S., and Rachel Swords. *Code-Switching: Teaching Standard English in Urban Classrooms.* Urbana: National Council of Teachers of English, 2006.

Young, Vershawn Ashanti. "Your Average Nigga." *College Composition and Communication* 55 (2004): 693–715.

——. *Your Average Nigga: Performing Race, Literacy, and Masculinity.* Detroit: Wayne State UP, 2007.

Understanding the Text

1. What is meant by the term *double consciousness*? How does Young believe that it is "continually manufactured in writing classrooms" (par. 9)?

2. Why does Young disapprove of code switching?

3. In what ways are the quotes Young gives from Geneva Smitherman and other scholars (pars. 17–18) examples of code meshing?

Reflection and Response

4. In your own educational history, have you encountered the view that some ways of speaking are more appropriate for home and others are more appropriate for school? How have you felt about such distinctions?

5. Young spends much of this piece arguing against what other teachers and scholars have said about Black English. In the process, he provides an interesting example of how complex scholars' opinions of one another's work can be. Consider his treatment of Geneva Smitherman and of John and Russell Rickford (pars. 14–19). How does Young make clear that he respects some parts of their work while disapproving of others? Based on what you see Young doing, how do you think that acknowledging the strengths of someone's work, even while critiquing it, might add to a writer's credibility?

Making Connections

6. How do Rusty Barrett in "Rewarding Language" (p. 130) and/or Carmen Fought in "Are White People Ethnic?" (p. 114) support Young's assertion that "students who speak black English . . . are simultaneously required to recognize the superiority of standard English and the people associated with it" (par. 11)?

7. How might the concept of *linguistic double consciousness* help explain the experiences of Amy Tan in "Mother Tongue" (p. 24) and/or Gloria Anzaldúa in "How to Tame a Wild Tongue" (p. 31)? In what way have these authors experienced pressure to evaluate their language from the perspectives of others?

Writing That Matters: A Paradigm Shift

Nancy Sommers and Laura Saltz

Nancy Sommers is a pioneer in the field of writing studies, having been a writing researcher, teacher, and program director for over thirty years. Her award-winning research has included numerous articles about students' writing and revising practices and about teacher response to student writing. Starting in 2001, she was the principal investigator in the Harvard Study of Undergraduate Writing, which followed four hundred undergraduates throughout their college careers, using surveys and writing samples to examine how they developed as writers. Laura Saltz, now a professor of American studies at Colby College, was a research associate for the Harvard Study of Undergraduate Writing. The excerpt below comes from Sommers and Saltz's coauthored 2004 *College Composition and Communication* article, "The Novice as Expert: Writing the Freshman Year."

When asked what advice she would give future freshmen, one student responds: "See that there is a greater purpose in writing than completing an assignment. Try to get something and give something when you write." This idea, that a student might "get something" other than a grade and that there might be a "greater purpose in writing than completing an assignment," represents the most significant paradigm shift of the freshman year. When, just three weeks into the freshman year, we asked students, "Why do you think faculty assign writing?" the most common responses focused upon evaluation—"so that professors can evaluate what we know"—and upon an abstract notion that "writing is an important skill in the real world." What is missing from these responses is any sense that students might "get something" other than a grade or career advancement, or that they might "give" something to their professors beyond a rehearsal of the course material. These early responses stand in stark contrast to those given at the end of the year, when so many students report that writing allows them not only to bring their interests into a course but also to discover new interests, to make writing a part of themselves. When students begin to see writing as a transaction, an exchange in which they can "get and give," they begin to see a larger purpose for their writing. They have their first glimmerings of audience; they begin to understand that they are writing for flesh-and-blood human beings, readers who want them to bring their interests into a course, not simply teachers who are poised with red pens, ready to evaluate what they don't know. One student describes her great surprise freshman year when she realizes, after receiving detailed feedback, "someone is actually reading my papers, someone who is trying to understand what I care about in a subject."

If there is one great dividing line in our study between categories of freshmen writers, the line falls between students who continue throughout the year not to see a "greater purpose in writing than completing an assignment" and freshmen who believe they can "get and give" when they write—between students who make the paradigm shift and those who don't. Students who continue to see writing as a matter of mechanics or as a series of isolated exercises tend never to see the ways writing can serve them as a medium in which to explore their own interests. They continue to rely on their high school idea that academic success is reflected in good grades. When one such student is asked about his best writing experience freshman year, he responds, "Do you want me to tell you about the paper I got the best grade on?" If freshmen focus on college writing as a game, where someone else makes up the rules and doles out the grades, it doesn't matter if they write twenty papers or ten. Practice and instruction are, of course, important during freshman year; the more a student writes, the more opportunities she has to become familiar with the new expectations of academic writing and to use writing to discover what is important to her. But it is not practice per se that teaches reciprocity. Students who refuse to be novices,[1] who continue to rely on their high school methods and see writing as a mere assignment, often end up writing versions of the same paper again and again, no matter how different their assignments.

> "Someone is actually reading my papers, someone who is trying to understand what I care about in a subject."

What characterizes the experience of freshmen who discover they can "get and give" something in their writing? Looking closely at the ways in which freshmen describe their best writing experiences, we see the crucial role faculty play in designing and orchestrating these experiences, whether by creating interesting assignments, mentoring through feedback, or simply moving aside and giving students freedom to discover

---

[1] Editor's note: In an earlier section of their article from the September 2004 issue of *College Composition and Communication,* not included here, Sommers and Saltz assert that "freshmen who see themselves as novices are most capable of learning new skills" (127) because they possess "an open attitude to instruction and feedback" and "a willingness to experiment" (134). On the other hand, they say, "freshmen who cling to their old habits and formulas and who resent the uncertainty and humility of being a novice have a more difficult time adjusting to the demands of college writing" (134).

what matters to them. The paradigm shift is more likely to occur when faculty treat freshmen as apprentice scholars, giving them real intellectual tasks that allow students to bring their interests into a course.

Yet for freshmen, another force is at work, one that shapes their course selection, engagement with faculty, or choice of writing assignments. In the transitional first year, students often discover themselves as subjects of inquiry when they think about their ethnic, racial, religious, or sexual identities for the first time. One student from New Mexico, for instance, speaks of having "culture shock," the sudden awareness of her culture that comes from leaving it. She describes her first-semester course in Chicano Literature:

Chicano culture was just something I figured was a part of me, but now I'm really examining it, and trying to form my own identity. I like being in a class where I hear other people's points of view rather than being surrounded by the culture and the stereotypes that I've grown up with. I'm trying to decide for myself what I agree with and what I don't.

Another student speaks of her decision freshman year to learn more about her mother's Italian heritage:

When I arrived at college, I realized that there is no social group called "Children of Fifth-Generation British Americans," which is what I am on my father's side, but there is an Italian Cultural Club, so I joined the club and got involved. I also started taking Italian and an art history course on Michelangelo, and even wrote about Italian cooking practices in an anthropology paper.

Free to set their own intellectual agendas, many freshmen, particularly those who grew up in relatively homogeneous communities, set off to explore their identities by selecting courses that enable them, however covertly, to study themselves. It is most frequently in these courses that novices discover they can "give and get" something through writing.

When we asked students about their best freshmen writing experience, 5 they described opportunities to write about something that matters to them, whether in Chicano literature or Italian, political science or computer science. Maura, for instance, used many of her freshman papers to think through her doubts about religion and her own social conscience. Since she does not refer to herself in her papers, her professors might not notice the connection between her writing and her religious identity, but she returns in course after course to themes of individuality, responsibility, and culpability. As a senior looking back on her freshman papers, she comments, "I spent much of my freshman year trying to figure out what I am contributing to the world through the study of religion. I was disenchanted by academia and struggled to understand what a life of action versus a life of contemplation would look like. My papers helped me think through some of these issues."

Understanding the Text

1. What is the difference, according to Sommers and Saltz, between first-year writers who can and cannot see themselves as novices?

2. What does it mean to "get something and give something when you write" (par. 1)?

3. Sommers and Saltz describe the view "that academic success is reflected in good grades" as a "high school idea" (par. 2). What other forms can academic success take?

Reflection and Response

4. Sommers and Saltz describe two stages that many first-year writers go through: Most students come from high school believing that writing has no "greater purpose . . . than completing an assignment"; eventually, some "believe they can 'get and give' when they write" (par. 2). Which of these stages do you believe you are in and why?

5. Sommers and Saltz mention that first-year students "often discover themselves as subjects of inquiry" by researching and writing about aspects of their own identity (par. 4). How have you done this, in this class or others?

6. How has the subject matter of this course affected your attitude toward your own writing?

Making Connections

7. Sommers and Saltz note, "students report that writing allows them not only to bring their interests into a course but also to discover new interests, to make writing a part of themselves" (par. 1). Use Kevin Roozen's "Writing Is Linked to Identity" (p. 227) to support and elaborate on this point.

8. Use Sommers and Saltz's article, along with Kevin Roozen's "Writing Is a Social and Rhetorical Activity" (p. 224) and Susan E. Schorn's "A Lot Like Us, but More So" (p. 294), to explain why it is important for student writers to have a sense of their audience.

"I Just Turned In What *I* Thought": Authority and Voice in Student Writing

Anne Elrod Whitney

Anne Elrod Whitney is an associate professor of language and literacy education at Penn State University, where her research interests focus on the teaching of writing. In the piece below, originally published in the December 2011 issue of *Teaching English in the Two-Year College*, Whitney explores the case of one of her former students. As you read Whitney's account of Keith's struggles and efforts and her responses, keep in mind that her primary audience for this piece is other teachers of writing.

Keith stepped into my cubicle on Monday morning, tentatively looking around. "Is this it?" he asked hesitantly.

"This is it . . . you've found the Nerve Center," I joked. Keith's eyes passed over the peeling pasteboard cubicle dividers, the flickering fluorescent light, the dented (and empty) metal bookcases. It looked more like a storage space than an office. I smiled a little sheepishly; I knew what the cubicle revealed about my status. "Have a seat," I invited warmly, "it's great to see you."

Keith sniffled, eyes watering. This was his first time to be sick at the university, away from home and the old comfort of staying home ill. Instead of watching TV and drinking soup prepared by Mom, he was dragging himself to classes, doing his best to keep up. He was a first-year student taking the first-year composition course. Writing wasn't easy for Keith; he mentioned even the first day of the course that he had to come early over the summer to take a remedial course for those deemed not prepared for regular college English, and that he wasn't sure he was ready for the papers he'd be writing this quarter. Now he was about to receive his first graded paper for the quarter; other than his preparatory work over the summer, it would be his first graded work in college, period.

Keith was a student in my first college writing class in the fall of 2002. As he undertook a transition from high school to college writer, I was transitioning from high school to college teacher: after beginning my career teaching secondary English, I had now returned to graduate school, moving into a career in English education.

When he'd gotten settled and looked across the desk at me, my expression was pained. "Keith, I have your paper, and I want to make sure you understand what's going on. Basically, you're getting an F because you 5

339

didn't use any examples from the text." I put the graded essay on the desk between us, and I waited, watching his response.

I had been dreading this moment all weekend. When I'd read Keith's paper and discovered to my horror that he had not referred to any of the assigned readings, I had felt both confusion and anger. Had he not understood the assignment? It clearly called for "Examples from at least two of the readings and from your own experience"; I even double-checked. Had he written it at the last minute? It couldn't be; students had brought rough drafts to class the week before, Keith included. What happened? Did he just not care? Did he think I wouldn't notice? Why hadn't he included textual examples? My mind raced into the future: Would he freak out when he saw the failing grade? Would this be my first complaint to the director of the program? Would he fail the next paper too? Did I fail him as a teacher? Now, I had broken the news: *you failed*. How would he react?

Keith looked at the paper without touching it. He saw the rubric and comment sheet stapled to the front of his paper; he'd seen that same rubric when the essay was assigned, and he'd used it in class as a guide to revision. Somehow, though, it seemed like another animal entirely now, covered in my crinkly handwriting, comments squeezed in between the typed lines and squirreling up the margins. And the grade: 56 out of 100. He'd known it was coming, knew it the day he handed it in. Still, there it was: his first graded assignment, failed. He took a deep breath; then he looked up at me and smiled. "I knew exactly what you were going to say when I got here. I knew what was going to happen."

His explanation revealed that this was true. Keith knew a lot about what had happened and why: "I've always had a problem incorporating textual examples."

I started a little at his use of the term. Is this the way an "F" writer talks?

"I had to take [the remedial course], you know, this summer. In that class, we didn't really have to deal with any readings; it was all based on your experience. The papers were all about what we thought, our opinions and our reasons for them. I think I'm comfortable writing that sort of paper, *my* argument. But the problem is the same problem I had in high school: I don't really know how to work the readings in. I thought, going into this paper, that I'd just write a draft first, without any quotes or anything. I just write better that way, if I focus on what I think."

Keith then opened his course reader to show its bookmarked, highlighted pages—passages he had identified and annotated where they might be added to his paper. He continued: "Then I planned to go back, and work the quotes in later, in between. Then I put it off and put it off, and I never got back to it. I kept thinking about it, but for some reason I never did it. I just turned in what *I* thought."

A Problem of Voice and Authority

The day the essay was due, Keith had written a process piece (a post-assignment reflection I collected from all students), which he titled "A. D. D." In the piece, he described *not* a diagnosed case of attention deficit disorder or learning disability but his own "writing process, or better called, procrastination process" and the myriad activities he found to engage in other than revision: laundry, housecleaning, watching television, and checking email. I had read that piece before reading his essay, and I had interpreted Keith's tendency to procrastinate as an example of developing study habits in a first-year student. He delayed revising because he wanted to avoid writing. I often have the same problem, and I had planned to speak with Keith about strategies for organizing his time, breaking up a writing task into manageable pieces, and other tricks for motivation and planning in writing.

Now, after listening to him speak, I saw it differently: when Keith avoided revising his paper, he was not avoiding writing altogether but was instead avoiding making a shift away from his own ideas and into the readings' ideas. To use quotations and other specific examples was, to Keith, an exercise in communicating someone else's ideas rather than his own. The paper as he had written it, without examples, documented his own thought process and conclusions. He felt that referring to the texts would make it into a paper about someone else's thought process and conclusions. Whereas I see the essay as a piece of writing in which the writer's ideas are the main event and the textual examples serve as mere tools for illumination and support, Keith resisted the encroachment of the readings into the territory of his own argument.

In Keith's comments I also heard, of course, echoes of Bartholomae's notion: "Every time a student sits down to write for us, he has to invent the university for the occasion . . . to appropriate (or be appropriated by) a specialized discourse" (4). Understood this way, writers must first understand the swirl of existing discourse on their subject (in this case, readings on obesity in America); then they must assert themselves as more qualified, or sensitive, attentive, or otherwise authoritative readers of these texts than the reader of their paper. And indeed this frame offers one way of understanding Keith's situation, but I thought then and still think now that Keith's task was less about establishing authority for invention and more about finding ways to express his already-invented argument and to position that argument within the arguments of others. That is, Keith had something to say, a position he had developed in response to and within the discourse of the course readings. His was not a question of entering the room in which the conversation was being held, nor of generating responsive things to add to that conversation; instead, he was reaching for a strategy for composing texts that reflected the authority he had already claimed. He was aware of the need for examples, too, and had plans for which ones to use and where they might go; he can synthesize texts in service of an argument—at least in talking with me about it. The problem then, for Keith, was that to include those texts in his paper would be to make the paper no longer about "what *I* thought." In other words, using explicit references to the very texts from which Keith worked in building his argument drowned out the sound of Keith saying what he thought.

This conference helped both Keith and me to think differently about 15 the task of writing an essay. Over the course of the quarter, Keith managed to find ways to make use of outside texts in his essays without sacrificing his sense of control over his writing. Watching him work, I began to find new ways of thinking about the writer's voice in relation to the voices found in source texts. And in the nine years that have passed since I worked with Keith—years in which I have been engaged in research related to authority in writing—I have further come to link concerns about authority and acquiring a discourse to concerns about voice.

Voice?

At the beginning of my career, I unwittingly approached voice as a kind of flavoring for student writing, like salt. I noticed "voice" in students' language when they sounded like their adolescent or young adult selves: when they used surprising word choices or slang, or when their writing sounded conversational or even quirky. I thought of voice (and encouraged my students to use it) as flair, as personal touches one added to the language of a piece of writing to make it "sound like you." The problem with that view is one of several that Peter Elbow lays out in "Voice in Writing Again—Embracing Contraries": the metaphor of voice, particularly when used in the way I've just described, activates unhelpful notions of fixed identity and individual uniqueness (183). And flair wasn't what Keith needed. In fact the writing "sounded like Keith," but it wasn't saying the right things. It failed to accomplish the assigned task, which was to make an argument extending from the ideas of others. In this case not voice but *voices* were the problem—that is, his sense that his own voice was somehow not powerful enough or entitled to speak alongside or even over the voices of more authoritative, published, and expert speakers. It was less a problem in flavor but in volume (as he seemed to experience it), or perhaps in register (insofar as register can index positioning of speakers relative to one another).

And, in fact, I think my teaching of voice in the past, grounded in an understanding of voice as individual, "authentic," and more or less stable for students has actually discouraged students from taking on such a sense of authority. I characterized their writing as "voiceful" when it was specific to personal experience, when it vividly characterized personal reactions, or when it conjured unique images that resonated with what I already knew about the student. Yet for Keith to write

> "It is successful integration of the words and ideas of others, without loss of one's own authority over the ideas, that is called for when writing in an academic voice."

with voice, in that sense, would mean for him to pull away from the words and ideas of others. It is successful integration of the words and ideas of others, without loss of one's own authority over the ideas, that is called for when writing in an academic voice.

Working with References

At the time I met Keith, however, I had not developed this perspective much beyond a sense that Keith could be encouraged to "speak up." We ended our conference on his first essay by talking about how Keith might revise his paper for an improved grade. We read his essay aloud together, and after every point I asked him questions like "how?," "when?," "how do you know?" I hoped that these would serve as entry points for Keith to include relevant passages from the readings in support of his original ideas; I wanted him to consider the readings as strengthening beams to tuck *behind* his own argument rather than structures erected on top of it or in place of it. As Keith answered those elaborating questions, I hoped he would notice that the answers were his, even when he used others' words to explain those answers.

I was surprised at Keith's rueful but good-natured response to having received a failing grade. Students at this university were typically high achievers in high school, and many have difficulty adjusting to the drop in grades that often accompanies the new challenges of college courses. I wondered whether the high level of engagement in class Keith had shown at the beginning of the quarter would continue after he received his F. I was happy, then, when Keith emailed me well before the next essay was due and asked if he could come in for another conference for some feedback on a rough draft.

His draft reflected progress from the first paper; he laid out his argu- 20
ment point by point, and he had penciled notes in the margins at points
where he thought references to the readings might be appropriate. Our
conference was brief, and he left with a plan to insert the textual examples and advice from me to "be sure to explain what each quotation
means and why you're using it; don't just dump them in." While I was
encouraged to see Keith beginning to incorporate material from the text
into the paper, I was a little dismayed at his process. I wanted students
responding to and commenting on the readings, not just dropping bits
of them in as adornments for an already-written paper.

It was with interest, then, that I pulled his finished essay from the
stack to grade a few days later. I immediately noted that he had included
a number of direct quotations from the assigned readings. In fact, in the
introductory paragraph, he incorporated perhaps too many quotations:

*Obesity has been quite a controversial and intriguing topic in the recent few
years. Obesity has become the center of attention for many people because
it has been spreading so rapidly. Now, more than half of the adults in our
nation can be classified as being overweight and about "22% of the U.S.
population is obese" (Koplan and Dietz, p. 440). This percentage of obese
Americans has been on the rise for many years and does not look like it will
slow down soon. Health problems that have been related to obesity are on
the rise as well. "More than 300,000 deaths each year have been linked to
obesity" (Goodman and Witaker, p. 497). Soon obesity could be the number
one cause of death in our nation. Right now "only smoking exceeds obesity
in its contribution to total mortality rates in the United States" (Koplan and
Dietz, p. 440). Because of these facts, something needs to be done in order
to reverse this rise in obesity. And because of the impressionability of teens,
it seems very likely that this change could be brought on during the years of
adolescence.*

Keith's introduction shares problems with many of its kind I have seen in
high school, introductory college courses, and even graduate seminars.
In the paragraph's last sentence, Keith states his own thesis: to effectively
combat widespread obesity in the United States, we should focus our
attack on teenagers. However, in the course of providing needed background information, he provides a string of facts that threaten to take
over the paragraph; it is for a moment as Keith feared it would be. As
quotation after quotation is added to the pile, the writing sounds less
and less like the thoughtful and opinionated student I know. Indeed, by
the end, Keith can state his thesis only timidly, using qualifiers such as
"seems very likely" and "could be."

However, as he moves into the body of the paper Keith again emerges as the paper's speaker. He explains that he offers an idea the class readings failed to address:

In our readings during class, we went over a lot of information regarding obesity in adulthood and we also went over a lot of information regarding obesity during childhood. One topic that wasn't covered, however, was the one that covers the years between *these two stages. This group of years may also be known as adolescence. Adolescents are not only impressionable, but they seem to be the most widely affected age group as well. "Although obesity is increasing in all age groups and among all racial/ethnic groups and educational levels, young adults ages 18 to 29 are experiencing the highest rate of increase" (Goodman and Witaker, p. 497)*

Here Keith articulates his point as an alternative to those positions found in the readings. In the conference I described at the beginning of this essay, Keith said that quoting the readings distracted the paper's energy from what *he* thought into what *they* (the articles' authors) thought. Here, though, Keith's position is not obscured behind or overshadowed by the experts' voices; instead, he steps up alongside the readings and shows where they have failed. While the paragraph is rough, it represents a significant shift in Keith's stance relative to the texts. Keith enters into dialogue with and even disagrees with the texts rather than competing with them for authorial power.

As the essay draft continues, Keith becomes more and more comfortable engaging in discussion of the texts, noting degrees of agreement and points of departure. He begins to walk through the assigned readings, noting how each overlooks adolescents and proposing that the solutions in each article be redirected at this important group:

I agree with Greg Crister when he says in his article "Too Much of a Good Thing" that overeating should be stigmatized (2001, p. 461), but I think that this stigmatization should be focused on young-adults and teens. . . The minds of today's youth are very delicate and could be stigmatized very easily.

That Keith can agree with parts of an author's argument even while pointing out its flaws reflects Keith's increasing tendency to *use* the texts for his own purpose rather than simply recounting them — and it is the practice of recounting texts without discussion or elaboration that enables sources' voices to "take over" a student paper. While in revision he will work on detailing his solution more clearly — what might "stigmatization of youth" look like, and how would its results differ from what Crister proposes?—Keith now can quote the text and advance his own points within the same paragraph.

Why So Difficult?

As Keith began to cite assigned texts, detailing his own position in relation to the voices of the readings, he began to demonstrate awareness that his voice is one in a field of many, that others have spoken on his subject in the past and will again. He located his particular position within that field of voices. As Thonney points out in a recent article in this journal, academic writers across disciplines make some similar moves in their published work. In adopting one of these moves, "respond[ing] to what others have said about their topic," students struggle with synthesizing and using references rather than simply mentioning them (348). In another move, Thonney notes, students "adopt a voice of authority" by "learn[ing] to imitate techniques of experienced writers" to navigate between first or third person and to write concisely (348, 353).

Yet doing this is not so simple. I see working from sources and 25 voice as much more intimately connected problems (see also Elbow, "Reflections"). Some of the difficulty students have writing in an academic, authoritative voice while using source texts appropriately stems from the complex set of abstractions required to position one's argument relative to those of authoritative others in print, while also positioning oneself relative to readers (in this case classmates and teacher). As Graff and Birkenstein explain,

the underlying structure of effective academic writing . . . resides not just in stating our own ideas, but in listening closely to others around us, summarizing their views in a way that they will recognize, and responding with our own ideas in kind . . . to argue well you need to do more than assert your own ideas, You need to enter a conversation, using what others say (or might say) as a launching pad or sounding board for your own ideas. (3)

Graff and Birkenstein offer templates writers can use to make these moves, but the mental activity involved in using those goes beyond simply filling in the blanks. To use them successfully, writers construct a vision from the texts they have read and may write. They must envision the discourse on a topic as a conversation—meaning also that they must envision each author as a speaker, even though their contributions have been asynchronous and encoded in writing rather than speech. They must envision themselves as speakers among the other speakers, though in fact student writers are usually beginners in disciplines where the authors of the source texts are key figures. When a writer like Keith struggles to make use of readings in his papers, he learns to set his own worldview ("what *I* thought") in the context of what others think and have said. As James Moffett points out, "[d]ifferentiating among modes of discourse, registers of speech, kinds of audiences is essentially a matter of decentering, of seeing alternatives, of standing in others' shoes, of knowing that one has a private or local point of view and knowledge structure" (57). For a student writing in a course context, this differentiation is complicated by the different authority positions the student writer must simultaneously occupy: a novice citing experts must nonetheless take a stance of authority over his or her own argument; a student seeking approval and awaiting evaluation must write without reference to that most immediate context for the writing. These problems can present themselves in writing as problems with voice.

Rethinking Voice

Thus, on that day in 2002, I first imagined Keith's problem to be a problem of voice and authority, and I still do. However, the way I think about voice and authority has changed. At the time, in my working model of students' writing processes, I had imagined students "finding" their voices through readings, and though I probably wouldn't have articulated this, operationally I conceptualized authority in writing as having something to say to a given audience. That is, I then imagined, students come in with nothing to say, writing in "no voice." Through engagement with the readings and class discussion, they find things to say, and as they write about those new opinions their writing begins to have voice. Students struggle with the problems inherent in writing about topics on which they are *not* yet authorities, and I had imagined the assigned readings as little toeholds for students to use as they climbed onto the topic.

I think now that my model was incorrect and even unhealthy. The high school and beginning college writers I have worked with were "voiceful" most of the time. Their language, both spoken and written, featured novel uses of familiar words, slang terms, and turns of phrase that signal their memberships and stances, rich in connotation. I always encouraged my students to capitalize on these when composing narratives and personal essays (as Keith was able to do in his high school courses and the introductory college course). However, for reasons of audience and register such terms and phrasing don't typically find their way into the academic essay (it wouldn't have helped Keith much for his paper to include the witticisms that peppered his speech, and he happened not to have much personal experience with the obesity issues in the paper). The task instead was to situate his voice among the voices of others, not by adding flair but by claiming his right to speak on a topic about which he had read and thought, articulating those thoughts clearly and with reference to the others' ideas that had informed those thoughts.

Further, Keith did not enter my class "voiceless" in any sense of the term; in fact, he had much to say and had been an opinionated and lively speaker and writer. My deficit model° for voice and authority kept me from seeing Keith's situation clearly. He struggled not with finding something to say but with saying it loudly enough to be heard amid more expert voices. His failure to use the readings in the first paper was not a retreat from serious engagement with the ideas of the course, but a defensive move that preserved space in which he *could* engage with them effectively. Instead of moving from having nothing to say, through the readings, to an eventual opinion, Keith had to learn to move from having much to say, to negotiating differences between his views and those presented in the texts, to presenting both in proper relation to one another.

Sperling and Appleman, synthesizing scholarship on the notion of voice, ultimately characterize voice as "a language performance—always social, mediated by experience, and culturally embedded" (71). That is, voice is something writers make rather than something they already have and then express. Further, that *making* is a situated activity in every sense. Voice, in other words, is just as composed as the text itself. My challenge, then, is to work with student writers to understand and manipulate voice in the context of an academic discourse in which source texts are cited, synthesized, and put to work in service of a writer's argument. This is no easy task, but seeing it now as an act of composing, I can approach it the way I approach so many other composing tasks with students: by modeling my own practices as I compose, by engaging students in similar practices, and—most important—by engaging students in analysis of and talk about those practices. For, as Elbow states:

learning new intellectual practices is not just a matter of practicing them; it's also a matter of thinking and talking about one's practice. Or, speaking academically, students need metacognition and metadiscourse to help them understand just what these new intellectual practices are that they are being asked to learn. ("Reflections" 149)

Further, to teach in this manner is not, as some might charge, to pretend again that the writer works alone in shaping voice or that he or she claims

---

deficit model: the view that an observed difference from the norm is a weakness or deficiency.

authority simply by deciding to claim it. In emphasizing metacognition and metadiscourse,° I am not only emphasizing "process talk" focused on individual decisions in crafting a piece of writing but also talk about the complex ways our processes as writers both follow from and push back against our situations as readers, writers, students, and practitioners of the disciplines in which we write. Sperling and Appleman call for just such an approach: "Teaching voice, then, means that we understand with students how and whether one discourse infiltrates or meshes with another, and to what rhetorical, academic, and, not least, political ends" (81). This is a self-conscious, reflexive, and reflective teaching around both voice and authority, taken together as elements of the composed text rather than as preconditions for it.

I keep thinking what I might do differently with Keith now, were he to visit me in office hours these nine years later. What I think is this: instead of engaging him in discussion of the obesity epidemic, his argument about the role of adolescents, and the sources he might use in forwarding that argument, I'd like to engage Keith in a discussion of the very kind in which I have engaged here. It is the discussion Keith himself opened when he named his own problem "incorporating textual examples" and placed that activity in opposition to "just turn[ing] in what *I* thought." I think Keith might have learned something from that kind of discussion that could have helped him that quarter—and I *know* I would have.

Works Cited

Bartholomae, David. "Inventing the University." *Journal of Basic Writing* 5.1 (1986): 4–23. *Google Scholar*. Web.

Elbow, Peter. "Reconsiderations: Voice in Writing Again—Embracing Contraries." *College English* 70.2 (2007): 168–88. Print.

———. "Reflections on Academic Discourse: How It Relates to Freshmen and Colleagues." *College English* 53.2 (1991): 135–55. Print.

Graff, Gerald, and Cathy Birkenstein. *They Say, I Say: The Moves That Matter in Academic Writing*. New York: Norton, 2006. Print.

Moffett, James. *Teaching the Universe of Discourse*. Boston: Houghton Mifflin, 1968. Print.

Sperling, Melanie, and Deborah Appleman. "Review of Research: Voice in the Context of Literacy Studies." *Reading Research Quarterly* 46.1 (2011): 70–84. *ProQuest*. Web.

Thonney, Teresa. "Teaching the Conventions of Academic Discourse." *Teaching English in the Two-Year College* 38.4 (2011): 347–62. Print.

metacognition and metadiscourse: One meaning for the prefix *meta* is "referring to itself." Thus, metacognition is thinking about thinking, and metadiscourse is talking or writing about talking or writing.

Understanding the Text

1. What problems does Keith have when writing a paper that requires the use of sources? What reasons does Whitney suggest are at the root of his problems?

2. How did Whitney define and think about the concept of *voice* when she began teaching? How has her definition changed?

Reflection and Response

3. Whitney's article frequently takes the form of narrative. Her story is especially personal toward the beginning, particularly in paragraph 6, where she talks about her emotional reaction to Keith's work. What effect do you think the personal nature of Whitney's story might have on a reader who is a teacher of writing? What effect does it have on you?

4. How does your own process of working with sources compare to Keith's? Do you tend, as he describes doing in paragraphs 10 and 11, to write your ideas first and work sources in later, or do you first plan out how your sources will develop and support your argument and then write with them in mind?

5. Consider Whitney's description of Keith's feelings in paragraph 13: "He felt that referring to the texts would make it into a paper about someone else's thought process and conclusions." Do you ever feel similarly when writing with sources? What strategies have you developed for keeping track of your own points so that your sources don't take over a paper?

Making Connections

6. Evaluate Keith's progress as a writer from the perspective of either Nancy Sommers and Laura Saltz in "Writing That Matters" (p. 335) or Dan Berrett in "Students Come to College Thinking They've Mastered Writing" (p. 284).

7. Below is a quote from literary and rhetorical theorist Kenneth Burke, from his book *Philosophy of Literary Form* (University of California Press, 1974; originally published in 1941). His metaphor of a social gathering in a parlor is often used to describe academic writing.

> *Imagine that you enter a parlor. You come late. When you arrive, others have long preceded you, and they are engaged in a heated discussion, a discussion too heated for them to pause and tell you exactly what it is about. In fact, the discussion had already begun long before any of them got there, so that no one present is qualified to retrace for you all the steps that had gone before. You listen for a while, until you decide that you have caught the tenor of the argument; then you put in your oar. Someone answers; you answer him; another comes to your defense; another aligns himself against you, to either the embarrassment or gratification of your opponent, depending upon the quality of your ally's assistance. However, the discussion is interminable. The hour grows late, you must depart. And you do depart, with the discussion still vigorously in progress.*

How could you apply this metaphor to academic writing? How do you see it comparing with Whitney's description of writing as conversation in paragraph 26?

Sentence Guides for Academic Writers

Being a college student means being a college writer. No matter what field you are studying, your instructors will ask you to make sense of what you are learning through writing. When you work on writing assignments in college, you are, in most cases, being asked to write for an academic audience.

Writing academically means thinking academically — asking a lot of questions, digging into the ideas of others, and entering into scholarly debates and academic conversations. As a college writer, you will be asked to read different kinds of texts; understand and evaluate authors' ideas, arguments, and methods; and contribute your own ideas. In this way, you present yourself as a participant in an academic conversation.

What does it mean to be part of an *academic conversation*? Well, think of it this way: You and your friends may have an ongoing debate about the best film trilogy of all time. During your conversations with one another, you analyze the details of the films, introduce points you want your friends to consider, listen to their ideas, and perhaps cite what the critics have said about a particular trilogy. This kind of conversation is not unlike what happens among scholars in academic writing — except they could be debating the best public policy for a social problem or the most promising new theory in treating disease.

If you are uncertain about what academic writing *sounds like* or if you're not sure you're any good at it, this booklet offers guidance for you at the sentence level. It helps answer questions such as these:

How can I present the ideas of others in a way that demonstrates my understanding of the debate?

How can I agree with someone, but add a new idea?

How can I disagree with a scholar without seeming, well, rude?

How can I make clear in my writing which ideas are mine and which ideas are someone else's?

The following sections offer sentence guides for you to use and adapt to your own writing situations. As in all writing that you do, you will have to think about your purpose (reason for writing) and your audience (readers) before knowing which guides will be most appropriate for a particular piece of writing or for a certain part of your essay.

The guides are organized to help you present background information, the views and claims of others, and your own views and claims — all in the context of your purpose and audience.

Academic Writers Present Information and Others' Views

When you write in academic situations, you may be asked to spend some time giving background information for or setting a context for your main idea or argument. This often requires you to present or summarize what is known or what has already been said in relation to the question you are asking in your writing.

SG1   Presenting What Is Known or Assumed

When you write, you will find that you occasionally need to present something that is known, such as a specific fact or a statistic. The following structures are useful when you are providing background information.

As we know from history, _____.

X has shown that _____.

Research by X and Y suggests that _____.

According to X, _____ percent of _____ are/favor _____.

In other situations, you may have the need to present information that is assumed or that is conventional wisdom.

People often believe that _____.

Conventional wisdom leads us to believe _____.

Many Americans share the idea that _____.

_____ is a widely held belief.

In order to challenge an assumption or a widely held belief, you have to acknowledge it first. Doing so lets your readers believe that you are placing your ideas in an appropriate context.

Although many people are led to believe X, there is significant benefit to considering the merits of Y.

College students tend to believe that _____ when, in fact, the opposite is much more likely the case.

SG2 Presenting Others' Views

As a writer, you build your own *ethos*, or credibility, by being able to fairly and accurately represent the views of others. As an academic writer, you will be expected to demonstrate your understanding of a text by summarizing the views or arguments of its author(s). To do so, you will use language such as the following.

X argues that _____.

X emphasizes the need for _____.

In this important article, X and Y claim _____.

X endorses _____ because _____.

X and Y have recently criticized the idea that _____.

_____, according to X, is the most critical cause of _____.

Although you will create your own variations of these sentences as you draft and revise, the guides can be useful tools for thinking through how best to present another writer's claim or finding clearly and concisely.

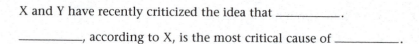 **Presenting Direct Quotations**

When the exact words of a source are important for accuracy, authority, emphasis, or flavor, you will want to use a direct quotation. Ordinarily, you will present direct quotations with language of your own that suggests how you are using the source.

X characterizes the problem this way: ". . ."

According to X, _____ is defined as ". . ."

". . . ," explains X.

X argues strongly in favor of the policy, pointing out that ". . ."

Note: You will generally cite direct quotations according to the documentation style your readers expect. MLA style, often used in English and in other humanities courses, recommends using the author name paired with a page number, if there is one. APA style, used in most social sciences, requires the year of publication generally after the mention of the source, with page numbers after the quoted material. In *Chicago* style, used in history and in some humanities courses, writers use superscript numbers (like this[6]) to refer readers to footnotes or endnotes. In-text citations, like the ones shown below, refer readers to entries in the works cited or reference list.

MLA   Lazarín argues that our overreliance on testing in K-12 schools "does not put students first" (20).

APA   Lazarín (2014) argues that our overreliance on testing in K-12 schools "does not put students first." (p. 20)

Chicago   Lazarín argues that our overreliance on testing in K-12 schools "does not put students first."[6]

Many writers use direct quotations to advance an argument of their own:

Standardized testing makes it easier for administrators to measure   *Student*
student performance, but it may not be the best way to measure it. Too much   *writer's idea*
testing wears students out and communicates the idea that recall is the
most important skill we want them to develop. Even education policy advisor   *Source's*
Melissa Lazarín argues that our overreliance on testing in K-12 schools "does   *idea*
not put students first" (20).

SG4   Presenting Alternative Views

Most debates, whether they are scholarly or popular, are complex—often with more than two sides to an issue. Sometimes you will have to synthesize the views of multiple participants in the debate before you introduce your own ideas.

> On the one hand, X reports that _____, but on the other hand, Y insists that _____.

> Even though X endorses the policy, Y refers to it as " . . ."

> X, however, isn't convinced and instead argues _____.

> X and Y have supported the theory in the past, but new research by Z suggests that _____.

Academic Writers Present Their Own Views

When you write for an academic audience, you will indeed have to demonstrate that you are familiar with the views of others who are asking the same kinds of questions as you are. Much writing that is done for academic purposes asks you to put your arguments in the context of existing arguments—in a way asking you to connect the known to the new.

When you are asked to write a summary or an informative text, your own views and arguments are generally not called for. However, much of the writing you will be assigned to do in college asks you to take a persuasive stance and present a reasoned argument—at times in response to a single text, and at other times in response to multiple texts.

SG5   Presenting Your Own Views: Agreement and Extension

Sometimes you agree with the author of a source.

X's argument is convincing because _____.

Because X's approach is so _____, it is the best way to _____.

X makes an important point when she says _____.

Other times you find you agree with the author of a source, but you want to extend the point or go a bit deeper in your own investigation. In a way, you acknowledge the source for getting you so far in the conversation, but then you move the conversation along with a related comment or finding.

X's proposal for _____ is indeed worth considering. Going one step further, _____.

X makes the claim that _____. By extension, isn't it also true, then, that _____?

_____ has been adequately explained by X. Now, let's move beyond that idea and ask whether _____.

SG6   Presenting Your Own Views: Queries and Skepticism

You may be intimidated when you're asked to talk back to a source, especially if the source is a well-known scholar or expert or even just a frequent voice in a particular debate. College-level writing asks you to be skeptical, however, and approach academic questions with the mind of an investigator. It is OK to doubt, to question, to challenge — because the end result is often new knowledge or new understanding about a subject.

Couldn't it also be argued that _____?

But is everyone willing to agree that this is the case?

While X insists that _____ is so, he is perhaps asking the wrong question to begin with.

The claims that X and Y have made, while intelligent and well-meaning, leave many unconvinced because they have failed to consider _____.

A Note about Using First Person "I"

Some disciplines look favorably upon the use of the first person "I" in academic writing. Others do not and instead stick to using third person. If you are given a writing assignment for a class, you are better off asking your instructor what he or she prefers or reading through any samples given than *guessing* what might be expected.

First person (*I, me, my, we, us, our*)

I question Heddinger's methods and small sample size.

Harnessing children's technology obsession in the classroom is, I believe, the key to improving learning.

Lanza's interpretation focuses on circle imagery as symbolic of the family; my analysis leads me in a different direction entirely.

We would, in fact, benefit from looser laws about farming on our personal property.

Third person (names and other nouns)

Heddinger's methods and small sample size are questionable.

Harnessing children's technology obsession in the classroom is the key to improving learning.

Lanza's interpretation focuses on circle imagery as symbolic of the family; other readers' analyses may point in a different direction entirely.

Many Americans would, in fact, benefit from looser laws about farming on personal property.

You may feel as if not being able to use "I" in an essay in which you present your ideas about a topic is unfair or will lead to weaker statements. Know that you can make a strong argument even if you write in the third person. Third person writing allows you to sound more assertive, credible, and academic.

 Presenting Your Own Views: Disagreement or Correction

You may find that at times the only response you have to a text or to an author is complete disagreement.

X's claims about _____ are completely misguided.

X presents a long metaphor comparing _____ to _____; in the end, the comparison is unconvincing because _____.

It can be tempting to disregard a source completely if you detect a piece of information that strikes you as false or that you know to be untrue.

Although X reports that _____, recent studies indicate that is not the case.

While X and Y insist that is _____ so, an examination of their figures shows that they have made an important miscalculation.

SG8 Presenting and Countering Objections to Your Argument

Effective college writers know that their arguments are stronger when they can anticipate objections that others might make.

Some will object to this proposal on the grounds that _____.

Not everyone will embrace _____; they may argue instead that _____.

Countering, or responding to, opposing voices fairly and respectfully strengthens your writing and your *ethos*, or credibility.

X and Y might contend that this interpretation is faulty; however, _____.

Most _____ believe that there is too much risk in this approach. But what they have failed to take into consideration is _____.

Academic Writers Persuade by Putting It All Together

Readers of academic writing often want to know what's at stake in a particular debate or text. Aside from crafting individual sentences, you must, of course, keep the bigger picture in mind as you attempt to persuade, inform, evaluate, or review.

SG9   Presenting Stakeholders

When you write, you may be doing so as a member of a group affected by the research conversation you have entered. For example, you may be among the thousands of students in your state whose level of debt may change as a result of new laws about financing a college education. In this case, you are a *stakeholder* in the matter. In other words, you have an interest in the matter as a person who could be impacted by the outcome of a decision. On the other hand, you may be writing as an investigator of a topic that interests you but that you aren't directly connected with. You may be persuading your audience on behalf of a group of interested stakeholders—a group of which you yourself are not a member.

You can give your writing some teeth if you make it clear who is being affected by the discussion of the issue and the decisions that have or will be made about the issue. The groups of stakeholders are highlighted in the following sentences.

Viewers of Kurosawa's films may not agree with X that _____.

The research will come as a surprise to parents of children with Type 1 diabetes.

X's claims have the power to offend potentially every low-wage earner in the state.

Marathoners might want to reconsider their training regimen if stories such as those told by X and Y are validated by the medical community.

SG10   Presenting the "So What"

For readers to be motivated to read your writing, they have to feel as if you're either addressing something that matters to them or addressing something that matters very much to you or that should matter to us all. Good academic writing often hooks readers with a sense of urgency—a serious response to a reader's "So what?"

Having a frank discussion about _____ now will put us in a far better position to deal with _____ in the future. If we are unwilling or unable to do so, we risk _____.

Such a breakthrough will affect _____ in three significant ways.

It is easy to believe that the stakes aren't high enough to be alarming; in fact, _____ will be affected by _____.

Widespread disapproval of and censorship of such fiction/films/art will mean _____ for us in the future. Culture should represent _____.

_____ could bring about unprecedented opportunities for _____ to participate in _____, something never seen before.

New experimentation in _____ could allow scientists to investigate _____ in ways they couldn't have imagined _____ years ago.

SG11 Presenting the Players and Positions in a Debate

Some disciplines ask writers to compose a review of the literature as a part of a larger project—or sometimes as a freestanding assignment. In a review of the literature, the writer sets forth a research question, summarizes the key sources that have addressed the question, puts the current research in the context of other voices in the research conversation, and identifies any gaps in the research.

Writing that presents a debate, its players, and their positions can often be lengthy. What follows, however, can give you the sense of the flow of ideas and turns in such a piece of writing.

_____ affects more than 30% of children in America, and signs point to a worsening situation in years to come because of A, B, and C. Solutions to the problem have eluded even the sharpest policy minds and brightest researchers. In an important 2003 study, W found that _____, which pointed to more problems than solutions. [. . .] Research by X and Y made strides in our understanding of _____ but still didn't offer specific strategies for children and families struggling to _____. [. . .] When Z rejected both the methods and the findings of X and Y, arguing that _____, policy makers and health-care experts were optimistic. [. . .] Too much discussion of _____, however, and too little discussion of _____, may lead us to solutions that are ultimately too expensive to sustain.

Student writer states the problem.

Student writer summarizes the views of others on the topic.

Student writer presents her view in the context of current research.

Appendix: Verbs Matter

Using a variety of verbs in your sentences can add strength and clarity as you present others' views and your own views.

When you want to present a view fairly neutrally

acknowledges	observes
adds	points out
admits	reports
comments	suggest
contends	writes
notes	

X points out that the plan had unintended outcomes.

When you want to present a stronger view

argues	emphasizes
asserts	insists
declares	

Y argues in favor of a ban on _____; but Z insists the plan is misguided.

When you want to show agreement

agrees
confirms
endorses

An endorsement of X's position is smart for a number of reasons.

When you want to show contrast or disagreement

compares	refutes
denies	rejects
disputes	

The town must come together and reject X's claims that _____ is in the best interest of the citizens.

When you want to anticipate an objection

admits
acknowledges
concedes

Y admits that closer study of _____, with a much larger sample, is necessary for _____.

Acknowledgments *(continued from page iv)*

H. Samy Alim."Hip Hop Nation Language." *Language in the U.S.A.: Themes for the Twenty-First Century.* Ed. Edward Finegan and John R. Rickford. Cambridge: Cambridge UP, 2004.

Gloria Anzaldúa. "How to Tame a Wild Tongue." *Borderlands/La Frontera.* San Francisco: Aunt Lute, 1987.

Naomi S. Baron. "Are Digital Media Changing Language?" *Educational Leadership* 66.6 (2009): 42–46.

Rusty Barrett. "Rewarding Language: Language Ideology and Prescriptive Grammar." *Other People's English: Code-Meshing, Code-Switching, and African American Literacy.* Ed. Vershawn Ashanti Young, Rusty Barrett, Y'Shanda Young-Rivera, and Kim Brian Lovejoy. New York: Teacher's College P, 2014. 15–23.

Edwin L. Battistella. "Slang as Bad Language." *Bad Language: Are Some Words Better than Others?* Oxford: Oxford UP, 2005. 84–90.

Dan Berrett. "Students Come to College Thinking They've Mastered Writing." *Chronicle of Higher Education* 60.28 (2014): 12.

Cheryl J. Boucher, Georgina S. Hammock, Selina D. McLaughlin, and Kelsey N. Henry. "Perceptions of Competency as a Function of Accent." *Psi Chi Journal of Psychological Research* 18.1 (2013): 27–32.

Kathryn Campbell-Kibler. "Intersecting Variables and Perceived Sexual Orientation in Men." *American Speech* 86.1 (2011): 52–68.

Tom Chatfield. "OMG—It's the Textual Revolution." *New Scientist* 217.2911 (2013): 40.

Connie Eble. "Culture." *Slang & Sociability: In-Group Language among College Students.* Chapel Hill: U of North Carolina P, 1996. 130–43.

Peter Elbow. "Speaking and Writing" from *Vernacular Eloquence: What Speech Can Bring to Writing.* Oxford UP, 2012, pp. 14–17; 140–45.

Louise Erdrich. "Two Languages in Mind, but Just One in the Heart." *New York Times* 22 May 2000.

Carmen Fought. "Are White People Ethnic? Whiteness, Dominance, and Ethnicity." *Language and Ethnicity.* Cambridge: Cambridge University Press, 2006. 112–21.

Helen Fox. "Worldwide Strategies for Indirection" (excerpt). *Listening to the World: Cultural Issues in Academic Writing.* NCTE, 1994. 15–21.

Carie Gauthier. "Metaphors in the Writing Process of Student Writers." *Oshkosh Scholar* 8 (2013): 87–96.

Paul A. Johnson and Ethan Krase. "Affect, Experience, and Accomplishment: A Case Study of Two Writers, From First-Year Composition to Writing in the Disciplines" (excerpt). *Journal of Teaching Writing,* vol. 27, no. 2, 2012, pp. 12–22.

Rosina Lippi-Green. "Standard (American) English," from "The Standard Language Myth." *English with an Accent.* 2nd ed. New York: Routledge, 2012. 57–61. Print.

Robert MacNeil. "English Belongs to Everybody." *Wordstruck: A Memoir.* New York: Neely, 1989. 217–23. ("English Belongs to Everybody" isn't a title in the text, but it's the title this excerpt was given when it was in *Language Awareness.*)

Robert MacNeil and William Cran. "The Language Wars." *Do You Speak American?* New York: Doubleday, 2005. 9–24.

Paul Kei Matsuda. "The Image of College Students and the Myth of Linguistic Homogeneity" excerpt from "The Myth of Linguistic Homogeneity in U.S.

College Composition." *College English*, Vol. 68, no. 6 (July 2006), pp. 639–41.

Paul Kei Matsuda. "Writing Involves the Negotiation of Language Differences." *Naming What We Know: Threshold Concepts in Writing Studies*, edited by Linda Adler-Kassner and Elizabeth Wardle, Utah State UP, 2015, pp. 68–70.

Erin McKean. "How Are Dictionaries Made?" *The 5-Minute Linguist: Bite-Sized Essays on Language and Languages*. 2nd ed. Ed. E.M. Rickerson and Barry Hilton. London: Equinox, 2012.

John McWhorter. "Straight Talk: What Harry Reid Gets about Black English." *The New Republic* 4 February 2010: 10–11.

Mark Peters. "He Said, Sheme Said." *Boston Globe*, 31 Jan. 2016.

Dennis Preston. "Some Plain Facts about Americans and Their Language." *American Speech* 75.4 (2000): 398–401.

Douglas Quenqua. "They're, Like, Way Ahead of the Linguistic Currrrve." *New York Times* 27 February 2012. Web.

Lee Romney. "Revival of Nearly Extinct Yurok Language Is a Success Story." *Los Angeles Times* 6 Feb. 2013.

Kevin Roozen. "Writing Is a Social and Rhetorical Activity." *Naming What We Know: Threshold Concepts in Writing Studies*, edited by Linda Adler-Kassner and Elizabeth Wardle, Utah State University Press, 2015, pp. 17–19.

Kevin Roozen. "Writing Is Linked to Identity." *Naming What We Know: Threshold Concepts in Writing Studies*, edited by Linda Adler-Kassner and Elizabeth Wardle, Utah State University Press, 2015, pp. 50–52.

Mike Rose. "Rigid Rules, Inflexible Plans, and the Stifling of Language." *College Composition and Communication* 31.4 (1980): 389–401.

Susan E. Schorn. "A Lot Like Us, but More So: Listening to Writing Faculty Across the Curriculum." *What Is "College-Level" Writing?* Ed. Patrick Sullivan and Howard Tinberg. Urbana, IL: NCTE, 2006. 330–40.

Marybeth Seitz-Brown. "Young Women Shouldn't Have to Talk Like Men to Be Taken Seriously." *Slate*, 16 Dec. 2014.

Nancy Sommers and Laura Saltz. "Writing that Matters: A Paradigm Shift" (excerpt from "The Novice as Expert: Writing the Freshman Year"). *College Composition and Communication*, vol. 56, no. 1, 2004, pp. 139–41.

Emily Strasser. "Writing What Matters: A Student's Struggle to Bridge the Academic/Personal Divide." *Young Scholars in Writing* 5 (2007): 146–50.

Susan Tamasi and Lamont Antieau. "Social Variables." *Language and Linguistic Diversity in the US: An Introduction*. New York: Routledge, 2015. 127–35.

Amy Tan. "Mother Tongue." Threepenny Review Fall 1990. Rpt. in *Making Sense: A New Rhetorical Reader*. Ed. Cheryl Glenn. Boston: Bedford, 2002. 301–06.

Chris Thaiss and Terry Myers Zawacki. "What Is Academic Writing? What Are Its Standards?" *Engaged Writers, Dynamic Disciplines: Research on the Academic Writing Life*. Portsmouth, NH: Boynton, 2006. 4–7.

Anne E. Whitney. "'I Just Turned In What I Thought': Authority and Voice in Student Writing." *Teaching English in the Two-Year College*, Dec. 2011, pp. 184–93.

Susan Wyche. "Time, Tools, and Talismans." *The Subject is Writing*. 4th ed. Ed. Wendy Bishop and James Strickland. Portsmouth, NH: Heinemann, 2006.

Vershawn Ashanti Young. "The Problem of Linguistic Double Consciousness" (excerpt from "'Nah, We Straight': An Argument against Code Switching"). *JAC* 29.1-2 (2009): 51–59.

Index of Authors and Titles